HOUGHTON MIFFLIN HARCOURT

JOURNEYS

Program Authors

James F. Baumann · David J. Chard · Jamal Cooks
J. David Cooper · Russell Gersten · Marjorie Lipson
Lesley Mandel Morrow · John J. Pikulski · Héctor H. Rivera
Mabel Rivera · Shane Templeton · Sheila W. Valencia
Catherine Valentino · MaryEllen Vogt

Consulting Author

Irene Fountas

HOUGHTON MIFFLIN HARCOURT
School Publishers

Cover illustration by Brandon Dorman.

Printed in the U.S.A.

ISBN 10:   0-547-25156-4
ISBN 13:   978-0-547-25156-1

3456789 - 1421 – 18 17 16 15 14 13 12 11 10
4500234242

HOUGHTON MIFFLIN HARCOURT

JOURNEYS

HOUGHTON MIFFLIN HARCOURT
School Publishers

Reaching Out

Big Idea Helping brings out the best in us.

Do You Know What I Mean?

 Big Idea We express ourselves in many ways.

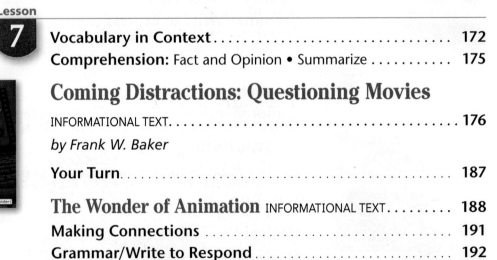

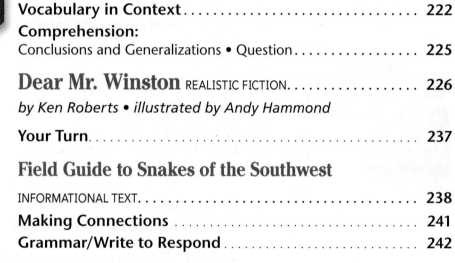

Unit 3

NATURAL ENCOUNTERS

Big Idea Nature can amaze us.

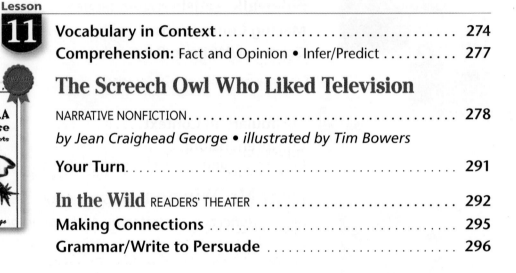

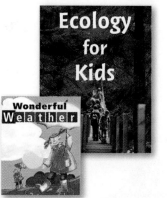

Unit 4

NEVER GIVE UP!

Big Idea There is more than one secret to success.

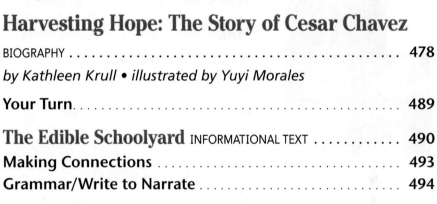

CHANGE Is All Around

Big Idea Change happens to us and because of us.

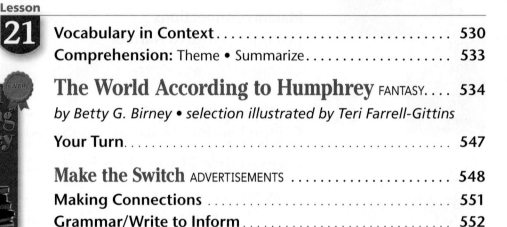

Welcome, Reader!

You're about to set out on a reading journey that will take you from the underwater world of a Japanese folktale to the American wilderness of Sacagawea in 1804. On the way, you'll learn amazing things as you become a better reader.

Your reading journey begins with a story about a remarkable dog named Winn-Dixie.

Many other reading adventures lie ahead. Just turn the page!

Sincerely,

The Authors

Reaching Out

Unit 1

Big Idea

Helping brings out the best in us.

Paired Selections

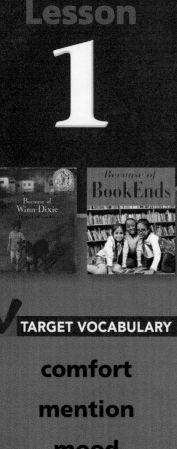

✓ **TARGET VOCABULARY**

comfort

mention

mood

properly

intends

consisted

positive

advanced

peculiar

talent

Vocabulary Reader	Context Cards

Vocabulary in Context

1 comfort
Friends often comfort each other. They help each other get through hard times.

2 mention
Do not mention one friend's faults to another. Keep them to yourself instead.

3 mood
Friends remain friends even when one is in a bad mood, or emotional state.

4 properly
Friends often greet each other properly. A handshake is the correct way.

- **Study each Context Card.**
- **Use two Vocabulary words to tell about an experience you had.**

5 intends

This girl intends to keep in touch with a friend. She plans to send e-mail every day.

6 consisted

This lively day consisted of, or was made up of, bike riding and fresh air.

7 positive

These friends are positive that they're having a good time. They are sure of it.

8 advanced

With his advanced chess skills, this man can teach his young friend to play.

9 peculiar

Friends may act in peculiar, or unusual, ways when taking photos.

10 talent

These friends share a talent for music. This ability gives them hours of fun.

Background

What Makes a Good Friend?

Do you look for someone with advanced skills or a special talent, someone who is always in a good mood, or someone who intends to comfort or be kind to others? If all friendships consisted of the same traits, you could properly predict who would be a good friend.

However, no one is ever sure, or positive, that a new person will become a friend. Friendship is more peculiar than that. Many people simply mention that they feel good around a certain person, and that's reason enough to be that person's pal.

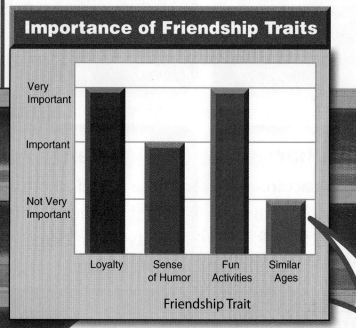

Importance of Friendship Traits

This bar graph shows what one person values in a friendship. How do the friendship traits compare in importance? What is the most important trait?

Comprehension

✔ **TARGET SKILL** **Story Structure**

As you read "Because of Winn-Dixie," ask yourself what the most important parts of the story are. Who are the main characters? Where does the action take place? In the story's plot, what are the most important events? Use a graphic organizer like the one below to keep track of the story's elements.

Characters:
•
•

Setting:
•
•

Plot:
•
•

✔ **TARGET STRATEGY** **Summarize**

You can use the information in your graphic organizer to help you summarize, or briefly describe, the main events in "Because of Winn-Dixie." At the end of each page, pause to briefly summarize what you have just read to make sure you understand it. Your summary should include the characters, what they said, and what happened to them.

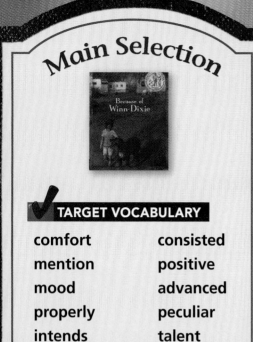

✔ **TARGET VOCABULARY**

comfort	consisted
mention	positive
mood	advanced
properly	peculiar
intends	talent

✔ **TARGET SKILL**

Story Structure Examine details about characters, setting, and plot.

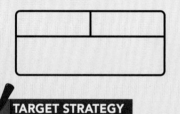

✔ **TARGET STRATEGY**

Summarize Briefly tell the important parts of the text in your own words.

GENRE

Realistic fiction is a present-day story that could take place in real life.

MEET THE AUTHOR

Kate DiCamillo

Kate DiCamillo grew up in Florida, where this story takes place. She wrote *Because of Winn-Dixie* during the first time in her life that she did not own a dog. DiCamillo believes that looking closely at the world and paying attention are the most important ways to become a good writer.

Because of
WINN-DIXIE

BY KATE DiCAMILLO

Essential Question

How do friends help each other?

Ten-year-old Opal is a newcomer in the town of Naomi, Florida. She hasn't made any friends yet and feels a little lonely. Opal's only pal is a very big dog, named after the grocery store where she found him: Winn-Dixie.

I spent a lot of time that summer at the Herman W. Block Memorial Library. The Herman W. Block Memorial Library sounds like it would be a big fancy place, but it's not. It's just a little old house full of books, and Miss Franny Block is in charge of them all. She is a very small, very old woman with short gray hair, and she was the first friend I made in Naomi.

It all started with Winn-Dixie not liking it when I went into the library, because he couldn't go inside, too. But I showed him how he could stand up on his hind legs and look in the window and see me in there, selecting my books; and he was okay, as long as he could see me. But the thing was, the first time Miss Franny Block saw Winn-Dixie standing up on his hind legs like that, looking in the window, she didn't think he was a dog. She thought he was a bear.

This is what happened: I was picking out my books and kind of humming to myself, and all of a sudden, there was this loud and scary scream. I went running up to the front of the library, and there was Miss Franny Block, sitting on the floor behind her desk.

"Miss Franny?" I said. "Are you all right?"

"A bear," she said.

"A bear?" I asked.

"He has come back," she said.

"He has?" I asked. "Where is he?"

"Out there," she said and raised a finger and pointed at Winn-Dixie standing up on his hind legs, looking in the window for me.

"Miss Franny Block," I said, "that's not a bear. That's a dog. That's my dog. Winn-Dixie."

"Are you positive?" she asked.

"Yes ma'am," I told her. "I'm positive. He's my dog. I would know him anywhere."

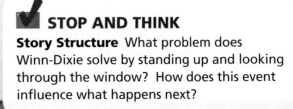

✔ STOP AND THINK

Story Structure What problem does Winn-Dixie solve by standing up and looking through the window? How does this event influence what happens next?

Miss Franny sat there trembling and shaking.

"Come on," I said. "Let me help you up. It's okay." I stuck out my hand and Miss Franny took hold of it, and I pulled her up off the floor. She didn't weigh hardly anything at all. Once she was standing on her feet, she started acting all embarrassed, saying how I must think she was a silly old lady, mistaking a dog for a bear, but that she had a bad experience with a bear coming into the Herman W. Block Memorial Library a long time ago and she never had quite gotten over it.

"When did that happen?" I asked her.

"Well," said Miss Franny, "it is a very long story."

"That's okay," I told her. "I am like my mama in that I like to be told stories. But before you start telling it, can Winn-Dixie come in and listen, too? He gets lonely without me."

"Well, I don't know," said Miss Franny. "Dogs are not allowed in the Herman W. Block Memorial Library."

"He'll be good," I told her. "He's a dog who goes to church." And before she could say yes or no, I went outside and got Winn-Dixie, and he came in and lay down with a "huummmppff" and a sigh, right at Miss Franny's feet.

She looked down at him and said, "He most certainly is a large dog."

"Yes ma'am," I told her. "He has a large heart, too."

"Well," Miss Franny said. She bent over and gave Winn-Dixie a pat on the head, and Winn-Dixie wagged his tail back and forth and snuffled his nose on her little old-lady feet. "Let me get a chair and sit down so I can tell this story properly."

"Back when Florida was wild, when it consisted of nothing but palmetto trees and mosquitoes so big they could fly away with you," Miss Franny Block started in, "and I was just a little girl no bigger than you, my father, Herman W. Block, told me that I could have anything I wanted for my birthday. Anything at all."

STOP AND THINK

Author's Craft Authors sometimes use a **flashback** to tell about events that happened before the time in which the larger story is set. Which details in the text tell you that a flashback is part of this selection?

Miss Franny looked around the library. She leaned in close to me. "I don't want to appear prideful," she said, "but my daddy was a very rich man. A very rich man." She nodded and then leaned back and said, "And I was a little girl who loved to read. So I told him, I said, 'Daddy, I would most certainly love to have a library for my birthday, a small little library would be wonderful.'"

"You asked for a whole library?"

"A small one," Miss Franny nodded. "I wanted a little house full of nothing but books and I wanted to share them, too. And I got my wish. My father built me this house, the very one we are sitting in now. And at a very young age, I became a librarian. Yes, ma'am."

"What about the bear?" I said.

"Did I mention that Florida was wild in those days?" Miss Franny Block said.

"Uh-huh, you did."

"It was wild. There were wild men and wild women and wild animals."

"Like bears!"

"Yes ma'am. That's right. Now, I have to tell you, I was a little-miss-know-it-all. I was a miss-smarty-pants with my library full of books. Oh, yes ma'am, I thought I knew the answers to everything. Well, one hot Thursday, I was sitting in my library with all the doors and windows open and my nose stuck in a book, when a shadow crossed the desk. And without looking up, yes ma'am, without even looking up, I said, 'Is there a book I can help you find?'"

"Well, there was no answer. And I thought it might have been a wild man or a wild woman, scared of all these books and afraid to speak up. But then I became aware of a very peculiar smell, a very strong smell. I raised my eyes slowly. And standing right in front of me was a bear. Yes ma'am. A very large bear."

"How big?" I asked.

"Oh, well," said Miss Franny, "perhaps three times the size of your dog."

"Then what happened?" I asked her.

"Well," said Miss Franny, "I looked at him and he looked at me. He put his big nose up in the air and sniffed and sniffed as if he was trying to decide if a little-miss-know-it-all librarian was what he was in the mood to eat. And I sat there. And then I thought, 'Well, if this bear intends to eat me, I am not going to let it happen without a fight. No ma'am.' So very slowly and very carefully, I raised up the book I was reading."

"What book was that?" I asked.

"Why, it was *War and Peace*, a very large book. I raised it up slowly and then I aimed it carefully and I threw it right at that bear and screamed, 'Be gone!' And do you know what?"

"No ma'am," I said.

"He went. But this is what I will never forget. He took the book with him."

"Nuh-uh," I said.

"Yes ma'am," said Miss Franny. "He snatched it up and ran."

"Did he come back?" I asked.

"No, I never saw him again. Well, the men in town used to tease me about it. They used to say, 'Miss Franny, we saw that bear of yours out in the woods today. He was reading that book and he said it sure was good and would it be all right if he kept it for just another week.' Yes ma'am. They did tease me about it." She sighed. "I imagine I'm the only one left from those days. I imagine I'm the only one that even recalls that bear. All my friends, everyone I knew when I was young, they are all dead and gone."

She sighed again. She looked sad and old and wrinkled. It was the same way I felt sometimes, being friendless in a new town and not having a mama to comfort me. I sighed, too.

Winn-Dixie raised his head off his paws and looked back and forth between me and Miss Franny. He sat up then and showed Miss Franny his teeth.

"Well now, look at that," she said. "That dog is smiling at me."

"It's a talent of his," I told her.

"It is a fine talent," Miss Franny said. "A very fine talent." And she smiled back at Winn-Dixie.

"We could be friends," I said to Miss Franny. "I mean you and me and Winn-Dixie, we could all be friends."

Miss Franny smiled even bigger. "Why, that would be grand," she said, "just grand."

And right at that minute, right when the three of us had decided to be friends, who should come marching into the Herman W. Block Memorial Library but old pinch-faced Amanda Wilkinson. She walked right up to Miss Franny's desk and said, "I finished *Johnny Tremain* and I enjoyed it very much. I would like something even more difficult to read now, because I am an advanced reader."

"Yes dear, I know," said Miss Franny. She got up out of her chair.

Amanda pretended like I wasn't there. She stared right past me. "Are dogs allowed in the library?" she asked Miss Franny as they walked away.

"Certain ones," said Miss Franny, "a select few." And then she turned around and winked at me. I smiled back. I had just made my first friend in Naomi, and nobody was going to mess that up for me, not even old pinch-faced Amanda Wilkinson.

STOP AND THINK
Summarize Summarize the main events in Miss Franny's bear story.

Your Turn

Two for One

Short Response Sometimes an author writes a story within a story. What is the "story within the story" in "Because of Winn-Dixie"? Who tells this story? What lesson about real life can you learn from it? Write a paragraph that answers these questions.

AUTHOR'S CRAFT

Wild Kingdom

Draw a Picture With a partner, draw a picture based on Miss Franny Block's childhood memories of Florida. Use her descriptions of the wild animals and plants she remembers to help you. Include labels that give the names of all the wild things in your picture. PARTNERS

Making Friends

Turn and Talk With a partner, discuss how Opal and Miss Franny Block help each other as friends. Do you think they would have become friends if they had met somewhere besides the library? Why or why not? How might the story have been different if Winn-Dixie had not been at the library with Opal? Use details and your own experiences to explain your thoughts. STORY STRUCTURE

Because of BookEnds

by John Korba

Think about what you're doing right now. You're learning something new. How are you doing it? You're reading a book.

You learn all kinds of things from books, things that are fun, or important, or even peculiar. Books can make you smile and can comfort you when you're sad.

What if you didn't have this book, or any books? An eight-year-old boy named Brandon once thought about that, and then he had a great idea.

A Little Boy's Big Idea

One day in 1998, Brandon Keefe was home from school with a cold. His mother, Robin, had to go to a meeting, so she brought Brandon with her. The meeting was at a place called Hollygrove in Los Angeles, California. Hollygrove is a community organization for children and families.

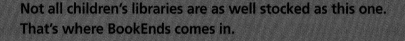

Not all children's libraries are as well stocked as this one.
That's where BookEnds comes in.

At the meeting, Brandon played in a corner. The adults were in a serious mood. They wanted to buy books for the children's center, but they didn't have much money. Brandon thought about this. He was positive he could use his problem-solving talent to help.

The next day Brandon was back at school. His teacher talked to the class about helping the community and asked for ideas. Brandon told the class about the children's center and its need for books. Then he announced his idea to hold a giant book drive.

Brandon's class organized the book drive. Soon, donations of new and used books poured in. Teams of volunteers, which consisted of students, teachers, and administrators from the school, collected and sorted the books. Meanwhile, Brandon did not mention this project to his mother.

Then one day Robin drove to school to pick up Brandon. He was waiting in the driveway with a great surprise: 847 books for the new library!

"That was one of the best days of my life," said Robin.

BookEnds Is Born

Robin knew there were many places that needed children's books. She saw that Brandon's idea could help them, too, so she started an organization called BookEnds.

BookEnds helps school kids set up book drives and get the books to children who need them. Since 1998, BookEnds volunteers have donated more than a million books to more than three hundred thousand children.

Brandon is an adult now. He is still involved with BookEnds and intends to stay involved.

You Can Do It, Too!

Do you and your schoolmates have many books that you'll never read again? Then your school might want to hold a book drive.

Step 1: Find a place that needs books.
Step 2: Collect books that are still in good shape.
Step 3: Sort the books properly by reading level. (You don't want children to get books that are too easy or too advanced.)
Step 4: Deliver your books and watch the smiles appear!

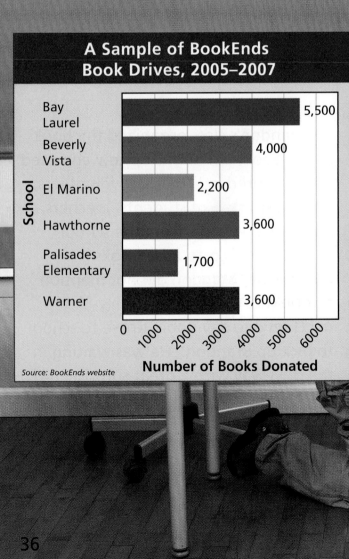

A Sample of BookEnds Book Drives, 2005–2007

- Bay Laurel: 5,500
- Beverly Vista: 4,000
- El Marino: 2,200
- Hawthorne: 3,600
- Palisades Elementary: 1,700
- Warner: 3,600

School (y-axis)

Number of Books Donated (x-axis): 0, 1000, 2000, 3000, 4000, 5000, 6000

Source: BookEnds website

Making Connections

Text to Self

Write a Narrative Think about a time you made a new friend. Write about that experience and why it was important to you. Be sure to include descriptive details about the place and time to help readers visualize the story.

Text to Text

Compare Actions How do the characters in "Because of Winn-Dixie" and the students in "Because of BookEnds" help others? Give an example of someone helping someone else from each selection.

Text to World

Write a Proposal Think of a place in your community that might like to receive a donation of books. Write a step-by-step plan for how you and your classmates might organize a book drive. Then pitch the idea to your class.

Grammar

What Is a Sentence? A **sentence** is a group of words that tells a complete thought. Every sentence has a subject and a predicate. The **simple subject** is the main word that names the person or thing being spoken about. The **simple predicate** is the main word or words that tell what the subject is or does.

Complete Sentences

simple subject   simple predicate
A small woman sits at the desk.

simple subject   simple predicate
Many children visit the library.

A group of words that does not tell a complete thought is called a **sentence fragment**.

Sentence Fragments

A newcomer in town.

Looking at books about animals.

Turn and Talk **With a partner, find the two complete sentences. What is the simple subject in each? What is the simple predicate in each?**

❶ Several students borrow books from the library.

❷ The book about dogs.

❸ The kind librarian stands by the door.

Sentence Fluency When you write, make sure each sentence states a complete thought. Sometimes you can fix a sentence fragment by adding it to a complete sentence.

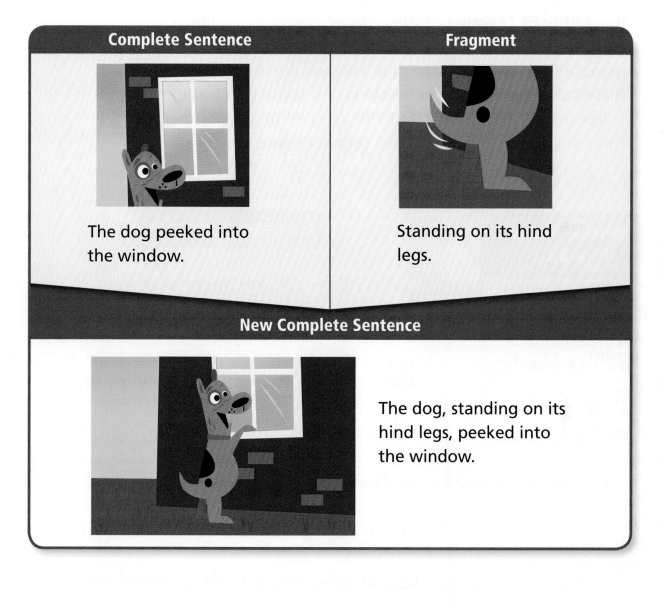

Complete Sentence	Fragment
The dog peeked into the window.	Standing on its hind legs.

New Complete Sentence

The dog, standing on its hind legs, peeked into the window.

Connect Grammar to Writing

As you revise your descriptive paragraph, make sure each sentence has a subject and a predicate. Change any fragments you find into complete sentences.

Write to Express

A good **descriptive paragraph** has clear, colorful details to describe real or imaginary places. For example, the author of "Because of Winn-Dixie" describes the library as "just a little old house full of books." Find places in your paragraph to add vivid details to keep readers interested. Use the Writing Traits Checklist below as you revise your writing.

For a story, Vanessa drafted a description of an apartment. Later, she added more details to help her readers picture it.

Writing Traits Checklist

☑ **Ideas**
   Did I include vivid details?

☑ **Organization**
   Did I put my details in a logical order?

☑ **Word Choice**
   Did I use sense words and phrases?

☑ **Voice**
   Did I give my description a special mood or feeling?

☑ **Sentence Fluency**
   Did I write smooth, complete sentences?

☑ **Conventions**
   Did I use correct spelling, grammar, and mechanics?

Revised Draft

Mrs. Henry's apartment was very small and cheery. When you walked in, it always smelled ~~good~~. There were two

like pancakes

sunny windows and funny photographs, such as a Chihuahua on a doll chair on the walls. Mrs. Henry's sofa had a

fuzzy blue

cover that she crocheted herself, and

by her sofa was a table covered with seashells, china birds, and family pictures ~~interesting things~~.

40

Mrs. Henry's Place
by Vanessa Brune

Mrs. Henry's apartment was very small and cheery. When you walked in, it always smelled like pancakes. There were two sunny windows and funny photographs on the walls, such as a Chihuahua on a doll chair. Mrs. Henry's sofa had a fuzzy blue cover that she crocheted herself, and by her sofa was a table covered with seashells, china birds, and family pictures. The best thing was the fish tank with goldfish and blue-and-red striped guppies. In the sand at the bottom of the tank, a scuba diver explored for treasure. The diver's air tube bubbled quietly as the fish swam in smooth circles or darted around. Mrs. Henry's apartment was a fascinating place to visit.

In my final paper, I added some vivid details. I also made sure I had written complete sentences.

Reading as a Writer

What makes Vanessa's details vivid? Where can you add clear and colorful details in your description?

✓ **TARGET VOCABULARY**

injustice

numerous

segregation

nourishing

captured

dream

encounters

preferred

recall

example

Vocabulary
Reader

Context
Cards

Vocabulary in Context

1 injustice

Some people spend their entire lives fighting injustice, or unfairness.

2 numerous

If numerous people sign a petition, their many voices can change the laws.

3 segregation

Laws on segregation once kept African Americans and white Americans separate.

COLORED   WHITE

4 nourishing

Many groups hope to end hunger by giving people healthy, nourishing food.

- Study each Context Card.
- Make up a new context sentence that uses two Vocabulary words.

5 captured
Some leaders have captured, or caught, people's attention with moving speeches.

6 dream
Many people have a dream of fair treatment for all. It is their goal.

7 encounters
Brief encounters, or meetings, with heroes can inspire kids to work for change.

8 preferred
Some Americans have preferred, or chosen, to work for change as a group.

9 recall
Most people can look back and recall a situation when they were treated unfairly.

10 example
It is easy to admire a leader who set an example of fairness and equality.

Background

Dr. Martin Luther King Jr. Do you have a dream that could change the whole world? Dr. Martin Luther King Jr. did. King worked for the end of segregation in the South during the 1950s and 1960s. He led thousands of people to fight bigotry and injustice against African Americans, and he preferred using nonviolent ways. He led numerous marches. He gave nourishing speeches that inspired listeners. He was sometimes jailed with supporters after encounters with police.

Most of all, King led by his example. He captured African Americans' desire for a change in society and helped make that change a reality. Those who knew him recall a remarkable, important man.

Dr. Martin Luther King Jr.

The Civil Rights Movement

1955: Rosa Parks, an African American, won't give up her bus seat to a white person and is arrested.

1960: Four African American students in North Carolina ask to be served at a lunch counter for whites only.

1963: Martin Luther King Jr. tells hundreds of thousands of supporters at the March on Washington, "I have a dream."

1964: Many people from the North and the South help African Americans in Mississippi register to vote.

1965: King leads thousands on a march to defend the voting rights of African Americans. Later, Congress passes the Voting Rights Act.

1968: King is killed in Memphis, Tennessee.

Today: Every January millions of Americans celebrate Martin Luther King Jr.'s birthday.

1955   1960   1970   TODAY

Use this timeline to summarize and explain the events of the Civil Rights Movement.

Comprehension

✓ **TARGET SKILL** **Author's Purpose**

As you read "My Brother Martin," think about the author's reasons for writing. Does she want to inform, entertain, or persuade readers? For clues, look at details in the text. Why does the author focus on certain events in Martin's life? Why does she choose certain words to describe a person or event? Use a graphic organizer like this one to help you figure out and explain the author's purpose.

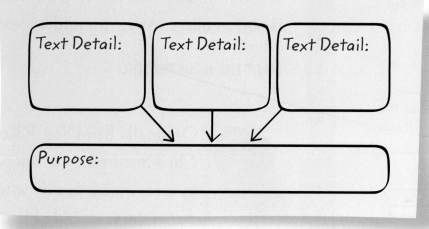

Text Detail:

Text Detail:

Text Detail:

Purpose:

✓ **TARGET STRATEGY** **Monitor/Clarify**

Monitor, or pay attention to, your understanding of "My Brother Martin" as you read. If something does not make sense, stop to clarify it, or make it clear. A graphic organizer can help you clarify the text because knowing the author's purpose for writing helps you better understand the selection.

✔ TARGET VOCABULARY

injustice	dream
numerous	encounters
segregation	preferred
nourishing	recall
captured	example

✔ TARGET SKILL

Author's Purpose Use text details to figure out the author's reasons for writing.

✔ TARGET STRATEGY

Monitor/Clarify Notice what is confusing as you read. Pause to confirm your understanding

GENRE

Biography tells about events in a person's life, written by another person.

MEET THE AUTHOR

CHRISTINE KING FARRIS

Christine King Farris is the sister of Martin Luther King Jr. *My Brother Martin* is her second book about the famous civil rights leader. The first one was *Martin Luther King: His Life and Dream*. In addition to being a writer, she is also a college instructor and a speaker.

MEET THE ILLUSTRATOR

CHRIS SOENTPIET

Originally from South Korea, Chris Soentpiet was adopted by a Hawaiian family when he was eight years old. He met members of his birth family while researching his book *Peacebound Trains*. Research and accuracy are very important to Soentpiet. He uses live models, makes costumes for them, and photographs the models before he begins painting.

my brother
MARTIN

A SISTER REMEMBERS
GROWING UP WITH
THE REV. DR. MARTIN LUTHER KING JR.

by CHRISTINE KING FARRIS
illustrated by CHRIS SOENTPIET

Essential Question

How can an author show what it takes to be a leader?

We were born in the same room, my brother Martin and I. I was an early baby, born sooner than expected. Mother Dear and Daddy placed me in the chifforobe drawer that stood in the corner of their upstairs bedroom. I got a crib a few days afterward. A year and a half later, Martin spent his first night in that hand-me-down crib in the very same room.

The house where we were born belonged to Mother Dear's parents, our grandparents, the Reverend and Mrs. A. D. Williams. We lived there with them and our Aunt Ida, our grandmother's sister.

And not long after my brother Martin—who we called M. L., because he and Daddy had the same name—our baby brother was born. His name was Alfred Daniel, but we called him A. D., after our grandfather.

They called me Christine, and like three peas in one pod, we grew together. Our days and rooms were filled with adventure stories and Tinkertoys, with dolls and Monopoly and Chinese checkers.

And although Daddy, who was an important minister, and Mother Dear, who was known far and wide as a musician, often had work that took them away from home, our grandmother was always there to take care of us. I remember days sitting at her feet, as she and Aunt Ida filled us with grand memories of their childhood and read to us about all the wonderful places in the world.

And of course, my brothers and I had each other. We three stuck together like the pages in a brand-new book. And being normal young children, we were almost *always* up to something.

Our best prank involved a fur piece that belonged to our grandmother. It looked almost alive, with its tiny feet and little head and gleaming glass eyes. So, every once in a while, in the waning light of evening, we'd tie that fur piece to a stick, and, hiding behind the hedge in front of our house, we would dangle it in front of unsuspecting passersby. Boy! You could hear the screams of fright all across the neighborhood!

Then there was the time Mother Dear decided that her children should all learn to play piano. I didn't mind too much, but M. L. and A. D. preferred being outside to being stuck inside with our piano teacher, Mr. Mann, who would rap your knuckles with a ruler just for playing the wrong notes. Well, one morning, M. L. and A. D. decided to loosen the legs on the piano bench so we wouldn't have to practice. We didn't tell Mr. Mann, and when he sat . . . *CRASH!*
Down he went.

STOP AND THINK

Author's Craft If the author is in the story, he or she uses **first person point of view**. If the author or narrator is outside the story, he or she speaks in **third person**. Which point of view does the author use here?

But mostly we were good, obedient children, and M. L. did learn to play a few songs on the piano. He even went off to sing with our mother a time or two. Given his love for singing and music, I'm sure he could have become as good a musician as our mother had his life not called him down a different path.

But that's just what his life did.

My brothers and I grew up a long time ago. Back in a time when certain places in our country had unfair laws that said it was right to keep black people separate because our skin was darker and our ancestors had been captured in far-off Africa and brought to America as slaves.

Atlanta, Georgia, the city in which we were growing up, had those laws. Because of those laws, my family rarely went to the picture shows or visited Grant Park with its famous Cyclorama. In fact, to this very day I don't recall ever seeing my father on a streetcar. Because of those laws, and the indignity that went with them, Daddy preferred keeping M. L., A. D., and me close to home, where we'd be protected.

We lived in a neighborhood in Atlanta that's now called Sweet Auburn. It was named for Auburn Avenue, the street that ran in front of our house. On our side of the street stood two-story frame houses similar to the one we lived in. Across it crouched a line of one-story row houses and a store owned by a white family.

When we were young all the children along Auburn Avenue played together, even the two boys whose parents owned the store.

And since our house was the favorite gathering place, those boys played with us in our backyard and ran with M. L. and A. D. to the firehouse on the corner where they watched the engines and the firemen.

The thought of *not* playing with those kids because they were different, because they were white and we were black, never entered our minds.

Well, one day, M. L. and A. D. went to get their playmates from across the street just as they had done a hundred times before. But they came home alone. The boys had told my brothers that they couldn't play together anymore because A. D. and M. L. were Negroes.

And that was it. Shortly afterward the family sold the store and moved away. We never saw or heard from them again.

Looking back, I realize that it was only a matter of time before the generations of cruelty and injustice that Daddy and Mother Dear and Mama and Aunt Ida had been shielding us from finally broke through. But back then it was a crushing blow that seemed to come out of nowhere.

"Why do white people treat colored people so mean?" M. L. asked Mother Dear afterward. And with me and M. L. and A. D. standing in front of her trying our best to understand, Mother Dear gave the reason behind it all.

Her words explained the streetcars our family avoided and the WHITES ONLY sign that kept us off the elevator at City Hall. Her words told why there were parks and museums that black people could not visit and why some restaurants refused to serve us and why hotels wouldn't give us rooms and why theaters would only allow us to watch their picture shows from the balcony.

But her words also gave us hope.

She answered simply, "Because they just don't understand that everyone is the same, but someday, it will be better."

And my brother M. L. looked up into our mother's face and said the words I remember to this day.

He said, "Mother Dear, one day I'm going to turn this world upside down."

✔ STOP AND THINK

Author's Purpose Authors often send a message through the way they tell a story. Sometimes the author states the message and sometimes it is implied. How can you tell the difference?

In the coming years there would be other reminders of the cruel system called segregation that sought to keep black people down. But it was Daddy who showed M. L. and A. D. and me how to speak out against hatred and bigotry and stand up for what's right.

Daddy was the minister at Ebenezer Baptist Church. And after losing our playmates, when M. L., A. D., and I heard our father speak from his pulpit, his words held new meaning.

And Daddy practiced what he preached. He always stood up for himself when confronted with hatred and bigotry, and each day he shared his encounters at the dinner table.

When a shoe salesman told Daddy and M. L. that he'd only serve them in the back of the store because they were black, Daddy took M. L. somewhere else to buy new shoes.

Another time, a police officer pulled Daddy over and called him "boy." Daddy pointed to M. L. sitting next to him in the car and said, "This is a boy. I am a man, and until you call me one, I will not listen to you."

These stories were as nourishing as the food that was set before us.

Years would pass, and many new lessons would be learned. There would be numerous speeches and marches and prizes. But my brother never forgot the example of our father, or the promise he had made to our mother on the day his friends turned him away.

And when he was much older, my brother M. L. dreamed a dream . . .

STOP AND THINK

Monitor/Clarify Explain what the phrases "the example of our father" and "the promise he had made to our mother" refer to. If you have difficulty, reread pages 54–56.

. . . that turned the world upside down.

Your Turn

Role Model

In Your Own Words Martin Luther King Jr. and his sister and brother learned about pride and dignity from their father. Think about something important you have learned from an adult. Write a paragraph about that lesson and explain how it can help you to be a strong leader.

PERSONAL RESPONSE

Free at Last!

Make a Timeline In a small group, look back through the selection and list the most important events in M. L.'s childhood. Then use the list to create a timeline of these events. Add illustrations to your timeline to help show what was happening at important times. SMALL GROUP

Why Writers Write

Turn and Talk With a partner, discuss why the author might have written about M. L.'s childhood rather than about what he did as an adult. What important point does the author make about how people become leaders?

AUTHOR'S PURPOSE

59

Poetry

Langston
HUGHES:
A Poet and a Dreamer

✓ TARGET VOCABULARY

injustice	dream
numerous	encounters
segregation	preferred
nourishing	recall
captured	example

GENRE

Poetry, such as this lyrical poetry, uses the sound and rhythm of words to suggest images and express feelings.

TEXT FOCUS

Repetition Poetry often repeats certain sounds to create a rhythm, focus on an image, or heighten an emotion. Discuss how this poet uses repetition in his lyrical poetry to help express his feelings.

Langston HUGHES:
A Poet and a Dreamer

Langston Hughes was a famous African American poet whose words inspired and affected people all over the world. Like Martin Luther King Jr., Hughes believed that a person's dream, or goal, could change the future. In the following poems, Hughes writes about dreams and why they are so important.

Langston Hughes,
1902–1967

As a child, Langston Hughes moved from city to city in the Midwest. Without a permanent home, he found comfort in reading. Books were as nourishing to him as food. He grew into a strong reader and writer. He published his first poems and stories when he was in high school.

As a young man, Hughes traveled the world. He wrote about his encounters with all kinds of people. At home, he had to deal with the unfair laws of segregation that kept people apart because of race. He thought deeply about injustice.

Hughes moved to Harlem, an African American neighborhood in New York City. Harlem became the place he preferred to all others. Here, writers, artists, and musicians were creating great works of art. Hughes's career as a writer blossomed. He went on to write numerous poems, stories, plays, and articles. Many of his works captured the culture and experiences of African Americans, to be shared with readers around the world.

Langston Hughes is known as one of the most important poets of the twentieth century. His work has set an example for writers to come.

To You

To sit and dream, to sit and read,
To sit and learn about the world
Outside our world of here and now—
　　Our problem world—
To dream of vast horizons of the soul
Through dreams made whole,
Unfettered, free—help me!
All you who are dreamers too,
　　Help me to make
　　Our world anew.
I reach out my dreams to you.

by Langston Hughes

Dreams

Hold fast to dreams
For if dreams die
Life is a broken-winged bird
That cannot fly.

Hold fast to dreams
For when dreams go
Life is a barren field
Frozen with snow.

by Langston Hughes

The Dream Keeper

Bring me all of your dreams,
You dreamers,
Bring me all of your
Heart melodies
That I may wrap them
In a blue cloud-cloth
Away from the too-rough fingers
Of the world.

by Langston Hughes

Write a Dream Poem

Do you have a special dream? Write a poem about it. Try to recall the important details and show how you feel. Your dream might be big or small. It might be something you hope to accomplish tomorrow, next month, or in many years.

See where your dreams take you!

Making Connections

 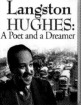

Text to Self

Write a Paragraph Martin Luther King Jr. and Langston Hughes both dreamed about making the world a better place. Write about a dream you have for making your neighborhood, your city, or even the world better.

Text to Text

Compare and Contrast How were the challenges faced by the King children when they moved like the experiences of Opal in "Because of Winn-Dixie"? How were they different?

Text to World

Connect to Social Studies Martin Luther King Jr. worked hard to help improve his community. With a partner, research different ways that people can help others in your community or state. Use the Internet or other reference sources to make your list. Present your findings to the class.

Grammar

What Is a Complete Subject? What Is a Complete Predicate? The **complete subject** includes all the words that tell *who* or *what* is doing the action in a sentence. The **complete predicate** includes all the words that tell what the subject of the sentence is or does.

Academic Language

complete subject
complete predicate
compound subject

Complete Subjects and Complete Predicates

complete subject | complete predicate

An important minister | lives in the house.

complete subject | complete predicate

This minister | travels often for work.

A **compound subject** is made up of two or more simple subjects that perform the same action.

simple subject | simple subject

An important minister and a famous musician live in the house.

compound subject

Turn and Talk **With a partner, identify the complete subject and the complete predicate in each sentence. Which sentence has a compound subject?**

1. Young Christine sat near her grandmother.

2. Her grandmother told wonderful stories.

3. Christine and her two brothers played pranks on people.

Sentence Fluency Too many short sentences can make your writing sound choppy. If two short sentences have the same predicate, you can combine them by joining the subjects with the word *and*. The new sentence will have a compound subject. Make sure the verb agrees with the compound subject.

Short Sentence	Short Sentence
Michael lives in Atlanta.	Rebecca lives in Atlanta.

Longer, Smoother Sentence

Michael and Rebecca live in Atlanta.

Connect Grammar to Writing

As you revise your narrative composition, look for sentences that repeat a predicate. Try combining these sentences by creating a compound subject.

Write to Express

☑ **Word Choice** When the author of "My Brother Martin" says that segregation was "a crushing blow" or that her family's pride was "nourishing," her words help us understand people's feelings. In your **narrative**, use words that capture feelings. Use the Writing Traits Checklist below as you revise your writing.

Victor drafted a scene about a boy who stood up for his rights. Later, he added some words that show more clearly how his characters felt.

Writing Traits Checklist

☑ **Ideas**
Did I show the events vividly?

☑ **Organization**
Did I tell the events in order?

☑ **Word Choice**
Did I use words that express feelings?

☑ **Voice**
Does my dialogue sound natural?

☑ **Sentence Fluency**
Did I combine sentences so they flow smoothly?

☑ **Conventions**
Did I use correct spelling, grammar, and punctuation?

Revised Draft

James could hardly believe his luck. His
~~James's~~ new house was right next to
a basketball court. He ~~got~~ grabbed his ball and
raced ~~went~~ over.

A boy was already shooting baskets.

"Can I shoot some?" James asked.

"Not now," said the boy. "I was here
first." His face ~~was~~ and voice were unfriendly. ~~His voice was unfriendly too.~~

James sat on the bench. He waited patiently
for a whole hour and then asked again.

66

Fair Play: A Story Scene

by Victor Alvez

James could hardly believe his luck. His new house was right next to a basketball court. He grabbed his ball and raced over.

A boy was already shooting baskets. "Can I shoot some?" James asked.

"Not now," said the boy. "I was here first." His face and voice were unfriendly.

James sat on the bench. He waited patiently for a whole hour and then asked again. The boy just kept on shooting baskets. James's face grew hot. He stood up. "Hey!" he said in a loud, firm voice. "This court's for everyone, not just you."

The boy stopped. His look of surprise turned to an embarrassed grin.

"Yeah, you're right," he said. "It's your turn." Then he said, "My name's Cole. What's yours?"

In my final paper, I added words to better show how my characters feel. I also combined two sentences by forming a compound subject.

Reading as a Writer

How does Victor make the story more exciting? Where in your paper can you make your characters' feelings clearer?

✓ **TARGET VOCABULARY**

welcomed

sensitive

observes

unspoiled

prepared

negative

honor

included

glances

encouragement

Vocabulary Reader   Context Cards

Vocabulary in Context

1 welcomed

Newcomers to the United States feel welcomed when others greet them.

2 sensitive

Be caring and sensitive about the customs of newcomers.

3 observes

This boy observes, "Our new city is big!" His family agrees with what he has said.

4 unspoiled

Some city dwellers come from areas that seem untouched, or unspoiled, by people.

- **Study each Context Card.**

- **Discuss one picture. Use a different Vocabulary word from the one on the card.**

5 prepared

These people have prepared, or created, some traditional food from their homeland.

6 negative

Recent immigrants might have gloomy or negative feelings at first in their new land.

7 honor

If a relative talks about "the old country," listen with respect, or honor.

8 included

Everyone can be included as a citizen of the world at an international festival.

9 glances

When a newcomer glances, or looks, at you, smile and say hello.

10 encouragement

Encouragement and support can make an immigrant feel at ease in new surroundings.

Background

Moving to a New Home Think of a time when you felt homesick. You may have gone off to cry by yourself. Perhaps you even prepared to return home immediately. Did anyone give you encouragement and cheer you up, or did you face your negative feelings alone?

A sensitive person can make shy newcomers feel welcomed and included by talking to them. For example, if someone new glances your way, invite that person to join you and your friends. If a friend observes to you that a new classmate is feeling homesick, make an effort to help out. Often when people move, they have happy, unspoiled memories of their old communities. If you let newcomers share these stories, you can help them feel right at home.

What Can You Do to Make a Newcomer Feel Welcome?

- Smile and introduce yourself.
- Be a good listener.
- Invite the person to join you and your friends.
- Throw a small party in that person's honor.

70

Comprehension

✓ **TARGET SKILL** **Cause and Effect**

As you read "How Tía Lola Came to Stay," note how some events can cause other events to happen. In this story, Tía Lola's arrival has an effect on the behavior of other characters, especially Miguel. Clue words such as *because*, *then*, *so*, and *since* can help you identify a cause-and-effect relationship. Use a graphic organizer like this one to show causes and effects as you read about this family.

Cause	Effect
•	•
•	•
•	•

✓ **TARGET STRATEGY** **Visualize**

As you read, visualize the characters' actions and reactions to form pictures of the story events in your mind. Use this strategy to help clearly identify the causes and effects of the characters' behavior in the story.

Main Selection

✔ TARGET VOCABULARY

welcomed	negative
sensitive	honor
observes	included
unspoiled	glances
prepared	encouragement

✔ TARGET SKILL

Cause and Effect Tell how events and characters' actions are related and how one event causes another.

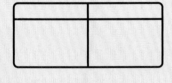

✔ TARGET STRATEGY

Visualize Use text details to form pictures in your mind of what you are reading.

GENRE

Realistic fiction is a present-day story that could take place in real life.

MEET THE AUTHOR

JULIA ALVAREZ

Julia Alvarez was raised in the Dominican Republic. She has lived in Vermont, on a farm that grows fruits and vegetables. She and her partner, Bill Eichner, also began a coffee farm in the Dominican Republic with a school on it that teaches people to read.

MEET THE ILLUSTRATOR

DAVID DIAZ

As an artist, David Diaz likes to experiment with new ideas and different techniques. He does some work by hand and some on the computer. He says, "I think that by changing techniques I add more interest to the books that I do."

How Tía Lola Came to ~~Visit~~ Stay

by Julia Alvarez
selection illustrated by
David Diaz

Essential Question

What happens when one person helps another?

Miguel (mee GEHL) has recently moved from New York City to Vermont with his mother and his sister, Juanita (hwah NEE tah). Now Tía (TEE ah) Lola (or Aunt Lola) has just come from the Dominican Republic to live with them and to help his mother. Miguel thinks his aunt is unusual, and he's having a hard time getting used to her.

That night, a snowstorm blows in. When Miguel glances out the window the next morning, flakes are still falling in the light by the front porch. Downstairs, Tía Lola is not at breakfast.

"Good news," Juanita says as Miguel sits down. "No school today!"

"I do have to go to work," their mother reminds them. "I'm so glad Tía Lola is here so I don't have to worry about you. Where is she anyhow?" Their mother glances up at the clock. "She's usually up at this hour. She seemed a little sad last night."

"She wouldn't tell us a story," Miguel admits.

"Did you hurt her feelings?" Since she is a psychologist (sy KAHL uh jihst), their mother always guesses everything that happens has to do with people's feelings.

"How could I hurt *her feelings*?" Miguel says, trying not to sound annoyed at his mother. Her feelings are awfully sensitive these days. "I don't know enough Spanish to hurt Tía Lola's feelings."

"Tía Lola is a special person," Miguel's mother observes. "She can tell the secret feelings in a person's heart." Miguel's mother gives him a look as if *she* can tell what is in his heart.

The truth is Miguel has mixed feelings about having Tía Lola around. She is fun, but he sure doesn't think having her here will improve his chances of making new friends. Why can't Tía Lola act more like his teacher, Mrs. Prouty, who speaks without moving her jaw and is so proper that she says, "Pardon me," *before* she sneezes. Or like farmer Becky, their shy next-door neighbor, who dresses in a white pullover sweater as if she wants to blend in with the sheep she shears and tends. Or even like their mother's new friend, Stargazer, who, although she wears fanciful, long skirts and dangly earrings, speaks in a soft voice in order not to stir up negative energies.

STOP AND THINK

Visualize In your mind, picture what farmer Becky in her white pullover might look like next to the sheep.

"You have to love people for who they are," his mother is saying, "then they will become all they can be."

That sounds like a riddle, but it makes sense. When Miguel first started playing baseball, Papi would always say, "Great swing, Miguel," or "Nice try," even when Miguel missed the ball. Over time, his playing actually got better because of Papi's encouragement.

"Remember," his mother continues, "Tía Lola might be a little homesick. She needs to feel really welcomed."

Miguel looks down at his cereal. He is sorry that he has made Tía Lola feel unwelcomed. He knows what that feels like. At school, an older kid in his class named Mort has nicknamed him Gooseman, because that's what Miguel's last name, Guzmán (goos MAHN), sounds like in English. Now other kids are calling out, "Quack, quack!" whenever they pass him in the hall. Maybe they are trying to be funny, but it makes him feel embarrassed and unwelcomed.

"What's the word for welcome in Spanish?" Miguel asks his mother.

"*Bienvenido* (byehn veh NEE doh) for a man, *bienvenida* (byehn veh NEE dah) for a woman." His mother spells out the words. "Why do you ask?"

"I've got a great idea. Nita, I'll need your help."

Juanita nods. She loves to be included in her brother's Great Ideas. She doesn't even have to know what they are ahead of time.

The snow is deep, almost to his knees. Miguel trudges down to the back field, keeping close to the fence line. The sun has broken through the clouds. All around him, the field is fresh and unspoiled by footprints and sparkling with diamonds of light.

He starts by walking in a straight line, kicking the snow to either side. Then he walks in a half circle, out and back to the straight line, and then out and back again. Every step of the way, he has to imagine what each mark will look like from the house.

STOP AND THINK

Author's Craft An author uses **metaphors** to describe something by using the characteristics of another thing. For example, *the clouds are cotton balls in the sky.* Find a metaphor on page 77.

He thinks of his father in New York. Although he works setting up department store windows at night, Papi's real love is painting. Today, Miguel feels the closest he has felt to his father since his mother and Juanita and he moved to Vermont. He is an artist like his father, but working on a larger canvas. He is trying to create something that will have the same result: making somebody happy.

At one point, he glances up, and he thinks he sees his little sister waving. It is her job to keep Tía Lola from looking out the windows.

The sun is right above his head when Miguel is done.

Inside, the house smells of something delicious baking in the oven. Tía Lola has prepared a special pizza with lots of cheese and black beans and *salchichón* (sahl chee CHOHN), a tasty sausage that she has brought from the island.

"*Pizza dominicana* (doh mee nee KAH nah)," Tía Lola calls it. "*Buen provecho* (bwehn proh VEH choh)," she adds. It is what she always says before they eat. Their mom has told them it is sort of like wishing somebody a happy meal.

"Pizza Tía Lola," Miguel renames the pizza in honor of his aunt.

STOP AND THINK

Cause and Effect As he works on his idea, what causes Miguel to feel closer to his father?

When they have finished eating, Miguel announces there is a surprise for his aunt in the back field.

"*¿Para mí* (PAH rah mee)?" Tía Lola says, pointing to herself.

Miguel can see the color coming back into her cheeks, the sparkle in her eyes. The beauty mark that was above her upper lip on the right side is now on the left side. Tía Lola tends to forget little things like that. It winks like a star.

Miguel leads the way up the stairs to the landing. They line up at the big picture window and look out at the snowy fields where large letters spell out *¡Bienvenida, Tía Lola!*

Tía Lola claps her hands and hugs Miguel.

Your Turn

Snowy Surprise

Short Response The author says that Miguel "is an artist like his father, but working on a larger canvas." What do you think the author means? Write a paragraph explaining what you think the author is saying about Miguel and his actions. AUTHOR'S CRAFT

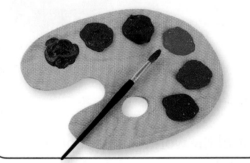

Guess the Letter

Play a Drawing Game Work in a group. Each member of the group chooses one letter of the alphabet, keeping it a secret. Each person then writes a short set of directions for how to make that letter in the snow, as Miguel did. Group members take turns reading the directions aloud as your other group members follow them to draw and identify the letter.

SMALL GROUP

Getting Results

Turn and Talk With a partner, talk about how Miguel changes throughout the story. What causes him to change? What effect do his actions have on his aunt? What does Miguel learn about treating others with kindness? Use details from the story to explain your thoughts.

CAUSE AND EFFECT

✓ TARGET VOCABULARY

welcomed	negative
sensitive	honor
observes	included
unspoiled	glances
prepared	encouragement

GENRE

Informational text, such as this recipe article, gives facts and examples about a topic.

TEXT FOCUS

Directions A text may include a set of instructions telling how to do something by following a series of steps. As you read each recipe, note how the steps are in sequence. What would happen if the steps were done out of order?

Pizza Pizzazz

by Peter Sylvia

Pizza, one of the world's most popular foods, has not been around as long as you might think. America's first pizza parlor did not open until 1905. At first, this strange Italian food wasn't welcomed. Pizza did not become popular until after World War II.

Even in Italy, cheese was not included on pizzas until 1889, when a pizza like this one was prepared in honor of the queen. Note the colors of the Italian flag: red (tomatoes), green (basil), and white (cheese).

Pizza Dominicana

What pizza toppings do you like? The Japanese enjoy eel and squid. People living in Brazil prefer peas. This Dominican Republic recipe uses beans and salchichón, a special kind of sausage.

Tips

- Wash your hands.
- Make sure an adult is present.
- Be careful with knives.
- Use oven mitts.

Ingredients

pizza dough

1 tablespoon vegetable oil

1 can black beans, rinsed and drained

1 can diced tomatoes

1 package shredded cheese

6 ounces of salchichón, sliced (You can also use sausage or salami.)

1. Preheat oven to 425 degrees.

2. Press dough into a greased baking dish. Bake about 5 minutes until the crust browns. Carefully remove the dish from the oven.

3. Heat oil in a frying pan. (Have an adult help.) Add beans and tomatoes. Cook for two minutes, uncovered, until thick.

4. Sprinkle 2/3 of a cup of cheese over the crust.

5. Spoon bean mixture onto the crust. Top with cheese and salchichón.

6. Bake 8 to 10 minutes more.

Is Your Pizza Ready?

Is your pizza ready? A good pizza cook always glances at the crust and observes whether it is crispy. Have an adult remove the pizza from the oven. Before slicing it into pieces, admire your pizza while it is still perfect and unspoiled.

Design Your Own Pizza!

Use the following recipe to make your own pizza. What topping will you add? Be creative but sensitive to what others might like.

Ingredients

4 English muffins
1 jar of pizza sauce
4 ounces of shredded Mozzarella cheese
your favorite pizza topping

1 Preheat oven to 375 degrees.

2 Split English muffins and arrange them on a baking sheet.

3 Spoon 1 tablespoon of pizza sauce on each muffin half.

4 Add your own topping.

5 Sprinkle cheese on each half.

6 Bake 10 to 12 minutes.

You can name your pizza. Make the name fun but not negative. Then share the pizza with a friend. With some encouragement, maybe your friend will invent a pizza for you!

Heat It Up!

Pizza chefs know that high temperatures and long baking times make pizza taste better. Scientists are now finding that pizza dough cooked this way may also be healthier for you. Why? The heat releases a substance that is good for your health.

Making Connections

Text to Self

Write About Comforts Sometimes simple things can bring people great comfort, such as the *pizza dominicana* Tía Lola makes. Write a paragraph about some simple things you find comforting. Include a topic sentence and several supporting details.

Text to Text

Describe a Process With a partner, write a script for a TV cooking show about pizza-making. Draw on details from both selections you have read as you plan what viewers will see on the show. Include a set of instructions for the pizza recipe in your script.

Text to World

Research Wheat Flour, used in pizza dough, is made from wheat. Use an online source to create a poster about one country where wheat is an important crop. Describe the climate, including the average temperature and rainfall. Share your poster with the class.

Grammar

What Are the Four Kinds of Sentences? A sentence that tells something is a **statement**. A statement ends with a period. A sentence that asks something is a **question**. A question ends with a question mark. A sentence that tells someone to do something is a **command**. A command ends with a period and sometimes an exclamation mark. A sentence that shows strong feeling is an **exclamation**. It ends with an exclamation point.

Sentence	Kind of Sentence
period Our aunt lives with us.	statement
question mark Does she speak Spanish?	question
period Bring me a warm sweater.	command
exclamation point How beautiful the snow looks!	exclamation

Turn and Talk **Take turns reading each sentence below with a partner. Tell what kind of sentence it is.**

1. How can we make our aunt feel welcome?

2. What a great idea that is!

3. Bring me a marking pen.

4. This will really make her feel welcome and happy.

Sentence Fluency Avoid using too many statements when you write. Turn some statements into questions, commands, or exclamations. This will make your writing livelier and help to keep your readers' attention.

Statements	Varied Sentence Types

My aunt came to visit all the way from Mexico. She made pizza. It is the best pizza in the world. You may want to come over to try it.

Can you believe my aunt came to visit all the way from Mexico? She made pizza! It is the best pizza in the world. Come over to try it!

✏ Connect Grammar to Writing

As you revise your writing, look for opportunities to use questions, commands, and exclamations as well as statements.

Write to Express

☑ **Voice** In "How Tía Lola Came to Stay," the **dialogue**—what the characters say to each other—sounds like real people talking. People don't always speak in complete sentences, and how they talk fits their ages, feelings, and personalities. Use the Writing Traits Checklist below as you revise your writing.

Iris drafted a story dialogue between a sister and brother. Then she revised it to sound more true to life.

Writing Traits Checklist

☑ **Ideas**
Did I include some gestures and actions?

☑ **Organization**
Does the sequence make sense?

☑ **Word Choice**
Did I use words that fit my characters?

☑ **Voice**
Does my dialogue sound natural and show expression?

☑ **Sentence Fluency**
Did I use different kinds of sentences?

☑ **Conventions**
Did I use correct spelling, grammar, and mechanics?

Revised Draft

Ashley and Daniel were eating a snack after school. "Let's make get-well cards for Dad," Ashley said.

Daniel made a face. "~~I don't like~~ Boring! ~~making cards.~~"

"Well, what else would Dad like?"

"I know," said Daniel. "Let's bake brownies!"

"~~Would they be~~ for him or for you? Dad's got stomach flu!"

The Get-Well Gift: A Dialogue
by Iris Panza

Ashley and Daniel were eating a snack after school. "Let's make get-well cards for Dad," Ashley said.

Daniel made a face. "Boring!"

"Well, what else would Dad like?"

"I know," said Daniel. "Let's bake brownies!"

"For him or for you? Dad's got stomach flu!"

"Oops. Duh. I forgot. Hmmm."

Suddenly, Ashley slapped the table. "You gave me a great idea. We can make him a surprise gift certificate. When he's better, he can turn it in, and the surprise will be—"

"Homemade brownies!" Daniel said. "Let's go for it!"

My final dialogue has more expression. I made sure to use statements, questions, commands, and exclamations.

Reading as a Writer

Which parts make Ashley and Daniel sound like real people? Where can you make your own dialogue sound more natural?

4

✓ **TARGET VOCABULARY**

assist

burglaries

innocent

scheme

regretfully

misjudged

suspect

favor

speculated

prior

Vocabulary
Reader

Context
Cards

Vocabulary in Context

1 assist

Everyone appreciates people who **assist**, or help, others to solve a problem.

2 burglaries

Finding robbers who commit **burglaries** is a job for the police.

3 innocent

If you are accused of mischief and are not **innocent**, be honest! Admit your mistake.

4 scheme

When a solution involves many steps, a **scheme**, or plan, is helpful.

90

- Study each Context Card.
- Ask a question that uses one of the Vocabulary words.

5 regretfully

At times people must regretfully, or sadly, admit that a problem can't be solved.

6 misjudged

People who have bought too little pet food have misjudged how much pets eat.

7 suspect

This teacher has a good idea who hid the desk keys. She has a suspect in mind.

8 favor

If an adult helps you solve a problem, you might mow his or her lawn as a favor.

9 speculated

This weather reporter has speculated, or supposed, that winter frosts are over.

10 prior

Checking a map prior to a road trip can help you know where to go beforehand.

Background

✓ **TARGET VOCABULARY** **Do Young People Care About Their Communities?** Regretfully, some adults have speculated that young people are guilty of not caring about their communities. In reality, young people are innocent of this charge—they do care about their communities. Adults who look at young people as suspects have misjudged them.

Young people assist their communities in many ways. They are energetic and resourceful, and they don't give up easily. In the next selection, a group of young people thinks of a creative scheme to save the local bookmobile, a large vehicle used as a "library on wheels." Will their scheme succeed?

The list below shows some examples of how young people have done their community a favor by getting involved. In what other ways might young people help their communities?

- Young people can work with adults to organize "neighborhood watch" groups to help protect residents from crime, such as burglaries.

- Young people can raise money to support community centers or other local resources.

- Young people can write letters to city council members to let them know how they feel about prior decisions the council has made.

92

Comprehension

✔ **TARGET SKILL** **Theme**

As you read "The Power of W.O.W.!", notice how the elements of the play come together to teach a lesson or message to the audience. This lesson is the theme of the play. To figure out the theme, look at the play's setting, the cast of characters, and their actions in each scene. A graphic organizer like this one can help you see how these elements come together to create the theme.

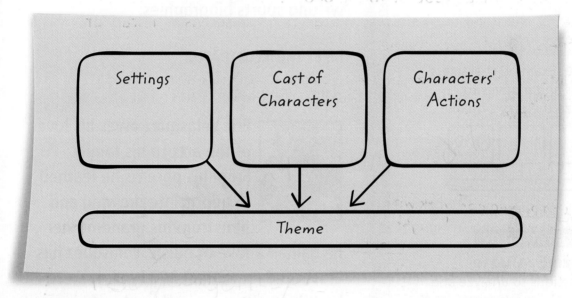

✔ **TARGET STRATEGY** **Analyze/Evaluate**

Use your graphic organizer to keep track of the characters' actions in "The Power of W.O.W.!" As you read, ask yourself why the characters in the play say and do certain things. The answers to these questions can help you understand the author's message.

Main Selection

The Power of W.O.W.!

✓ TARGET VOCABULARY

misjudged	assist
burglaries	innocent
suspect	scheme
regretfully	favor
prior	speculated

✓ TARGET SKILL

Theme Examine characters' qualities and motives to recognize the play's theme.

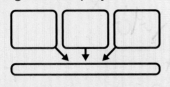

✓ TARGET STRATEGY

Analyze/Evaluate
Ask questions to analyze and evaluate the text's meaning.

GENRE

A **play** tells a story through both words and actions.

Set a Purpose Before reading, set a purpose based on the genre and what you want to find out.

MEET THE AUTHOR

Crystal Hubbard

As a child growing up in St. Louis, Missouri, Crystal Hubbard dreamed of being a writer. She lives near Boston, Massachusetts with her family and two goldfish named Eyeballs and Rocks. Hubbard has written for Boston-area newspapers, and especially likes writing sports biographies.

MEET THE ILLUSTRATOR

Eric Velasquez

Eric Velasquez owes his love of the arts to his family. From his parents he learned to appreciate drawing and film; from his grandmother he gained a love of music. Velasquez has illustrated more than 300 book jackets. He has also written several books of his own.

The Power of W.O.W.!

by Crystal Hubbard
illustrated by Eric Velasquez

Essential Question

How can characters'
actions inspire us to
do good things?

CHARACTERS

Ileana	Shane	Mr. Diaz
Jake	Jason	Mrs. Nguyen
Erica	Camera Operator	

Maria Kopanas, *television news reporter*

ACT ONE

SCENE ONE

Time: Present

Setting: Inside a bus used as a bookmobile—a traveling library—in a Dallas, Texas neighborhood. Mrs. Nguyen (WIN) sits at the checkout counter. Ileana steps inside and sets a heavy stack of books on the counter.

Mrs. Nguyen: Hi, Ileana! How did you enjoy the books?

Ileana: I liked everything but Greek mythology. *(Pause)* I *loved* that!

Mrs. Nguyen: *(Smiling)*: I almost misjudged you. Which myth was your favorite?

Ileana: The one where King Midas turns everything to gold. That wish didn't work out too well.

Mrs. Nguyen: *(Sighing)*: I wouldn't mind having the golden touch today.

Ileana: Why? Is something wrong?

Mrs. Nguyen: *(Forcing a smile)*: Nothing *you* need to worry about. By the way, we just got the latest Sam Thorne mystery. It's called *The Case of the Pet Store Burglaries.* I won't give away who the prime suspect is …

Ileana: I think you're changing the subject, Mrs. Nguyen.

Mrs. Nguyen: *(Looking down regretfully)* I'm afraid Words on Wheels won't be back after next week.

Ileana: What?? Why not?

Mrs. Nguyen: Words On Wheels is a pilot program. The prior plan—for this past year—was for the library to fund W.O.W. But the year's almost up. Now there's no more money to pay for gas or to buy new books. I'll have to go back to the downtown branch.

Ileana: But that's too far away! The only time my grandmother can use a computer is when the W.O.W. bus comes. And I'll never get to see you, Mrs. Nguyen. Can't the library give you some more money?

Mrs. Nguyen: The library does its best to assist us, but the money doesn't go as far as we'd like. We rely on community support, and people just don't seem to be interested in contributing to W.O.W.

Ileana: I have some money saved. You can have it—all of it.

Mrs. Nguyen: *(Smiling sadly)* That's very generous, Ileana, but I'm afraid it would take King Midas to save W.O.W., and I doubt if he's going to show up.

SCENE TWO

Setting: Shane's backyard. Ileana, Shane, and Jason are sitting at a picnic table, sipping juice and munching snacks.

Shane: *(Shaking his head)* Wow. That's bad news about W.O.W.

Ileana: Could we do without the puns, Shane? This is serious.

Shane: *(Looking innocent)* What did I say?

Jason: So, what did Mrs. Nguyen mean by "community support"?

Ileana: She meant that donations from people in the community help pay for the library's special programs.

Jason: Well, we're the community, and if we want to save W.O.W., we have to find a way to make money to pay for it.

Ileana: Does anyone have something we can sell? A rare baseball card?

Shane: I'd sell my bike, but I need it to get to school.

Ileana: Right. Maybe there's something we could do to raise money.

Shane: I could ask my brother. He and his friends raised money for their school picnic last year.

Jake: *(Calling from the back door)* Hey, Squirt. Mom says your friends can stay for dinner. We're having mutant chicken.

Ileana: *(Looking confused)* Mutant chicken?

Shane: Jake and I used to fight over the drumsticks, so my mom uses skewers to attach extra legs to a regular chicken. *(To Jake)* Hey, we have a question.

Jake: *(Sits at picnic table)* Make it fast. I'm a busy man.

Ileana: We need a way to make some cash. The W.O.W. program ran out of money. So tell us how your class paid for last year's picnic.

Jake: We did a lot of things. *(Picks up a handful of snacks)* You could have a bake sale.

Jason: Is that what you did?

Jake: Nope. We held a car wash one Saturday morning, and we earned enough money to pay for the picnic.

Ileana: (*Perking up*) A car wash!

Jason: Let's do it!

Shane: Works for me.

Jake: Whoa. Hold on. You can't just stand on the street and yell "Car Wash!" You have to organize it. You need a place and supplies. You especially need a water source, and you have to advertise.

Shane: (*Resigned*) Wow. I guess it's going to take a lot of work to save W.O.W.

Ileana: You did it again, Shane.

Shane: Oops. Sorry.

Jake: (*To Ileana and Jason*) Tell you what. If you guys are staying for mutant chicken, we can discuss ways to save W.O.W.

Ileana: Great!

STOP AND THINK
Analyze/Evaluate Why do you think raising money for W.O.W is so important to Ileana and her friends?

ACT TWO

SCENE ONE:

Setting: Diaz Bakery. Mr. Diaz stands beside a counter next to a glass case filled with pastries. Ileana, Shane, and Jason enter the shop wearing hand-lettered buttons that read "P.O.W.W.O.W." Each of them carries a stack of papers of assorted colors.

Mr. Diaz: *Hola, niños*[1]. *(He reads buttons.)* What's "pow-wow"?

Shane: It stands for "Please Open Wallets for Words On Wheels." Ileana thought of it.

Mr. Diaz: What scheme are you kids cooking up now?

Ileana: *(Taking a deep breath)* We'd like to ask you for a favor, Uncle Carlos. Words on Wheels needs money so it can keep coming to the neighborhood.

Mr. Diaz: *(Reaching for his wallet)* So, you'd like a donation?

[1] *Hola, niños.*: Hi, kids.

> **STOP AND THINK**
> **Author's Craft** The setting is an important **element of a drama**. Reread the setting on this page. How does it help you stay connected to the scene that follows?

Ileana: Not that kind of donation. See, we'd like to have a car wash this Saturday to raise the money. Our parents donated all the cleaning supplies and we used the W.O.W. computer and printer to make advertisements. (*She hands Mr. Diaz a bright-blue flyer, which he reads.*)

Jason: All we need now is a place to hold the car wash.

Mr. Diaz: (*Chuckling softly*) And that's where I come in, right?

Ileana: Well, you are a part of the community, Uncle Carlos.

Mr. Diaz: True. (*He rubs his chin.*) The "Texas Longhorn" recipe Mrs. Nguyen found online last month has been one of my best sellers. Sure. You can use my parking lot. You can hook up your hose right to the building.

Ileana: (*Slaps high-fives with Shane, Jason, and Mr. Diaz*) Gracias², Uncle Carlos! Thank you!

Shane: You won't be sorry. Just think of all the people who'll want to buy Texas Longhorns while we're washing their cars.

Jason: (*Turns to Ileana and Shane*) The next step is to get the word out. We have to add the location to these flyers and hand them out. Let's stick to the places that we know. I'll go to the Spotless Cleaners and to Teddy's Barbershop and see if we can put flyers there. Mr. Diaz, may I leave a stack of flyers for your customers?

Mr. Diaz: Of course, and I'll give a discount on baked goods to anyone who lets you wash their car.

Jason: *Muchas gracias,*³ Mr. Diaz.

Mr. Diaz: *De nada,*⁴ Jason.

Shane: I'll go to Big Hit Card store and Dr. Bonzo's Used CDs.

Ileana: And I'll take my flyers to Mrs. Romero's market, the Bead Shop, and the Flower Basket.

Mr. Diaz: (*Impressed*) You're very organized.

Ileana: The bookmobile has a lot of information on fundraising.

Shane: That's the power of W.O.W.

Mr. Diaz: After you finish handing out your flyers, meet back here and I'll show you the power of a Texas Longhorn!

---

² *gracias*: Thank you.
³ *muchas* gracias: Thank you very much.
⁴ *de nada*: You're welcome.

SCENE TWO

Setting: Parking lot of Diaz Bakery. Jake uses a hose to rinse his father's car. Shane and Jason towel-dry a second car. Erica accepts a few bills from the driver and hurries over to Ileana, who holds the cash jar.

Erica: (*Excitedly*) How much do we have so far?

Ileana: (*Sarcastically*) A whopping sixty-five dollars.

Erica: We've been out here for three hours and that's it?

Ileana: I thought for sure we'd have tons of cars. I guess . . .
(*Her voice trails off as she stares over Erica's shoulder.*)

Erica: (*Turns to see*) Hey, check out the van. We should charge extra to wash that big silver pole on top.

Jake: (*Jogging over with Shane and Jason*) That's the Dallas News 7 van! We're going to be famous.

Maria Kopanas: (*She exits the van while the driver shoulders a video camera. They walk over.*) Hi, my name is Maria Kopanas. I'm a reporter for Channel 7.

Shane: I've seen you on the news.

Maria: Well, today you're the news. My aunt Della owns Spotless Cleaners, and she told me about the car wash today. May I speak to the organizer?

(*Ileana reluctantly allows the others to push her forward.*)

Maria: Do you mind if I ask you a few questions?

Ileana: (*Shyly*) I guess not.

Camera Operator: We're on the air in five . . . four . . . three . . .
(*Raises two fingers, then one, and points to Maria*)

Maria: (*Speaking into microphone*) I'm Maria Kopanas with five remarkable young people. They decided to do something after learning that their beloved bookmobile, Words on Wheels, lacked the funds to operate. I'll let them introduce themselves. (*Holds microphone to each*)

Ileana: Hi. I'm Ileana, and this is my sister Erica.

Erica: I can say my own name! (*Sweetly, to camera*) I'm Erica. And Diaz Bakery makes the best bread in town!

Jason: I'm Jason.

Jake: I'm Jake.

Shane: He's my brother. I'm Shane. (*Waving*) Hi, Mom!

Maria: (*To Ileana*) Why is the bookmobile so important to you?

Ileana: It's the only way a lot of kids in my neighborhood can get library books and use a computer. The downtown branch is too far away, so it's nice to have a library come to us. (*Showing her button*) P.O.W. stands for "Please Open Wallets"—or "Power of Words."

Erica: Yeah, a book can give you an adventure.

Jason: Or teach you something.

Shane: Or make you laugh.

Maria: (*Speaking to camera*) Some have speculated that when a community is in trouble, no one's around. But here's a group of kids who have come together to help one of their own. What about you? It's a beautiful day for a car wash, folks!

Camera Operator: And we're out. Nice job, Maria.

Maria: Thanks. But before we head back to the station, I think the news van could use a good wash.

103

SCENE THREE

Setting: Parking lot of Diaz bakery. Kids, parents, and the camera operator are washing a long line of cars. The W.O.W. bus lumbers into the parking lot. Mrs. Nguyen exits the bookmobile.

Ileana: Look, Mrs. Nguyen! (*Holding up the money jar*) This is all for W.O.W.

Mrs. Nguyen: Ileana, this is unbelievable!

Ileana: After Maria Kopanas put us on the news, tons of cars showed up. I don't know if there's enough money here to save W.O.W., but it looks like a good start, doesn't it?

Mrs. Nguyen: That's what I came to tell you, Ileana. Thanks to your flyers and the news story, people have promised to help. (*She pulls envelopes from her pocket.*) All of these contain checks! They're from Spotless Cleaners, Teddy's Barbershop, the Bead Shop, Mrs. Romero's Market, Channel 8, your parents, and so many others in the neighborhood. W.O.W. can keep running for a long time to come!

Ileana: (*jumping in the air*) Wow! Guys! We saved W.O.W!

Shane: I couldn't have said it better myself.

> ✔️ **STOP AND THINK**
> **Theme** How do the characters' actions reveal the **theme**, or central idea, of the play in this last scene?

Your Turn

Take Action!

Short Response "The Power of W.O.W.!" shows that taking action can have a positive effect on a community. What would you do if you found out your favorite after-school activity or community program was going to stop? Write a paragraph explaining what you might do to help that activity or program continue. Tell what effect you think your actions might have. PERSONAL RESPONSE

Places, Everyone

Perform a Scene Now that you have read the play, you will perform part of it. In a small group, choose one scene to act out together. Choose one person to be the director. Have each of the other group members play a character from the scene. Take time to rehearse. Then perform the scene for the class. SMALL GROUP

Dramatic Messages

Turn and Talk A story or play may have more than one theme. With a partner, talk about some different themes "The Power of W.O.W.!" suggests. How do the characters' actions help clarify the themes? Use evidence from the play to support your conclusions. THEME

Social Studies

✓ TARGET VOCABULARY

assist	misjudged
burglaries	suspect
innocent	favor
scheme	speculated
regretfully	prior

GENRE

Informational text, such as this magazine article, gives factual information about a topic, organized around main ideas and supporting details.

TEXT FOCUS

Headings Identify the main ideas of sections of a text, such as chapters, paragraphs, and sidebars. Before you begin reading, scan the headings and topic sentences to gain an overview of the text.

KNOWING NOSES

SEARCH-AND-RESCUE DOGS

by Ellen Gold

Search-and-rescue dogs are trained to perform some very special jobs. They often assist in finding someone who is lost. Sometimes they help police officers solve crimes such as burglaries. These hard-working dogs are also known as SAR dogs. SAR stands for "Search And Rescue."

FROM THE PAGES OF
WEEKLY READER

WR

Noses to the Rescue!

Dogs have a great sense of smell. They have about twenty-five times more smell receptors than people have. This makes them good at search-and-rescue work. SAR dogs are trained to follow scents in the air, on the ground, and even underwater!

Air-scent dogs are the most common type of SAR dog. They can find a lost person by smelling the scent that person has left behind. The dogs follow the scent as it gets stronger. Then, they lead the rescuers to the lost person.

Qualities of a Good SAR Dog

SAR dog trainers look for certain qualities in dogs prior to teaching them SAR skills. They look for dogs that like to play and like to please their trainers. Dogs with these qualities will respond to rewards when being trained. SAR dogs should also be friendly, healthy and smart. They should not be afraid of strangers. Certain types of dogs have a natural talent for search-and-rescue work. These are usually bloodhounds, German shepherds, and golden retrievers.

The SAR Dog and the Lost Boy: A Happy Ending

In March of 2007, a twelve-year-old Boy Scout wandered away from his troop's campsite in North Carolina. He misjudged the seriousness of being alone in the wilderness and soon found himself lost.

The boy survived for four days by drinking stream water and finding safe places to sleep. His father speculated that the boy was trying to live out his favorite story. It is about a boy who survives in the wilderness on his own.

Meanwhile, a search-and-rescue team with dogs was looking for the boy. One of the dogs, named Gandalf, picked up the boy's scent and found him. What a great favor Gandalf did for the boy and his family!

SAR Training and Work

Training SAR dogs is a big job. It can take more than a year to get a dog ready for a search-and-rescue mission. Regretfully, some dogs that go through training don't have what it takes to be SAR dogs.

Those that do become SAR dogs deal with different types of jobs. Sometimes they search for a suspect who is part of a crime scheme. Often their searches help innocent people. They might search for someone lost in the wilderness or trapped in fallen buildings.

Whatever their mission might be, SAR dogs are a big help to their human teams.

Making Connections

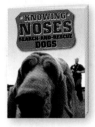

📖 Text to Self

Write About Teamwork In "The Power of W.O.W.!," a group of students work together to save their bookmobile. Think about a time when you worked with a group to benefit other people. Describe what your group's goal was, the steps you took to reach the goal, and what happened as a result.

📖 Text to Text

Compare Community Services Based on what you read in "The Power of W.O.W.!" and "Knowing Noses," which service is more important— search-and-rescue dogs or bookmobiles? Why? Use text evidence to support your opinion.

🌐 Text to World

Research an Animal According to "Knowing Noses," dogs have about twenty-five times more smell receptors than people have. Use an online source to research another animal with a great sense of smell. Then write a paragraph about the animal, explaining how its sense of smell helps it survive. Share your findings with the class.

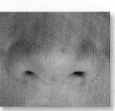

Grammar

What Is a Simple Sentence? What Is a Compound Sentence? A **simple sentence** has one subject-verb relationship. A **compound sentence** is a sentence made up of two smaller sentences joined by a comma and a **conjunction** such as *and, but,* or *or*.

Simple and Compound Sentences	
two simple sentences	subject verb subject verb The kids had a car wash. They made fifty dollars.
compound sentence	subject verb comma conjunction subject verb The kids had a car wash, and they made fifty dollars.

Turn and Talk   **Work with a partner. Find the errors in these compound sentences. Tell how each should be corrected. Then identify the conjunction.**

❶ Adults and children needs books to read, but not all families live near libraries.

❷ A library van come to our town and I borrow books from it.

❸ The van program are almost out of money, but my friends and I are helping.

110

Sentence Fluency You might find pairs of sentences in your writing that are related in some way. Try combining the sentences using a comma and a conjunction such as *and,* *but,* or *or.*

Related Sentences

A few kids fuss during story time.

Most of them listen intently.

Compound Sentence

A few kids fuss during story time, but most of them listen intently.

Connect Grammar to Writing

As you revise your story next week, look for related sentences that you can rewrite as compound sentences, using a comma and a conjunction. Be sure all subjects and verbs agree.

Write to Express

✓ **Ideas** When planning your **fictional narrative**, first brainstorm for characters, setting, and a story problem. Then plot out what happens in the beginning, middle, and end. A story map can help you categorize your ideas and plan what happens. Use the Writing Process Checklist below as you develop your writing.

Mei Ann thought of ideas for her story. She circled the ones to write about. Then she developed her ideas in more detail using a story map.

Writing Process Checklist

▶ **Prewrite**
- ✓ Did I think of ideas that my audience and I will both enjoy?
- ✓ Are my characters and setting worked out?
- ✓ Did I plan a problem for my characters?
- ✓ Did I think of exciting events for the middle of the story?
- ✓ Did I decide how the story problem will turn out?

Draft

Revise

Edit

Publish and Share

Exploring a Topic

Who? a dog walker

two friends

a young guitarist

Where? attic

city park

talent show

What? find a mysterious box

loses a dog

wants to win a contest

Story Map

Setting	Characters
Attic: dusty, full of toys, furniture, camping equipment.	Matt: afraid of spiders, smart Sarah: bossy, brave Attic is in her house.

Plot

Beginning: Sarah discovers a locked suitcase.

Middle: They find a photo with numbers on the back. The numbers unlock the suitcase. Inside the suitcase is an old newspaper and a jacket with a ring in the pocket.

End: Matt reads the newspaper and learns that a jewelry thief used to live in Sarah's house. They return the ring to the jewelry store owner.

> As I filled out my story map, I added details about the setting, characters, and events.

Reading as a Writer

Which parts of Mei Ann's story map sound interesting to you? What interesting events and details can you add to your own story map?

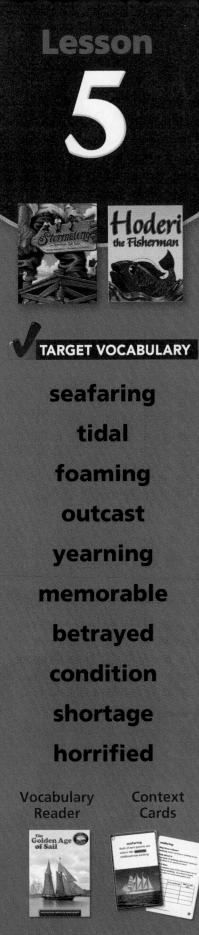

✓ **TARGET VOCABULARY**

seafaring

tidal

foaming

outcast

yearning

memorable

betrayed

condition

shortage

horrified

Vocabulary
Reader

Context
Cards

Vocabulary in Context

1 seafaring

Both of Jen's parents are sailors. Her seafaring childhood was exciting.

2 tidal

An earthquake in the ocean caused a great tidal wave.

3 foaming

Foaming waves crashed against the sea wall, spraying mist into the air.

4 outcast

The lonely girl felt like an outcast in her new town. She did not know anyone.

- **Study each Context Card.**
- **Tell a story about two or more pictures, using the Vocabulary words.**

---

5 yearning

After traveling for months, Daniel felt a yearning to be home.

6 memorable

The vacation was very memorable. She will never forget it.

7 betrayed

If someone betrayed you, he or she let you down.

---

8 condition

Abe has a fever. In his condition, he should be resting.

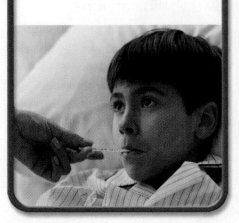

9 shortage

There are long lines for gas because of the gas shortage.

10 horrified

He was horrified when he accidentally dropped his plate of food.

Background

TARGET VOCABULARY   **A Sailor's Life** The age of the clipper ship was a memorable time in seafaring history. Clipper ships were developed in the United States in the mid-1800s. These sleek, graceful sailing ships got their name because of their amazing speed. Sailors claimed that they sailed so fast, they "clipped off" the miles of a voyage.

A sailor's life aboard a clipper ship was tough. In fact, modern sailors might be horrified by the conditions on a clipper ship. It was hard to keep food fresh at sea. At the end of a voyage, there was a shortage of most supplies, especially fruit. A sailor's life was also dangerous. In a storm, tidal surges or giant waves could easily sink a ship. Despite these risks, most sailors loved their work. If they spent too long on land, they often expressed a yearning to once again sail the foaming seas.

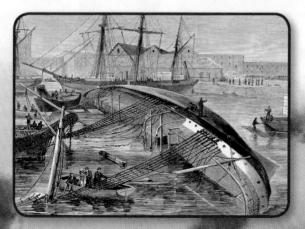

A ship's crew was a community. A sailor who didn't do his job well or who betrayed his mates quickly became an outcast.

Comprehension

✔ **TARGET SKILL** **Understanding Characters**

As you read "Stormalong," look for details in the text that help you understand the personality of the main character. Pay attention to how Stormalong feels, what he does, and what his relationships are like with other characters. Use a graphic organizer like the one below to help you understand Stormalong and the changes he experiences.

Thoughts and Feelings	Actions	Relationships with Others

✔ **TARGET STRATEGY** **Infer/Predict**

When you infer, you use details in the story to figure out something that the author has left unsaid or has not stated directly. As you read, infer what kind of person Stormalong is by using the details you have collected in your graphic organizer. Then predict what he might do next based on your thoughts.

yearning	shortage
memorable	tidal
betrayed	outcast
condition	foaming
seafaring	horrified

✔ **TARGET SKILL**

Understanding Characters
Examine the characters'
relationships and how they
change throughout the story.

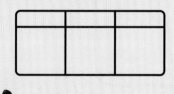

✔ **TARGET STRATEGY**

Infer/Predict Use text clues
to figure out what isn't exactly
stated by the author.

GENRE

A **tall tale** is a humorous
story about impossible or
exaggerated events.

MEET THE AUTHOR

Mary Pope Osborne

Mary Pope Osborne, the author of
the Magic Tree House series, has
written more than fifty books.
As a child, she traveled widely
with her family and continued
to seek adventure as a young adult. Once she
slept in a cave on the Greek island of Crete!
Osborne's love of research has led to many
other journeys through her writing.

MEET THE ILLUSTRATOR

Greg Newbold

Greg Newbold always loved
art and began drawing and
painting at a very early age.
He has illustrated many
children's books and has even
made designs for advertisements. Newbold
also teaches college art classes.

Stormalong

by Mary Pope Osborne   illustrated by Greg Newbold

Essential Question

What motivates one character to help another?

One day in the early 1800s a tidal wave crashed down on the shores of Cape Cod in New England. After the wave had washed back out to sea, the villagers heard deep, bellowing sounds coming from the beach. When they rushed to find out what was going on, they couldn't believe their eyes. A giant baby three fathoms tall—or eighteen feet!—was crawling across the sand, crying in a voice as loud as a foghorn.

The villagers put the baby in a big wheelbarrow and carried him to town. They took him to the meetinghouse and fed him barrels and barrels of milk. As ten people patted the baby on the back, the minister said, "What will we name him?"

"How about *Alfred Bulltop Stormalong*?" a little boy piped up. "And call him Stormy for short."

The baby smiled at the boy.

"Stormy it is!" everyone cried.

STOP AND THINK

Author's Craft The author uses **hyperbole,** or exaggeration, to show how extraordinary Stormy is. In the first paragraph on page 120, she compares Stormy's voice to a foghorn. Look for other examples of hyperbole as you read the selection.

As he grew older Stormy was the main attraction of Cape Cod. He didn't care for all the attention, however. It reminded him that he was different from everyone else. After school he always tried to slip away to the sea. He liked to swim out into the deep water and ride the whales and porpoises. Stormy's love for the ocean was so strong that folks used to say he had salt water in his veins.

By the time Stormy was twelve, he was already six fathoms tall—or thirty-six feet! "I guess you're going to have to go out into the world now," his friends said sadly. "The truth is, you've grown too big for this town. You can't fit in the schoolhouse, and you're too tall to work in a store. Maybe you should go to Boston. It's a lot bigger than Cape Cod."

Stormy felt like an outcast as he packed his trunk, hoisted it over his shoulder, and started away. And when he arrived in Boston, he discovered something that made him even sadder. Although the city had more buildings than Cape Cod, they were just as small. Worse than that, his huge size and foghorn voice scared the daylights out of everyone he met.

"A sailor's life is the only one for me," he said, staring longingly at Boston Harbor. "The sea's my best friend. It's with her that I belong." And with his back to Boston, Stormy strode toward the biggest Yankee clipper docked in the harbor, *The Lady of the Sea.*

"Blow me down!" said the captain when Stormy stood before him. "I've never seen a man as big as you before."

"I'm not a man," said Stormy. "I'm twelve years old."

"Blow me down again!" said the captain. "I guess you'll have to be the biggest cabin boy in the world then. Welcome aboard, son."

The sailors were a bit shocked when the captain introduced the thirty-six-foot giant as their new cabin boy. But the day soon came when all the sailors of *The Lady of the Sea* completely accepted Stormy's awesome size. It happened one morning when the clipper was anchored off the coast of South America.

"Hoist the anchor!" the captain shouted after a few hours of deep-sea fishing. But when the crew pulled on the great chain, nothing happened. The sailors heaved and hoed, and still could not move the anchor off the bottom of the ocean.

"Let me take care of it!" Stormy boomed. Then the cabin boy climbed onto the bowsprit, and dived into the sea.

After Stormy disappeared, terrible sounds came from the water. The ship began pitching and tossing on wild, foaming waves. It seemed that all aboard were about to be hurled to a wet grave, when suddenly the sea grew calm again—and Stormy bobbed to the surface!

Hand over hand he climbed the anchor chain, nearly pulling the ship onto her side with his great weight. As soon as he was safely aboard, he yanked up the anchor, and once again *The Lady of the Sea* began to glide through the ocean.

"What happened?" cried the crew.

"Just a little fight with a two-ton octopus," said Stormy.

"Octopus!"

"Aye. He didn't want to let go of our anchor."

"What'd you do to him?" the others cried.

"Wrestled eight slimy tentacles into double knots. It'll take a month o' Sundays for him to untie himself."

From then on Stormy was the most popular sailor on board. Over the next few years his reputation spread too, until all the Yankee clipper crews wanted him to sail with them.

But Stormy still wasn't happy. Partly it was because no ship, not even *The Lady of the Sea*, was big enough for him. She would nearly tip over when he stood close to her rail. All her wood peeled off when he scrubbed her decks. And giant waves rolled over her sides when he sang a sea chantey.

Worst of all, Stormy was still lonely. The clipper's hammocks were so small that at night he had to sleep by himself in a rowboat. As he listened to the other sailors singing and having a good time, he felt as if his best friend, the sea, had betrayed him. Maybe it was time for the giant sailor to move on.

STOP AND THINK

Infer/Predict In the third paragraph on page 127, Stormy says he'll settle down where the first person asks him what he's carrying on his shoulder. Why would that question tell him he has found the right place?

One day, when *The Lady of the Sea* dropped anchor in Boston, Stormy announced to his friends that he'd decided to give up his seafaring life. "I'm going to put an oar over my shoulder and head west," he said. "I hear there's room enough for any kind of folks out there, even ones as big as me."

"Where will you settle down, Stormy?" a sailor asked.

"I'm going to walk till the first person asks me, 'Hey, mister, what's that funny thing you got on your shoulder there?' Then I'll know I'm far enough away from the sea, and I won't ever think about her again."

Stormy walked through the cities of Providence and New York. He walked through the pine barrens of New Jersey and the woods of Pennsylvania. He crossed the Allegheny Mountains and floated on flatboats down the Ohio River.

Pioneers often invited Stormy to share their dinner, but these occasions only made him homesick, for folks always guessed he was a sailor and asked him questions about the sea.

It wasn't until Stormy came to the plains of Kansas that a farmer said, "Hey, mister, what's that funny thing you got on your shoulder?"

"You asked the right question, mate," said Stormy. "I'm going to settle down on this spot and dig me some potatoes!"

And that's just what Stormy did. Soon he became the best farmer around. He planted over five million potatoes and watered his whole crop with the sweat of his brow.

But all the time Stormy was watering, hoeing, picking, and planting, he knew he still had not found a home. He was too big to go square dancing in the dance hall. He was too big to visit other farmhouses, too big for the meetinghouse, too big for the general store.

And he felt a great yearning for the sea. He missed the fishy-smelling breezes and salt spray. Never in the prairies did a giant wave knock him to his knees. Never did a hurricane whirl him across the earth. How could he ever test his true strength and courage?

One day, several years after Stormy's disappearance, the sailors of Boston Harbor saw a giant coming down the wharf, waving his oar above his head. As he approached, they began to whoop with joy. Stormy was back!

But as happy as they were to see him, they were horrified when they discovered how bad he looked. He was all stooped over. His face was like a withered cornstalk, and there were pale bags under his eyes.

After word spread about Stormy's condition, thousands of sailors met to talk about the problem.

"We've got to keep him with us this time," one said.

"There's only one way to do it," said another. "Build a ship that's big enough."

"Aye!" the others agreed. "We can't be having him trail behind us at night in his own rowboat!"

So the New England sailors set about building the biggest clipper ship in the world. Her sails had to be cut and sewn in the Mojave Desert, and after she was built, there was a lumber shortage all over America. It took over forty seamen to manage her pilot's wheel—unless, of course, the captain happened to be Alfred Bulltop Stormalong, who could whirl the ship's wheel with his baby finger!

Stormalong named the clipper *The Courser*. On her maiden voyage, he clutched *The Courser's* wheel and steered her out of Boston Harbor. As he soared over the billowing waves, his cheeks glowed with sunburn, his hair sparkled with ocean spray, and the salt water began coursing through his veins again.

Soon Stormy and *The Courser* were taking cargoes all over the world—to India, China, and Europe. It took four weeks to get all hands on deck. Teams of white horses carried sailors from stem to stern. The ship's towering masts had to be hinged to let the sun and the moon go by. The tips of the masts were padded so they wouldn't punch holes in the sky. The trip to the crow's nest took so long, the sailors who climbed to the top returned with gray beards. The vessel was so big that once, when she hit an island in the Caribbean Sea, she knocked it clear into the Gulf of Mexico!

But one of *The Courser's* most memorable escapades took place in the English Channel. When she was trying to sail between Calais and the dark cliffs of Dover, her crew discovered the width of her beam was wider than the passageway.

✔ **STOP AND THINK**

Understanding Characters What can you tell about the New England sailors by their actions after seeing Stormy again?

"It's impossible to wedge her through!" the first mate cried. "We have to turn back!"

"Hurry, before she crashes on the rocks!" said another.

"No, don't turn her back!" bellowed Stormy from the captain's wheel. "Bring all the soap on deck!"

The crew thought Stormy had lost his mind, but they went below and hauled up the three-ton shipment of soap just picked up in Holland.

"Now swab her sides until she's as slippery as an eel," Stormy ordered.

"Aye!" the sailors shouted, and they sang a chantey as they plastered *The Courser's* sides with white soap.

"Now we'll take her through!" said Stormy. And as the ship's sails caught the wind, Stormalong eased her between the Dover cliffs and Calais. Ever since then the white cliffs of Dover have been as milky white as a whale's belly, and the sea below still foams with soapsuds.

For years Stormalong was the most famous sea captain in the world. Sailors in every port told how he ate ostrich eggs for breakfast, a hundred gallons of whale soup for lunch, and a warehouseful of shark meat for dinner. They told how after every meal he'd pick his teeth with an eighteen-foot oar—some said it was the same oar he once carried to Kansas.

But it was also said that sometimes when the crew sang chanteys late at night, their giant captain would stand alone on the deck, gazing out at the sea with a look of unfathomable sorrow in his eyes.

After the Civil War, steamships began to transport cargo over the seas. The days of the great sailing ships came to an end, and the courageous men who steered the beautiful Yankee clippers across the oceans also began to disappear.

No one remembers quite how old Stormalong died. All they recollect is his funeral. It seems that one foggy twilight thousands of sailors attended his burial. They covered him with a hundred yards of the finest Chinese silk, and then fifty sailors carried his huge coffin to a grave near the sea. As they dug into the sand with silver spades and lowered his coffin with a silver cord, they wept tears like rain.

And for years afterward they sang about him:

Old Stormy's dead and gone to rest—
To my way, hey, Stormalong!
Of all the sailors he was the best—
Aye, aye, aye, Mister Stormalong!

Ever since then seamen first class put "A.B.S." after their names. Most people think it means "Able-Bodied Seaman." But the old New England seafaring men know different. They know it stands for the most amazing deep-water sailor who ever lived, Alfred Bulltop Stormalong.

Your Turn

Fitting In

Short Response Stormy struggled his whole life to fit in. Using examples from the story, write a paragraph about why he struggled so much. Include your thoughts about why people feel the need to fit in. PERSONAL RESPONSE

Local Legend

Write a Song With a partner, write your own humorous song about a huge baby or other tall-tale character that shows up in your town. Include a description of the main character and a problem his or her arrival creates. How does your town solve this problem? Decide on a tune for your song and perform it for the class. Use ready-made or handmade instruments if you wish. PARTNERS

Friends Forever

Turn and Talk The sailors in New England spent a lot of time and money building a boat that was big enough for Stormy. With a partner, discuss why the sailors worked so hard to make Stormy's boat. What do the sailors' actions show about their feelings for Stormy? Would you do something that hard for a friend? Why or why not? UNDERSTANDING CHARACTERS

133

Traditional Tales

✓ TARGET VOCABULARY

yearning	memorable
betrayed	condition
seafaring	shortage
tidal	outcast
foaming	horrified

GENRE

A **folktale** is a story that the people of a country tell to explain or entertain. This folktale is in the form of a **play.**

TEXT FOCUS

Scenes help show when the **setting**, or time and place, changes in a play and separates the action of the play into different sections. How does each scene differ from the others?

Hoderi the Fisherman

retold by Kate McGovern

❋

Cast of Characters

Narrator
Hoderi (hoh DEH ree)
Hikohodemi (HIH koh hoh DEH mee)
Katsumi (kat SOO mee)
Sea King

❋

Scene 1

[Setting: A small Japanese fishing village in the 1500s.]

Narrator: One day, two brothers—Hoderi, a hunter, and Hikohodemi, a fisherman— decide to trade jobs for a day.

Hoderi: Brother, let us make this day memorable by doing something special. I have always had a yearning to fish.

Hikohodemi: Good idea! But do not lose my fishing hook. With the shortage in iron, I cannot easily replace it.

Narrator: Alas, Hoderi is not a seafaring man. The first fish he catches swims away with the fishing hook.

Hoderi: *[To Hikohodemi]* I am afraid I lost your hook.

Hikohodemi: *[Looking horrified]* Hoderi! You betrayed my trust! By now the sea's tidal shifts have taken it far away.

Hoderi: *[Sorrowfully]* Then I shall search the entire sea until I find it. *[Hoderi dives into the water.]*

Scene 2

[Setting: Underwater, near the Sea King's palace.]

Narrator: Soon, Hoderi meets Katsumi, a Sea Princess.

Katsumi: Welcome! What brings you to our palace?

Hoderi: Forgive me. I am looking for a lost fishing hook. It belongs to my brother.

Katsumi: Perhaps my father, the Sea King, can help.

Narrator: Hoderi tells the Sea King his story.

Sea King: The condition of the sea can make it dangerous, friend. We will help you search.

Scene 3

[Setting: The Sea King's palace, weeks later.]

Narrator: Hoderi stayed in the palace. Soon, he and Katsumi fell in love. Then they received news.

Hoderi: *[Sadly]* The sea creatures have found the lost hook, Katsumi. Now I must return home.

Katsumi: I will go with you, Hoderi.

Narrator: Katsumi hurries to tell her father.

Sea King: *[Upset]* You cannot leave! If you do, you will turn into a sea dragon! You will be an outcast!

Narrator: Katsumi did not listen to her father. She traveled with Hoderi back to his village. But her father was right. One day, without warning, the Sea Princess became a dragon and disappeared into the foaming sea. Hoderi never saw her again.

Making Connections

Text to Self

Describe an Interest In "Stormalong," the main character becomes happy only when he finds his true calling as a sailor. Think of an activity, such as a sport, game, or hobby, that makes you especially happy. Write a short paragraph describing this activity. Explain why you like it so much.

Text to Text

Compare Traditional Tales Both "Stormalong" and "Hoderi the Fisherman" are traditional tales. How are Stormy's adventures similar to Hoderi's adventures? How are they different?

Text to World

Research Steamships The era of the clipper ships described in "Stormalong" ended when ships powered by steam were invented. Use one online and one print source to learn about steamships. Then create a list of facts about steamships, including how they changed the way goods could be transported. Share what you learned with the class.

Grammar

What Are Singular and Plural Nouns? What Are Common and Proper Nouns? A noun that names only one person, place, or thing is called a **singular noun**. A noun that names more than one is a **plural noun**. A noun that names any person, place, or thing is called a **common noun**. A noun that names a particular person, place, or thing is called a **proper noun**. Proper nouns are capitalized.

Academic Language

singular noun

plural noun

common noun

proper noun

Singular and Plural Nouns

| plural noun | singular noun | | plural noun |

The villagers near the beach heard bellowing sounds.

Common and Proper Nouns

| common noun | | common noun | proper noun |

A big wave had crashed on the shores of Cape Cod.

Try This! **Read the sentences below. The nouns have been underlined. Make lists of the common nouns and the proper nouns. Then note which nouns are singular and which nouns are plural.**

① <u>Residents</u> of <u>New England</u> had never seen a gigantic <u>baby</u> before.

② The <u>nickname</u> of the <u>child</u> was <u>Stormy</u>.

③ After twelve <u>years</u> in a <u>village</u>, the <u>giant</u> traveled to <u>Boston</u>.

④ The huge <u>fellow</u> stared at the <u>ships</u> in <u>Boston Harbor</u>.

Word Choice When you write, use exact nouns to create clear pictures for your readers. Exact nouns also help to make your writing more interesting and easier to understand for the reader.

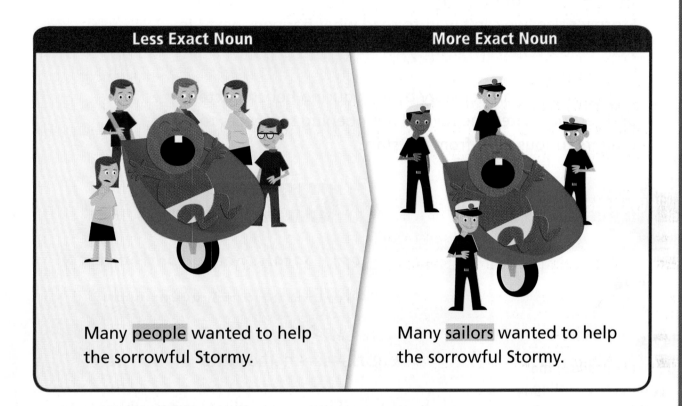

Less Exact Noun	More Exact Noun
Many people wanted to help the sorrowful Stormy.	Many sailors wanted to help the sorrowful Stormy.

Less Exact He crossed mountains and floated down rivers.

More Exact He crossed the Allegheny Mountains and floated on flatboats down the Ohio River.

✏ Connect Grammar to Writing

As you revise your story, look for nouns that you can replace with more exact nouns. Be sure to create clear pictures for the reader in your writing.

Write to Express

✅ **Organization** "Stormalong" grabs our interest right from the beginning of the story. As the narrator tells us about Stormy's size, we can't wait to read what happens next. In your **fictional narrative**, will your beginning get your readers wondering?

Mei Ann began her story by introducing her characters and setting. Later, she revised her opening sentences to make readers curious right from the start.

Writing Process Checklist

Prewrite

Draft

▶ **Revise**

✅ Did I introduce the characters, setting, and problem in an interesting way?

✅ Do my characters deal with the problem in the middle part?

✅ Does the end show how the problem worked out?

✅ Did I use vivid details and dialogue?

Edit

Publish and Share

Revised Draft

"Achoo!" Sarah sneezed in the dusty air. "Looks like no one's been in this attic for years."

~~A girl was in the attic of her new house.~~ There was dust everywhere. Camping gear, old toys, furniture, and trash were stacked along the walls. "This is so cool!" she said to her friend Matt.

Matt didn't agree. "There are probably
spiders
~~bugs~~ up here!"

"We can't turn back now!" Sarah said.

In the Attic

by Mei Ann Lee

"Achoo!" Sarah sneezed in the dusty air. "Looks like no one's been in this attic for years." There was dust everywhere. Camping gear, old toys, furniture, and trash were stacked along the walls. "This is so cool!" she said to her friend Matt.

Matt didn't agree. "There are probably spiders up here!"

"We can't turn back now!" Sarah said. "I've lived in this house for a whole week, and I haven't been up here yet." She pointed to an old brown suitcase. "I wonder what's in that." Sarah tried to open the suitcase, but it was protected by a heavy combination lock. "We'll never get this open!" she said.

In my final draft, I made my beginning more interesting. I also used exact nouns.

Reading as a Writer

Which parts of Mei Ann's opening make you curious about the story? What can you do to make your own beginning more exciting?

141

Read this selection. Think about how the main
character changes by the end of the story.

The Name of the Game

Javier had been in Bay City for only a few weeks. It had been hard to leave his friends and relatives in Mexico and come to a place where everything was different.

At Javier's new school, many kids smiled at him. Some boys in his class even made room for him at the lunch table. Still, Javier worried that he would never make friends. He was learning more English every day, but it was still hard to talk with the other kids. None of them spoke Spanish. Javier had to concentrate so much on the strange-sounding words that he sometimes got a headache. He missed being able to read and understand everything around him.

Other things were different, too. Javier often thought about the big midday meals he used to share with his family. In Mexico, everyone in the family came home in the middle of the day and ate a meal together. They talked and laughed, and no one was in a hurry. Now his father ate lunch at work, and Javier ate lunch at school. Javier was not used to the food they served in the cafeteria, and everyone had to eat so quickly.

Most of all, Javier missed playing *futbol*. In Mexico, Javier and his friends played *futbol* whenever they could. Sometimes older brothers, fathers, and uncles joined in the games. They played in the evenings until it got too dark to see the ball. No one seemed to play Javier's favorite game in Bay City.

Then one day at recess, one of the boys called, "Hey, Javier! Do you want to play football with us?

At last! Here was something familiar. Here was something Javier loved. He nodded excitedly and ran over to the group of kids. When the game began, it was not at all what Javier had expected. This was American football. It was fun, but it was not the same. When Javier walked back to class, his shoulders drooped a little bit.

"I don't think the kids here know how to play *futbol*," Javier told his family that night at dinner.

"Maybe you'll need to learn American football," said his mother.

Javier shrugged. "I guess so."

For the next few days at recess, Javier played American football. He became quite good at throwing and catching the ball. He liked the game well enough, but he really missed the game he used to play.

Then one Saturday afternoon, Javier grabbed his old ball and took it to the park. He was dribbling it across the grass when he heard someone call his name. Some boys from his class were waving to him.

"Can we play soccer with you?" one of them yelled to Javier.

Javier was confused. What was this soccer they were talking about?

"Come on, Javier! Pass the ball to me!" another called.

Javier grinned and kicked the ball. Before he knew it, he was in the middle of the game he loved best. When they finally stopped playing, the boys gathered around Javier.

"You're a great soccer player, Javier!" one of the boys said. "Did you play soccer a lot in Mexico?"

Javier figured it out. He smiled and nodded. "In Mexico, it is called *futbol*."

The boys looked surprised. "Well, let's play some more *futbol*!" one of them said.

Javier grinned. Whatever it was called, he was glad to be playing his favorite game again.

Unit 1 Wrap-Up

The Big Idea

Helpful Hints In Unit 1, you read about people helping others or helping themselves. Work with a group of two or three classmates. Think of ways to be helpful at home, at school, in your community, and outdoors. Illustrate the different ways to be helpful and gather your illustrations in a pamphlet. Present your pamphlet to the class.

Hints for Helping, at Home and Away from Home

Listening and Speaking

A Helpful Act Play a game of charades with a small group. Take turns acting out a helpful act or a character from one of the selections. The student who guesses what is being acted out presents the next charade.

Do You Know What I Mean?

Unit 2

Big Idea

We express
ourselves in
many ways.

Paired Selections

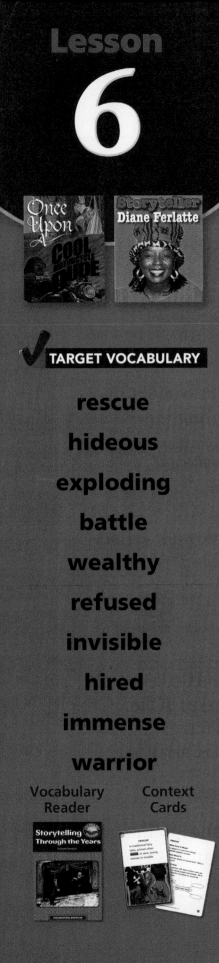

✓ **TARGET VOCABULARY**

rescue

hideous

exploding

battle

wealthy

refused

invisible

hired

immense

warrior

Vocabulary
Reader

Context
Cards

Vocabulary in Context

1 rescue

In traditional fairy tales, princes often rescue, or save, young women in trouble.

2 hideous

Some tales feature a hideous ogre or another extremely ugly character.

3 exploding

Many fairy tale movies end with fireworks exploding in the sky.

4 battle

The hero of a tale sometimes must fight an enemy in a dangerous battle.

- **Study each Context Card.**

- **Use a dictionary to help you learn the meanings of these words.**

5 wealthy

Some characters in fairy tales may be wealthy, while others may be very poor.

rich

6 refused

This fairy tale princess has refused to marry the man chosen to wed her.

no

7 invisible

These heroes wish their capes could make them invisible, or unable to be seen.

8 hired

Long ago, storytellers were hired by kings and queens, who paid them to entertain.

9 immense

Fairy tales may be set in places of immense size, such as huge castles.

10 warrior

Some tales feature a strong, brave warrior who fights to protect the kingdom.

Background

Planning a Story People love stories, but telling a story isn't easy. Good storytellers know how to begin and end as well as to keep listeners interested in between.

Every decision a storyteller makes is important. For example, is the main character someone like you? Perhaps the character is a girl who has hired someone to rescue her dog from a deep well. On the other hand, maybe the main character is extremely wealthy, or hideous, or even invisible. What about the plot? If your story is about a warrior, should the main battle happen near the beginning or at the end? Suppose your story is about an immense spaceship flying toward an exploding star, and the captain has refused to turn back. What happens next? Anything is possible in a story you create, but if you don't plan it carefully, it might take some funny turns.

Did you know that some stories, such as *Cinderella*, exist in many different versions from all over the world? This table shows a few examples.

Name of Cinderella Tale	Country
Cinderella, or The Glass Slipper	France
Yeh-hsien	China
Little One-eye, Little Two-eyes, and Little Three-eyes	Germany
Hearth Cat	Portugal
Vasilisa the Beautiful	Russia
The Little Red Fish and the Clog of Gold	Iraq
Nomi and the Magic Fish	Africa
How the Cowherd Found a Bride	India
The Story of Tam and Cam	Vietnam

Comprehension

✓ **TARGET SKILL** **Compare and Contrast**

As you read "Once Upon a Cool Motorcycle Dude," compare and contrast the two versions of the tale. Find ways in which the characters, events, and art styles are similar and different. Create a graphic organizer like this one to help you compare and contrast these details.

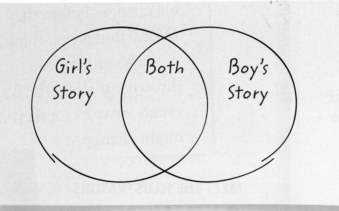

Girl's Story   Both   Boy's Story

✓ **TARGET STRATEGY** **Infer/Predict**

When you infer, you try to figure out something that is not directly stated in the text. Use your graphic organizer to help you infer what the boy and the girl are like and predict what story events might happen next.

Main Selection

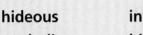

✓ **TARGET VOCABULARY**

rescue	refused
hideous	invisible
exploding	hired
battle	immense
wealthy	warrior

✓ **TARGET SKILL**

Compare and Contrast
Examine how details or ideas are alike and different.

✓ **TARGET STRATEGY**

Infer/Predict Use text clues to figure out what is not directly stated by the author.

GENRE

A **fairy tale** is a story with magical things and characters.

Set a Purpose Before reading, set a purpose based on the genre and what you want to find out.

MEET THE AUTHOR-ILLUSTRATOR
Kevin O'Malley

In addition to writing "Once Upon a Cool Motorcycle Dude," Kevin O'Malley also worked with a team to ilustrate the fractured fairy tale. O'Malley says that his story ideas usually begin with a visual idea of what the characters will look like. He says that projects often go through big changes before they are finished. "Many things you think might work in the beginning of a project get thrown out along the way." Story events, artwork, and even the title might change.

MEET THE ILLUSTRATORS
Carol Heyer and Scott Goto

Carol Heyer loves to illustrate fantasy stories because "characters and creatures can be painted any way that you choose to see them. After all, no one can tell you your dragon is wrong!" Scott Goto not only illustrates children's books, he also creates advertisements and magazine covers. A child at heart, Goto says, "I still love playing video games, watching cartoons, and buying toys."

Once Upon a

by KEVIN O'MALLEY

ILLUSTRATED BY
Kevin O'Malley
Carol Heyer
Scott Goto

COOL MOTORCYCLE DUDE

Essential Question

How are old and new fairy tales alike and different?

151

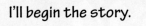

Every day Princess Tenderheart would play with her eight beautiful ponies. She named them Jasmie, Nimble, Sophie, and Polly. And Penny and Sunny and Monica . . .

Her favorite pony of all was called Buttercup.

Please . . . don't call him Buttercup. Call him Ralph or something.

One night a terrible thing happened. A giant came and stole away poor little Jasmie. All the other ponies cried and cried, but Princess Tenderheart cried hardest of all.

The very next night the giant came and took Nimble and Sophie. Princess Tenderheart wept all day and refused to eat.

It was very sad.

Oh please . . . get a grip, Princess!

Her father, the king, hired all the princes he could find to protect the ponies, but night after night another pony was stolen away.

The poor princess just sat in her room and spun straw into gold thread. She cried and cried and cried. When only Buttercup was left, Princess Tenderheart thought her heart would break.

Oh, who would protect Buttercup?

That's it . . . I can't take it anymore. I'll tell the story from here.

STOP AND THINK
Author's Craft Fairy tales often include **hyperbole**, or exaggeration. How is the princess's behavior so far in the story an example of hyperbole?

155

Dudes . . .

One day this really cool muscle dude rides up to the castle on his motorcycle. He says he'll guard the last pony if the king gives him all the gold thread that the princess makes. The king says okay, and the dude sits and waits for the giant.

As if . . . He's not even cute or anything.

So that night the giant heads up to the castle. Man, this giant was a hideous dude. He was big and mean and he had four teeth in his mouth that were all rotten and yellow and black . . .

He needs eight ponies to make a tasty pony stew and he only has seven. So that night he goes to steal the last horsey.

. . . and his breath smelled like rotten, moldy, stinky wet feet.

That's just gross!

157

The muscle dude has this really big sword. The giant and the dude battled all over the place. The Earth was shaking and there was lightning and thunder and volcanoes were exploding.

It was HUGE!

Volcanoes? Where'd the volcanoes come from?

Night after night the giant comes back, but the dude beats him. Night after night the princess makes gold thread and gives it to the dude. He gets really wealthy . . .

STOP AND THINK

Infer/Predict Are you able to predict how the kids' story will end? Why or why not?

THE END!

That's it? The princess just sits around making thread?

Yep!

I don't think so . . . I'll tell you what happened, bubba!

Princess Tenderheart goes to the gym and pumps iron. She becomes Princess Warrior. She tells the dude to make his own thread.

So that night the princess has this immense and tremendous battle. The giant runs back to his cave.

The End.

And the dude just sits there making gold thread.

Nuh-uh! See, this is what really happened . . .

160

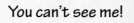

The dude makes this really cool blanket out of the gold thread, and when he puts it over his head he turns INVISIBLE. Then he goes to rescue the ponies.

The dude and the princess get into this big fight over who gets to free the ponies. The giant hears voices and gets so scared he jumps off the cliff.

The End.

☑ STOP AND THINK

Compare and Contrast How is Princess Tenderheart the same at the end of the story as she was at the start? How is she different?

COOL!

COOL!

Your Turn

Different Styles

Short Response Write a paragraph that briefly describes the narrators' storytelling styles. What point is the author making about the kinds of stories boys like and the kinds of stories girls like? Do you agree or disagree with the author? Tell why. PERSONAL RESPONSE

Then What, Dude?

Draw a Cartoon With a partner, imagine the next scene of the fairy tale you have just read. What will Princess Warrior and the motorcycle dude do after defeating the giant and rescuing the ponies? Work together to create several illustrations showing their next adventure.
PARTNERS

Something Old, Something New

Turn and Talk "Once Upon a Cool Motorcycle Dude" is a mix of two styles of fairy tale—old and modern. With a partner, make a T-map that lists the features of old-style fairy tales and those of modern fairy tales. How are they alike? How are they different?
COMPARE AND CONTRAST

Old	Modern

STORYTELLER

Diane Ferlatte

by Ellen Gold

Do you enjoy hearing a good story? Even better, do you love to tell tales to others? Now imagine doing that for a living as an adult. That's what internationally known storyteller Diane Ferlatte has been doing from the bayous of Louisiana to theaters, schools, and festivals as far away as Australia.

Childhood Memories

Much of Diane Ferlatte's early childhood was spent on her grandparents' Louisiana porch, where friends and family told and traded stories. These family gatherings played an immense part in guiding her to her future occupation as a professional storyteller.

Ferlatte's family treasured a rich tradition of passing stories and knowledge from one generation to the next by the spoken word. She explains that, for her culture, oral storytelling is a strong tradition that was passed down from times tracing back to life in Africa. "When the slaves were brought here, they were forced to be totally oral," Ferlatte says. "They weren't allowed to read or to write. . . . They did a lot of talking, a lot of telling stories and singing. . . ."

Ferlatte's family moved to California before she was a teenager, but she visited Louisiana every year. She has happy memories of these times spent with relatives talking, cooking, singing, and, most of all, simply *listening*.

"There wasn't television back when I was a child. They had no computers . . . so people did a lot more talking."

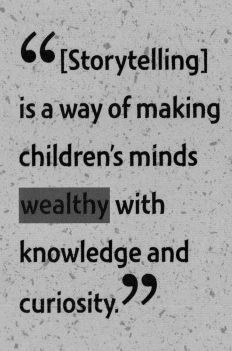

" [Storytelling] is a way of making children's minds **wealthy** with knowledge and curiosity. **"**

Diane's stories inspire children to express themselves.

Storytelling Develops

As an adult, Ferlatte noticed that her young son spent a lot of time watching TV. He **refused** to read books. To **rescue** him from too much TV, she became a "word **warrior**." She read him books in an exciting way and even sang them. She captured his interest with powerful storytelling, without relying on TV images of **hideous** monsters in **battle** or of buildings **exploding**.

Ferlatte told her first public story at a church gathering. People loved it. Stories became her career as people **hired** her to do what she loved.

Today, Ferlatte uses music as an **invisible** but vital tool to support the stories she tells. She likes to visit schools and libraries best. She says, "This is where the tradition of storytelling is to be nurtured and the lessons of the stories most need to be heard."

Making Connections

📖 Text to Self

Be a Storyteller The narrators in "Once Upon a Cool Motorcycle Dude" had very different storytelling styles. With a partner, take turns telling a part of the story, using your own style. Listen carefully and give each other feedback.

📕 Text to Text

Compare and Contrast What fairy tales or other traditional tales do you know? Choose one of them. Compare and contrast the main characters and their adventures in the tale you chose with the main characters of "Once Upon a Cool Motorcycle Dude." Organize your thoughts in a Venn diagram.

🌐 Text to World

Connect to Social Studies Like Diane Ferlatte, many Native American groups have rich storytelling traditions. Research a Native American group from Texas, using the Internet or other resources. Find a traditional story from that group. Share your findings with the class.

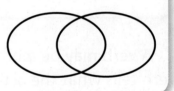

Grammar

What Is a Verb? A verb is a word that can show action. When a verb tells what people or things do, it is called an **action verb**. When a verb tells what someone or something is or is like, it is called a **linking verb**. Most linking verbs are forms of the verb *be*.

Action Verb	Linking Verb
The princess fed her ponies.	The ponies were beautiful.
She gave her ponies names.	Buttercup was her favorite pony.

A verb may be more than one word. The main verb tells what the action is. The **helping verb** comes before the main verb and tells more about the action.

helping verb   main verb
The princess was crying.

helping verb   main verb
A giant had stolen a pony.

Turn and Talk **Work with a partner. Find the sentence that has a linking verb. Then find three sentences with action verbs. Pick out the sentence that has a main verb and a helping verb.**

❶ The giant had stolen another six ponies.

❷ The motorcycle dude approached the castle.

❸ His sword was very sharp.

❹ The voices of the dude and the princess scared the giant.

Word Choice You can make your writing clearer and more interesting by choosing stronger verbs.

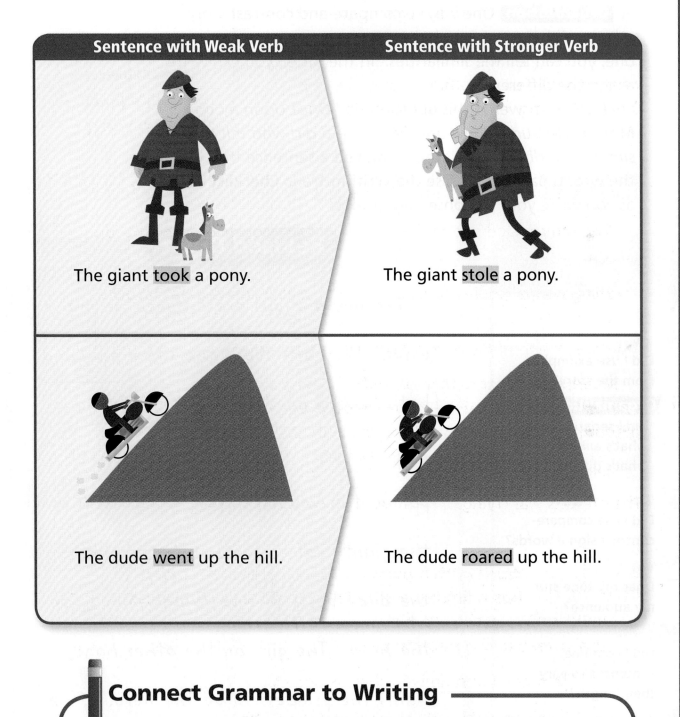

Sentence with Weak Verb	Sentence with Stronger Verb
The giant took a pony.	The giant stole a pony.
The dude went up the hill.	The dude roared up the hill.

Connect Grammar to Writing

As you revise your writing, replace weak verbs with stronger verbs to help keep the reader interested and engaged.

Write to Respond

One way to compare and contrast story events or characters is to write two **response** paragraphs. In one, you can tell the similarities. In the other, you can write about the differences.

   Warren answered this question: *In "Once Upon a Cool Motorcycle Dude," how are the boy and girl who tell the story similar and different?* Later, he moved a sentence that was in the wrong paragraph. Use the Writing Traits Checklist below as you write your response paragraphs.

Writing Traits Checklist

☑ **Ideas**
Did I use examples from the story?

☑ **Organization**
Did I separate what's alike and what's different?

☑ **Word Choice**
Did I use compare-contrast signal words?

☑ **Voice**
Does my tone suit my audience?

☑ **Sentence Fluency**
Did I combine sentences to vary their length?

☑ **Conventions**
Did I use correct spelling, grammar, and mechanics?

Revised Draft

The boy and girl are different in many ways. They are about the same age, and both have a good imagination. While the girl likes sweet things such as pretty ponies, the boy likes gross things such as the giant's rotten teeth. The boy likes the dude best, and ~~The boy~~ wants him to be the hero. The girl, on the other hand, wants the princess to be the hero. ¶ The boy and girl have similarities too.

Final Copy

Comparing Storytellers
by Warren Donovan

The boy and girl are different in many ways. While the girl likes sweet things such as pretty ponies, the boy likes gross things such as the giant's rotten teeth. The boy likes the dude best and wants him to be the hero. The girl, on the other hand, wants the princess to be the hero.

The boy and girl have similarities too. They are about the same age, and both have a good imagination. They each want their favorite character to be powerful. That's why the princess pumps iron and ends up as strong as the dude. Another similarity is that the boy and girl both like happy endings. For example, they both want the ponies to be saved, and they like having the giant jump off the cliff at the end.

In my final paper, I moved an idea that was out of place. I also combined two sentences by forming a compound predicate.

Reading as a Writer

Why did Warren arrange his ideas in two paragraphs? As you write your response this week, look for ways you can organize your paper more clearly.

✓ **TARGET VOCABULARY**

entertaining

promote

focus

advertise

jolts

critics

target

thrilling

angles

generated

Vocabulary
Reader

Context
Cards

Vocabulary in Context

1 entertaining

Going to a movie has been a fun and entertaining pastime for generations.

2 promote

Moviemakers show clips of exciting scenes to promote their movies.

3 focus

Moviemakers use cameras to focus, or concentrate, on each film shot.

4 advertise

Posters advertise movies. People know a film is coming when they see the poster.

- **Study each Context Card.**
- **Use a dictionary to help you pronounce these words.**

5 jolts

Movies often include chase scenes so that viewers feel jolts, or bursts, of excitement.

6 critics

Critics give reviews of movies. Many people pay attention to these reviewers' opinions.

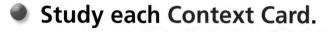

7 target

Some movies are made for kids. Kids are the target audience.

8 thrilling

Seeing a movie on a giant screen can be thrilling. Many people find it exciting.

9 angles

A movie scene is usually filmed from several angles, or positions.

10 generated

Sometimes a movie's success is generated, or created, mainly by word of mouth.

173

Background

Messages in the Media We all know that media are forms of communication, but can they communicate more messages than they seem to? Video games, for example, give players jolts of thrilling excitement, but some critics argue that they promote violence. Websites can be fun and informative, but companies advertise on those sites. They hope that you, their target Internet surfer, will buy their products. People who create magazine ads and television commercials focus their cameras carefully and use certain angles to make the ads and commercials more entertaining. Cinematographers, people who film movies, also make careful decisions about each movie scene. Some people think that all of these media-generated images affect how we think and what we buy.

Every detail of films, commercials, and advertisements must be carefully planned.

Comprehension

✔ TARGET SKILL **Fact and Opinion**

As you read "Coming Distractions: Questioning Movies," notice the facts and opinions that the author provides. A fact can be proved true by checking a reference book or other resource. An opinion tells a thought, feeling, or belief. Create a graphic organizer like this one to help you separate facts from opinions.

Fact	Opinion

✔ TARGET STRATEGY **Summarize**

As you read, periodically retell the most important parts of the text in your own words to confirm your understanding. Record the most important ideas, both facts and opinions, in a graphic organizer as you read.

entertaining	critics
promote	target
focus	thrilling
advertise	angles
jolts	generated

✓ **TARGET SKILL**

Fact and Opinion Decide if an idea can be proved or if it is a feeling or belief.

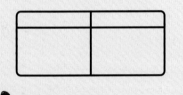

✓ **TARGET STRATEGY**

Summarize Briefly tell the important parts of the text in your own words.

GENRE

Informational text gives facts about a topic.

Set a Purpose Before reading, set a purpose for reading based on what you know about the genre and your background knowledge.

MEET THE AUTHOR

Frank W. Baker

Frank W. Baker was once a television news reporter. Today he travels around the United States, encouraging students to question messages in the media. Movies are only one of his concerns. He also cautions young people about toy commercials that may be dishonest, about the health risks of not exercising enough, and about the problems caused by eating too much junk food.

HOT

FRESH

DELICIOUS

Pop Corn

COMING DISTRACTIONS

Questioning Movies

by
Frank W. Baker

Essential Question

How can movies express facts and opinions?

Movies are fun. There's no doubt about that. But sometimes movies don't give us the whole story. And that can be a problem. But never fear! There is an easy way to make sure we aren't influenced without knowing it. Think about what you see and ask questions.

What Is Left Out of the Message?

Every time cinematographers look through their camera they frame their shot. They focus on one thing. But just as important as what's in their frame is what isn't. Sometimes moviemakers leave things out of the frame or out of the script on purpose. But why would they do that? Well, there are a few reasons.

The "Numbing" Effect

One reason filmmakers leave things out is simply a length issue. If our legs fall asleep because the movie is too long, we're not going to like it. Moviemakers have to decide what to keep and what to cut.

LINGO
frame: to focus the camera on an object or scene

Painting a "Bad" Picture

Sometimes movies leave things out that would make them lose momentum. Fast-paced, action-packed car chase movies are exciting to watch. Violent fight scenes are thrilling to see. But movies don't always show the effects of these actions.

Watching people clean up the damage or go to the hospital just isn't as fun. So even though the movie is entertaining, we have to remember that it's not really how things would go down in real life.

> ✔ **STOP AND THINK**
>
> **Fact and Opinion** "Fast-paced, action-packed car chase movies are exciting to watch" is the author's opinion. Find a fact in the first paragraph on this page and explain how to verify that it is a fact.

Cameron Diaz in *Charlie's Angels* makes fighting in heels look easy.

Painting a "Pretty" Picture

Think about a movie dealing with ordinary people with real problems. Maybe a dad loses his job. Even without a job, the family still has a brand new car, a beautiful home, and fashionable clothes. How can they afford it? Moviemaking magic, that's how. A leading man doesn't look as good driving a rusty old car. A leading lady, even when she's fighting the bad guys, wears high heels. These tricks make for entertaining viewing, but they don't paint an accurate picture of real life.

Try It Out!

Imagine that you're writing a screenplay about your life. It's getting long, so you have to decide what to leave out. Make a list of things you would not put in a movie about you. Here are some things to consider:

+ Do you show your bad habits? Why or why not? If you don't, does that change the story of the real you?

+ Do you include situations where you got in trouble? Why or why not?

How Does the Message Get My Attention?

So now we know studios think a lot about who the movie is for, what they'd put in the movie, and what to leave out. But how do they get the word out? Movie studios advertise their movies like crazy. They market their films in places where their target audience will see it. Trailers for *Revenge of the Mighty Hamburger* won't be running during the evening news. Kids aren't watching TV then. But they'll be all over the TV right around the time school lets out!

Movie studios use more than trailers to grab our attention. They use every marketing trick in the book.

Movie posters tell about important features of a movie. They list the title, the stars, and what happens.

Stars of the movie give lots of interviews on TV, on the radio, in magazines, and even on Web sites. Moviemakers hope the more you hear about the movie, the more interested you'll be.

Blogs, or Web logs, are becoming a popular way to promote movies. Bloggers write about movies to create more buzz.

Movie critics get to see movies before the public. Their reviews carry a lot of weight. Many people will go to see a movie that gets "two thumbs up."

STOP AND THINK

Summarize Summarize the above advertisement techniques and explain how they positively and negatively impact people's behavior.

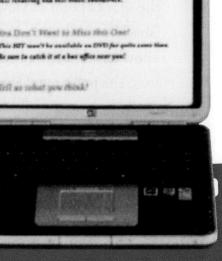

Blogs are sometimes used to market movies.

181

Different types of lighting can make two images of the same person look very different.

Mixing Up a Movie

It takes a lot of ingredients to mix up a film. These ingredients all have to work together to keep us in our seats. Why does that matter? Well, if we aren't interested, we won't buy the products featured in the film or tell our friends to buy tickets.

In a movie, we see only what the camera sees. And moviemakers use this to their advantage. In a scene in *Jaws*, the director wanted the shark's point of view. So the camera became the shark. When the "shark" moved, the camera was panned. We don't see the shark, but we know it's after the swimmer.

The position of the lights can tell us a lot about what's happening. A character in a well-lit area is safe and happy. When a person's face is half in shadow, half in light we know she is doing something evil.

Moviemakers use CGI (Computer Generated Imagery) to keep the action going. Dangerous or imaginary scenes can be digitally created to look like anything they want. The character Gollum from the *Lord of the Rings* trilogy was made using CGI.

The character of Gollum was created using CGI.

LINGO
pan: to move the camera back and forth

Could you imagine *Star Wars* without the music? Music is a great trick to keep our attention. Generally, we don't even think about the music. But without it, movies just wouldn't be as exciting. Did you know editors dub in the sound track after the movie is filmed? The actors may not even hear the finished sound track until they see the final cut of the movie.

LINGO
dub: adding a sound track to a movie after filming is complete

Jolts Per Minute

Lighting, music, camera angles, and special effects are all ingredients that make movies exciting and fun. But moviemakers have other tricks they use to keep us watching. One of these tricks is called jolts per minute (JPM). JPMs are fast, exciting quick cuts or action sequences that get you excited.

LINGO
quick cut: fast scene changes that are meant to jolt and excite you

STOP AND THINK
Author's Craft Words that are used mainly in one type of business are called **jargon**. *Dub* is an example of movie jargon, or lingo, on page 184. Find another example of movie jargon on page 184.

Try It Out!

Music can play a big role in a movie's JPMs. Suppose *Revenge of the Mighty Hamburger* needs a sound track. Get out your CD collection. Pick out some songs that would fit these scenes.

✦ The Mighty Hamburger is rolling down the hill on his skateboard going 60 miles per hour. The cops are chasing him and getting closer and closer.

✦ The Mighty Hamburger and a beautiful cheeseburger take a stroll along the beach at sunset.

Did you use different kinds of music for each scene? Why or why not? Could you use something other than music to beef up a movie's JPMs?

The End

Movies are great entertainment. And sometimes they even teach us a thing or two. That's why we watch them. What's cool, though, is that we don't have to believe everything a movie shows. It's totally our choice. So let's go pop some popcorn, watch a movie, and enjoy asking questions.

Your Turn

Movie Critic

Analyze a Film "Coming Distractions" tells how filmmakers use techniques, such as jolts per minute and music, to influence how we experience movies. Think about one of your favorite movies. What techniques described in "Coming Distractions" does the film use? Write a paragraph that describes how these techniques helped make the movie memorable.

PERSONAL RESPONSE

Coming Soon

Design a Poster Work with a partner. Come up with an idea for a movie that you think would be a big hit. Decide on a title. Then create a poster to advertise your movie. Include on the poster techniques that will persuade people to see it.

PARTNERS

Movie Madness

Turn and Talk Make a list of movie genres, such as action movies, fantasy films, and documentaries. With a partner, discuss which of these genres are likely to have more facts than opinions and which are likely to have more opinions than facts. Based on "Coming Distractions," discuss whether or not you think any movie can be completely free of opinions. FACT AND OPINION

The Wonder of Animation

by Grace V. Montek

Viewers of all ages enjoy animated movies. Do you prefer simple cartoons or thrilling films? Either way, one thing is certain. Animated films are entertaining.

Have you ever wondered how these films are made? Animation is the art of capturing motion in a drawing. At one time, every part of an animated film had to be drawn by hand. These days much of the work is done on computers. Even with all the modern technology, it takes many people and months of work to make a full-length animated film.

The Early Days of Animation

J. Stuart Blackton made the first American animated cartoon in 1906. Called *Humorous Phases of Funny Faces*, it showed an artist drawing faces on a chalkboard. The faces seemed to come to life.

A mouse called Mickey first appeared on film in 1928. An animator named Walt Disney created him. Mickey Mouse became famous in *Steamboat Willie,* one of the first animated cartoons with sound.

The first full-length animated film in the United States was *Snow White and the Seven Dwarfs*, created by Disney in 1937. It was a huge hit. Because *Snow White* was so popular, film studios worked to promote more full-length animated films.

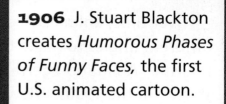

1906 J. Stuart Blackton creates *Humorous Phases of Funny Faces,* the first U.S. animated cartoon.

1928 Walt Disney creates *Steamboat Willie*, one of the first animated films with sound.

1937 *Snow White and the Seven Dwarfs* is the first full-length animated film.

1995 *Toy Story* is the first full-length film created with computer animation.

2001 The first Academy Award for Best Animated Feature is awarded to *Shrek*.

Animation Grows Up

Over time, animators learned to draw from different angles to make their films look more realistic. Animation generated by computers started in the 1990s. Viewers who enjoy jolts of excitement in movies love the constant action in these films.

Children are not the only target audience for animated movies. Film studios advertise them for viewers of all ages. Both audiences and critics continue to enjoy these films. Animation is an art that provides entertainment for everyone.

An animator must focus on one image at a time.

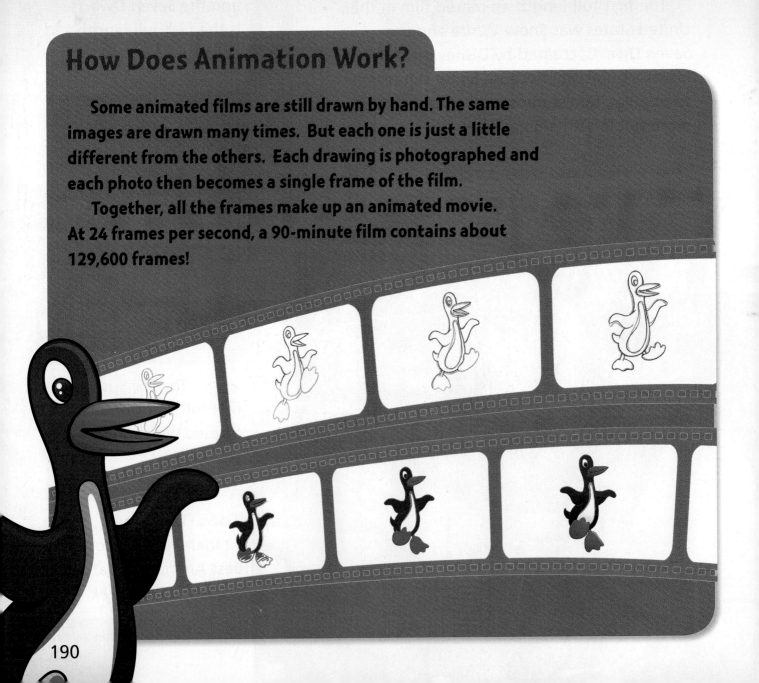

How Does Animation Work?

Some animated films are still drawn by hand. The same images are drawn many times. But each one is just a little different from the others. Each drawing is photographed and each photo then becomes a single frame of the film.

Together, all the frames make up an animated movie. At 24 frames per second, a 90-minute film contains about 129,600 frames!

Making Connections

Text to Self

Analyze Advertising Think of an advertisement you have seen recently for sodas or snack foods. What effect are these ads supposed to have on viewers? How do you know? Discuss with a partner whether you think this effect is positive or negative.

Text to Text

Write a Movie Review Write a short movie review. What was the movie's message? How did the sound effects, close-ups, and other "moviemaking magic" influence its message? Use details from "Coming Distractions" and "The Wonder of Animation" to support your thoughts.

Text to World

Chart Opinions Discuss with the class your favorite animated film. Explain why it is your favorite by giving reasons to support your opinions. As a class, list the five most popular films. Vote for your favorite one, and make a chart or graph showing the results.

Grammar

What Are the Simple Verb Tenses? A verb in the **present tense** tells about action that is happening now or that happens over and over. A verb in the **past tense** tells about action that happened in the past. Many verbs in the past tense end with *-ed*. A verb in the **future tense** tells about what will happen in the future. Verbs in the future tense use the helping verb *will*.

Academic Language

present tense
past tense
future tense

Sentence	Tense of Verb
Filmmakers include exciting scenes.	present tense
The director filmed a car chase.	past tense
You will see this chase in an ad.	future tense

Try This! **Copy these sentences onto another sheet of paper. Circle the verb in each sentence. Label each as present tense, past tense, or future tense.**

❶ Pilar will write about the film on her blog.

❷ She started her blog last month.

❸ Anquan watched four films yesterday.

❹ He likes realistic films.

❺ Rick prefers fantasy films.

Sentence Fluency When you write, use verb tenses carefully to make your meaning clear. Change tense only to show a change in time. Make sure your subjects and verbs agree.

Incorrect Verb Agreement	Correct Verb Agreement
NOW PLAYING! The Robot That Ate Chicago Hayley and I went to the movies. We watch *The Robot That Ate Chicago*. The movie were scary and funny.	Hayley and I went to the movies. We watched *The Robot That Ate Chicago*. The movie was scary and funny.

Connect Grammar to Writing

As you revise your writing, look carefully at verb tenses. Change tenses only to show a change in time.

Write to Respond

☑ Voice When a question asks for your opinion, you can add interest and variety to your writing voice by including a question, a command, or an exclamation. Try this out as you revise your **opinion** paragraph about "Coming Distractions." Use the Writing Traits Checklist below to help you revise.

Marcela drafted a response to answer which is the best way of advertising movies. Later, she made changes to vary sentence types.

Writing Traits Checklist

☑ **Ideas**
Did I use examples to explain my ideas?

☑ **Organization**
Did I state my opinion in the first sentence?

☑ **Word Choice**
Did I vary my transition words?

☑ **Voice**
Did I add interest with a question, a command, or an exclamation?

☑ **Sentence Fluency**
Did I change tense only when needed?

☑ **Conventions**
Did I use correct spelling, grammar, and mechanics?

Revised Draft

In my opinion, trailers are the best
                    Think of all the people who
way to advertise a movie. ~~Thousands~~
~~of people~~ go to the movies. Nearly all
of them watch the trailers, but many
probably don't look at posters or read
reviews. Another reason trailers are best
is that they show parts of the movie.
            Can't you
It's like food. ~~You can~~ tell more by
tasting it than by reading the label?

Movie Trailers Work Best
by Marcela Cabral

In my opinion, trailers are the best way to advertise a movie. Think of all the people who go to the movies. Nearly all of them watch the trailers, but many probably don't look at posters or read reviews. Another reason trailers are best is that they show parts of the movie. It's like food. Can't you tell more by tasting it than by reading the label? Finally, trailers are the best advertisement because they can be shown as a TV commercial. A cartoon show's commercials could be trailers for animated movies. Detective shows could show trailers for mystery movies. This is smart advertising! Why? People who like TV cartoons or mysteries will go see those kinds of movies too.

> In my final paper, I added two questions, a command, and an exclamation. I also made sure not to change verb tense without a reason.

Reading as a Writer

Find a question, a command, and an exclamation in Marcela's paper. Where can you vary the kinds of sentences in your own paper?

✓ **TARGET VOCABULARY**

glorious

studio

model

concerned

smeared

ruined

yanked

streak

schedule

feast

Vocabulary
Reader

Context
Cards

Vocabulary in Context

1 glorious

Fine arts, such as collage and painting, are stunning, glorious forms of expression.

2 studio

A studio is an artist's workshop. Painters paint and potters make pots there.

3 model

As they design a building, architects may create a small, model version.

4 concerned

This photographer is concerned, or worried, that the penguin will move.

- Study each Context Card.
- Use context clues to determine the meanings of these words.

5 smeared

Paint may be lightly dabbed or thickly smeared onto a surface.

6 ruined

This handmade pot was perfect at first, but then it collapsed and became ruined.

7 yanked

This girl must have accidentally yanked, or pulled, the base from the vase.

8 streak

In this lively artwork, some colors seem to streak across the painting.

9 schedule

Some artists stick to a regular schedule, or timetable, as they work.

10 feast

A photographer took a picture of this delicious feast full of food.

Background

Creating Collages In the selection
you're about to read, the artist Romare Bearden makes
collages. What is a collage? Some people think of it as a
scrapbook page full of memorable objects. A collage might
include a birthday invitation or a page yanked from a sports
schedule. Some sections might be smeared with thick paint.
Working like an artist in a studio, you can make a collage using
paper, paints, pieces of cloth, and much more. A collage can
be about anything, such as building a model rocket, watching
a comet streak through the night sky, or eating a Thanksgiving
feast. Don't be concerned that your creation might be ruined
by something you add. As long as it expresses your feelings,
your collage will be glorious.

Art © Romare Bearden Foundation/Licensed by VAGA, New York, NY

Romare Bearden was
a twentieth-century
African American artist
who loved to make
collages about the people
and places he knew.

Comprehension

✔ **TARGET SKILL** **Understanding Characters**

As you read "Me and Uncle Romie," notice details in the text that help you understand the personalities of James, Aunt Nanette, and Uncle Romie. How do they think, act, speak, and interact in the story? Think, too, about how you might react in a similar situation. Use a graphic organizer to help you organize a character's thoughts, actions, and words to give you a better understanding of the characters.

Thoughts	Actions	Words

✔ **TARGET STRATEGY** **Visualize**

To visualize, use details from the text to form a picture in your mind. You can use the details in your graphic organizer to visualize scenes that include these characters. Visualizing characters' actions can help you better understand the story.

Main Selection

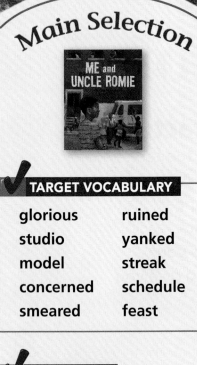

ME and UNCLE ROMIE

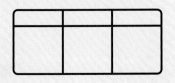

TARGET VOCABULARY

glorious	ruined
studio	yanked
model	streak
concerned	schedule
smeared	feast

✓ TARGET SKILL

Understanding Characters Use details to tell more about characters.

✓ TARGET STRATEGY

Visualize Use text details to form pictures in your mind of what you are reading.

GENRE

Realistic fiction is a present-day story that could take place in real life.

Set a Purpose Set a purpose for reading based on the genre and your background knowledge.

MEET THE AUTHOR
CLAIRE HARTFIELD

Claire Hartfield was born in Chicago. She works as a lawyer, making schools fairer and more equal for all children. For many years she was a dance teacher, helping students to express themselves through movement. She became interested in the artist Romare Bearden because of his ability to tell stories with art. In this story, the character of Uncle Romie is based on Bearden.

MEET THE ILLUSTRATOR
JEROME LAGARRIGUE

Jerome Lagarrigue was born in Paris, France. He won awards and praise for his illustrations in the book *Freedom Summer*. In addition to his work as an illustrator, Lagarrigue spends much of his time as a painter. Recently, he has exhibited oil paintings in Italy. Look closely at the illustrations in "Me and Uncle Romie" to find printed materials Lagarrigue used to create collages in the style of artist Romare Bearden.

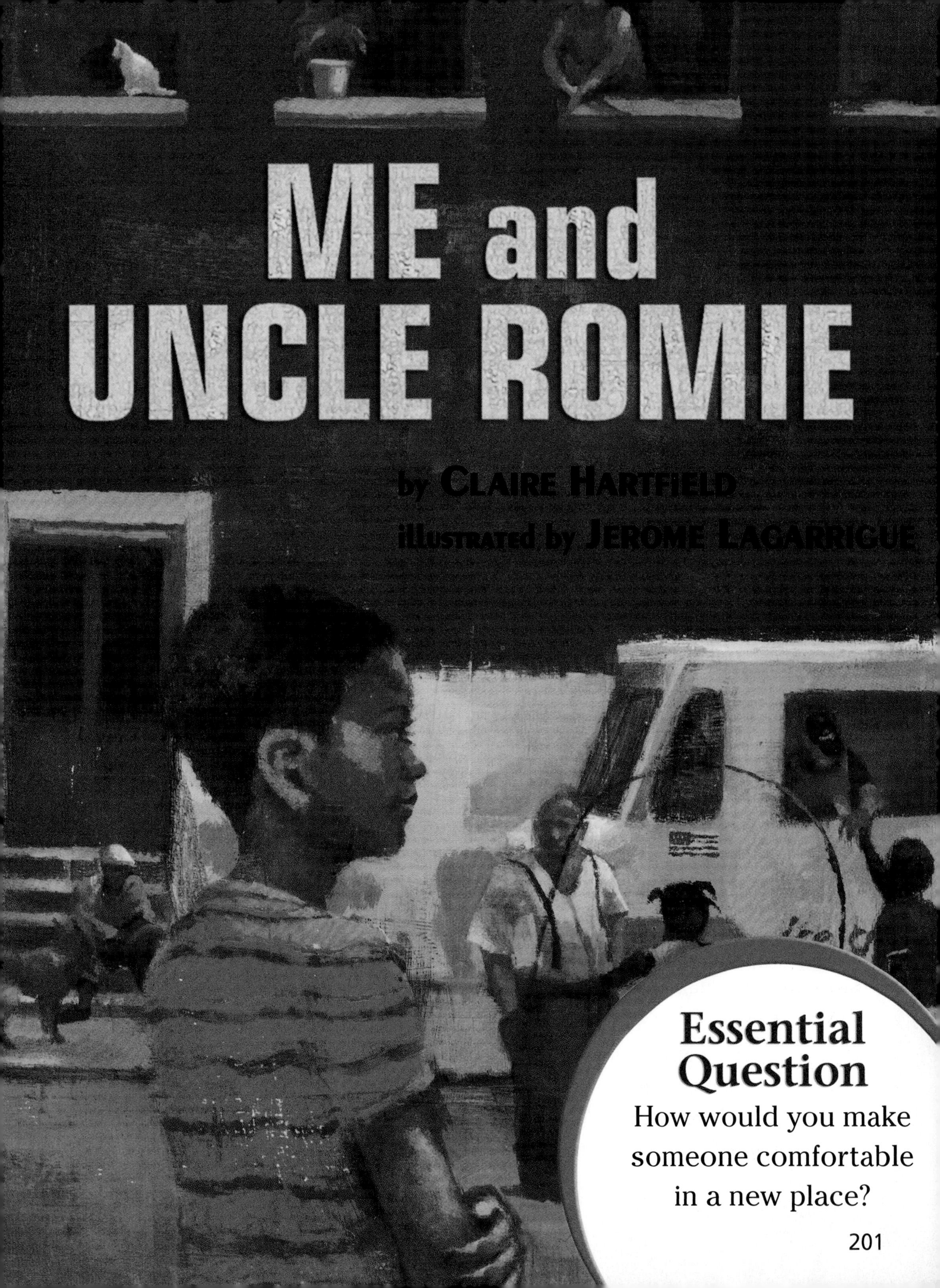

ME and UNCLE ROMIE

by CLAIRE HARTFIELD

illustrated by JEROME LAGARRIGUE

Essential Question

How would you make someone comfortable in a new place?

201

James is on a train from North Carolina to New York City to visit his Aunt Nanette and Uncle Romie. He's never met them before, and he's a little concerned. James has left behind his friend B. J., his dad, and his mom, who will soon have twin babies. James hopes he will have fun on this summer vacation, especially since his birthday is coming up.

Then I saw it . . . New York City. Buildings stretching up to the sky. So close together. Not like North Carolina at all.

"Penn Station! Watch your step," the conductor said, helping me down to the platform. I did like Daddy said and found a spot for myself close to the train. Swarms of people rushed by. Soon I heard a silvery voice call my name. This had to be Aunt Nanette. I turned and saw her big smile reaching out to welcome me.

She took my hand and guided me through the rushing crowds onto an underground train called the subway. "This will take us right home," she explained.

STOP AND THINK

Author's Craft Authors tell stories from different perspectives. When a story is first person point of view, the narrator is part of the story. When a story is third person point of view, the narrator is outside of the story. From what point of view is this story told?

Home was like nothing I'd ever seen before. No regular houses anywhere. Just big buildings and stores of all kinds—in the windows I saw paints, fabrics, radios, and TVs.

We turned into the corner building and climbed the stairs to the apartment—five whole flights up. *Whew!* I tried to catch my breath while Aunt Nanette flicked on the lights.

"Uncle Romie's out talking to some people about his big art show that's coming up. He'll be home soon," Aunt Nanette said. She set some milk and a plate of cookies for me on the table. "Your uncle's working very hard, so we won't see much of him for a while. His workroom—we call it his studio—is in the front of our apartment. That's where he keeps all the things he needs to make his art."

"Doesn't he just paint?" I asked.

"Uncle Romie is a collage artist," Aunt Nanette explained. "He uses paints, yes. But also photographs, newspapers, cloth. He cuts and pastes them onto a board to make his paintings."

"That sounds kinda easy," I said.

Aunt Nanette laughed.

"Well, there's a little more to it than that, James. When you see the paintings, you'll understand. Come, let's get you to bed."

Lying in the dark, I heard heavy footsteps in the hall. A giant stared at me from the doorway. "Hello there, James." Uncle Romie's voice was deep and loud, like thunder. "Thanks for the pepper jelly," he boomed. "You have a good sleep, now." Then he disappeared down the hall.

The next morning the door to Uncle Romie's studio was closed. But Aunt Nanette had plans for both of us. "Today we're going to a neighborhood called Harlem," she said. "It's where Uncle Romie lived as a boy."

Harlem was full of people walking, working, shopping, eating. Some were watching the goings-on from fire escapes. Others were sitting out on stoops greeting folks who passed by—just like the people back home calling out hellos from their front porches. Most everybody seemed to know Aunt Nanette. A lot of them asked after Uncle Romie too.

We bought peaches at the market, then stopped to visit awhile. I watched some kids playing stickball. "Go on, get in that game," Aunt Nanette said, gently pushing me over to join them. When I was all hot and sweaty, we cooled off with double chocolate scoops from the ice cream man. Later we shared some barbecue on a rooftop way up high. I felt like I was on top of the world.

STOP AND THINK

Visualize The descriptions of James's activities in Harlem, on pages 204 and 205, involve many different senses. For example, people's greetings involve the sense of hearing. Which details focus on the sense of sight?

204

As the days went by, Aunt Nanette took me all over the city—we rode a ferry boat to the Statue of Liberty . . . zoomed 102 floors up at the Empire State Building . . . window-shopped the fancy stores on Fifth Avenue . . . gobbled hot dogs in Central Park.

But it was Harlem that I liked best. I played stickball with the kids again . . . and on a really hot day a whole bunch of us ran through the icy cold water that sprayed out hard from the fire hydrant. In the evenings Aunt Nanette and I sat outside listening to the street musicians playing their saxophone songs.

On rainy days I wrote postcards and helped out around the apartment. I told Aunt Nanette about the things I liked to do back home—about baseball games, train-watching, my birthday. She told me about the special Caribbean lemon and mango cake she was going to make.

My uncle Romie stayed hidden away in his studio. But I wasn't worried anymore. Aunt Nanette would make my birthday special.

4 . . . 3 . . . 2 . . . 1 . . . My birthday was almost here!

And then Aunt Nanette got a phone call.

"An old aunt has died, James. I have to go away for her funeral. But don't you worry. Uncle Romie will spend your birthday with you. It'll be just fine."

That night Aunt Nanette kissed me good-bye. I knew it would not be fine at all. Uncle Romie didn't know about cakes or baseball games or anything except his dumb old paintings. My birthday was ruined.

When the sky turned black, I tucked myself into bed. I missed Mama and Daddy so much. I listened to the birds on the rooftop—their songs continued into the night.

The next morning everything was quiet. I crept out of bed and into the hall. For the first time the door to Uncle Romie's studio stood wide open. What a glorious mess! There were paints and scraps all over the floor, and around the edges were huge paintings with all sorts of pieces pasted together.

I saw saxophones, birds, fire escapes, and brown faces. *It's Harlem*, I thought. *The people, the music, the rooftops, and the stoops*. Looking at Uncle Romie's paintings, I could *feel* Harlem—its beat and bounce.

> ✔️ **STOP AND THINK**
> **Understanding Characters** How does James' opinion of Uncle Romie change throughout the story?

Then there was one that was different. Smaller houses, flowers, and trains. "That's home!" I shouted.

"Yep," Uncle Romie said, smiling, from the doorway. "That's the Carolina I remember."

"Mama says you visited your grandparents there most every summer when you were a kid," I said.

"I sure did, James. *Mmm.* Now that's the place for pepper jelly. Smeared thick on biscuits. And when Grandma wasn't looking . . . I'd sneak some on a spoon."

"Daddy and I do that too!" I told him.

We laughed together, then walked to the kitchen for a breakfast feast—eggs, bacon, grits, and biscuits.

"James, you've got me remembering the pepper jelly lady. People used to line up down the block to buy her preserves."

"Could you put someone like that in one of your paintings?" I asked.

"I guess I could." Uncle Romie nodded. "Yes, that's a memory just right for sharing. What a good idea, James. Now let's get this birthday going!"

He brought out two presents from home. I tore into the packages while he got down the pepper jelly and two huge spoons. Mama and Daddy had picked out just what I wanted—a special case for my baseball cards, and a model train for me to build.

"Pretty cool," said Uncle Romie. "I used to watch the trains down in North Carolina, you know."

How funny to picture big Uncle Romie lying on his belly!

"B. J. and me, we have contests to see who can hear the trains first."

"Hey, I did that too. You know, it's a funny thing, James. People live in all sorts of different places and families. But the things we care about are pretty much the same. Like favorite foods, special songs, games, stories . . . and like birthdays." Uncle Romie held up two tickets to a baseball game!

It turns out Uncle Romie knows all about baseball—he was even a star pitcher in college. We got our mitts and set off for the game.

Way up in the bleachers, we shared a bag of peanuts, cracking the shells with our teeth and keeping our mitts ready in case a home run ball came our way. That didn't happen— but we sure had fun.

Aunt Nanette came home that night. She lit the candles and we all shared my Caribbean birthday cake.

After that, Uncle Romie had to work a lot again. But at the end of each day he let me sit with him in his studio and talk. Daddy was right. Uncle Romie is a good man.

The day of the big art show finally came. I watched the people laughing and talking, walking slowly around the room from painting to painting. I walked around myself, listening to their conversations.

"Remember our first train ride from Chicago to New York?" one lady asked her husband.

"That guitar-playing man reminds me of my uncle Joe," said another.

All these strangers talking to each other about their families and friends and special times, and all because of how my uncle Romie's paintings reminded them of these things.

209

Later that night Daddy called. I had a brand-new brother and sister. Daddy said they were both bald and made a lot of noise. But he sounded happy and said how they all missed me.

This time Aunt Nanette and Uncle Romie took me to the train station.

"Here's a late birthday present for you, James," Uncle Romie said, holding out a package. "Open it on the train, why don't you. It'll help pass the time on the long ride home."

I waved out the window to Uncle Romie and Aunt Nanette until I couldn't see them anymore. Then I ripped off the wrappings!

And there was my summer in New York. Bright sky in one corner, city lights at night in another. Tall buildings. Baseball ticket stubs. The label from the pepper jelly jar. And trains. One going toward the skyscrapers. Another going away.

Back home, I lay in the soft North Carolina grass. It was the first of September, almost Uncle Romie's birthday. I watched the birds streak across the sky.

Rooftop birds, I thought. *Back home from their summer in New York, just like me.* Watching them, I could still feel the city's beat inside my head.

A feather drifted down from the sky. In the garden tiger lilies bent in the wind. *Uncle Romie's favorite flowers.* I yanked off a few blossoms. And then I was off on a treasure hunt, collecting things that reminded me of Uncle Romie.

I painted and pasted them together on a big piece of cardboard. Right in the middle I put the train schedule. And at the top I wrote:

Your Turn

Made by Hand

Write About Gifts James made Uncle Romie a birthday gift because he cared about him. Write a paragraph that tells about a time you made a special gift for someone. Describe the gift and the experience you had making it. Tell why you made it and how the person you made it for reacted.

PERSONAL RESPONSE

Welcome!

Plan a Tour Imagine you are giving a tour of your school to a new student. Work with a partner to draw a simple map of your school. Label the places you would include on the tour and discuss why those places are important to show the new student. PARTNERS

Our school

Class rooms

Play ground

Class rooms

Class rooms   Library   Auditorium

Reading Uncle Romie

Turn and Talk Think of the various ways in which Uncle Romie makes James's birthday special for him. Using story details and your own experience, discuss with a partner what Uncle Romie's actions tell you about his personality.

UNDERSTANDING CHARACTERS

Connect to
Art

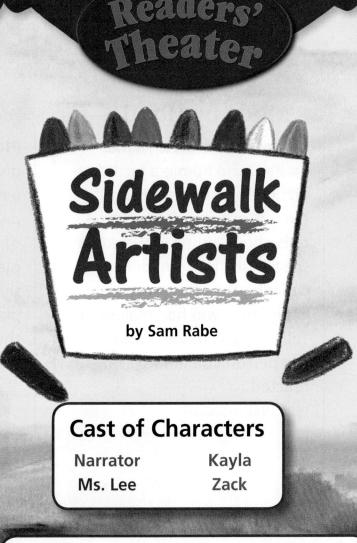

GENRE

Readers' theater is a text that has been formatted for readers to read aloud.

TEXT FOCUS

Directions A text may include a set of instructions telling how to do something, often by following a series of steps. Review the steps presented in the text to create sidewalk art.

Sidewalk Artists

by Sam Rabe

Cast of Characters

Narrator	Kayla
Ms. Lee	Zack

Narrator: On a sunny day in southern Texas, Ms. Lee's students gathered in the school playground.

Ms. Lee: Tomorrow is the day of the sidewalk chalk-art festival. The principal has given us permission to practice our wet-chalk drawing on the playground pavement, which will be our studio. Remember, whenever you want to draw on a sidewalk, always ask an adult in charge for permission before you draw. Now let's review the steps of wet-chalk drawing. What do we do first?

Narrator: As the students told her the steps in order, Ms. Lee wrote them on a large pad of paper. When she finished writing, she yanked the sheet off the pad and displayed the directions so everyone could read them. Then the students chose and soaked their pieces of chalk. Meanwhile, Kayla and Zack planned their drawing.

Kayla: Let's draw a jungle feast. Parrots can be eating all kinds of fruit.

Zack: I'll draw a model train carrying food to the birds.

Narrator: The students removed their pieces of chalk from the water and drew. As Zack drew a sweeping curve of train track, his hand knocked over the jar of water. He and Kayla watched water streak across their drawing.

Zack: Our drawing is ruined!

Kayla: Don't be so concerned! Quick, blend the water and the chalk together! Now let's layer on more chalk and smear it around.

Narrator: Kayla and Zack worked quickly. The smeared colors looked glorious, like rich, thick frosting on a cake.

Ms. Lee: That looks great! That's a neat technique you're using, kids. Are you two interested in taking part in the chalk-art festival tomorrow? The schedule for the festival says that drawing starts at 9:00 A.M.

Kayla and Zack: Sure!

Kayla: Tomorrow we'll spill water on our drawing on purpose.

Zack: Then we'll know just what to do!

Making Wet Chalk Drawings

1. Choose your pieces of chalk, and put them in a jar.
2. Fill the jar with water to cover three quarters of the length of the chalk. Let the chalk soak for a few minutes, but don't let it dissolve.
3. Remove the wet chalk from the jar.
4. Draw!
5. Let your drawing dry.

Making Connections

 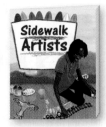

Text to Self

Write a Description Think of an adult who is important to you. What items would you include in a collage about that person? Write a paragraph describing the collage you would make. Tell how each item reminds you of the person.

Text to Text

Compare and Contrast Think about the forms of art featured in "Me and Uncle Romie" and "Sidewalk Artists." How are these forms of art alike and how are they different? Use evidence from the text to make a list of the similarities and differences.

Text to World

Biography and Fiction "Me and Uncle Romie" is a fictional story based on a real artist. Read an online biography of the artist Romare Bearden. Then identify the things that were the same in both his real life and in this story. Share your findings with a partner.

Grammar

What Is a Conjunction? A **conjunction** is a connecting word. *And, but,* and *or* are conjunctions that connect two sentences to form a **compound sentence**. Conjunctions such as *if, because,* and *unless* can connect two sentences to form a **complex sentence**. Some conjunctions are used in pairs. They are called **correlative conjunctions**. Common ones are *either/or, neither/nor,* and *both/and*. Correlative conjunctions can be used in simple sentences to make a strong connection between ideas.

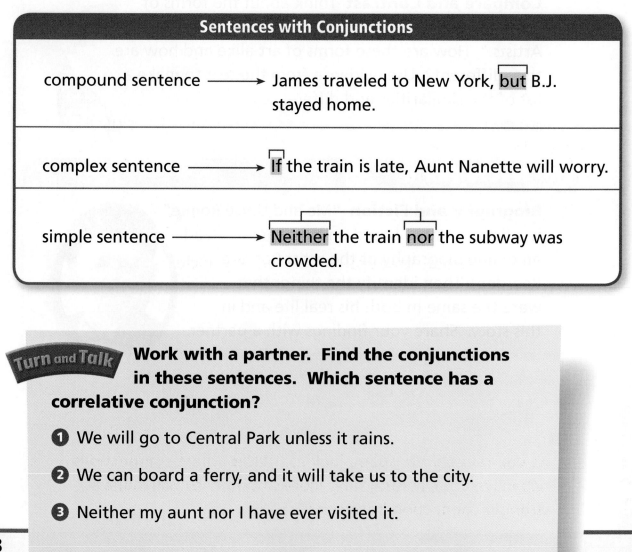

Sentences with Conjunctions	
compound sentence	James traveled to New York, but B.J. stayed home.
complex sentence	If the train is late, Aunt Nanette will worry.
simple sentence	Neither the train nor the subway was crowded.

Turn and Talk **Work with a partner. Find the conjunctions in these sentences. Which sentence has a correlative conjunction?**

1. We will go to Central Park unless it rains.

2. We can board a ferry, and it will take us to the city.

3. Neither my aunt nor I have ever visited it.

218

Ideas Similar ideas can be linked in a single sentence to help readers see the connection between the ideas. If two sentences are about the same idea, sometimes you can use correlative conjunctions to combine the sentences, making a stronger connection between the ideas.

Separate Sentences

My aunt does not disturb my uncle.

I do not disturb my uncle.

One Sentence

Neither my aunt nor I disturb my uncle.

Connect Grammar to Writing

As you revise your poem, look for places where conjunctions will make your writing flow more smoothly or will make a stronger connection between ideas.

Write to Respond

☑ **Word Choice** One way to respond to literature is to write a **poem** based on what you read. Your poem should include details that appeal to the five senses: sight, sound, taste, touch, and smell. It may also contain conventions of poetry, such as rhyme, rhythm, and stanzas, or lines that are grouped together. Use the Writing Traits Checklist as you revise your poem.

Davey drafted a poem about New York City in response to "Me and Uncle Romie." Then he changed words in his poem to improve the rhyme and the details that appeal to the senses.

Writing Traits Checklist

☑ **Ideas**
Are my ideas clear?

☑ **Organization**
Did I arrange my ideas in a clear way?

☑ **Word Choice**
Did I choose words that create vivid sounds or images?

☑ **Voice**
Did I express my ideas in my own way?

☑ **Sentence Fluency**
Did I use conjunctions to join ideas?

☑ **Conventions**
Did I use correct spelling, grammar, and mechanics?

Revised Draft

There's ~~a lot~~ so much to see and do,

from Harlem to ~~the statue of Liberty~~ Fifth Avenue.

Buildings ~~going~~ stretching to the sky

and tons of ~~many~~ people ~~going~~ rushing by.

New York, Big City
by Davey Chu

There's so much to see and do,

from Harlem to Fifth Avenue.

Buildings stretching to the sky

and tons of people rushing by.

There are so many treats to taste:

Caribbean lemon mango cake,

huge hot dogs in Central Park,

rooftop barbecue in the dark.

Listen to the city sounds!

Subways rumbling underground,

street musicians and saxophones—

in New York you're never alone.

For my final poem, I replaced weak words with words that help readers imagine vivid tastes, sounds, and images. I also used conjunctions to link ideas together.

Reading as a Writer

Which words did Davey replace to make his poem stronger? As you write your own poem, look for words you could replace to make the poem come alive with sights and sounds.

FIELD GUIDE
to
Snakes
of the
Southwest

✓ **TARGET VOCABULARY**

fault

borrow

reference

fainted

genuine

local

apologize

proof

slimy

insisted

Vocabulary
Reader

Context
Cards

Vocabulary in Context

1 fault

A misunderstanding between friends is often no one's **fault**, or responsibility.

2 borrow

If you **borrow** an item from someone, make sure to return it soon.

3 reference

A **reference** book is a good source of information. It can explain things clearly.

4 fainted

This person has not **fainted**. She is just taking a short nap.

● **Study each Context Card.**

● **Use a dictionary to help you understand the meanings of these words.**

5 **genuine**

If you say something that is not genuine, or sincere, someone's feelings could be hurt.

6 **local**

Visitors from another region may not understand local practices and customs.

7 **apologize**

If you do something wrong, it's best to apologize by saying you're sorry.

8 **proof**

Your parents might want proof that you really have done your homework.

9 **slimy**

These boys didn't mind that the soccer field had patches of slimy mud!

10 **insisted**

This boy's mom demanded, or insisted, that he fix the mess he made.

Background

✓ TARGET VOCABULARY **Why Apologize?** When we do something wrong, it's important to apologize. Sometimes we have to apologize for things done on purpose, such as putting a slimy frog into a friend's backpack! At other times we have to apologize for mistakes we made, such as asking to borrow a reference book from a teacher and then losing it.

In the next selection, a girl writes a letter to the local librarian to say that a recent disturbance in the library was her fault. Someone even fainted! Her parents have insisted she provide proof that she is sorry. See whether you think her apology is genuine.

Ways to Apologize to Someone

- Write a letter.

- Say "I'm sorry" in person.

- Do something special for him or her.

Comprehension

✔ TARGET SKILL   Conclusions and Generalizations

Sometimes an author expects readers to figure something out, or draw a conclusion, on their own. A generalization is a kind of conclusion that is true about something *most* of the time, but not always. As you read, notice details from the text that might help you draw a reasonable conclusion about the story. Create a graphic organizer to show how text details support a conclusion or a generalization.

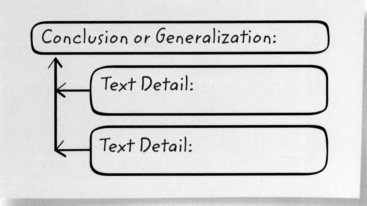

Conclusion or Generalization:

Text Detail:

Text Detail:

✔ TARGET STRATEGY   Question

Use your graphic organizer and the question strategy to draw conclusions about the narrator's attitudes and feelings. As you read, ask yourself questions such as *How?* or *Why?* to gain a better understanding of ideas not stated directly.

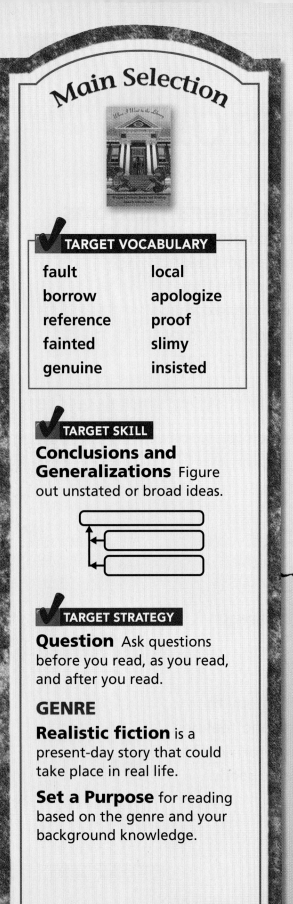

✓ **TARGET VOCABULARY**

fault	local
borrow	apologize
reference	proof
fainted	slimy
genuine	insisted

✓ **TARGET SKILL**

Conclusions and Generalizations Figure out unstated or broad ideas.

✓ **TARGET STRATEGY**

Question Ask questions before you read, as you read, and after you read.

GENRE

Realistic fiction is a present-day story that could take place in real life.

Set a Purpose for reading based on the genre and your background knowledge.

MEET THE AUTHOR

KEN ROBERTS

Like Mr. Winston, Ken Roberts is a librarian. He also writes books and plays and is a storyteller. "I am good at many things," he says, "but a master at none, really." Sometimes he works on many projects at once. At other times he reads quietly by the fireside.

MEET THE ILLUSTRATOR

ANDY HAMMOND

Andy Hammond has been a busy cartoonist for more than thirty years. He works in pen and ink and watercolor, often finishing his work on the computer. His favorite cartooning jobs are the ones that let him use his own style and allow his sense of humor to run free.

Dear Mr. Winston

from When I Went to the Library

by Ken Roberts

selection illustrated
by Andy Hammond

**Essential
Question**

Why would
someone make an
insincere apology?

Dear Mr. Winston,

My parents said that I have to write and apologize. Dad says he is going to read this letter before it's sent and that I'd better make sure my apology sounds truly genuine. So, I am truly, genuinely sorry for bringing that snake into the library yesterday.

My parents say that what I did was wrong, even though the cardboard box was shut, most of the time, and there was no way that snake could have escaped if you hadn't opened the box and dropped it on the floor.

My parents say it's my fault for having brought that snake into the library and I truly, genuinely apologize but I still don't know how I was supposed to find out what kind of snake I had inside that box without bringing the snake right into the library so I could look at snake pictures and then look at the snake and try to find a picture that matched the snake.

STOP AND THINK

Question The beginning of a story can raise many questions. What is one question you want this story to answer, now that you've read one page?

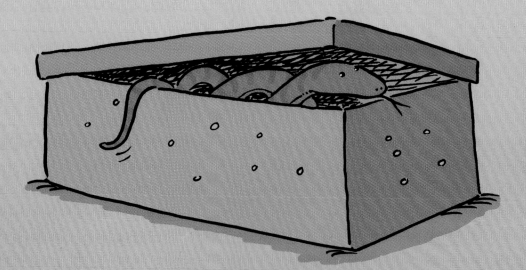

228

229

230

I told my parents something that I didn't get a chance to remind you about before the ambulance took you away. I did come into the library without the snake, first. I left the box outside, hidden under a bush and tried to borrow a thick green book with lots of snake pictures. You told me that the big green book was a reference book which meant that it had to stay inside the library and I couldn't take it out, even for ten minutes.

My parents say I still shouldn't have brought that snake into the library and that I have to be truly, genuinely sorry if I ever hope to watch *Galactic Patrol* on television again. My parents picked *Galactic Patrol* because it's my favorite show, although I'm not sure what not watching a television program has to do with bringing a snake into the library.

The people at the library say you hate snakes so much that you won't even touch a book with a picture of snakes on the cover and that is why you won't be back at the library for a few more weeks. If you want, you could watch *Galactic Patrol*. It's on at 4:00 P.M. weekdays, on channel 7. There are no snakes on the show because it takes place in space.

Did the flowers arrive? Dad picked them out but I have to pay for them with my allowance for the next two months. The flowers are proof that I am truly, genuinely sorry for having brought that snake into the library. I hope the people who work at the library find that snake soon! Did they look under all the chairs?

WILD FLOWERS

That snake isn't dangerous. It is a local snake, and there are no poisonous snakes in Manitoba. The people at the library say you know that too because that was one of the reasons you decided to move here. I bought that snake from a friend. I paid one month's allowance for it, which means that snake has cost me a total of three months' allowance and I only owned it for one hour!

Mom says I don't have to tell who sold me that snake so I won't tell you either because Dad says he is going to read this letter. Besides, I don't want you to be mad at anyone else when I am the one who brought that snake into the library yesterday. I am truly, genuinely sorry.

I want you to know that I didn't plan to show you that snake. I didn't mean to scare you at all. I knew where the big green snake book was kept. I put the box on a table close to the book and tried to find the right picture. I looked at a picture, then at the snake, at another picture, and then the snake. I did that five times and can tell you that the snake inside the library is not a python, a rattlesnake, an anaconda, an asp, or a cobra.

Anyway, I was surprised when you wanted to see what was inside the box because I didn't ask for any help and there were plenty of people in the library who did need help.

Dad says that the fact that I said, "Nothing," instead of "A snake," is proof that I knew I was doing something wrong when I brought that snake into the library. I am truly, genuinely sorry even though my friend Jake Lambert promised me that the snake I bought from him is perfectly harmless.

233

I did tell you that I didn't need any help and I did have a snake book open in front of me, so I don't know why you insisted on looking inside the box if you are so afraid of snakes and everything. I don't know why you picked up that box before opening a flap, either. If you had left the box on the table and maybe even sat down next to it, then maybe the box would have been all right when you screamed and fainted. You wouldn't have fallen so far, either, if you were sitting down.

Did you know that you broke out in a rash after you fainted? I thought a person had to touch something like poison ivy to get a rash. I didn't know it was possible to get a rash by just thinking about something but my parents say it really can happen. I think maybe you did touch something. Maybe, when you were lying on the floor, that snake slithered over to you and touched you! Did you know that snake skin feels dry, not wet and slimy at all?

I just thought of something. Maybe everyone's looking in the library for that snake but it's not in the library. Maybe it crawled into one of your pockets or up your sleeve and rode with you to the hospital! Wouldn't that be funny? Why don't you get one of the nurses to check? If it's not in your clothes, it might have crawled out and might be hiding inside the hospital someplace. I think people should be looking there, too.

✔ **STOP AND THINK**
Conclusions and Generalizations
Look at the first paragraph on page 235. What conclusion can you draw about the letter writer's attitude from her suggestions to Mr. Winston?

235

I am sure you will be talking to the people in the library, to make sure they find that snake before you go back to work. I hope they do find it, even though my parents say that I can't keep it. If that snake is found, could you ask the people at the library to give me a call? I would be interested in knowing that it is all right. And if they do find that snake and do decide to give me a call, could you ask them if they could compare that snake with the snake pictures in that big green reference book before they call me? I would still like to know what kind of snake I owned for an hour.

I am truly, genuinely sorry.

Your friend,
Cara

STOP AND THINK

Author's Craft Sometimes authors will repeat words, or use **repetition**, if they want readers to pay close attention to those words. Do you believe Cara when she repeatedly says, "I am truly, genuinely sorry"? Why or why not?

Your Turn

Dear Cara

Write a Reply How do you think Mr. Winston will react to Cara's apology? Imagine you are Mr. Winston, and write a reply to Cara's letter. Tell whether you accept her apology, and explain why or why not. PERSONAL RESPONSE

Cara

Snake-free Zone

Role-Play Imagine that Mr. Winston has read Cara's letter and he is still too scared to return to the library. With a group, role-play a scene in which Cara, her mother, and her father all try to persuade Mr. Winston to return to his job. Each person should take the role of one of the characters. SMALL GROUP

Who's to Blame?

Turn and Talk With a partner, discuss what led Cara to make an apology that doesn't seem completely sincere. What parts of the incident in the library does she think are someone else's fault? Do you think most people would feel the same way? Why?

CONCLUSIONS AND GENERALIZATIONS

FIELD GUIDE
to
Snakes
of the
Southwest

by Patrick Sutter

Snakes are amazing. They have no arms or legs, but they move quickly. They have no ears, but heat-sensing organs help them find their prey. Snakes survive in almost every ecosystem on Earth.

Many people fear snakes. Some individuals have even fainted at the sight of these reptiles, but this is no one's fault. It's true that some snakes are dangerous. Yet many are not. In fact, most snakes help local farmers by eating pests. People imagine a snake's skin is slimy, but it is made of dry scales.

This reference guide gives information about three snakes from the Southwest.

Common name: Mountain King Snake
Scientific name: *Lampropeltis zonata*
Size: 20–40 inches
Habitat: mountains, damp woods
Nonvenomous

Black, cream, and red bands circle the body and tail of this snake. The pattern and colors are very similar to those of the deadly coral snake, but the king snake is not venomous. Both snakes seem to borrow each other's colors, but a genuine king snake will have red and black bands touching each other. This color pattern is proof that the reptile is a king snake. The diet of the king snake includes lizards, small mammals, birds, and other snakes.

Common name: Western Diamond-Backed Rattlesnake
Scientific name: *Crotalus atrox*
Size: 30–90 inches
Habitat: dry areas, such as deserts and rocky foothills
Venomous

This is the largest snake in the West. It eats small mammals, birds, and reptiles. People fear this snake because it is very dangerous. Even a dead rattlesnake can bite! Its jaws can still open when touched and can still inject venom. Scientists do not apologize for trying to protect rattlesnakes, though. They have insisted that in spite of the danger, rattlesnakes are important. This snake will not attack, but it will defend itself. First, it shakes its tail to make a rattling sound. This is a signal to back off!

Common names: Desert Threadsnake or Western Blind Snake
Scientific name: *Leptotyphlops humilis*
Size: 6–13 inches
Habitat: mountain slopes, deserts, rocky foothills
Nonvenomous

This tiny, harmless snake can be brown, purple, or pink in color. One of its two common names refers to its thin, wormlike body. The other refers to its lack of eyes. Instead of eyes that see, this snake has two black spots on its face. The threadsnake burrows for its food under plant roots and rocks and in ant nests. It eats ants and other small insects.

Traits of Southwestern Snakes

TRAITS	MOUNTAIN KING SNAKE	DIAMOND-BACKED RATTLESNAKE	DESERT THREADSNAKE
venomous		🐍	
nonvenomous	🐍		🐍
desert habitat		🐍	🐍
mountain habitat	🐍		🐍
large size	🐍	🐍	
small size			🐍

Making Connections

Text to Self

Write a Letter Everyone makes mistakes sometimes. Write a short letter of apology to a friend you should have said "I'm sorry" to but didn't. Include a date, a salutation, and a closing.

Text to Text

Compare and Contrast Choose one snake from "Field Guide to Snakes of the Southwest" and complete a Venn diagram to compare and contrast that snake with Cara's snake. Use the details that Cara gives about her snake and the information in the "Field Guide" to guess what kind of snake Cara may have brought into the library.

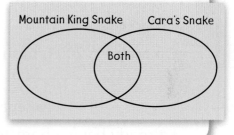

Text to World

Snake Research Research a snake that lives somewhere other than the Southwest. Make a chart with facts such as where the snake lives, what it eats, how long it is, and whether it is or is not venomous. Present your chart to the class.

Grammar

Where Are Commas Used? A **comma** is used after an introductory word in a sentence. One or two commas are needed to set off the name of a person being addressed. A comma separates the day and the year in a date and the city and the state in a place name. Also, commas are needed to separate items in a **series**, a list of nouns or actions.

Academic Language

comma

series

Commas in Sentences
after introductory word to set off a name Yes, it is a local snake, Dad.
in a date in a place name On May 17, 2009, I found it in Houston, Texas.
to separate items in a series I already have a hamster, a mouse, and a rabbit.

Try This! **Copy these sentences onto another sheet of paper. Add commas where they are needed.**

❶ Robbie do you like turtles lizards or frogs best?

❷ Wow I wasn't expecting a snake!

❸ Last year my relatives traveled to Startzville Texas.

❹ Yes my uncle aunt and cousin visited a snake farm.

❺ They sent me a postcard dated July 18 2008.

Conventions Sentences with commas used incorrectly can be difficult to understand. Check your writing carefully to make sure you have used commas correctly.

Sentences with Comma Errors

Cara we looked, in the storeroom the book bin and, the closet for your snake. Yes we finally found it on April 4 2009 on a shelf behind a book about, Denver Colorado.

Sentences with Correct Comma Usage

Cara, we looked in the storeroom, the book bin, and the closet for your snake. Yes, we finally found it on April 4, 2009, on a shelf behind a book about Denver, Colorado.

Connect Grammar to Writing

As you plan your response, be sure that you use commas correctly with introductory words, names, dates, places, and items in a series.

Write to Respond

✅ **Organization** As you plan your **response to literature**, think about the prompt and review the story. Begin by listing your ideas. Then organize them in a chart and add details. Use the Writing Process Checklist below as you prewrite.

Trudy planned her response to this question: *In "Dear Mr. Winston," does the author want readers to feel sorry for Mr. Winston or to think he is silly?* After listing her ideas, Trudy organized them in a chart and added details.

Writing Process Checklist

▶ **Prewrite**

- ✔ Did I make sure I understood the question?
- ✔ Did I think of strong reasons for my opinion?
- ✔ Did I find examples in the story to support my reasons?
- ✔ Did I put my ideas in an order than makes sense?

Draft

Revise

Edit

Publish

Share

Exploring a Topic

Sorry

Mr. W. faints, gets a rash

Goes to the hospital

Silly

Mr. W. opens box—should suspect snake is in it

Snake's not dangerous—doesn't even touch him

Mr. W. won't even touch picture of snake

Cara's letter—really funny

Opinion Chart

The author wants readers to think that Mr. Winston is kind of silly.

Reason: Mr. W. is silly to open the box.

Details: He sees Cara look at the snake book then peek in box.

Mr. W. is very scared of snakes, even just pictures.

Reason: The snake isn't dangerous.

Details: He knows there are no poisonous snakes in Manitoba.

It doesn't touch him, but he faints and gets a rash.

> In my chart, I organized my reasons and details. I added more details, too.

Reason: Cara's letter makes the whole situation funny.

Details: She tells him to watch Galactic Patrol because there are no snakes in space.

She tells him the snake might be in the hospital.

Reading as a Writer

What other details could Trudy add to support her opinion? What details could you add to your own opinion chart?

debut

stubborn

permission

hauling

mournful

towered

triumph

discouraged

toured

border

Vocabulary Reader   Context Cards

Vocabulary in Context

1   debut

A performing artist is always excited at his or her debut, or first public show.

2   stubborn

Performers with a stubborn desire to succeed will continue to work hard.

3   permission

This musician is allowed to play in the subway. She was given permission.

4   hauling

When a band is traveling, workers are hauling equipment from city to city.

- **Study each Context Card.**
- **Use a dictionary to help you pronounce these words.**

5 mournful

The mournful songs of some singers are more memorable than their happy ones.

6 towered

Performers on stilts have always towered above their audiences.

7 triumph

Becoming a star is a triumph, or victory, most performance artists long for.

8 discouraged

Some musicians become discouraged, or disappointed, after a poor performance.

9 toured

A performer who has toured, or traveled, has gained new fans in every location.

10 border

Touring performers often cross an international border such as this one.

Background

What Does It Take to Become a Dancer? Many people think it requires stubborn determination. Competition can be fierce. Dancers might feel discouraged if they are not given permission to join a dance company. But if dancers are talented enough to join a company, a choreographer creates dances for them. They must practice, practice, practice to music of all kinds, from mournful to lively. Those dancers who finally make their debut often feel a great sense of triumph.

Several famous dance companies have toured the world, crossing border after border, hauling costumes and sets. Perhaps one of them will be performing on a stage near you!

Have you ever had a goal that towered over others? Dancer José Limón did. He founded the world-famous Limón Dance Company.

Comprehension

Author's Purpose

As you read "José! Born to Dance," think about the author's reasons for writing. Does she want to entertain, to inform, to persuade, or to describe? Does she have more than one purpose? For clues, focus on the way she describes the characters, events, and setting. Create a graphic organizer like this one to help you explain the author's implied purpose.

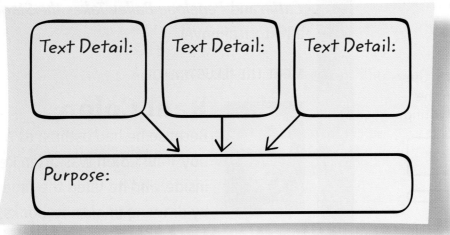

Text Detail:

Text Detail:

Text Detail:

Purpose:

✔ TARGET STRATEGY   **Analyze/Evaluate**

You can use the analyze and evaluate strategy to help you understand the author's purpose. Ask yourself questions about why José worked so hard to become a dancer and why this is important to the author. Keep track of these details in the graphic organizer.

✔ **TARGET VOCABULARY**

debut	towered
stubborn	triumph
permission	discouraged
hauling	toured
mournful	border

✔ **TARGET SKILL**

Author's Purpose Use text details to explain the author's reasons for writing.

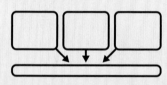

✔ **TARGET STRATEGY**

Analyze/Evaluate Ask questions to analyze and evalute the author's purpose.

GENRE

Biography tells about events in a person's life, written by another person.

MEET THE AUTHOR

Susanna Reich

A former professional dancer, Susanna Reich is the author of *Clara Schumann: Piano Virtuoso*, an NCTE Orbis Pictus Honor Book, an ALA Notable, and a School Library Journal Best Book of the Year. Her other books include *Painting the Wild Frontier: The Art and Adventures of George Catlin* and *Penelope Bailey Takes the Stage*, a historical novel.

MEET THE ILLUSTRATOR

Raúl Colón

Because he had asthma as a boy, Raúl Colón was often kept inside, and he filled the time by drawing in his notebooks. "So my illness as a child," he recalls, "which kept me from going outside to play, became a blessing." He even created his own comic book. He began his official art training in the tenth grade and has since illustrated many children's books.

JOSÉ!

Born to Dance

by Susanna Reich
illustrated by Raúl Colón

Essential Question

Why do authors write biographies?

In 1908 a baby boy was born in Culiacán (koo lyah KAHN), Mexico, kicking like a roped steer. BAM! BAM! BAM! His name was José Limón (hoh SEH lee MOHN).

When José was a toddler, Mama used to take him to his grandmother's house for breakfast. The pet canary sang to him while he ate. TRILLIA-WEET! TRILLIA-WEET!

Surrounded by flowers, José feasted on mango and papaya, pineapple and banana, sweet rolls and eggs. His mouth watered as Grandmother whisked the hot chocolate with her *molinillo* (moh lee NEE yoh). When the hot chocolate was cool enough to drink, José gulped it down.

Sometimes Papa took José to the theater where Papa worked as a musician. José loved to watch the dancers on the stage. The cancan dancers lifted their petticoats and kicked their legs. OH LA LA!

The flamenco dancers flipped their skirts and clicked their heels. *¡Sí (see)! ¡Sí! ¡Sí!*

The ballet dancers leapt into the air. Raising their arms high above their heads, they seemed to fly. AHHHHH!

One afternoon Papa took José to the *corrida de toros* (koh REE dah deh TOH rohs). In the bullfight ring a torero swirled his red cloak to anger the black bull. *¡Olé (oh LEH)! ¡Olé! ¡Olé!* The bull pawed the ground. It ran straight toward the bullfighter, its head down and its eyes ablaze. José gripped Papa's hand.

Later that night, when Mama tucked José into bed, her sweet voice echoed in the darkness. SORA-SORA-SO, SORA-SO. That night José dreamed of the bullfight.

One spring day when José was five, he saw government soldiers marching in the street. A civil war had broken out in Mexico. José slung a stick over his shoulder and marched through the house. *¡Uno (OO noh)! ¡Dos (dohs)! ¡Uno! ¡Dos!*

The next day at breakfast, shots rang out. The rebels had attacked their town. Surrounded by fighting, José's family hid in the cellar for three days and three nights.

STOP AND THINK

Analyze/Evaluate How well do the expressions "OH LA LA!," "¡Sí! ¡Sí! ¡Sí!," and "AHHHHH!" help you understand José's reaction to the dancers? Explain your answer.

Months passed and the war raged on. Safety lay across the border—in the United States. Perhaps Papa could find a job there.

José's family took a train to Nogales (noh GAH lehs), close to the border. Soldiers sat on top of the train, their guns at the ready. The train crawled through the hot desert. As the sun set, José heard the sound of an accordion—a slow, mournful song. *"O, soñador . . ."* (oh so nyah DOHR)

For two years José and his family lived in Nogales, waiting and waiting for permission to enter the United States. Finally Papa's work permit arrived, stamped with an official seal. They packed their bags and set out across the northern frontier. *Adiós* (ah DYOHS), Mexico.

At José's new school the children gathered around the teacher to read aloud from their books. When José read, the other children laughed at his poor English. At first José cried. Then he stamped his foot in fierce determination. PUM!

I will learn this language better than any of you, he said to himself—though it seemed nearly impossible.

But within three years José could speak English with confidence. He was quick to learn new words and translated for Mama wherever she went. *Carmesí* (kahr meh SEE). *Radiante* (rah DYAHN teh). *Liberación* (lee beh rah SYON). Crimson. Radiant. Liberation.

By sixth grade José had become known for his colorful drawings. Among his many younger brothers and sisters he was famous for his pictures of trains. Everyone thought he would become an artist.

But José loved music, too. As a teenager he practiced the piano at all hours of the day and night. When his fingers flew, his spirit soared. AHH!

After José finished high school in Los Angeles, Mama became very sick. When she died, sadness lay on José's heart.

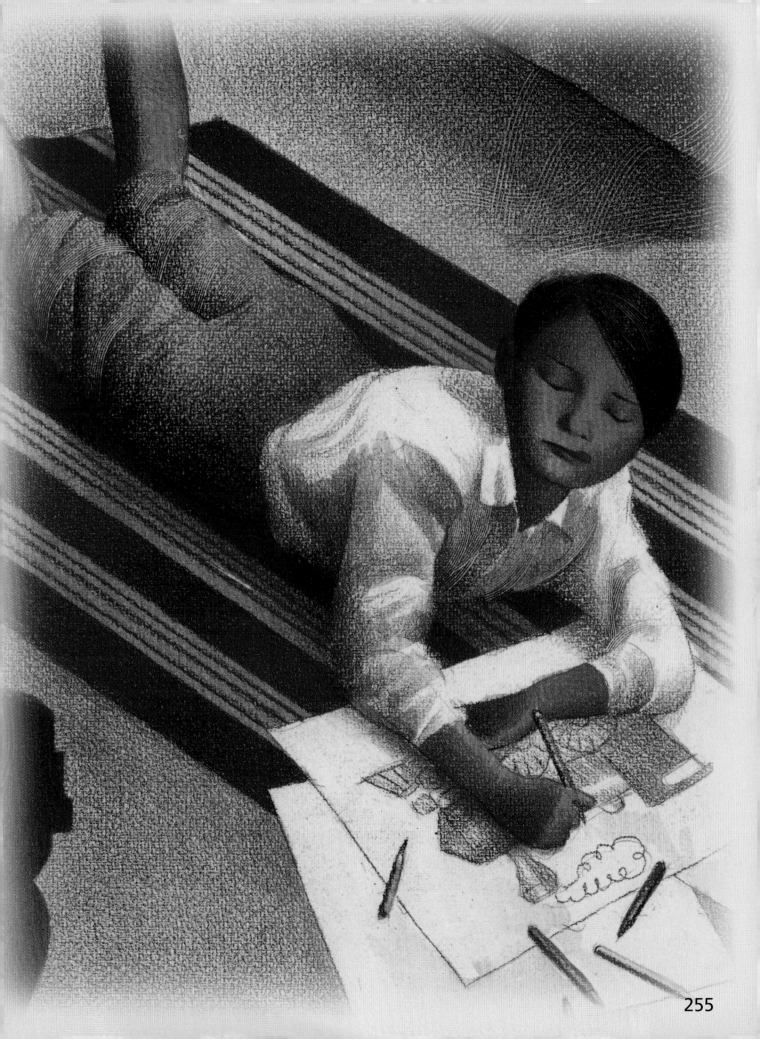

He went to work in a factory. All day long he took tiles from one wheelbarrow and loaded them into another. At night he dreamed of painting and drawing. He dreamed of living in New York among the artists. But he didn't know if Papa could manage without him.

José waited, and brooded, and argued with himself. Finally, after a year, he made up his mind. "Papa," he announced, "I'm going."

Adiós, José. Farewell.

He headed east across the continent, two thousand four hundred and sixty-two miles.

When José reached New York, the shimmering city towered above him: marble, stone, brick, and steel. José floated down the sidewalk. He would become a great artist, *un artista grandioso y magnífico*. He would fill his sketchbooks with drawings like none the world had ever seen.

He took a job as a janitor, scooping ashes out of a coal furnace and hauling garbage cans to the curb. But as winter wore on, a cold loneliness settled over José. He missed his family, far away in sunny California.

Discouraged, he wandered the halls of the great museums. *Manet* (muh NAY), *Renoir* (ruhn WAHR), *and Picasso* (pih KAH soh), he thought. Perhaps they had already painted everything. His drawings would never compare. The music in his heart fell silent.

"New York is a cemetery," he said. "A jungle of stone."

José put away his drawings. He felt sad and lost. How could he be an artist without an art? He wanted to give a gift to the world, but he didn't know what it could be.

One day José's friend Charlotte invited him to a dance concert. The dancer twisted his body and leapt into the air. AIEEEEE!

STOP AND THINK
Author's Craft A **metaphor** compares one thing to something entirely different without using the words *like* or *as*. One example of a metaphor is "New York is a jungle of stone." Find another one on this page.

The dance lit a fire in José's soul. Ideas exploded in his mind. "I do not want to remain on this earth unless I can learn to do what this man is doing!" he said.

A few days later, José stepped into a dance studio for the first time. As soon as the pianist began to play, the sound of the music carried José away. He swooped. He stretched. He swirled. And then he flew—AHHHHH!

I embrace the dance! ¡La danza será mi vida!

From then on, José took classes from teachers Doris Humphrey and Charles Weidman (WYD muhn) nearly every day. Dripping with sweat, he struggled with his stiff and stubborn body. And at night he hobbled home, his muscles sore and aching.

Six weeks later, he made his debut (day BYOO), performing for the first time. As he waited to go onstage, he felt shy and nervous. All those people in the audience would be watching him.

But once he heard the thundering applause, his spirits lifted. "That night I tasted undreamed-of exaltation, humility, and triumph," he said.

Ankles and feet, knees and hips, chest and arms, head and neck, up and down and back and forth and in and out, José Limón became a dancer.

For eleven years José studied and danced with Doris and Charles. He learned to make his muscles sing. He learned to move his bones every which way. He learned to flow and float and fly through space with steps smooth as silk. He learned to be fierce like a bullfighter—¡Olé! Strong like a soldier—¡Uno! ¡Dos! ¡Uno! ¡Dos! And proud like a king—PUM!

He learned to make dances sweet as birdsong—TRILLIA-WEET! Hot as the desert sun—¡Sí! ¡Sí! Sad as broken dreams—O, soñador . . . Loving as a mother's lullaby floating on a Mexican breeze—SORA-SORA-SO, SORA-SO.

In time José became a world-famous choreographer and toured the globe with his own dance company. For forty years, with bare feet and broad shoulders, he graced the concert stage. From New York to Mexico City and London to Buenos Aires (BWEH nohs EYE rehs), he danced for presidents and princesses, builders and bricklayers, bankers and bus drivers, fiddlers and firemen.

259

And each night before the curtain rose, he whispered to himself, "Make me strong so I can give."

BRAVO! BRAVO! BRAVO!

✔ STOP AND THINK

Author's Purpose Explain what you think the author wants you to learn from José's story.

Your Turn

Take My Advice

Letter to a Young Dancer It took José a long time to figure out how to use his many talents. What advice might he give young people who want to pursue a career in the arts? Write a letter of advice José might give to someone who wants to be a dancer or another kind of artist.

SOCIAL STUDIES

SORA-SORA-SO!

Write a Poem With a partner, make a list of "sound words," such as *SORA-SORA-SO* and *TRILLIA-WEET*; other descriptive adjectives the author used to help readers picture José's movements; and Spanish words from the selection. Use words from your list to write a poem about dancing.

PARTNERS

The Writer's Reasons

Turn and Talk With a partner, discuss what you think the author's purpose was for writing "José! Born to Dance." Remember that authors often have more than one purpose for writing. Do you think the author succeeded in achieving her purpose or purposes?

AUTHOR'S PURPOSE

✓ **TARGET VOCABULARY**

debut	towered
stubborn	triumph
permission	discouraged
hauling	toured
mournful	border

GENRE

Poetry uses the sound and rhythm of words to suggest images and express feelings.

TEXT FOCUS

Rhythm, the regular pattern of stress in words, is part of the sound and tone of poems. As you read, note how the rhythm is different in each poem. How does the rhythm affect the form, or type, of poem?

dance to the beat

by Adam Fogelberg

Dancers move their bodies to the beat, or rhythm, of music. Poems are like music and dance: They, too, have rhythm. As you read the following three poems about dancing, listen for their rhythm.

The Song of the Night

I dance to the tune
of the stars and the moon.
I dance to the song of the night.

I dance to the strains
of a cricket's refrain.
I dance to the fireflies' light.

I dance to the breeze
and the whispering trees.
I dance to the meteor's flight.

I dance to the beat
of the summertime heat.
I dance to the pulse of the night.

by Leslie D. Perkins

from Lines Written for Gene Kelly to Dance To

Can you dance a question mark?
Can you dance an exclamation point?
Can you dance a couple of commas?
And bring it to a finish with a period?

Can you dance like the wind is pushing you?
Can you dance like you are pushing the wind?
Can you dance with slow wooden heels
   and then change to bright and singing silver heels?
Such nice feet, such good feet.

by Carl Sandburg

Gene Kelly
(1912–1996)

Gene Kelly was a famous actor, dancer, and director. He was born in Pittsburgh, Pennsylvania, in 1912. As a child he was small, and his peers towered above him. He wanted to become a professional athlete, but his mother would not give him permission. Instead of being discouraged, Kelly became a dancer. He ran a dancing school and toured with shows.

In 1938 he crossed the Pennsylvania border and headed to New York City. That year he made his Broadway debut.

During his career, Kelly enjoyed one triumph after another. He starred and danced in many movies.

Gene Kelly was famous for his athletic dancing style.

263

Three/Quarters Time

Dance with me . . . dance with me . . . we are the song . . . we
  are the music . . .
Dance with me . . .
Dance with me . . . dance with me . . . all night long . . .
We are the music . . . we are the song . . .

by Nikki Giovanni

Write a Dance Poem

How do you dance? Does your body feel like it is
hauling a ton of bricks? Are your feet stubborn? Do
they refuse to move, or do they glide across the floor?
How does the music make you feel? Are you mournful or
overjoyed? Express your feelings about dance in a poem.

Making Connections

Text to Self

Creative Interests José Limón drew, painted, and played the piano before discovering dance. Write a paragraph about *your* main creative interest. Explain why you enjoy that activity.

Text to Text

Comparing Characters Compare and contrast the events and experiences of José Limón and James from "Me and Uncle Romie" as they visit New York City for the first time. Use a Venn diagram to chart your ideas.

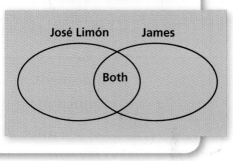

José Limón   James

Both

Text to World

The World of Dance There are many different styles of dance, such as Ballroom, Ballet, Tango, and Jazz. With a partner, use online sources or reference texts to make a list of dance styles. Then write a brief description of one dance style.

Grammar

What Is a Pronoun? A **pronoun** is a word, such as *he, she* or *they,* that takes the place of one or more nouns. An **antecedent** is the noun or nouns that the pronoun replaces. A pronoun should agree with its antecedent in number and gender. A **reflexive pronoun** is a pronoun whose antecedent is the subject of the sentence. Reflexive pronouns end with *-self* or *-selves.*

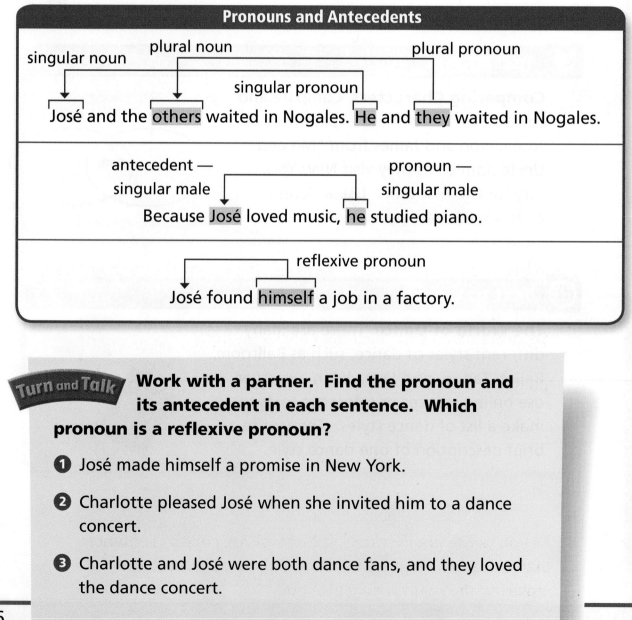

Pronouns and Antecedents

singular noun · plural noun · singular pronoun · plural pronoun

José and the **others** waited in Nogales. **He** and **they** waited in Nogales.

antecedent — singular male · pronoun — singular male

Because **José** loved music, **he** studied piano.

reflexive pronoun

José found **himself** a job in a factory.

Turn and Talk **Work with a partner. Find the pronoun and its antecedent in each sentence. Which pronoun is a reflexive pronoun?**

1. José made himself a promise in New York.

2. Charlotte pleased José when she invited him to a dance concert.

3. Charlotte and José were both dance fans, and they loved the dance concert.

Sentence Fluency To make your writing flow smoothly, you can use pronouns to help combine sentences. If two choppy sentences tell about the same noun, try replacing one of the nouns with a pronoun. Then, you can combine the two sentences without repeating the noun.

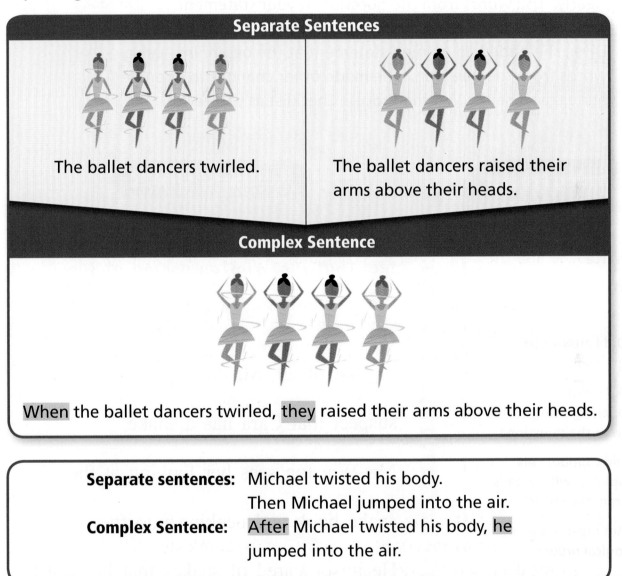

Separate Sentences

The ballet dancers twirled.

The ballet dancers raised their arms above their heads.

Complex Sentence

When the ballet dancers twirled, they raised their arms above their heads.

Separate sentences:	Michael twisted his body. Then Michael jumped into the air.
Complex Sentence:	After Michael twisted his body, he jumped into the air.

Connect Grammar to Writing

As you revise your writing, look for short, choppy sentences that repeat a noun. Try combining these sentences and replacing the noun with a pronoun.

267

Write to Respond

☑ **Organization** When a story question asks for your opinion, begin your **response to literature** by stating your opinion clearly. Use words from the question in your statement.

Trudy drafted her response essay about "Dear Mr. Winston." Later, she added an opinion statement at the beginning, using words from the question. She made other changes to improve her essay. Use the Writing Process Checklist as you revise.

Writing Process Checklist

Prewrite

Draft

▶ **Revise**

☑ Did I answer the question?

☑ Did I write an opening using words from the question?

☑ Did I support my opinion with details from the story?

☑ Are my ideas in a logical order?

☑ Did I sum up my reasons at the end?

Edit

Publish

Share

Revised Draft

I think the author wants readers to feel that Mr. Winston is kind of silly. Many events and details in the story show this.

First of all, Mr. Winston should suspect that Cara has a snake ^when he^ ~~Mr. Winston~~ sees her looking at the snake book and peeking into the box. He is so scared of snakes that he won't even touch one, so it's really silly of him to open the box.

268

Oh Dear, Mr. Winston
by Trudy Delgado

I think the author wants readers to feel that Mr. Winston is kind of silly. Many events and details in the story show this. First of all, Mr. Winston should suspect that Cara has a snake when he sees her looking at the snake book and peeking into the box. He is so scared of snakes that he won't even touch one, so it's really silly of him to open the box.

Another reason Mr. Winston seems silly is that Cara's snake isn't dangerous. Mr. Winston should know that too, since he moved to Manitoba because there are no poisonous snakes there.

> I began with a clear opinion statement. I also combined sentences to make them read more smoothly.

Reading as a Writer

Why was it a good idea for Trudy to state her opinion at the beginning? What will you say in your own opinion statement?

269

Wildfires!

Wildfires are fires that sweep across the land. They often occur in wilderness areas. There are about 100,000 wildfires in the United States each year. Of all the natural disasters, wildfires are the most terrifying.

A Scary Summer

In the summer of 1988, wildfires swept through Yellowstone National Park. In four months, they scorched over 793,000 acres of land. They burned 36% of the park.

Why were the fires of 1988 so damaging? For one thing, that summer was very dry. In fact, it was the driest summer in Yellowstone's recorded history. To make things worse, the weather was hot and windy. These conditions make fire spread quickly.

The Yellowstone fires began in June, with a few small fires. At first, there was no danger to people or their belongings. So park officials followed the "let the fire burn" policy. Letting a small fire burn helps clear the land of dead plants so that new plants can grow. Over time, though, the fires grew. New ones started. Lightning caused 42 new fires. Careless people caused 9 more. Not all of the fires began in the park, but they raced through the park.

Smoke billowed thousands of feet into the air. Ash rained down for miles around. In nearby Cooke City, someone had a good sense of humor. He or she added the letter "d" to the end of "Cooke" on the town sign. The overall situation wasn't funny, though. Local firefighters could not put out all the fires. Fire-fighting teams from across the country couldn't, either. In the end, 25,000 people took part in the effort and $120 million was spent. But it was rain and snow that finally stopped the fires in September.

Wilderness Firefighters

Have you seen photos or videos of city firefighters racing into burning buildings? These firefighters wear heavy clothing that protects them from flames and falling rubble. Wilderness firefighters do not wear the hot, heavy clothing that city firefighters wear. They have a different wardrobe and special fire-fighting equipment. They fight fires in different ways, too.

One way of fighting a wilderness fire is by using smokejumpers. Smokejumpers fight fires in remote wilderness areas. Some of them work from the West Yellowstone smokejumper base. These firefighters travel quickly to fires by plane, helicopter, ground vehicle, and on foot. They have to be in excellent condition. They also have to be brave. That's because smokejumpers parachute out of planes and land near wildfires. They travel quickly across rough terrain, packing up to 115 pounds of gear. They face long periods of smoke, fire, and heat. Sometimes food and water run short before they have finished their work.

Wilderness firefighting involves hard physical labor. Firefighters have to chop down trees, clear brush, and dig ditches to keep fires from spreading. If these firefighters wore hot, heavy clothing, their body temperatures would rise to a dangerous level. Scientists have invented special gear for them. Wilderness firefighters wear clothing made from a special lightweight fabric. They also carry tents made of a special foil. The foil reflects heat away from the tent. A firefighter who is covered by this emergency shelter can survive a fire with heat of more than 1,000° F.

Fighting wildfires is an important and challenging job. The men and women who do it risk their lives to save our lands. We should all be grateful to these courageous people.

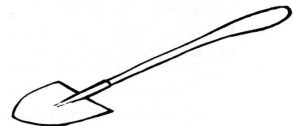

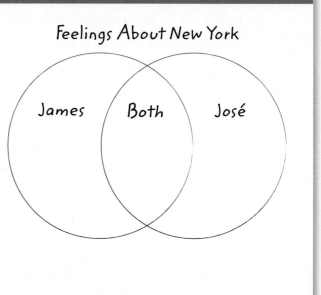

Unit 2 Wrap-Up

The Big Idea

Expressing Feelings Think about "Me and Uncle Romie" and "José! Born to Dance." James and José both go to New York City. Compare their descriptions of and feelings about the city. How are they the same? How do they differ? List details in a diagram. Then use it to write a paragraph comparing their feelings about New York.

Feelings About New York

James   Both   José

Listening and Speaking

A Soundtrack for a Tale Work with a partner to retell a fairytale. Choose music to go with it. Pick music that makes the funny parts of your tale funnier and the scary parts scarier. Sing or play the music, or use a recording. Play the soundtrack as you practice telling your tale. Then tell your tale with the music for the class.

NATURAL ENCOUNTERS

Unit 3

Big Idea

Nature can
amaze us.

Paired Selections

273

presence

disbelief

tempted

biological

endeared

arrangement

pounced

utter

hastened

incident

Vocabulary Reader

Context Cards

Vocabulary in Context

1 presence

Wild animals are everywhere. You can find signs of their presence.

2 disbelief

This girl stares in disbelief at the insect. She can't believe her eyes.

3 tempted

People might want, or be tempted, to pet wild animals, but they shouldn't.

4 biological

Like all living things, animals have a biological need for food.

- Study each Context Card.
- Use context clues to determine the meanings of these words.

5 **endeared**

Many raccoons have endeared themselves to people, who think they look loveable.

6 **arrangement**

Pigeons find that living among people is a fine plan, or arrangement.

7 **pounced**

Owls have often pounced, or jumped, on small animals.

8 **utter**

Coyotes in suburbs may utter, or express out loud, spooky cries during the night.

9 **hastened**

Animals have always hastened to flee from a wildfire. They hurry as fast as they can.

10 **incident**

An encounter with a skunk can be a smelly incident. It's not an enjoyable event.

Background

Instincts and Learning Have you ever watched in disbelief as a spider spins an amazing web? How does the spider know how to do that? Why does a human baby utter a cry when it wants something? Why are cats tempted to chase mice, and why do cats play with their prey after they have pounced? These are biological instincts, behaviors that animals and people are born with.

Learned behavior is the opposite of instinct. Has a pet ever hastened to greet you, showing joy at your presence? When a pet has endeared itself to a person, it has learned to be lovable. The animal has learned to show affection in return for something, such as food. It's a pleasing arrangement, for both the person and the pet.

This table shows how an animal might respond instinctively to an incident. How does an incident cause an instinctive response?

Incident	Instinctive Response
Seasons begin to change.	Birds migrate.
A squirrel runs across a road.	A dog chases the squirrel.
A bear cub is threatened by a larger animal.	The mother bear chases off the larger animal.

Comprehension

✓ **TARGET SKILL** **Fact and Opinion**

As you read "The Screech Owl Who Liked Television," notice the facts and opinions the author provides. A fact can be proved true. It can be verified in a reference book, for example. An opinion tells a thought, feeling, or belief. You might agree or disagree with an opinion, but you cannot prove it to be true or false. Use a graphic organizer like this one to help you separate the selection's facts from its opinions.

Fact	Opinion
•	•
•	•
•	•

✓ **TARGET STRATEGY** **Infer/Predict**

When you make an inference, you use text details to figure out something the author does not state directly. Use the facts and opinions in "The Screech Owl Who Liked Television" and the graphic organizer to help you make inferences about the author's point of view. Your inferences can help you predict what may happen next in the selection.

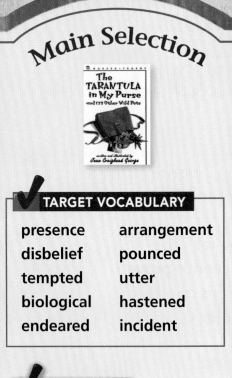

The TARANTULA
in My Purse
and 172 Other Wild Pets

written and illustrated by
Jean Craighead George

✔ **TARGET VOCABULARY**

presence	arrangement
disbelief	pounced
tempted	utter
biological	hastened
endeared	incident

✔ **TARGET SKILL**

Fact and Opinion Decide if an idea can be proved or if it is a feeling or belief.

✔ **TARGET STRATEGY**

Infer/Predict Use text clues to figure out what isn't directly stated by the author.

GENRE

Narrative nonfiction gives factual information by telling a true story.

Set a Purpose Set a purpose for reading based on the genre and what you want to know.

MEET THE AUTHOR
Jean Craighead George

Jean Craighead George has made a lifelong study of animals, their habitats, and the way they interact with people. "I have discovered I cannot dream up characters as incredible as the ones I meet in the wilderness," she says. George has kept and cared for more than 173 wild animals.

MEET THE ILLUSTRATOR
Tim Bowers

Tim Bowers loves to tell stories with his artwork. As a child he enjoyed the many animals at his grandparents' house, including an African Grey parrot and a squirrel monkey named Joe-Joe. Many of Bowers's illustrations feature animal characters, including a brave skunk, a dog that makes hats, chickens in a diner, and now, a screech owl who likes television.

The Screech Owl
Who Liked Television

from The Tarantula in My Purse

by Jean Craighead George   selection illustrated by Tim Bowers

Essential Question

How do animals influence your opinion of nature?

279

Children's author Jean Craighead George remembers how her three children, Twig, Craig, and Luke, raised a very special owl inside their house.

Twig's favorite pet was a small gray screech owl. Had he not fallen from his nest before he could fly, he would have lived in the open woodland, deciduous forest, park, town, or river's edge. But he had landed on a hard driveway instead and ended up in our house. He was round eyed and hungry. He looked up at Twig and gave the quivering hunger call of the screech owl. Twig named him Yammer.

Yammer quickly endeared himself to us. He hopped from his perch to our hands to eat. He rode around the house on our shoulders and sat on the back of a dining-room chair during dinner.

Before the green of June burst upon us, Yammer had become a person to Twig, who felt all wild friends were humans and should be treated as such.

Wild animals are not people. But Twig was not convinced. One Saturday morning she and Yammer were watching a cowboy show on television. They had been there for hours.

"Twig," I said, "you've watched TV long enough. Please go find a book to read, or do your homework." My voice was firm. I kept the TV in my bedroom just so the children wouldn't be constantly tempted to turn it on as they had when it was downstairs.

Reluctantly, Twig got to her feet. At the door she turned and looked at her little owl. He was on top of the headboard, staring at the screen. A rider on a horse was streaking across the desert. From an owl's point of view the pair were mouse sized.

"How come Yammer can watch TV and I can't?" she asked, pouting.

Hardly had she spoken than Yammer pushed off from the headboard, struck the prey with his talons, and dropped to the floor, bewildered.

Twig rushed to his rescue. She gathered him up and hugged him to her chest. With a scornful glance at me, she hurried to her room. The small owl's round yellow eyes were peering from between her gently curled fingers.

Twig was right: This otherworldly creature was a person. Wasn't his menu of mice and crickets included on the shopping list? Didn't he have his own bedroom in the gap between the Roger Tory Peterson field guides in the living-room bookcase? Didn't he run down into the cozy blanket-tunnels made by Twig at bedtime and utter his note of contentment? And didn't he like TV just as she did?

✔ **STOP AND THINK**

Fact and Opinion The last paragraph on page 282 contains both facts and opinions. Use your graphic organizer to distinguish the facts from the opinions. Then, explain how to verify the facts.

Most scientists are taught not to read human emotions into animals, but sometimes they wonder about the truth of it. When you live with animals, they often seem quite humanlike.

Later that morning of the TV incident, I looked in on Twig and Yammer. The owl was perched on the top of her open door, preening his feathers. She was sitting with her chin in her hands, looking at him.

"I feel sorry for Yammer," she said. "He's stuck in this house. He needs to see things that move like they do in the woods."

"So?" I said.

"So, I've finished my homework and made my bed. Can Yammer and I watch TV?"

I heard myself whisper, "Yes."

When I told Twig she could watch TV that day of the cowboy incident, she stood on her desk and held up her hand to Yammer. He stepped onto her finger. As she climbed down, she touched his toes and the talons curled around her forefinger.

"I wish I had Yammer's feet," she said. "Then I could sit on the teeny tiny branches of the apple tree."

Suddenly her brother Craig shouted, *"Road Runner's* on."

"Yammer loves *Road Runner*," Twig said, and dashed to the TV in my bedroom. Yammer flapped his wings to keep his balance, and the two joined Twig's brothers, Craig and Luke, before the television. Luke, not quite four, patted the pillow next to him.

"Put him here," he said. A chord of music sounded, lights flashed, and all eyes—particularly Yammer's—were riveted on that zany bird running on and off the screen.

Second to *Road Runner* was Yammer's love for the shower. He would fly into the bathroom when he heard one of us turn on the spray, sit on the top of the shower-curtain rod to orient himself, then drop into the puddles at our feet. Eyes half closed, he would joyfully flip the water up and into his wings and dunk his breast until he was soaked. A wet screech owl is as helpless as an ant in an ant lion's trap. Having bathed, Yammer couldn't climb out of the tub. We would have to pick him up and put him on a towel by the hot-air vent to dry.

This was a perfectly satisfactory arrangement until we failed to tell a visitor about Yammer's passion. In the morning, unaware of his quiet presence, she showered, stepped out of the tub, and left him there. It was almost noon before we discovered him.

Craig promptly put up a sign: "Please remove the owl after showering." It hung over the shower faucets for as long as Yammer lived with us.

Please remove the owl after showering.

Yammer was devoted to Twig. He sat on her shoulder at breakfast, flew to her hand for food when she whistled for him, and roosted on the window-curtain rod of her room when he was not watching TV.

He did like Craig's train set, however.

He had reason to. It moved like a garter snake. The tracks that Craig balanced on his big wooden blocks ran under the bed, then out across the floor past the chest of drawers, over the main line, and back under the bed again. When Yammer heard the train start up, he would fly to the back of the chair in Craig's room. Crouched to drop on this prey, he watched engine and cars ply the precarious route. The blocks would shudder as the little black locomotive swung around a curve or speedily crossed a ravine into the open stretch between the wall and the door. Yammer never struck this prey. The train was not the right size. Yammer was programmed to eat mice, insects, small snakes, and arthropods. The big owls, like the great horned, barred, and barn owls—pets of my childhood—might have pounced on Craig's train, but not Yammer. He just sat and watched. In a house that lacked diving blue jays and scurrying chipmunks, "Black Darling," as Craig called the Lionel train, was biological diversity to Yammer. His head fairly spun off his shoulders as his eyes followed the speeding engine around the room, under the bed, and out again.

> **STOP AND THINK**
> **Author's Craft** A **simile** compares two unlike things, using the word *like* or *as*. For example, "The setting sun was like an orange falling down from the sky." Find an example of a simile on this page.

Often the train wrecked. Craig ran it on the bleeding edge of disaster, and when the building blocks shifted too much, Black Darling would jump the tracks, knock down the trestles, and careen through the air before coming to rest on its side, wheels spinning. With every crash, Yammer took off for Craig's door top, where he would study the dead engine until its wheels stopped turning. Then he would look away. When the train didn't move, it wasn't there.

One evening, a screech owl's plaintive call of spring floated through our windows as we were going to sleep. The voice came from the spruce trees on the other side of the lane.

The next day at breakfast I put down my fork and leaned toward Twig, Craig, and Luke, smiling. They put down their forks and looked at me with that oh-boy-here-it-comes expression on their faces.

"It's time . . ." I said. The eyes widened, the fingers tightened on the table edge.

". . . to set Yammer free."

"NO."

"NO."

"NO NO NO NO." The third voice in the round came in. "Don't let him go."

"He'll stay around," I said. "It will be lovely to have Yammer in our woods, flying, calling to us at night and coming to the window for a mouse or two."

"NO NO NO NO NO NO."

"Maybe he'll even have owlets and bring them to us."

Silence, as they thought about that.

"I'm going to feed him on the windowsill of my bedroom for a few days," I said. "When he knows he can always get food there, I'll open the window and he'll fly off. I'll whistle and he'll come back."

"NO, NO," said Twig. "He won't."

"Yes, he will," I said. "Don't you remember Bubo, Twig?"

"No," she said. "I was just born when we had Bubo."

"Bubo was a great horned owl," I explained. "She lived with us for four years at Vassar College, and then we let her go."

"Don't let Yammer go," said Twig.

"Bubo came back every evening to be fed," I went on. "When she found a male great horned owl in the nearby woodsy graveyard, she moved off the campus and into the woods with him. They raised two owlets in an old crow's nest."

"NO, NO," shouted Luke and Craig.

"Don't let Yammer go," said Twig.

A week later we met in the bedroom.

"Yammer has been eating mice and chicken on the windowsill for a long time now," I said. "The moment has come to open the window." They looked at me as if I were an owl executioner.

STOP AND THINK

Infer/Predict Do you think Yammer will fly out the open window? If he does, will he return to the family regularly? Why or why not?

"He'll be back. He's very hungry."

Eyes widened in disbelief. No one spoke.

"He'll fly to the basswood tree to get his bearings," I said quickly. "Then I'll whistle the 'come get the food' call and he'll be right back."

"No, don't," said Twig.

"We'll feed him just a little bit tonight," I continued. "He'll still be hungry tomorrow, and he'll come back for more. We'll do this every night until he can hunt on his own."

I was facing an audience of skeptics. I had to convince them. "When I was a kid," I hastened to say, "we had a barn owl named Windy.

"He was Uncle John and Uncle Frank's lovable owl. They set him free, and he came to the sleeping porch every night to be fed. Yammer will too."

"Yammer's not a barn owl," said Craig.

That evening we let Yammer go. Twig was hopeful—she trusted that Yammer would come back. Craig was still skeptical. But Luke was brightened by a new awareness rising in him—freedom. The owl would go free. He liked that.

As we opened the window, Yammer blinked his golden eyes and swung his head in a wide circle. He saw the basswood tree, Mr. Ross's spruces, the sky, and the rising moon. Spreading his wings, he floated into the twilight.

We never saw him again.

Your Turn

Wild or Not?

Write About Animals Do you think it is right for people to keep wild animals as pets, as Twig did with Yammer? What are the positive and negative effects of keeping a wild animal? Write a paragraph that explains your opinion. Use support from your own experiences and other readings.

SCIENCE

Yammer Goes Free

Make a Comic Strip What do you imagine happened to Yammer after he flew away? In a group, brainstorm different versions of Yammer's future adventures. Discuss which version you think is most likely to happen and why. Then make a comic strip of the adventures, with each group member contributing a section. Add captions and speech balloons as appropriate.

SMALL GROUP

All About Owls

Turn and Talk Discuss with a partner some facts you learned about screech owls. Which fact did you find most surprising? How did the facts affect your opinion of owls in general? Discuss whether you think the author does a good job of teaching readers about owls and their habits. What do you still want to know about these birds?

FACT AND OPINION

Science

GENRE

Readers' Theater is text that has been formatted for readers to read aloud.

TEXT FOCUS

Persuasive text seeks to convince the reader to think or act a certain way. Sometimes the words and actions of a character reveal what the author wants the reader to think or do. What does Eliza say to persuade the other characters to be careful around the rabbit?

In the WILD

by Anne Patterson

Cast of Characters

Narrator	Luisa
Eliza	Joe
Sam	

Narrator: Friends Sam, Luisa, and Joe are visiting a state park in Texas. Eliza, a park ranger, is leading them on a nature walk.

Eliza: Our park has many amazing biological features, such as—

Sam: What does *biological* mean?

Eliza: Oh, it's anything that has to do with the lives of plants and animals. So, as I was saying, one remarkable biological feature of this park is—

Luisa: A bunny!

Eliza: Well, I wasn't going to say that, but—

Luisa: No, look! Right there. It's a little baby bunny.

Narrator: Everyone gathers around to look at a young rabbit lying in the grass. Sam reaches out his hand.

Eliza: Wait, Sam. Don't touch the rabbit.

Narrator: Eliza guides the group away from the rabbit. Sam looks at the ranger in disbelief.

Sam: But it's all alone! We have to help it.

Eliza: You're absolutely right! And let me tell you the best way we can help. When we see an animal that looks abandoned, we're tempted to touch it. But we may actually be hurting it by upsetting the natural arrangement of things.

Sam: So what should we do?

Eliza: The first thing to do is wait and watch. Usually, the mother is waiting nearby. If people stay too close to the baby, the mother can't come back to get it. If the animal seems hurt, you should call a wildlife center. They have trained people to rescue wild animals, help them recover, and return them to the wild.

Joe: But what if a bigger animal came and pounced on it?

Eliza: You can keep watch from a distance to protect the animal until the mother or the wildlife team comes.

Luisa: Look! Another bunny!

Narrator: A large rabbit hops through the grass towards the baby rabbit.

Eliza: Shhh! Don't utter a sound. We don't want to scare it away.

Luisa: I think it's the baby bunny's mother.

Narrator: As the group watches, the two rabbits hop away together.

Luisa, Joe, and **Sam:** YEAH!!

Eliza: That bunny endeared itself to us immediately. But what if we had hastened to pick it up?

Joe: Its mother wouldn't have been able to find it!

Eliza: That's right!

Joe: Aren't we lucky to have had this incident to teach us more about helping wild animals? We don't want our presence to upset the natural balance.

Sam: This park definitely has some amazing biological features. Let's go on our walk and find some more!

Making Connections

Text to Self

Write About an Animal Think about the George family's experiences with Yammer. Now think about the most unusual experience you have had with an animal or pet. Was it funny, scary, strange, or just plain amazing? Write a short paragraph about your experience.

Text to Text

Compare and Contrast Use a Venn diagram to compare and contrast the adventures of Yammer with the adventures of Winn-Dixie in "Because of Winn-Dixie."

Text to World

Conduct a Survey Ask classmates, friends, and family members what kinds of animals they have had as pets. Organize their responses into a chart. Which kind of animal is the most popular among the people you surveyed? Share your findings with the class and compare the results.

Grammar

What Are Proper Nouns? **Proper nouns** are nouns that begin with **capital letters**. Some examples are names, states, languages, and book titles. In book titles, all of the important words should be capitalized, including *is, are, was,* and *were*. The first and last words in titles should also be capitalized.

Academic Language
proper noun
capital letter

Proper Nouns

historical document

The Declaration of Independence was written and signed during

historical event

the Revolutionary War.

---

name   book   article

Calvin read *One Day in the Woods*, "Student Elections Held Monday"

essay

and "What Makes a Hero."

---

name   race   nationality   language

Marie checked the boxes for Caucasian, Swiss, and French on the form.

Try This! **The proper nouns in the sentences below appear in bold type. Rewrite the sentences with correct capitalization.**

❶ **lee** is **asian** and speaks both **english** and **japanese**.

❷ For her book report, Deb read ***wild birds*** and "**bird watching**."

❸ Our **constitution** was amended after the **civil war**.

Conventions When you use proper nouns in your writing, be sure to capitalize the appropriate words. This will help your reader know that you are using the names or titles of particular people, places, and things.

Incorrect	Correct
Two americans looked at their bill of rights.	Two Americans read the Bill of Rights.

Connect Grammar to Writing

As you edit your persuasive paragraph, check to see that you have capitalized all the important words in proper nouns. Rewrite any incorrect proper nouns so that they are capitalized correctly.

Write to Persuade

☑ **Ideas** A good **persuasive paragraph** states your opinion and gives strong reasons to support it. One way to strengthen your opinion is to include facts and examples. A good persuasive paragraph should end with a call to action to tell the readers exactly what you want them to do or think.

Grace wrote a persuasive paragraph explaining why people should support wildlife rescue centers. Later, she added facts and details to make her points stronger.

Writing Traits Checklist

☑ **Ideas**
Did I state a clear opinion and ideas to support it?

☑ **Organization**
Did I put my reasons in a certain order?

☑ **Word Choice**
Does my language make my meaning clear and strong?

☑ **Voice**
Did I express my own opinion in a convincing way?

☑ **Sentence Fluency**
Do my sentences vary in length?

☑ **Conventions**
Did I use correct capitalization in my title?

Revised Draft

People need to support wildlife rescue centers, or countless animals will suffer. Every day, wild animals become sick, injured, or orphaned. For example, Yammer was ∧Why should hurt when he fell onto a hard driveway. people support wildlife rescue centers?

People are responsible for many of the problems wild animals have—that's why. that end up in rescue centers For example, many animals∧have been hit by cars.

Support Wildlife Rescue Centers!
by Grace Martin

People need to support wildlife rescue centers, or countless animals will suffer. Every day, wild animals become sick, injured, or orphaned. For example, Yammer was hurt when he fell onto a hard driveway. Why should people support wildlife rescue centers? People are responsible for many of the problems wild animals have—that's why. For example, many animals that end up in rescue centers have been hit by cars. Last year my class visited a rescue center. Volunteers at the center helped us understand how to live in harmony with our wild "neighbors." Help us raise awareness of wildlife rescue centers by telling your friends and families about what they do for animals!

For my final paper, I added facts and details to make my ideas stronger. I also made sure my title was capitalized correctly.

Reading as a Writer

How did Grace make her persuasive paragraph stronger? What reasons, facts, or examples could you add to make your persuasive paragraph stronger?

Vocabulary in Context

✓ **TARGET VOCABULARY**

- **trembles**
- **wreckage**
- **slab**
- **possessions**
- **tenement**
- **crushing**
- **rubble**
- **debris**
- **timbers**
- **constructed**

Vocabulary Reader

Context Cards

1 trembles

People sense an earthquake when everything nearby shakes and trembles.

2 wreckage

Even an earthquake shorter than one minute can leave a lot of wreckage.

3 slab

A falling slab, or flat and thick piece, of concrete can destroy everything under it.

4 possessions

A quake can damage people's possessions. The things people own might be ruined.

- **Study each Context Card.**

- **Use a dictionary to help you understand the meaning of these words.**

5 tenement

A tenement, or poorly built apartment building, is especially at risk in a quake.

6 crushing

If falling structures are crushing everything inside them, the street is the safest place.

7 rubble

It can take a lot of time and effort to clean up broken bits of rubble.

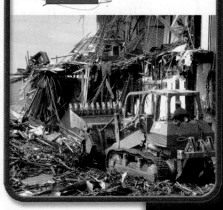

8 debris

After a quake, the debris from a badly damaged road can be dangerous.

9 timbers

Houses made of timbers, or wooden beams, can collapse like toothpick toys.

10 constructed

Buildings now can be constructed in a way that helps them survive quakes.

Background

The 1906 San Francisco Earthquake

Imagine this scene. You wake up suddenly. The bed trembles. A mirror falls from the wall. That is how the day began for many people in San Francisco on April 18, 1906. The huge earthquake was one of the worst natural disasters in United States history. The quake, along with a huge fire, destroyed tenement after tenement, business after business. Buildings had not been constructed to withstand such an event. They fell floor by floor, crushing hundreds. Large timbers snapped, and one slab of debris after another fell to the street. Afterward, residents wandered in the rubble with the few possessions they had saved. Wreckage surrounded them. Hundreds of thousands suddenly found themselves homeless.

San Francisco's city hall was rebuilt after being destroyed by the 1906 earthquake.

Comprehension

✔ **TARGET SKILL** **Sequence of Events**

As you read "The Earth Dragon Awakes," notice the sequence, or order, in which events take place. Notice also that the main sequence of events is interrupted once to tell the story from another point of view. To keep track of the sequence, look for dates and times of day as well as clue words such as *when*, *now*, *then*, and *again*. A graphic organizer can also help you keep track of the sequence of events.

Event:

↓

Event:

↓

Event:

✔ **TARGET STRATEGY** **Visualize**

You can use your graphic organizer and the visualize strategy to help you follow Chin and Ah Sing's story. Using text details to form pictures of the important events in your mind will help you to remember the sequence of those events.

trembles	crushing
wreckage	rubble
slab	debris
possessions	timbers
tenement	constructed

✓ **TARGET SKILL**

Sequence of Events
Examine the time order in which events take place.

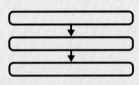

✓ **TARGET STRATEGY**

Visualize Use text details to form pictures in your mind of what you are reading.

GENRE

Historical fiction is a story whose characters and events are set in history.

Set a Purpose Set a purpose for reading based on the genre and what you want to find out.

MEET THE AUTHOR
LAURENCE YEP

During his childhood in San Francisco, Laurence Yep went to school in Chinatown but did not live there. As a young adult, Yep became increasingly interested in his Chinese-American culture. He began his writing career in high school, where he was paid one cent per word to write science fiction stories for a magazine. Now he is the author of many award-winning books, including "Dragonwings," which also tells about Chinese immigrants living in San Francisco.

MEET THE ILLUSTRATOR
YUAN LEE

Yuan Lee has created artwork for advertisements, posters, and magazines. He designed a series of stamps for the United Nations showing the endangered species of the world. Yuan also illustrated "The Parthenon," a book showing the construction of an ancient Greek temple.

The EARTH DRAGON AWAKES

The San Francisco Earthquake of 1906

by Laurence Yep

selection illustrated by Yuan Lee

Essential Question

How can nature influence events?

It is 5:12 A.M. on Wednesday, April 18, 1906. In San Francisco's Chinatown, Chin and his father, Ah Sing, are in their apartment. They are washing up, getting ready to go to the Travises' house, where Ah Sing works to send money to his wife in China. Their friend Ah Quon (kwahn) lives nearby.

Suddenly everything trembles. The bowl creeps across the table. Then even the table crawls away. Chin spills water everywhere.

"You can write your mother about your first earthquake," his father says unworriedly.

The floor rolls under them like a wooden sea. The bowl slips over the edge and crashes. Boxes tumble from the stack. Their possessions scatter across the boards. Chin and his father drop to their knees.

Ah Sing tries to sound brave. "The Earth Dragon must be scratching," he laughs.

Chin tries to be just as fearless. When the room stills, he tries to joke like his father. "He must really have an itch."

Before his father can answer, the trembling begins again.

Chin waits for it to stop. But it goes on and on. The tenement creaks and groans like an old giant. Their bed and bureau prowl like hungry animals.

Ah Sing crawls over. He puts his arms around Chin. "Don't be scared," he says. Ah Sing's voice sounds funny because he is shaking with the room.

Beneath them, unseen timbers crack like sticks. The next instant, one side of the room tilts upward. They slide helplessly with all the furniture toward the opposite wall. Chin feels like a doll. Their belongings crash and thump as they pile up.

His father forces him under the table.

"The tenement is falling!" his father shouts.

Walls crack and crumble. Windows shatter. Broken glass sprays like little daggers.

Chin's stomach feels funny when the room itself drops. They bounce against the floor as it stops with a jerk. For a moment, they lie there. Their neighbors scream from the middle level. Ah Sing and Chin's room is crushing them.

Then the floor twitches. It plunges again. There are more screams. This time it is the ground level that is smashed.

Their floor gives one final thump and stops.

Dazed, Chin peeks out from beneath the table. He sees cracks. They spread like a crazy spiderweb around all the walls. Spurts of powdery plaster puff out. The walls crumble like paper. The ceiling drops down on them.

STOP AND THINK

Visualize On these two pages, the author's detailed description makes it easy for you to visualize the action, or see it in your mind. As you read on, look for other words or phrases that help you to visualize the action.

5:15 A.M. to 5:20 A.M.
Wednesday, April 18, 1906
Underneath San Francisco

scare
Blood kill

The earthquake makes the ground bounce up and down, twisting it back and forth like an old towel. Horses bolt into the street from firehouses. On Mission Street, cattle are being herded from the docks to the slaughter yard. They stampede in terror. They trample and gore a man.

One sixth of the city is on landfill. Dirt, rock and debris (duh BREE) have been dumped along the shore of the bay and into the creeks and ponds. Homes and apartments and stores have been built on top. Valencia Street was constructed this way.

The earthquake tosses water from deep underground and mixes it with the landfill. The ground stops being solid then. That is called liquefaction. The soil becomes like quicksand and sucks entire houses down. That happens on Valencia Street.

Even on more solid ground, buildings collapse like houses of cards.

Thousands of people are trapped all over the city.

✔️ STOP AND THINK

Sequence of Events Summarize the events that have happened so far. What do these events tell you about what might happen next?

5:20 A.M.
Wednesday, April 18, 1906
Chin and Ah Sing's tenement
Chinatown

Chin cannot see. He cannot move. He can barely breathe.

In the darkness, he hears his father cough. "Are you all right, Chin?"

His father is holding him tight. Chin tries to answer. But dust fills his mouth and throat. So he simply nods. Since his father can't see him, Chin squeezes his arm.

Then he shifts around so he can raise one hand. He can feel the tabletop, but its legs have collapsed. Fallen pieces of ceiling and wall have turned the space into a tiny cave.

His father pushes at the wreckage around him. "It won't budge," he grunts.

Chin shoves with him. "The whole ceiling fell on us." If his father hadn't pulled him under the table, he would have been crushed.

But now they are buried alive.

Overhead, they hear footsteps.

"The Earth Dragon's mad," a man screeches in fear.

"Here!" cries Ah Sing.

"Help us!" Chin yells, too.

From nearby, someone hollers, "Fire!"

The footsteps run away.

Chin and his father shout until they are hoarse.

No one hears them though.

Trapped under the rubble, they will be buried alive.

"We'll have to rescue ourselves," his father says. "Try to find a loose section." They squirm and wriggle. There is a big slab of plaster near Chin's head. He gropes with his hands until they feel the plaster. Powdery chunks crumble into his hands.

He hears his father digging. Chin claws at the broken boards and plaster. Dust chokes their noses and throats. Still they scrabble away like wild animals.

6:00 A.M.
Wednesday, April 18, 1906
Chin and Ah Sing's tenement
Chinatown

Chin and his father dig in the darkness. He just hopes they are digging out of the rubble. His arms ache. He is covered with cuts and bruises. Dust chokes his mouth and throat. He feels as if he cannot even breathe. The earth has swallowed them up.

"Fire!" people cry from above. He feels the thumping of running feet.

He screams, "Let me out!"

His father stops digging and wraps his arms around him. "Don't panic!"

But fear twists inside Chin like a snake. He is so dry he cannot even cry. He just lies there. His fingernails are broken. His fingers are bleeding.

They will never escape. He thinks about his mother. She won't know how they died.

Suddenly a breeze brushes his face like a soft hand. He smells fresh air.

He forgets his pain. He forgets he is tired. He scrapes at the wreckage. But he can make only a narrow tunnel. It is barely big enough for him.

"Don't worry about me," urges his father. "Save yourself."

"I'll get help," Chin promises.

"You're the important one," his father says.

Chin crawls up through the passage, leaving his father behind. He would be scared to be left alone in the darkness. Until now he didn't realize how brave his father is. Or how much he loves Chin.

Chin's hands break into the open. They flap frantically like the wings of a scared bird.

"There's someone alive," a man shouts in Chinese.

All Chin can do is croak in answer.

Above him, he hears feet. Someone starts to dig. Boards and bricks and plaster chunks thump to the side. Blindly Chin helps his rescuer widen the hole.

Strong hands grip his wrists. He feels himself rising until he sees Ah Quon's big, grinning face.

"You're the biggest turnip that I ever pulled up," Ah Quon laughs in relief. He hauls Chin onto the rubble.

Chin has only one thought on his mind. "Father," he gasps and points below him.

As Ah Quon digs for his father, Chin manages to spit out the plaster dust. Then he tears at the debris, too.

STOP AND THINK

Author's Craft When authors or narrators are in the story, they are writing from **first person point of view**. When they are outside the story, they are writing from **third person point of view**. From which point of view is the author writing here?

Your Turn

Survivors

Write About Survival What lessons about surviving a disaster can readers learn from Chin and his father? Write a short paragraph answering this question. Then tell how people might use these lessons to help them survive another kind of disaster. HEALTH

Earth Dragon Alert

Research Earthquakes Chin and Ah Sing refer to the "Earth Dragon" as the cause of the earthquake. With a partner, research on the Internet the causes of earthquakes. Then discuss why an earthquake might be compared to a dragon in the Earth. PARTNERS

Living with Liquefaction

Reread **Student Book page 308.** List on a graphic organizer the sequence of events that led to liquefaction during the earthquake. Then compare graphic organizers with a partner and discuss how nature and human activity combined to influence the events of April 18, 1906. SEQUENCE OF EVENTS

TEXAS TWISTERS

Connect to

Science

TEXAS
TWISTERS

✓ TARGET VOCABULARY

trembles	crushing
wreckage	rubble
slab	debris
possessions	timbers
tenement	constructed

GENRE

Informational text, such as this magazine article, gives facts and examples about a topic.

TEXT FOCUS

Diagram Informational text may include a diagram, a picture that explains how something works or how parts relate to each other. How does the diagram on page 317 support the information in the text?

On March 28, 2000, a tornado passed through downtown Fort Worth, Texas. In about ten minutes, the tornado's crushing force left the city littered with debris. Right behind it, a second tornado damaged buildings in nearby towns. Each fallen slab added to the wreckage and rubble.

Around one thousand tornadoes form in the United States every year. Of all the states, Texas has the most tornadoes. It has an average of 153 twisters each year. Texas is an ideal setting for tornadoes. This is because it is located between the warm air of the Gulf of Mexico and the cool air of the Rocky Mountains.

Frequency of Tornadoes

1-2 a year

2-3 a year

3-4 a year

1 a year

less than 1
every two years

1 a year

Average number of tornadoes
in Texas per 2,500 square miles.

Supercells and Funnel Clouds

Tornadoes form when warm air moving in different directions rises and cools. If the air keeps rising and spinning, it can develop into a thunderstorm called a supercell. It can then turn into a tornado.

Meteorologists, scientists who study the weather, can't predict exactly when a tornado will strike. But, they can use radar to track storms. When a supercell grows stronger, the radar measures its rotation for changes in speed. Meteorologists can also spot tornadoes by studying jet streams. They do this by looking at computer models and satellite pictures for signs of thunderstorms.

Fort Worth braces for a tornado on March 28, 2000

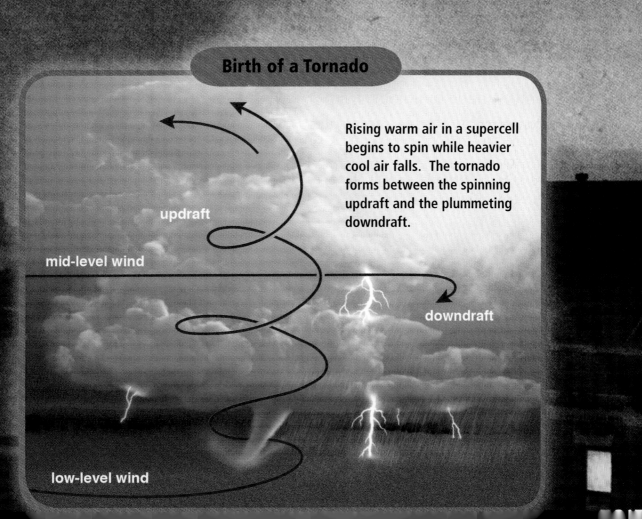

Birth of a Tornado

Rising warm air in a supercell begins to spin while heavier cool air falls. The tornado forms between the spinning updraft and the plummeting downdraft.

updraft

mid-level wind

downdraft

low-level wind

Tornado Safety

Buildings in tornado zones need to be constructed with strong roofs and foundations. Weaker buildings made from timbers can be made stronger with steel and concrete. Weather reports are used to alert residents that a tornado is on its way. Tornado sirens, used in several states, also warn people.

A tornado *watch* is announced when conditions are right for a tornado. A tornado *warning* means that a tornado has been seen. If you hear a tornado warning, don't stay outside and don't try to save your favorite possessions. Flying debris can injure people and damage buildings, from tenements to skyscrapers. Follow these simple rules:

- Get inside a sturdy building.
- Move to an inside room.
- Stay away from windows. If the glass trembles, it may break.
- Wait until the storm has passed before going outdoors.

A radar map shows a line of severe thunderstorms that may cause tornadoes south of Dallas and Fort Worth.

Fort Worth

Waco

Making Connections

Text to Self

Write a Disaster Plan What is one kind of natural disaster that happens where you live? What are the dangers associated with it? Write a step-by-step plan telling what people can do to be prepared for this kind of disaster. Then, with a group, take turns giving your instructions orally. After each partner speaks, restate the instructions in your own words.

Text to Text

Compare Experiences Chin and his father have quite an experience during the earthquake. Compare and contrast their experience with one of Stormy's adventures in "Stormalong" (Lesson 5). Use a Venn diagram to show your ideas.

Text to World

Connect to Technology Research what a seismograph is and what it does. Take notes from your research and use them to write a paragraph about the seismograph. Share your findings with the class.

Grammar

What Is a Possessive Noun? A noun that shows ownership is a **possessive noun**. Add an **apostrophe** and an *-s* (*'s*) to a singular noun to make it possessive. When a plural noun ends with *-s*, add an apostrophe to make it possessive (*s'*). When a plural noun does not end with *-s*, add an apostrophe and an *-s* to make it possessive.

Possessive Nouns
singular possessive noun
The boy's stomach felt odd during the quake.
plural possessive noun
The fire trucks' sirens wailed and screamed.
plural possessive noun
The children's pets ran away in fright.

Turn and Talk **Rewrite each sentence on another sheet of paper. Change the underlined phrase to a possessive noun. Exchange papers with a partner and discuss your changes.**

❶ The father <u>of the girl</u> holds her tight.

❷ They can hear the voices <u>of the rescuers</u>.

❸ The shovels <u>of the men</u> dig into the dirt.

❹ The efforts <u>of the diggers</u> free the father and daughter.

Ideas When you write, you can sometimes make a sentence clearer by adding a possessive noun to indicate ownership. Showing possession helps the reader better understand what is happening.

Unclear	Clearer

When we heard the calls, we shouted loudly for help.	When we heard the firefighters' calls, we shouted loudly for help.

Connect Grammar to Writing

As you revise your problem-solution paragraph, make your sentences clearer by adding possessive nouns to indicate ownership.

Write to Persuade

✔ Ideas A **problem-solution composition** first describes a problem and then explains how to solve it. As you write, include reasons and details to support your main idea. Try to be as persuasive as you can to convince a reader to agree to your solution. Use the Writing Traits Checklist below as you revise your writing.

Jeff wrote a problem-solution composition explaining why people should wear bicycle helmets. Later, he added persuasive details to make his points stronger.

Writing Traits Checklist

✔ Ideas
Did I clearly explain the problem and the solution?

✔ Organization
Do transition words make my ideas easy to follow?

✔ Word Choice
Did I use words that made my points in a positive way?

✔ Voice
Did I use a confident-sounding voice?

✔ Sentence Fluency
Did I use possessive nouns correctly?

✔ Conventions
Did I use correct spelling, grammar, and punctuation?

Revised Draft

Riding a bike is great exercise. It's a good way to get places, too. But riding your bike can be dangerous if you don't wear a helmet. Every year, more than 500,000 bicyclists go to emergency rooms with injuries. Many of the bicyclists' injuries happen to the brain. Experts say that up to 85 percent of these ~~many~~ brain injuries could have been prevented by helmets.

Wear Your Helmet
by Jeff Kowalski

Riding a bike is great exercise. It's a good way to get places, too. But riding your bike can be dangerous if you don't wear a helmet. Every year more than 500,000 bicyclists go to emergency rooms with injuries. Many of the bicyclists' injuries happen to the brain. Experts say that up to 85 percent of these brain injuries could have been prevented by helmets.

How can we make sure that people wear helmets? First, helmets should be made available to all bike riders. Second, people who make helmets should make them fit better and look cooler. Third, schools should have bicycle safety classes. Finally, we all need to wear our helmets, and tell our friends to wear theirs. If we do, we will save lives!

I added facts to make my points stronger. I also used a possessive noun.

Reading as a Writer

Which persuasive details did Jeff add to strengthen his points? What details could you include to show how serious your safety problem or hazard is?

Vocabulary
Reader

Context
Cards

Vocabulary in Context

1 display

The natural world is full of glorious scenes, such as this display of wildlife.

2 alert

These animals are alert. They are wide awake and ready to take action.

3 weariness

This bird can fly many miles. It may get tired, but it isn't stopped by its weariness.

4 fractured

In Antarctica, chunks of fractured, or broken, ice float through the icy sea.

- Study each Context Card.
- Use a dictionary to help you pronounce these words.

5 standards

By these polar bears' standards, or ways of measuring, cold air might be comfortable.

6 vision

Artists can have a vision, or mental image, of how to paint a scene from nature.

7 huddle

Baby goslings often huddle, or crowd, together to stay warm while they nap.

8 graceful

The delicate design of a spider's web is graceful and pleasing to see.

9 stranded

This fawn may seem stranded, or left helpless. Its mother is nearby, though.

10 concluded

Many people have concluded, or decided, that nature is full of beauty.

Background

✓ TARGET VOCABULARY **The Last Wilderness** If you have concluded that there is no place on Earth left to explore, think again. Scientists are still learning much about the continent of Antarctica. This frozen land seems stranded at the bottom of the world, yet it's a display of wonders. An alert visitor might see penguin parents huddle with their chick, or watch a graceful seal stretch out on the ice. Many people have a vision of exploring this amazing place, although it can be dangerous, even by adventurers' standards. Severe weather can lead to fractured ice, and extreme cold can make a person weak with weariness. Scientists and explorers, however, continue to visit this beautiful land.

Palmer Station

ANTARCTICA

South Pole Station

McMurdo Station

Of the many research stations on Antarctica, three are U.S. stations: Palmer, South Pole, and McMurdo. This photo shows the South Pole station.

Comprehension

✓ **TARGET SKILL** **Cause and Effect**

As you read "Antarctic Journal," note how some events cause other events, or effects, to happen. In the selection, the author discusses her adventures in Antarctica. Each thing that happens to her leads to something else. Sometimes, one cause might lead to several effects. Make a graphic organizer like this one to show how each cause leads to an effect.

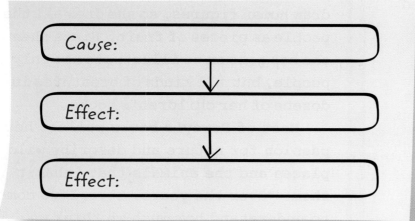

Cause:

Effect:

Effect:

✓ **TARGET STRATEGY** **Summarize**

As you read, summarize, or briefly retell, the most important parts of the selection. Summarizing will help you pull together ideas and better understand how each text event leads to the next.

Main Selection

✔ TARGET VOCABULARY

display	vision
alert	huddle
weariness	graceful
fractured	stranded
standards	concluded

 TARGET SKILL

Cause and Effect Notice how events cause other events, or effects, to happen.

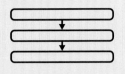

✔ TARGET STRATEGY

Summarize Briefly tell the important parts of the text in your own words.

GENRE

Narrative nonfiction gives factual information by telling a true story.

Set a Purpose Before reading, set a purpose based on the genre and what you want to find out.

MEET THE AUTHOR and ILLUSTRATOR

Jennifer Owings Dewey

When Jennifer Owings Dewey was ten, she wrote an illustrated autobiography. She doubted her ability to draw human figures, so she drew all the people as pieces of fruit. Since then she has gone on to illustrate not only people, but all kinds of creatures in dozens of her children's books.

Most of Dewey's books reflect her passion for nature and describe wild places and the animals that inhabit them. "Over the years. . . . I've come to understand how much we think we know and how much we do not know," says Dewey of her nature writing. She adds that she will never stop writing for children because, like herself, they "want to know the why of things."

Antarctic Journal

Four Months at the Bottom of the World

written and illustrated by
Jennifer Owings Dewey

The author has long had a vision of herself exploring Antarctica, what she calls "the windiest, coldest, most forbidding region on Earth." She has recently traveled by plane and ship to this icy continent. Her first exciting encounter was with humpback whales, when her ship stopped to let them pass. Now she has settled in at Palmer Station, where she'll be living for four months. During her visit to Antarctica, she plans to sketch, photograph, and write about this fascinating place.

the view looking away from Palmer Station

November 27th
Litchfield Island

In fair weather I go to Litchfield Island and spend the day, sometimes the night. Litchfield is three miles from Palmer by inflatable boat, a protected island visited by two or three people a year. Before going to Litchfield, I'm shown how to walk on open ground in Antarctica. An <u>inch</u> of moss takes one hundred years to grow. The careless scuff of a boot heel could rip out two hundred years of growth in seconds.

traveling by inflatable boat

I pack my food and extra clothes in a waterproof sea bag. A day pack holds pencils, pens, and paper for drawing and writing. There is no fresh water on the island. I carry two one-gallon canteens.

Each island has an emergency cache of food and supplies, marked with a flag, available if a person gets stranded during a storm.

Alone after being dropped on the island, I hear birds call, the whine of the wind, the waves pounding gravel shores, and no human sounds except my breathing.

Twilight falls and I crawl into my tent, alert and unable to sleep for a long time, listening to the sounds of the Antarctic night.

STOP AND THINK
Author's Craft The author uses **metaphors** in the third paragraph by comparing one thing to something entirely different without using the words **like** or **as**. One example is "waves pounding." Find another example in the third paragraph.

December 3rd
Litchfield Island

One of the larger islands offshore, Litchfield has a penguin rookery, or nesting area, on the gently sloping western edge. The ground is rocky but flat enough for penguins to build nests, with a beach close by for gathering small gray nest stones.

The rookery is occupied by two or three hundred penguins. It's small by penguin standards. The penguins are nearly all Adélies (uh DAY leez), named in 1838 by Dumont d'Urville (dur VEEL) after his wife. I wonder, did they look like her, act like her, or was he just missing her?

Pairs greet each other at the nest with calls like braying donkeys. They rub chests and bellies, flap wings, stretch necks, and reach for the sky with their bills—behavior called "ecstatic display."

I find a sheltered perch by the rookery and put my six-pound metal typewriter on a flat rock. The penguins begin to wander over.

They huddle close, smelling of guano (GWAH noh) and salt water, gently tugging at my clothing with their bills. One bold bird takes my hat and goes off with it.

They are curious about the tap-tap-tapping noise of the typewriter. They walk up and across it, tugging at the paper tucked into the roller. I let them have their way. Human visitors may not touch penguins, or any wildlife, but the penguins can take their time checking us out.

I follow penguins stone collecting, real work for an Adélie. They carry one stone at a time in their bills. It requires hundreds of trips to complete a nest.

Adélie penguin

Placing a stone takes time. With the stone in its bill, the penguin circles the nest, bowing like a butler. Finally deciding where the stone is needed most, the bird drops it and shuffles away to the beach for another. If one penguin steals a stone from another, a noisy argument erupts. Frustrated birds shriek like squabbling children, but they never come to blows.

✔ **STOP AND THINK**

Summarize The author observes several different kinds of penguin behavior while on Litchfield Island. Summarize the behaviors she observes.

blue whales

December 20th
Palmer Station

I have learned that the largest animal on
Earth, the hundred-ton blue whale, eats only one
of the smallest animals on Earth: krill. There
are more krill in the seas than there are stars
in the visible universe.

Krill is one link in a simple food chain.
Penguins, seals, and whales eat krill. In turn
the tiny shrimplike krill eat phytoplankton,
one-celled plants that bloom in the sea in
spring and summer.

My new friend, Carl, an oceanographer, said
we ought to try eating krill since so many
animals thrive on it.

In the bio lab we scooped krill into a jar.

We got a small fry pan, then melted butter
and cooked up the krill.

Someone said, "Add garlic."

Somebody said, "How about pepper and salt?"

These were added. When
the mixture looked ready,
we ate it.

"Tastes like butter,"
one person said.

krill

"More like garlic,"
another said.

"Tastes like butter *and*
garlic," Carl said.

"Krill don't have their
own taste," I concluded.

December 24th
Palmer Station

It was three in the morning, bright outside, and I couldn't sleep. I crept downstairs, signed out, and took the flagged trail up the glacier.

Dressed in a watchman's cap, three layers under my parka, and boots, I climbed in a stillness broken only by the noise of snow crunching under my soles. Greenish-purple clouds covered the sky from edge to edge. The sea was the color of pewter.

Near the top I heard a cracking sound, a slap magnified a million times in my ear. Another followed, then another. Echoes of sound, aftershocks, sizzled in the air. The sky began to glow with an eerie luminescence, as if someone in the heavens had switched on a neon light in place of the sun.

I felt myself dropping straight down. A crack had appeared under me, a crevasse (krih VAS) in the glacier.

I'm alive because the crack was narrow. I fell to my shoulders, my boot soles too wide to fit through the bottom of the crack. I stared below into a blue-green hole cut with facets like a diamond.

After a few deep breaths, I began to scramble out. Terrified the crack would keep growing, I moved slowly. It was an hour before I was on firm ice.

The color of the sky shifted to blue-gray with streaks of yellow along the western horizon. To my horror, I saw a pattern of cracks zig-zagging, like fractured window glass, across the glacier surface.

I checked my watch. I'd been gone three hours. I don't know why, but I didn't want anyone rescuing me. I decided to crawl down the glacier on hands and knees.

I felt my way inch by inch, rubbing the surface of the snow with my palms before making a move.

I have a new weariness tonight, born of having been frightened out of my wits while watching one of the most beautiful skies I'll ever see.

a green flash

January 6th
Palmer Station

Earlier today my friend Carl, the ocean
scientist, came to my room and said, "Let's go
see the green flash."

"The what?" I asked.

"Come on. You'll see. Hurry or we'll
miss it."

We headed up the glacier, and at the top we
sat facing west. The sun slipped slowly toward
the horizon. As it fell, its orb glowed a deep
orange. The shape of it was fat, like a squashed
pumpkin. Near the end of the drop the light on
top of the orb flashed green—the green flash.

"There it is," I said. "I saw it!"

The green flash is a rare, fleeting event
in the Earth's atmosphere. To catch it with
the naked eye, there must be a clear horizon at
sunset, as often seen over water. The green
flash comes with certain conditions in the sky
having to do with the way light bends. It lasts
less than a twentieth of a second.

March 12th
Winging Home

penguin egg

Before leaving, I collected (with
permission) a sterile penguin egg that would
never hatch. I made room for it in my suitcase
by giving a lot of my clothes away.

The airline lost my bag in Miami. I told
the airline people that I had to have it back,
pleading, begging. "It has a penguin egg in it,"
I said. They glanced at each other and eyed
me funny.

Fortunately for me, and them, they found
the bag.

The egg reminds me of my trip to the place
where penguins raise downy chicks, krill swarm
in numbers greater than stars in the sky, whales
have rights, and icebergs drift in graceful arcs
across Southern Ocean swells. At home, I'll
look out at the desert landscape and remember the
Antarctic desert, the last great wilderness
on Earth.

✔ **STOP AND THINK**
Cause and Effect The author says it's
fortunate for the airline people that they
found her bag. What do you think might
have happened if the bag wasn't found?

Your Turn

Which Is Worse?

Compare Extremes The bitterly cold continent of Antarctica is one of the most extreme environments on Earth. Write a paragraph in which you compare and contrast Antarctica in winter with a desert in the southwest United States. In which extreme environment do you think survival would be more difficult? Why? SCIENCE

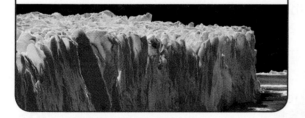

Krill, Anyone?

Create a Recipe As an experiment, the author of "Antarctic Journal" tried krill with garlic and butter. With a partner, make up your own recipe using krill as an important ingredient. In the recipe, include specific directions about how to prepare and serve your new dish.

PARTNERS

Follow the Food Chain

Turn and Talk Discuss this question with a partner: *How important are krill in the Antarctic food chain?* Give examples and details from the selection to support your answers. What effects might the disappearance of krill have on other animals and oceanic ecosystems? CAUSE AND EFFECT

✔ **TARGET VOCABULARY**

display	vision
alert	huddle
weariness	graceful
fractured	stranded
standards	concluded

GENRE
Informational text
gives facts and examples
about a topic.

TEXT FOCUS
Digital Media Each type of
digital media, such as online
articles or blogs, has certain
language conventions that
can be different from other
types of media. How is the
language, such as tone and
word choice, in the online
article alike and different
from the blog on p. 342?

File   Edit   View   Favorites

The
Coolest
Marathon!
by Misha Herenger

Welcome to the Antarctic Ice Marathon,
where people dare to run 26.2 miles on
our planet's coldest continent! Snow, ice, and
wind chills are as low as 40 degrees below zero.
This makes the race a challenge, even by extreme
sport standards.

Antarctica

AFRICA

ATLANTIC
OCEAN

SOUTH
AMERICA

SOUTHERN
OCEAN

Weddell
Sea

South
Pole

INDIAN
OCEAN

Location of
Ice Marathon

ANTARCTICA

SOUTHERN
OCEAN

Ross
Sea

PACIFIC
OCEAN

NEW
ZEALAND

AUSTRALIA

search   search

Home   Dashing Through the Snow   Runner's Blog

Dashing Through the Snow

The runners race on a marked course over snow and ice that has been smoothed and packed down. Antarctica is filled with fractured, jagged cuts in the ice called crevasses. So, the route of the race was well planned, with safety in mind. However, even the most graceful runner must keep alert for changing track conditions here.

Runners are given safety tips the morning of the race. In addition, snowmobiles and aid stations are set up along the route. Everyone stays safe this way, and no one can get stranded. There is no cut-off time for the race, and walking the course is allowed.

The Antarctic presents an icy but beautiful display for runners to enjoy. By the end of the race, however, runners sometimes feel a crushing weariness. Many runners may have a vision of being inside their dry tents. Here, they can huddle in the cozy warmth of their sleeping bags for a hard-earned rest.

341

Runner's Blog

The winner of the 2006 Ice Marathon was Evgeniy Gorkov, a runner from Russia. Below is an excerpt from the blog, or online journal, that Gorkov kept during the race, telling about his preparation and victory. (If you have concluded that Gorkov races in marathons around the world, you're right!)

January 7, 2006.　　The Race

45 minutes before the start. I have a cup of cocoa with a small piece of bread, applied sun block. Looks like I am ready to go. Jitters are no greater than before a regular marathon, wind remains the largest unknown variable. I have race bib number 2, I have folded it and pinned it to my hat. I set no specific time goal for today. The sole objective is to finish the race without major damage to my internal organs or skin. I'll make the next entry after I finish.

5 hrs., 10 min. later and I am the first to cross the finish line after a grueling 5.5 mile long final stretch against a headwind gusting up to 45 knots. Outside of the week-long desert races, this is by far the toughest marathon I have ever run. What makes it difficult is, first and foremost, the vicious wind. Secondly, the footing: even though the surface has been groomed by snowmobiles, the crust is relatively thin and often gives under foot, resulting in a mushy push-off... Would I run it again? Unlikely, unless they fix the wind. Would I recommend it to others? By all means.

Making Connections

📖 Text to Self

The Weather and You Think of a time when nature or the weather did something unexpected. How did you deal with it? Where were you? What were you doing? Write a paragraph about the experience and tell what you learned from it.

There was a big thunderstorm the last time I went camping.

📘 Text to Text

Danger in the Antarctic "The Coolest Marathon!" explains that runners of the Antarctic Ice Marathon "must keep alert for changing track conditions." Recall what you read about Jennifer Owings Dewey's fall into the crevasse in "Antarctic Journal." With a partner, discuss why runners might have to be aware of some of the same dangers.

🌐 Text to World

Diagram a Food Chain Create a diagram of an Antarctic food chain. Begin by choosing one of the animals you have learned about. Then research other plants and animals that belong in the same food chain as that animal.

Grammar

What Is a Regular Verb? To form the past tense of a **regular verb**, add *-ed* to its present form. Another way to show something that has already happened is to use a **helping verb**, such as *has*, *have*, or *had*, with the past participle. The helping verb *has* or *have* must agree with the subject of the sentence.

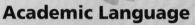

Academic Language

regular verb

helping verb

Agreement with Helping Verbs	
1. With singular subjects: Use *has* with the past participle.	The *author* has packed food. *She* has packed food.
2. With plural subjects: Use *have* with the past participle.	*Waves* have pounded the shore. *They* have pounded the shore.
3. With either singular or plural subjects: Use *had* with the past participle.	*Penguins* had collected stones. The *author* had observed this.

Turn and Talk **Work with a partner. Point out the main verb and helping verb in each sentence.**

❶ The author had dressed warmly.

❷ She has climbed the hill.

❸ Cracks have opened in the ice near the top.

❹ The author has dropped into a crevasse!

344

Conventions Edit your writing carefully. Check to be sure that when you use *has* or *have* with the past tense form of the verb, it agrees with the subject of the sentence.

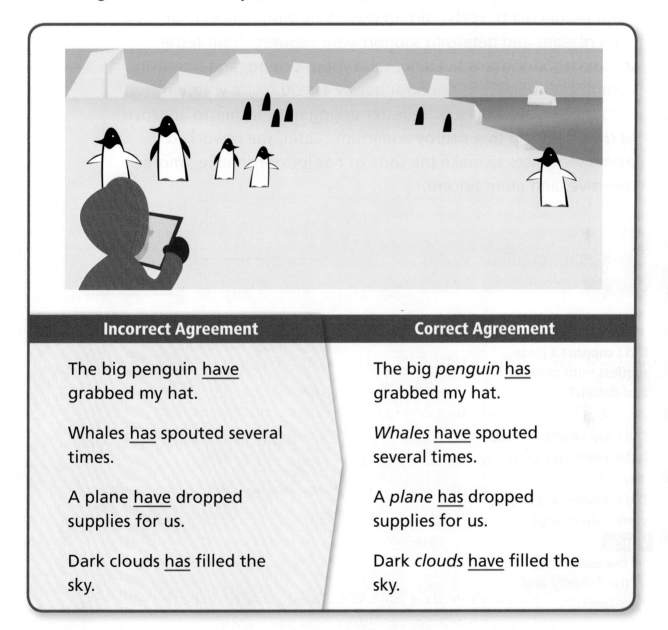

Incorrect Agreement	Correct Agreement
The big penguin <u>have</u> grabbed my hat.	The big *penguin* <u>has</u> grabbed my hat.
Whales <u>has</u> spouted several times.	*Whales* <u>have</u> spouted several times.
A plane <u>have</u> dropped supplies for us.	A *plane* <u>has</u> dropped supplies for us.
Dark clouds <u>has</u> filled the sky.	Dark *clouds* <u>have</u> filled the sky.

Connect Grammar to Writing

As you edit your persuasive letter, check to be sure that any helping verbs agree with the subjects of the sentences.

Write to Persuade

When you write a **persuasive letter**, you try to make your reader act or feel a certain way. You should include at least two reasons and details to support your request. Your letter should also include a heading, salutation, closing, and signature. Use the Writing Traits Checklist below as you revise your writing.

Jenna wrote a persuasive letter asking her teacher to approve a class field trip to a nearby aquarium. Later, she reworked some sentences to make the tone of her letter friendlier, more positive, and more sincere.

Writing Traits Checklist

☑ **Ideas**
Did I support a clear request with reasons and details?

☑ **Organization**
Did I use all parts of the letter correctly?

☑ **Word Choice**
Did I choose words that were convincing?

☑ **Voice**
Is the tone of my letter friendly and positive?

☑ **Sentence Fluency**
Did I use regular and helping verbs correctly?

☑ **Conventions**
Did I use correct spelling, grammar, and mechanics?

Revised Draft

I know you will agree that field trips are
∧ ~~Our class never gets to go anywhere.~~
a great way to make learning exciting.
~~exciting.~~ Since you are now
considering field trips for later in the
year, I hope you will consider my
idea. As you know, we have read about
penguins in Antarctica. Now we want
to learn more about these amazing birds.
Of course, we can't go on a field trip to
Antarctica! So instead we would like to
go to the New England Aquarium.

4680 Pine Avenue
Boston, MA 02101
October 18, 2010

Dear Ms. Beal,

I know you will agree that field trips are a great way to make learning exciting. Since you are now considering field trips for later in the year, I hope you will consider my idea. As you know, we have read about penguins in Antarctica. Now we want to learn more about these amazing birds. Of course, we can't go on a field trip to Antarctica! So instead we would like to go to the New England Aquarium. It's almost as good as Antarctica. Three kinds of penguins live there! The class would also see a lot of other amazing animals, such as sharks and seals. We could learn so much about ocean life by going to the aquarium. Please approve my idea for a class field trip.

Sincerely,
Jenna Morgan

> I replaced my first sentence to make it friendlier. I also checked that I used helping verbs correctly.

Reading as a Writer

How did Jenna change her first sentence to make her tone more friendly and positive? As you write your letter, revise sentences that sound unfriendly or insincere.

✓ **TARGET VOCABULARY**

social

exchanges

excess

reinforce

storage

transport

chamber

scarce

obstacles

transfers

Vocabulary Reader   Context Cards

Vocabulary in Context

1 social

Many animals are social. They live together in organized groups.

2 exchanges

Some people have seen exchanges in which dolphins give and receive food.

3 excess

People harvest only excess honey from a beehive. The bees need the rest to live.

4 reinforce

Elephants reinforce, or strengthen, their bond as they protect their young.

- **Study each Context Card.**
- **Use context clues to determine the meanings of these words.**

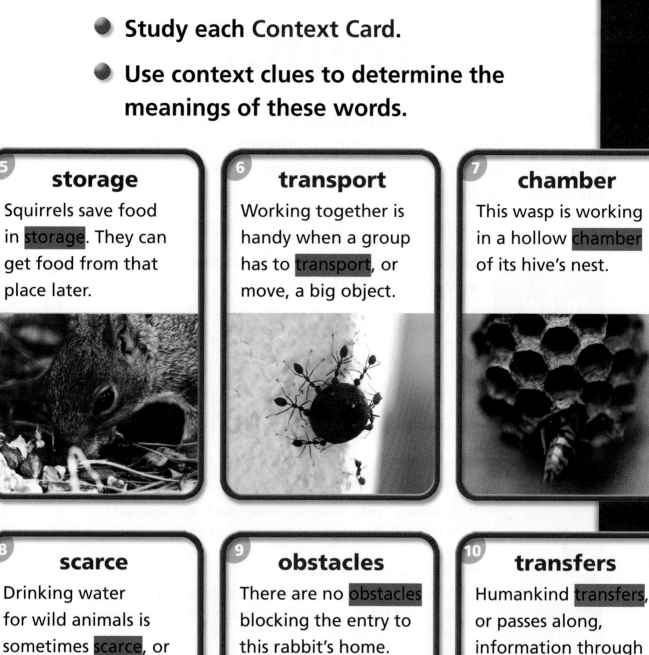

5 storage

Squirrels save food in storage. They can get food from that place later.

6 transport

Working together is handy when a group has to transport, or move, a big object.

7 chamber

This wasp is working in a hollow chamber of its hive's nest.

8 scarce

Drinking water for wild animals is sometimes scarce, or hard to find.

9 obstacles

There are no obstacles blocking the entry to this rabbit's home.

10 transfers

Humankind transfers, or passes along, information through teaching.

Background

The Amazing Ant Like humans, ants take part in different activities during different seasons. Use the timeline below to summarize the seasonal activities of an ant colony, or social group.

A Year in the Life of an Ant Colony

Spring
- Ants reinforce the anthill by fixing any damage.
- Ants leave the anthill to find food.

Summer
- There is plenty of food to be found now, maybe even excess food.
- The ants collect as much food as possible and transport it back to the anthill.
- Inside the anthill, an ant transfers food into a chamber for storage.
- However, "cold-weather ants," such as the small honey ant, are quiet at this time of year.

Fall
- The ants fight ants from other colonies over food, which is becoming scarce. These physical exchanges can be quite fierce.
- Ants close up the entrances into the anthill as they prepare for winter.

Winter
- Ants must deal with winter obstacles to survival: cold temperatures and shrinking supplies of food.
- Cold-weather ants are busy. They can often be found inside houses, looking for food.

Comprehension

Text and Graphic Features

As you read "The Life and Times of the Ant," notice the text and graphic features. Look for headings, captions, diagrams, timelines, and other features to help you understand the text and locate information. Use a graphic organizer to record the selection's text and graphic features and their purposes.

Text or Graphic Feature	Page Number	Purpose
•	•	•
•	•	•
•	•	•

☑ **TARGET STRATEGY** **Question**

Asking yourself questions before, during, and after you read will help you monitor your understanding of the selection. Use your graphic organizer to help you find answers to your questions.

✔ TARGET VOCABULARY

social	transport
exchanges	chamber
excess	scarce
reinforce	obstacles
storage	transfers

✔ TARGET SKILL

Text and Graphic Features Examine how text and graphics work together.

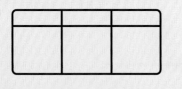

✔ TARGET STRATEGY

Question Ask questions before you read, as you read, and after you read.

GENRE

Informational text gives facts and examples about a topic.

Set a Purpose Before reading, set a purpose for reading based on the genre and what you want to know.

MEET THE AUTHOR AND ILLUSTRATOR

Charles Micucci

Charles Micucci takes a hands-on approach to his work. To research "The Life and Times of the Ant," he built his own ant farm and observed the ants' behavior. Micucci's other books in this series include "The Life and Times of the Apple," "The Life and Times of the Honeybee," and "The Life and Times of the Peanut." For the apple book, he planted twenty-three apple seeds and grew the plants in his apartment. Two of those plants were later relocated to Central Park in New York City. Micucci has also illustrated several books written by other authors.

The Life and Times

of the

ANT

written and illustrated by

Charles Micucci

Masters of the Earth

Ants have been digging through dirt for more than 100 million years. Their dynasty stretches from the time of dinosaurs to today.

They are one of the world's most important insects. They plow more soil than beetles, eat more bugs than praying mantises, and outnumber many insects by 7 million to 1.

Tunneling out of jungles and forests and into back yards on every continent except Antarctica, ants ramble on as if they own the Earth. Perhaps they do.

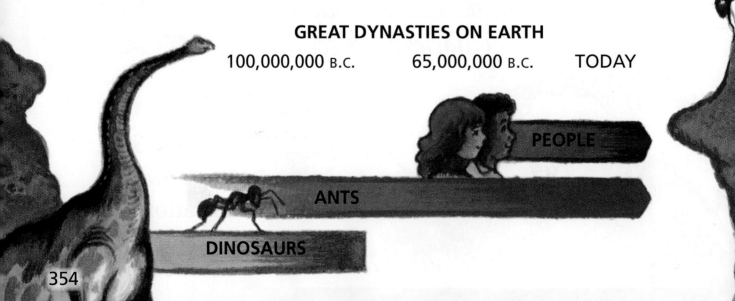

GREAT DYNASTIES ON EARTH

100,000,000 B.C.   65,000,000 B.C.   TODAY

PEOPLE

ANTS

DINOSAURS

Ounce for ounce, an ant is one of the strongest animals on earth. An ant can lift a seed five times its weight, while an elephant can lift a log only one fifth of its weight.

Each year, the world's ants dig up more than 16 billion tons of dirt—enough to fill 3 billion dump trucks.

Ants are frequently compared with people because they live in social communities and work together to solve their problems.

355

Inside an Ant Hill

Most ants build their homes underground. Ants dig by scooping dirt with their mandibles (jaws). As they chew the dirt, it mixes with their saliva to form little bricks. Then they pack the little bricks together to reinforce the tunnels. Finally, the ants carry the excess dirt outside with their mandibles, and it gradually forms an anthill.

Beneath the anthill lies the ant nest. Small nests have only one chamber just inches below the surface, while large nests may have thousands of chambers and may be as deep as twenty feet. All nests provide shelter from the weather and a safe environment for the queen ant to lay eggs.

Ants often nest beneath a rock or log, which protects the nest and traps moisture in the dirt. Ants require moisture so that their bodies do not dry out.

An anthill absorbs the sun's rays and transfers the heat down into the nest. An anthill can be ten degrees warmer than the surrounding area.

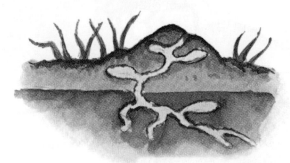

Ants dig their nests deep enough to reach damp dirt. As air dries out the nest, they dig new tunnels into the damp dirt.

STOP AND THINK
Question Is there anything that you do not understand on this page? What questions could you ask to help you better understand it?

356

As ants bring up dirt, they recycle nutrients that help plants grow.

In the daytime, workers move eggs into the upper chambers, which are heated by the sun.

Day nursery

The floor of an ant chamber slants down so water can drain off. The roof is curved to trap heat.

Queen laying eggs

At night, workers shift eggs to lower chambers, because the earth that stored the sun's heat during the day slowly releases the heat at night.

Food storage

Night nursery

357

A Life of Work

Ants begin their working lives by cleaning themselves. In a couple of days they start sharing food and licking each other. These food exchanges bond the colony together. There is no boss ant, but active ants usually begin doing chores and then other ants join in.

Younger ants work in the nest—tending the queen ant, feeding larvae (LAHR vee), and digging tunnels. After a couple of months, the ants leave the nest to search for food. There is no retirement; worn out or battle-scarred, ants work until they die.

Queen Tender
Young ants help the queen deliver her eggs by grabbing the eggs with their mandibles.

Nurse Ant
Ants lick larvae so they do not dry out, and feed them so they grow.

✔️ STOP AND THINK
Text and Graphic Features If you were trying to quickly find a fact about a type of ant on this page, what text and graphic features would help you locate that information?

Foragers
The oldest ants search for food. Most foragers search within fifty feet of the nest, but if food is scarce, they may travel thousands of feet.

Guard
When ants first leave the nest, they stand near the entrance, blocking strange ants from entering.

Tunnel Digger
As the population grows, ants dig more tunnels for the increased traffic and new chambers to store the eggs and larvae.

Digging holes can be hard work. To remove a pile of dirt 6 inches high, 6 inches wide, and 6 inches long requires 500,000 loads of dirt.

359

Grass Root Highways

Some ants connect their anthills to food sources by a system of ant trails. Unlike scent trails, which are invisible, these trails can be easily seen. Construction crews remove grass and twigs to form paths two to six inches wide that may stretch over six hundred feet. When food is plentiful, a thousand ants per foot crowd the trail. Established ant colonies may travel over the same grass root highways for many years.

STOP AND THINK

Author's Craft The author sometimes uses **imagery**, or words and phrases that help you form a mental picture of things not shown in an illustration. Find an example of imagery on page 360.

In forests, wood ants connect their anthills together by ant trails. Large wood ant colonies transport thousands of caterpillars and insects a day over their trails.

Harvester ants construct their trails to wildflowers, where they collect seeds. Surrounding their anthills, discarded seeds sprout into new plants.

Some ant trails are so well preserved that larger animals such as deer and even people may use them as footpaths.

Army ants form living bridges to cross streams by linking themselves together.

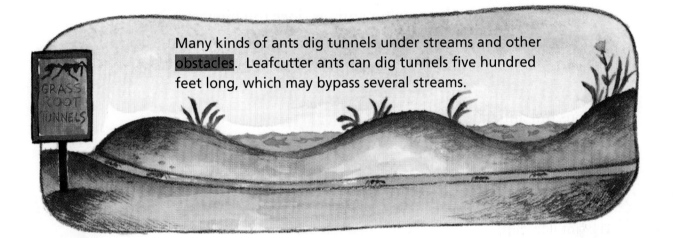

Many kinds of ants dig tunnels under streams and other obstacles. Leafcutter ants can dig tunnels five hundred feet long, which may bypass several streams.

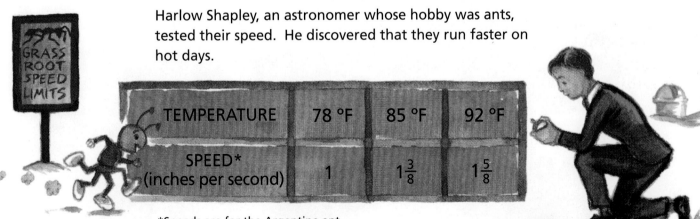

Harlow Shapley, an astronomer whose hobby was ants, tested their speed. He discovered that they run faster on hot days.

TEMPERATURE	78 °F	85 °F	92 °F
SPEED* (inches per second)	1	$1\frac{3}{8}$	$1\frac{5}{8}$

*Speeds are for the Argentine ant

woodpecker

horned lizard

armadillo

A Dangerous World

When you are only a quarter-inch tall, the world can be a dangerous place. Every time an ant leaves home, there is a risk that she will not return. Horned lizards lap up ants as they exit the nest, woodpeckers pick them off as they climb trees, and ant lions ambush them in sand pits.

Sometimes ants are not safe even in their own homes. Armadillos feast on burrowing ants, as does the biggest home wrecker of all: the giant anteater of Central and South America. Seven feet long and weighing as much as seventy pounds, a giant anteater can tear open an ant nest in minutes and devour twenty thousand ants in one meal.

Sand Trap of No Return

The ant lion digs a circular sand pit and waits at the bottom.

When an ant looks into the pit, the ant lion tosses sand into the air to trip up the ant.

The ant stumbles into the pit, and the ant lion grabs it with its large pincers.

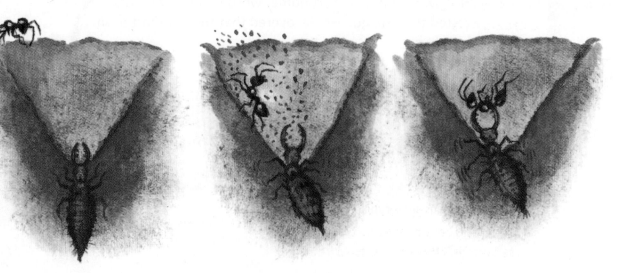

The Giant Anteater

The giant anteater is a slow, nearsighted, toothless animal that has escaped extinction for one reason only: it specializes in eating ants and termites.

Thick bristles of hair protect the body from insect stings.

The stomach wall absorbs ant stings and has special muscles that crush ants so they can be digested.

A three-foot-long tail with fifteen-inch hairs sweeps up escaping ants.

Four-inch claws can dig through hard dirt or tree trunks.

The long snout drives deep into the nest. Anteaters use their strong sense of smell to locate ants.

The mouth opens only a quarter-inch, about the width of a pencil.

The wormlike tongue stretches nineteen inches beyond the mouth. The tongue is coated with gluey saliva, which causes ants to stick to it.

How Ants Recycle Leaves

Leafcutter ants harvest leaves and take them to the nest. In the process, they thin jungle overgrowth and return mulch from the crushed leaves to the soil.

Using her mandibles like a saw, a foraging leafcutter cuts part of a leaf from a tree.

Marching home in long columns, thousands of foragers carry leaves over their heads.

Below ground, millions of ants work like a factory processing the leaves.

Workers chop the leaves. Smaller ants smash the leaf bits into damp paste.

When the leaf paste can no longer grow fungus, it is pushed into dump chambers. As it decomposes, nutrients are released into the soil, which helps plants grow.

Soon a fungus grows on the paste. Then garden ants, tinier than the foragers' heads, harvest the fungus, which all the ants eat as food.

364

Your Turn

Ants and Humans

Compare Social Systems
Think of the various ways that ants work together to create a society. Then write a paragraph that compares and contrasts ant colonies with human communities. How are the two alike? How are they different? SOCIAL STUDIES

Visitors Welcome!

Be a Guide Imagine that you are an ant. It is your job to show visiting ants around the anthill. Work with a partner to draw a map of your anthill. Decide where you will bring visitors, what you will show them, and what you will say about the different parts of the nest. Label each part of the map and add captions.
PARTNERS

Talk About Graphics

Turn and Talk
Page through the selection with a partner. Discuss how information is presented, focusing on what the text and graphic features add to each page. How might readers have reacted differently if only words were used, with no graphics illustrating the text?
TEXT AND GRAPHIC FEATURES

Traditional Tales

GENRE

A **fable** is a short story in which a character, usually an animal, learns a lesson.

TEXT FOCUS

A **moral** is the lesson that a character in a fable learns. What does this fable teach you about helping others?

THE DOVE AND THE ANT

retold by Anne O'Brien

This retelling of an old fable is set on the island of Puerto Rico, where a wide river, the Rio de la Plata, flows from the mountains down to the sea. Near the river stands a large ausubo tree.

A Dove sat in the branches of the ausubo tree. He was a social creature who liked to meet other animals.

At the base of the tree was an anthill. There an Ant was working to transport food for storage. The Dove watched her reinforce the anthill and clear the central chamber. He saw her moving obstacles from the tunnels.

"What a hard worker!" remarked the Dove.

Not long after, he heard the Ant say in a tiny voice, "I'm so thirsty!"

The Dove wanted to help. He flew down to a lower branch. "The river is not far," he called out to the Ant. "It is just beyond that tall grass."

At the riverbank, the Ant had a long drink. Then suddenly a gust of wind blew her into the water.

"Help!" cried the Ant. Hearing the Ant's cry, the Dove grabbed a twig in his beak and dropped it into the water.

"Climb on and save yourself!" the Dove called. Clinging to the twig, the Ant was soon washed to shore.

"How can I ever thank you?" the Ant asked the Dove. "Life is hard and such kindness is scarce."

"It was my pleasure," the Dove replied. "I like to help my fellow creatures. There can never be excess kindness in this world."

Thinking over the Dove's words, the Ant returned to work.

Later that day, a hunter named Rafael appeared, carrying a large sack. He spotted the Dove in the ausubo tree. He set to work near the anthill, building a bird trap.

The Ant saw the sack and the trap. "When the hunter catches a bird, he transfers it into the sack and carries it away," the Ant thought.

Just then the Ant saw the Dove flying toward the trap. "Oh no," said the Ant. "The Dove will be caught! I have to act quickly."

In a flash, the Ant crawled up Rafael's foot and bit his ankle. The hunter cried out in pain. Startled, the Dove flew higher up into the tree.

Rafael rubbed his ankle. "Too bad," he thought. "Now I will have to catch my dinner elsewhere."

When the hunter had gone, the Dove turned to his friend. "Now it is my turn to thank you," he said.

"It was my pleasure," the Ant replied.

The lesson of the tale is this: The best way to make friends is by exchanges of kind deeds.

Making Connections

Text to Self

Make a "Fun Facts" List "The Life and Times of the Ant" contains many facts about ants. Which facts were the most fun for you to learn about? Quickly skim the text again and make a list of five facts about ants that you found interesting or strange. Share your list with a partner.

Text to Text

Compare Traditional Tales Just like real ants, the ant in the fable is a hard worker. Think of another fable or traditional tale that has an ant as a character. Write a paragraph that compares and contrasts the two characters.

Text to World

Compare Ants Use reference texts and Internet search engines to research two kinds of ants. Then construct a chart to compare them. Include details that tell what they look like, where they live, and what their habits are. Present your findings to the class.

Grammar

What Are Participles? A **participle** is a verb form used as an adjective. Each verb has two forms that can be used as participles. The **present participle** form has *-ing* added to the verb. The **past participle** form usually has *-ed* added to the verb.

Participles

The growing larvae need food.

Ants make bricks out of chewed dirt.

A **participial phrase** begins with a participle and describes a noun.

participial phrase

The larvae growing in the ant nest need food.

participial phrase

The ants make bricks out of dirt mixed with saliva.

Turn and Talk Work with a partner. Identify the participle in each sentence. Tell whether it is a present participle or a past participle. If the participle begins a participial phrase, identify the phrase.

1. The expanded ant nest has new chambers.

2. Day nurseries are warm chambers filled with eggs.

3. Workers must move stored eggs each day.

4. The ants tending the eggs are young.

Sentence Fluency In your writing, sometimes you can combine two related sentences by making one a participial phrase, which is a participle and any accompanying words. The participial phrase in the new sentence tells more about the subject.

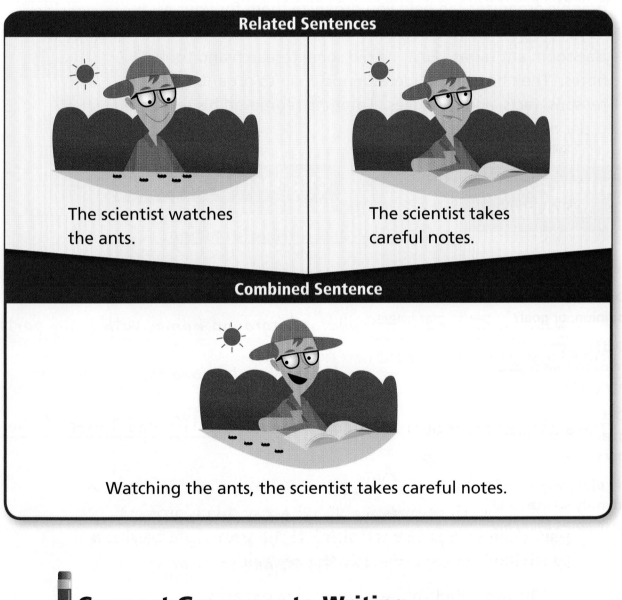

Related Sentences

The scientist watches the ants.

The scientist takes careful notes.

Combined Sentence

Watching the ants, the scientist takes careful notes.

Connect Grammar to Writing

As you revise your persuasive business letter next week, look for places to use a participial phrase to describe someone, something, or an action, or to combine sentences.

Write to Persuade

✓ Organization Good writers organize their ideas before writing a **persuasive essay**. Taking notes can help you identify reasons, facts, and examples to include in your essay. Making a graphic organizer can help you organize them for your essay.

For his persuasive essay, Julio chose to write about classroom ant farms. First, he did some research and took notes. Then he used an idea-support map to organize his reasons, facts, and examples. Later, he reordered his reasons in order of importance.

Writing Process Checklist

▶ **Prewrite**

✓ Did I state a clear opinion, or goal?

✓ Did I list strong reasons that support my goal?

✓ Did I include facts and examples to support my reasons?

✓ If I did research, did I identify sources and take notes using my own words?

Draft

Revise

Edit

Publish and Share

Exploring a Topic

<u>Why are ants interesting?</u>

—stronger than elephants for their size

— build underground homes with many parts

— work together to care for queen, eggs

Micucci, Charles. <u>The Life and Times of the</u>

<u>Ant.</u>

<u>How do ant farms work?</u>

— two types: gel; sand or soil

— get 25 ants; feed and water every day

"Setting Up a Classroom Ant Farm."

AllThingsAnt.com, 15 Nov. 2010.

Idea-Support Map

Goal: The students in room 6 want to get a classroom ant farm.

Reason: It would teach us responsibility.
Facts and examples:
We would have to choose the farm (sand, soil, or gel). There will be 25 ants to start with. We would have to feed and water them regularly.

Reason: Ants are fascinating.
Facts and examples:
Ants are stronger than elephants for their size. They have a complicated social structure.

Reason: We will be able to learn by observation.
Facts and examples:
We could observe how the ants build their homes and take care of each other. We could watch the community develop and grow.

I took notes about ants and ant farms. Then I used the notes to create an idea-support map. I listed reasons to support my goal. I added facts and examples to support my reasons. This helped me organize my ideas.

Reading as a Writer

How can Julio's idea-support map help him develop paragraphs? As you write your persuasive essay this week, look for ways that an idea-support map could help organize your thoughts.

Ecology for Kids

Wonderful
Weather

✓ TARGET VOCABULARY

organisms

directly

affect

traces

vast

habitats

variety

species

banned

radiation

Vocabulary
Reader

Context
Cards

Vocabulary in Context

1 organisms

Biologists study the organisms, or living things, on Earth.

2 directly

You can directly help the environment by planting trees. You can see results quickly.

3 affect

Smog and smoke negatively affect the air by making it unhealthy to breathe.

4 traces

Wash your hands thoroughly, or else traces of dirt and germs may remain.

- Study each Context Card.
- Use a dictionary to help you understand the meanings of these words.

5 vast

The vast desert stretched for hundreds of miles in every direction.

6 habitats

Forests and oceans are types of habitats that support different plants and animals.

7 variety

The rain forest contains a wide variety of animals and plants.

8 species

There are many different species of sharks, such as the hammerhead.

9 banned

Littering is banned in many public places. People should dispose of trash responsibly.

10 radiation

Invisible rays of energy called radiation are produced by the sun and other stars.

Background

How Do Our Actions Affect the Earth? It is important to remember how much the actions of individuals directly affect the environment. Earth seems so vast. It's tempting to think that our personal behavior does not matter much. In fact, our actions do leave traces on the planet in a variety of ways. For example, if people don't stay on the trail while hiking, their footsteps can damage delicate habitats. This may hurt the organisms that live there. Many species of animals and plants have died out as a result of habitat destruction.

Like individuals, governments also play an important role in protecting the environment. For example, several nations have banned the use of some chemicals because they weaken the atmosphere. Many scientists believe that these chemicals allow harmful radiation from the sun to reach Earth.

Comprehension

As you read "Ecology for Kids," look for the main ideas, or the most important points the author makes. Look for supporting details that give facts or examples of the main ideas. Use a graphic organizer like this one to help you see and summarize the relationship between a main idea and its supporting details.

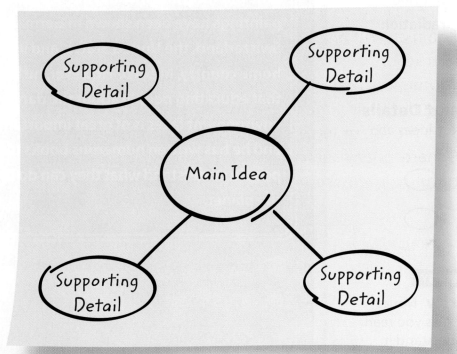

✓ **TARGET STRATEGY** **Monitor/Clarify**

Monitoring your understanding and stopping to clarify information that does not make sense will help you to fully understand what you read. Note the main ideas and supporting details on your graphic organizer to help you monitor and clarify.

Ecology for Kids

✓ **TARGET VOCABULARY**

organisms	habitats
directly	variety
affect	species
traces	banned
vast	radiation

✓ **TARGET SKILL**

Main Ideas and Details
Name a topic's key ideas and supporting details.

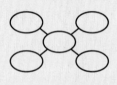

✓ **TARGET STRATEGY**

Monitor/Clarify Notice what is confusing as you read. Find ways to understand it.

GENRE

Informational text gives facts and examples about a topic.

Set a Purpose Set a purpose for reading based on the genre and what you want to know.

MEET THE AUTHOR

Federico Arana

Federico Arana has spent his life studying the environment and, as a science teacher, knows all about ecology. He also spends his time painting and making music. Federico's paintings have been shown in Germany, Switzerland, the United States, and in his home country, Mexico. However, he knows that educating people about the dangers the environment faces is of great importance, and he has written numerous books to help people understand what they can do to save the planet.

Ecology
for
Kids

By Federico Arana

Ecology

What does the word *ecology* mean? The term was invented by Ernst Haeckel (HEHK uhl), a German biologist. He joined two Greek words: *oikos*, meaning "house," and *logie*, meaning "the study of." Together they mean "the study of the house." The "house" Haeckel had in mind is our planet, Earth. Earth is home for all living things—humans, animals, plants, fungi, and even tiny microbes.

To study a house is to learn how its residents use it. An ecologist is a scientist who studies the relationships between organisms and their environment. The environment is an organism's surroundings. It may include water, gases, rocks, and temperature.

Ecologists also study the delicate balance of using the environment while protecting it.

An ecologist once asked a boy what he thought it meant to protect the environment.

The boy said, "You go into the forest and look for somebody who wants to cut down a tree. You take away his ax. You tell him about how important trees are. You say they are good for natural beauty, saving soil, putting oxygen into the air, and giving shelter to birds and other animals."

Trees give us resources and natural beauty.

"Good answer," said the ecologist, "but it may not be easy to find a woodcutter to talk to. Also, remember that sometimes it's necessary to cut down a tree. If we cut down too many trees, the forest will disappear. If we don't cut down any trees, we won't get any resources from the forest. We have to find the right balance."

"I get it," the boy said. "We need the forest's resources for wood and paper or we might not have desks or notebooks for school."

"Exactly—and school is a good place to learn about ecology," added the ecologist. "Then you will know how to protect the natural environment."

STOP AND THINK

Author's Craft How does the author adjust his **word choice** to suit the speakers on these two pages? Compare the words spoken by the boy with the words spoken by the ecologist. How are the word choices different? Why might the author have used different word choice for the speakers?

Ecosytem

Scientists call Earth and its surrounding atmosphere the biosphere. To study it, they divide it into parts called ecosystems.

An ecosystem is a natural area where groups of living and nonliving things interact with their environment. Forests, lakes, swamps, and deserts are all examples of ecosystems.

One ecosystem and the organisms that live in it may depend on other ecosystems. For example, a bear that lives in a forest might use a lake to find fish to eat and water to drink.

In the same way, the problems of one ecosystem often directly affect the organisms of other ecosystems. Take, for example, the problems of the tropical rain forest.

This bear relies on two different ecosystems.

Destruction of the Forests

Four of Earth's seven continents have traces of what used to be vast tropical forests. Now, these forests are gone.

How did they disappear? A large part of the forests was cut down to clear lands for farming. This caused problems. The layer of soil upon which a forest rests is thin. Without deeply rooted trees, the soil is washed away by rain. Soon nothing remains but dry, sandy soil in which very little can grow.

Without plants to eat, animals must leave their habitats. Huge amounts of oxygen are also lost. The Amazon rain forest alone is thought to produce one-third of all the oxygen in Earth's atmosphere. In addition, many rain forest plants are used to produce medicines. Preserving the rain forest is important to all living things.

Clearing a tropical forest can create problems for the world.

STOP AND THINK
Monitor/Clarify Monitor your understanding of how cutting down tropical forests caused other problems. Review the second paragraph. Why did the lack of trees cause animals to leave?

An Ocean of Resources

   The sea is another ecosystem to be both used and protected. The sea covers four-fifths of Earth's surface. It is an amazing world filled with a huge variety of creatures. These creatures include fish, crabs, jellyfish, corals, sponges, clams, snails, and algae. Marine mammals, such as dolphins and whales, spend their whole lives in the sea. Other mammals, including seals, walruses, and polar bears, live near the sea and spend much of their time in it. The sea turtle and some birds, such as penguins, spend most of their lives at sea. Scientists are still discovering new species of sea life.

The sea is home to an amazing variety of creatures.

Fish is an important food resource. The sea provides fifty million tons of fish each year. However, overfishing—harvesting too many fish—has put some species in danger. Ecology can show people how to fish responsibly. Learning about ocean animals and their relationships to their environments can help prevent their loss. With this information, fishing can be banned where necessary. People can use the correct nets to keep from trapping young fish and other sea animals.

The sea brings us other kinds of riches as well. It offers salt, iron, and copper. Fossil fuels, such as petroleum and natural gas, can be found beneath the sea.

The sea is used to transport people and goods. Thanks to the power of tides, the sea is also a promising source of new energy. We should use these resources while protecting the sea.

✔ STOP AND THINK

Main Ideas and Details For the topic of ecology, the author supports main ideas with details. In the first paragraph on this page, what details support the main idea that ecology teaches people how to fish responsibly?

The Protective Ozone Layer

Another important part of Earth's biosphere is the atmosphere. This is the blanket of air covering Earth. Part of the atmosphere is the ozone layer. It protects us from the sun.

The sun's light lets us see and is needed for growth. Its heat controls the temperature of Earth. All living things need the sun's light and heat to live and grow.

The sun also produces powerful radiation, including X rays, ultraviolet rays, and microwaves. If the ozone layer were to disappear, Earth would receive too many of these harmful rays. This would hurt all living things.

People have banned the use of chemicals that can weaken the ozone layer. By thinking ecologically, we can safely use the sun's resources.

The ozone layer protects the Earth from the sun's harmful rays.

How Can You Protect Biosphere Earth?

One important way to protect the environment is to help stop pollution. Here are a few ideas:

Put trash in its place. Trash does not belong in the streets, the rivers, or the oceans. Trash and other kinds of pollution harm all living things.

Use solar-powered clocks and calculators when you can. If you use battery-power, recycle used batteries.

When you leave a room, turn off the light. When you are not using televisions, radios, and computers, turn them off, too. That way, your family will use less electricity and will save money.

Save water in every way you can. Take short showers. Turn off the water while you brush your teeth. If a faucet is dripping, ask an adult to fix it.

Finally, remember that many people make mistakes because they don't know about ecology and pollution. Instead of getting mad, teach them! You will help make a better environment for yourself and for your own children.

A clean environment is everyone's responsibility.

Your Turn

Ecology in Action

Write a Paragraph We protect forests, but we also cut down trees for wood and paper. Write a paragraph explaining how we protect another natural resource, such as water, while still making responsible use of it. In your paragraph, use facts from the selection as well as your own knowledge. Include details that support your main idea. MAIN IDEAS AND DETAILS

Our House

Create a Poster In the selection, you learned that *ecology* comes from Greek words that mean "the study of the house"—and that our house is Earth. With a partner, create a poster that illustrates the idea that Earth is home to all living things. PARTNERS

Ocean Power

With a partner, discuss the details the author uses to support the idea that Earth's oceans are important. List five details that help you understand why oceans are such a valuable resource. What might happen if Earth's oceans were polluted beyond repair? CAUSE AND EFFECT

Poetry

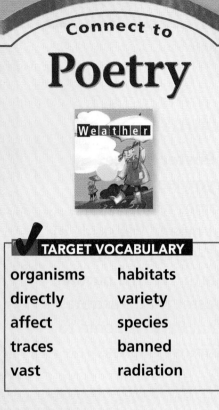

✔ **TARGET VOCABULARY**

organisms	habitats
directly	variety
affect	species
traces	banned
vast	radiation

GENRE

Poetry uses the sound and rhythm of words to suggest images and express feelings.

TEXT FOCUS

Rhyme is the repeated sounds at the end of two or more words. It helps give a poem rhythm and form.

Wonderful Weather

Get ready for a variety of weather and poems. "Lightning Bolt" is a concrete poem: its words form a picture. In the haiku "Spring Rain," and in "Umbrella," you may feel traces of a shower. Listen for the sounds in "Weather," and stop into "Weatherbee's Diner" for weather that suits all kinds of habitats.

Lightning Bolt

NEWS FLASH!
BEN
FRANKLIN
USES
KITE & KEY
TO UNLOCK
ELECTRICITY!

by Joan Bransfield Graham

Spring Rain

In the rains of spring,
An umbrella and raincoat
Pass by, conversing.

by Buson

Umbrella

Out there — wet
In here — dry
Cozy little roof
Between me and the sky

by Rob Hale

Weather

Weather is full
of the nicest sounds:
it sings
and rustles
and pings
and pounds
and hums
and tinkles
and strums
and twangs
and whishes
and sprinkles
and splishes
and bangs
and mumbles
and grumbles
and rumbles
and flashes
and CRASHES.

by Aileen Fisher

Weatherbee's Diner

Whenever you're looking for something to eat,
Weatherbee's Diner is just down the street.
Start off your meal with a bottle of rain.
Fog on the glass is imported from Maine.
The thunder is wonderful, order it loud,
with sun-dried tornado on top of a cloud.
Snow Flurry Curry is also a treat.
It's loaded with lightning and slathered in sleet.
Cyclones with hailstones are great for dessert,
but have only one or your belly will hurt.
Regardless of whether it's chilly or warm,
at Weatherbee's Diner they cook up a storm!

by Calef Brown

Write a Weather Poem

Organisms of every species, from a vast herd of buffalo to a swarm of tiny fleas, are directly affected by the weather. How does the weather affect you? What do you think of the sun's radiation? Should snow be banned? Write a poem about the weather you like or don't like. Include your reasons.

Making Connections

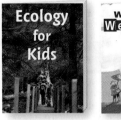

Text to Self

List Habits Reread the last page of "Ecology for Kids." Identify the five things you can do to help protect the environment. Then make a list of the things you already do to protect the planet. Make a second list of what you would like to begin doing.

What I Do to Help the Earth	What I Want to Start Doing

Text to Text

Compare Poems Compare two poems in "Wonderful Weather." Answer these questions about each poem: *Does the poem rhyme, or is it written in free verse? Does the poem contain metaphors or similes? Does the poem contain sound devices, such as alliteration?* Then create a Venn diagram to show how the poems are alike and different.

Text to World

Chart Rainfall Water is an important resource. Research the amount of rain that falls in your community or state in a typical year. Record the information in a chart.

My State's Rainfall Amounts

Annual Rainfall	Rainiest Month	Driest Month

Grammar

What Is an Irregular Verb? Verbs that do not add -*ed* to show past action are called **irregular verbs**. The spellings of irregular verbs can change in many different ways from present-tense to past-tense forms, so you must remember the spellings.

I **give** now   I **gave** earlier.   I **have given** already.

Present	Past	Past with helping verb
break	broke	(has, have, had) broken
bring	brought	(has, have, had) brought
come	came	(has, have, had) come
begin	began	(has, have, had) begun
eat	ate	(has, have, had) eaten
give	gave	(has, have, had) given
grow	grew	(has, have, had) grown
know	knew	(has, have, had) known
make	made	(has, have, had) made
say	said	(has, have, had) said
take	took	(has, have, had) taken
tell	told	(has, have, had) told

Try This! **Copy each sentence. Fill in the blank with the correct form of the verb in parentheses.**

❶ Our field trip _____ at 8 A.M. yesterday. (begin)

❷ Our teacher had _____ maps of the county park. (bring)

❸ The bus _____ us to the park. (take)

❹ A ranger _____ a talk about the park's ecology. (give)

Conventions The use of an incorrect verb form can confuse your readers. When you proofread your writing, be sure you have used the correct forms of irregular verbs to show past action. Also be sure that you have used correct forms of the helping verbs *has, have,* and *had.*

Incorrect Verb Form	Correct Verb Form
The science teacher has brung a poster of a typical food web. Yesterday I maked a drawing of a food web for our pond.	The science teacher has brought a poster of a typical food web. Yesterday I made a drawing of a food web for our pond.

Connect Grammar to Writing

As you edit your persuasive writing this week, look closely at each irregular verb form you use. Correct any errors you notice. Using verb forms correctly is an important part of good writing.

Write to Persuade

☑ **Ideas** In a **persuasive essay** good writers state a clear opinion about what they want their audience to think or do. As you revise your persuasive essay, you should include strong reasons to support your opinion and support those reasons with facts and examples. The words you use should be persuasive and confident.

Julio wrote a first draft of his persuasive essay about ant farms. Then he revised his draft. He replaced weak or vague words to make his revised essay stronger and more persuasive.

Writing Process Checklist

Prewrite

Draft

▶ Revise

☑ Did I state my opinion or goal clearly?

☑ Did I support it with reasons, facts, and examples?

☑ Did I use strong, specific words to make my points persuasive?

☑ Did I use irregular verbs correctly?

Edit

Publish and Share

Revised Draft

The most important reason we should get an ant farm is because ants are ~~cool.~~ fascinating.

They are among the most powerful insects on earth. They are stronger than elephants for their size. They have ~~an amazing~~ a complex social structure. The ants all work together.

They build homes and forage for food. They take care of the queen ~~and her babies~~, her eggs, and the larvae that hatch from the eggs.

396

Why Room 6 Should Have a Classroom Ant Farm

by Julio Cordoza

Chadbourne Elementary has a "no pets in the classroom" rule. This makes sense. A lot of people are allergic to animals such as hamsters, rabbits, and chicks. But wouldn't it be great if we could have classroom pets that no one is allergic to? The students in Room 6 think so. That's why we want to have a classroom ant farm.

The most important reason we should get an ant farm is because ants are fascinating. They are among the most powerful insects on earth. They are stronger than elephants for their size. They have a complex social structure. The ants all work together. They build homes and forage for food. They take care of the queen, her eggs, and the larvae that hatch from the eggs.

> In my final paper, I replaced weak and vague words with stronger, more specific words to show my ideas. I also made sure I used irregular verbs correctly.

Reading as a Writer

Which words did Julio replace to make his writing clearer? What words in your essay could be changed to make it clearer and more persuasive?

397

Read this selection. Think about how the sequence of events affects the plot.

The House Finches' Home

Charlie was eager to begin his assignment. This spring, Mr. Wooster had challenged everyone in class to keep a science journal about a bird's nest. The assignment had three parts. First, Charlie would need to find a bird's nest, study it, and describe it in his science journal. Next, Charlie would name and draw a picture of the bird that built the nest. Finally, he would observe the nest every day for two weeks and write down his observations.

As soon as Charlie got off the bus, he started looking for a bird's nest. He searched the shrubs along the road but found only prickly thorns. He peeked inside the wren house his grandfather had built. It was empty. He looked high into the old oak tree. No nest. Discouraged, Charlie headed inside. As he opened the front door, he spotted something brown in the wreath on the front porch. Stuffed into the straw and dried flowers was a small bird's nest!

Charlie snatched his science journal from his backpack and began to scribble notes. The oval-shaped nest was made of dried grass and tiny twigs. Charlie ran to the carport and returned carrying a stepstool. He climbed onto the stool and cautiously peered into the nest. Inside it were three tiny eggs. He was very careful not to touch the nest or the eggs. The eggs were very light blue, almost white, with a few black specks on them. Charlie gazed at the nest, making mental notes of what it looked like. In his science journal, he wrote down everything he saw.

Now Charlie needed to find out what kind of bird was using the nest. It would not be long until he had his answer.

Before going to school the next morning, Charlie looked out the front window at the bird's nest. Two birds were at the nest! A small brown bird sat in the nest. A second bird <u>perched</u> on the nest and fed the first bird. The birds looked alike, except that the second bird had a rosy color on its head, throat, and back. Charlie drew and colored pictures of the birds in his science journal. He flipped through his grandfather's bird book until he found a picture of the birds he had seen. The name under the picture was house finch. He recorded this information, finishing the second part of his assignment.

Charlie's next task was checking the nest every day for two weeks. Usually, the plain brown female bird sat alone on the nest. Sometimes the reddish-colored male bird was there, too. Whenever Charlie went near the nest, the birds flew to a nearby dogwood tree. Charlie carefully recorded his daily observations, but he was getting bored. Nothing was changing.

Finally, almost two weeks had passed since Charlie had discovered the nest. Today was the last day that he would have to write about the nest in his science journal. "I'll look at the nest when I get home from school," he thought as he ate breakfast. When it was time for the bus to come, Charlie grabbed his backpack and headed for the front door. He opened the door and heard a racket of chirps. Immediately, he looked toward the nest. The mother had not flown away as she usually did. Charlie stepped closer to the nest, and the mother flitted away. Charlie saw three tiny, V-shaped bills sticking out of the nest. The baby birds' mouths were wide open, and the chirping sounds got even louder. Charlie could not wait to record his observations. On the bus ride, he wrote about what he had heard and seen.

Charlie also thought about what would happen next. How would the parents feed the babies? How fast would the babies grow? When would they all fly away? Charlie decided this would not be his last science journal entry after all!

Unit 3 Wrap-Up

The Big Idea

How-to Manual In "The Life and Times of the Ant," you learned how ants build their homes. Choose one of the kinds of buildings where people live. Compare how ants and humans build their homes. Present your findings in an illustrated step-by-step manual.

Building an Ant Home

Ants start their homes by digging tunnels.

Building a Human Home

Human homes start with plans.

Listening and Speaking

Photos *versus* Drawings The selections in Unit 3 have different kinds of illustrations. Some of them have photos. Others have drawings. Work with a partner to compare the kinds of illustrations. Is one kind more helpful than another? Why? Discuss what makes them effective.

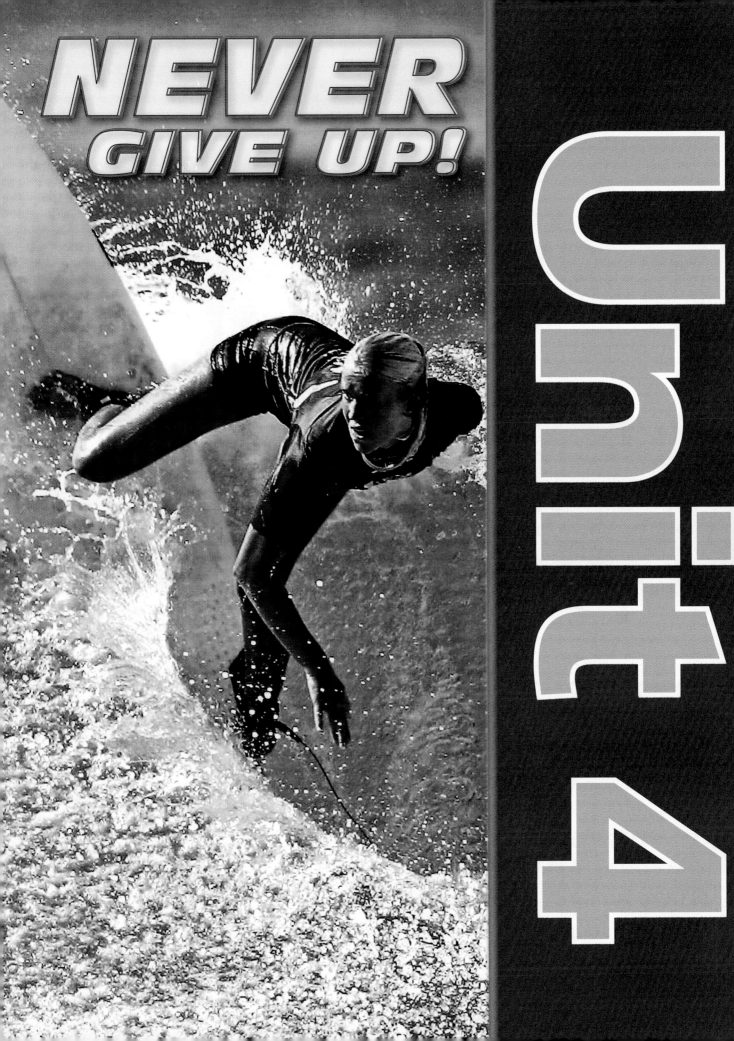

NEVER GIVE UP!

Unit 4

Essential Question
There is more than one secret to success.

Paired Selections

401

✓ **TARGET VOCABULARY**

escorted

swelled

relied

reputation

worthy

churning

situation

deserve

defended

satisfied

Vocabulary   Context
Reader   Cards

Vocabulary in Context

1 escorted

Guides who knew the western trails well often escorted, or led, travelers.

2 swelled

The number of wagons heading west swelled, or grew, in the 1850s.

3 relied

This family built a house of sod. They relied, or depended, on materials they found.

4 reputation

When customers were happy about a shop, its owner earned a good reputation.

● **Study each Context Card.**

● **Break the longer words into syllables. Use a dictionary to confirm.**

5 worthy

This plot of land was worthy, or valuable. It had rich soil and access to water.

6 churning

Dark clouds and churning winds over the plains could signal a tornado.

7 situation

Mail carriers were prepared for any situation, or event, as they rode alone.

8 deserve

Kids who worked hard on the farm would deserve an occasional treat.

9 defended

Westward travelers defended themselves from harm by circling their wagons.

10 satisfied

Despite the hard work and danger, some settlers were satisfied with life in the West.

Background

The Stagecoach In the 1800s, many people traveled west in covered wagons. Some, however, relied on the stagecoach, or stage. But passengers had to be ready for any situation. They might even have to get out and help guide the stage across a churning river!

Mail and gold also moved by stage. Guards often escorted these stages and defended them from attack. As the number of stages swelled, good drivers grew to deserve praise for their skills. One company, Wells Fargo, earned a reputation for being worthy because it usually got satisfied riders and cargo through safely.

Parts of a Stagecoach

Passengers' belongings were carried on the **luggage rack.** Each passenger was allowed up to twenty-five pounds of luggage.

The **boot**, or back area, held the mail that was shipped along with the passengers.

The **driver's seat** was high off the ground so that the driver could easily see ahead.

Window shades were made of oiled leather to keep out dust as well as rain and snow.

The **steps** into the coach could be folded up after passengers had climbed aboard.

Comprehension

Compare and Contrast

To help you understand the story, it can be useful to compare and contrast the characters' actions and thoughts. As you read "Riding Freedom," compare and contrast the two main characters. Look for places where Charlotte and James are similar and different. Use the graphic organizer below to compare and contrast these characters.

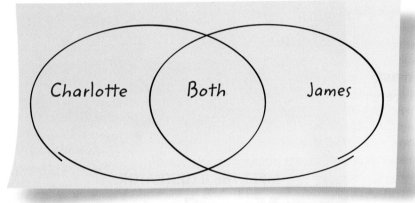

Charlotte   Both   James

Monitor/Clarify

Use your graphic organizer to help you monitor your understanding of the events in "Riding Freedom." Clarifying information that does not make sense will also help you to better compare and contrast story elements.

Main Selection

✓ **TARGET VOCABULARY**

swelled	churning
escorted	situation
relied	deserve
reputation	defended
worthy	satisfied

✓ **TARGET SKILL**

Compare and Contrast
Examine how characters are alike and different.

✓ **TARGET STRATEGY**

Monitor/Clarify Notice what is confusing as you read. Find ways to understand it.

GENRE

Historical fiction is a story whose characters and events are set in history.

Set a Purpose Before reading, set a purpose based on the genre and what you want to know.

MEET THE AUTHOR

Pam Muñoz Ryan

To research "Riding Freedom," Pam Muñoz Ryan recalls, "I wanted to travel on a dusty trail over rolling hills in a rutted-out road." She found an amusement park that offered rides in old stagecoaches. There she rode a coach, sat in the box seat, and even held the horses' reins. "Riding Freedom" is the winner of the national Willa Cather Award.

MEET THE ILLUSTRATOR

Marc Scott

Marc Scott knows a lot about illustrating an action-packed scene. In addition to working on books about whaling and mining, he has provided art for video games based on World Series baseball, trick skiing, and the movie *Star Wars*.

Riding Freedom

by Pam Muñoz Ryan

selection illustrated by Marc Scott

Essential Question

What traits do successful people have in common?

407

In the mid-1800s, when most girls are not allowed to have paid jobs, Charlotte Parkhurst disguises herself as a boy in order to work with horses. She goes by the name of "Charley" and keeps her true identity a secret. Years later, "Charley" moves from Rhode Island to an area near Sacramento, California. There, she and her friends, James and Frank, drive horse-drawn stagecoaches for a living. Suddenly, a bad accident leaves Charlotte partially blind. Now with only one good eye left, Charlotte must relearn how to drive a coach.

❦

The next day, she overturned the coach completely but was able to jump free. What was she doing wrong? She knew how to drive a team. She didn't need training with the horses or the ribbons. She knew those things by heart. It was her eye she didn't know. She needed to train her one good eye. She needed to learn how to use it all over again.

She started taking a smaller team out every day. First a two-horse team. Then a four. Finally, with six-in-the-hand. Charlotte had been proving herself her whole life and she wasn't about to stop now. She didn't even care if Frank and James caught on to what she was doing. They might as well see me trying, she thought.

She learned the different sounds the horses' hooves made on different types of roads. If the road was hard, the hooves made a hollow, clopping sound. If the road was soft, the hooves made a dull, thudding sound. She relied on her one good eye to take over for the other. She trusted her senses. And the sixth sense she had for handling horses.

Charlotte drove back and forth over her route and memorized every rock and tree. She set a goal for herself. If she made ten clean, round-trip runs, she'd know she was as good as the next driver. After that, she'd just have Frank and James to convince.

After the tenth clean run, Charlotte went to James. "I want to drive the stage run over the river."

"Now, Charley, we've been over all that. Me and Frank think . . ."

"You ride with me, and if you don't think I'm fit, then I won't bother you again," said Charlotte.

"What will the passengers say about your eye patch?" said James.

"Just tell them it's to frighten off bandits. They won't know any different."

"I don't know . . ."

Charlotte defended herself. "You know my reputation. I traveled all this way. Riding coaches is the whole reason I came to California. And I came because you asked me to come. You know I been practicin'. Go by my past drivin'. That's all I'm askin', and I wouldn't be askin' if I didn't know I could drive."

Reluctantly, James said, "The first sign that you can't handle the situation, I take the reins."

"I'll tell you if I need help. Don't go steppin' in unless I ask."

"Fair enough," said James.

"Tomorrow?"

"Tomorrow, if the weather holds."

"I ain't going to be a fair-weather driver," said Charlotte. "I want to drive, same as usual, like all the other drivers."

"Well, I guess you deserve that much. Tomorrow, rain or shine."

It was one of those storms where the rain came down in washtubs, but the stage was scheduled to go. The coach was chock-full of passengers, baggage, and mail pouches that had to get through. Charlotte was soaked clear through by the time the baggage was secured. James rode shotgun next to her.

The wind wouldn't let up, and the rain came flying in every which direction. James seemed nervous.

"Charley, I can't even see the road!" he yelled.

"Then it's a good thing I'm drivin', 'cause I can smell it, and I can hear it!" yelled Charlotte.

James sat back as the coach headed into the storm. The mud was so thick it reached the hubs, but Charlotte still found the road.

When they reached the river, it had swelled almost to the bridge supports. Charlotte stopped the stage on the north bank.

"Stay inside," she told the passengers. "I'll be checkin' the bridge."

Charlotte took off her gloves and carefully walked across the swaying timbers to see if the bridge was worthy. She stomped a few times and listened to the moans of the wood. She felt the swollen planks and pulled on the guard ropes until she was satisfied.

She walked back to the stage and told the passengers to get out.

"Ain't no reason to risk your lives," said Charlotte. "James, I'm going to walk you and these fine people over to the other side to wait for me there."

But a portly gentleman refused to budge.

"I'll take my chances inside the coach," he said.

"Not on my coach," said Charlotte.

"I'm familiar with adventure, young man," he argued.

"The bridge can't take any extra weight, and I'm not about to lose my first passenger to that river. Now, step out or I'll help you step out."

Still grumbling, the man reluctantly climbed down.

In the blinding rain, Charlotte escorted the group, a few at a time, across the bridge. When they were safely settled on the other side, she walked back for the stage.

STOP AND THINK

Author's Craft Authors sometimes use a type of **metaphor** called **personification**. Personification gives human characteristics to nonliving objects. For example, "the moans of the wood" makes the bridge seem alive. Find an example of personification as you continue reading.

413

She got back in the box. Thunder growled nearby. She knew what was coming next. She held tight to the ribbons and waited for the lightning. It hit within a mile but she kept the horses reined. Trusting her instincts, she inched the horses and the stage across the bridge. The timbers groaned as the iron-capped wheels clacked across the wooden planks. Ahead, the passengers huddled together and watched anxiously from the other side. The river raced a few feet beneath the wheels.

The bridge rocked and the horses reared and whinnied. The coach was smack in the middle of the bridge.

Charlotte kept her sights on the far bank.

She heard the splintering and cracking of weathered wood that meant the bridge was coming apart.

She stood up in the box. "Keep them straight on the bridge, Charlotte." Dashing the water from her good eye and gathering the reins in a firm grip, she cracked her whip and yelled, "Away!"

She was thrown back into the box. The horses jibbed, side to side, but she held tight to the ribbons. They flew across like scared jackrabbits. The back wheels barely turned on solid ground when the bridge collapsed and dropped into the churning river.

"Whoa, my beauties! Whoa!" yelled Charlotte.

STOP AND THINK

Compare and Contrast Compare and contrast the thoughts and emotions of Charlotte to those of the passengers as she guides the stagecoach across the bridge.

The passengers hurried back to the stage, clamoring about the excitement, while Charlotte settled the team.

"We could've all fallen in," one woman gasped.

"My heart's a-pounding," a man exclaimed as others joined him.

"We would've drowned."

"He saved my life!" said the gentleman who had almost refused to leave the coach.

And by the way they were talking and James was nodding his head, Charlotte knew there wouldn't be a question about her driving a stage again.

STOP AND THINK

Monitor/Clarify Think about all of Charlotte's achievements. How do you know that James will let her keep her job as a stagecoach driver?

Your Turn

What an Attitude!

Short Response Charlotte must keep her true identity as a woman a secret in order to drive a stagecoach. What does this tell you about attitudes toward women in the mid-1800s? Write a paragraph comparing attitudes toward women in Charlotte's day to attitudes toward women today.

SOCIAL STUDIES

Steal the Scene

Perform a Play Charlotte had some challenging and exciting experiences. Work with a small group to choose a scene from the story. Choose roles. Use details from the story to make your scene realistic and exciting. Rehearse the scene and then perform it for classmates.

SMALL GROUP

Do You Trust Me?

Turn and Talk Think about the point in the story where Charlotte tries to convince James that she can drive the stage again. With a partner, discuss the problems the characters face as they try to come to a decision. How are their problems similar and different? How do each character's traits affect the way the problem is solved?

COMPARE AND CONTRAST

Social Studies

Spindletop

✓ **TARGET VOCABULARY**

swelled	escorted
relied	reputation
worthy	churning
situation	deserve
defended	satisfied

GENRE
Informational text, such as this **web encyclopedia entry,** gives factual information about a topic.

TEXT FOCUS
Digital Media Conventions
Different kinds of digital media, such as web articles and e-mail, have different conventions of writing for different purposes. Compare and contrast the forms and purposes of this web encyclopedia entry and the e-mail on page 420.

File   Edit   View   Favorites

TEXAS HISTORY: Online

Spindletop

News • Publications • Education • Events

In the 1890s Texas produced only small amounts of oil. But one risk-taker thought that east Texas was worthy of further study. In 1892, Pattillo (puh TIH loh) Higgins, a self-taught geologist, began drilling for oil. He drilled near Beaumont, Texas in an area called Spindletop Hill. Spindletop was a salt dome, a hill formed by rising underground mineral salts. Higgins's first drills found nothing. His financial situation was looking bad. So he hired Captain Anthony F. Lucas to take over.

OIL: Spindletop

The Lucas Geyser

Lucas was a leading geologist with a reputation as an expert on salt domes. He began drilling at Spindletop in 1899. At first, he, too, had no luck. The money he relied on was running out. Lucas escorted businessmen to Beaumont, hoping that they would invest in the well. Most of them felt that he did not deserve their help. But Lucas defended his ideas about salt domes and oil. Finally, his investors were satisfied that his project was worthwhile, and the funds came in.

On the morning of January 10, 1901, Lucas's team drilled down 1,139 feet—and found oil. "The Lucas Geyser," as it came to be called, blew oil more than 150 feet in the air. In time, it would produce 100,000 barrels per day. Until then, few oil fields in Texas had produced more than 25 barrels per day!

The Spindletop Gusher, 1901

Birth of an Industry

Spindletop was the largest oil well the world had ever seen. Nearby Beaumont became one of the first oil-fueled boomtowns. Its population of 10,000 tripled in three months, and eventually swelled to 50,000. Spindletop is now known as the birthplace of the modern oil industry.

We welcome input from our readers. Please e-mail us your comments!

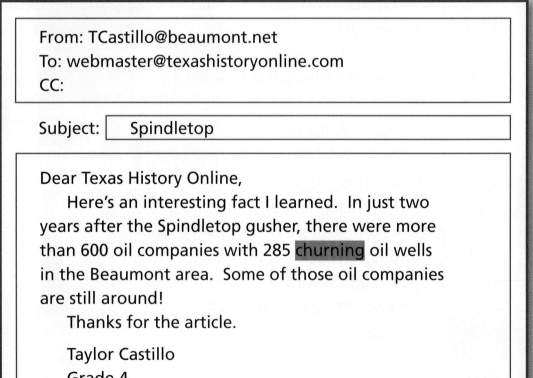

From: TCastillo@beaumont.net
To: webmaster@texashistoryonline.com
CC:

Subject: Spindletop

Dear Texas History Online,
    Here's an interesting fact I learned. In just two years after the Spindletop gusher, there were more than 600 oil companies with 285 churning oil wells in the Beaumont area. Some of those oil companies are still around!
    Thanks for the article.

Taylor Castillo
Grade 4
Beaumont Hill School

Making Connections

Text to Self

Write a Letter Imagine that you have traveled back in time to the mid-1800s. What differences do you notice between your neighborhood now and in the past? Write a letter to a friend in which you compare and contrast the two settings.

Text to Text

Compare and Contrast How are the challenges faced by Charlotte Parkhurst similar to those faced by Pattillo Higgins (right) and Anthony Lucas in Texas? How are they different? Show evidence from the text.

Text to World

Connect to Social Studies In "Riding Freedom," Charlotte Parkhurst overcomes a physical challenge in order to continue doing what she loves. Work in a group to identify a famous person you have heard or read about who has done something similar, and discuss his or her experiences.

Grammar

What Is an Adjective? An **adjective** is a word that gives information about a noun. Some adjectives tell *what kind*. Others tell *how many*. They often appear right before the nouns they describe. Sometimes adjectives appear after a form of the verb *be*. They give information about the noun in front of the verb.

What Kind	How Many
Charlotte used her good eye.	She made ten runs successfully.

An **adjective of purpose** is a special type of adjective. It tells what a noun is used for.

The campers slept in sleeping bags. (bags for sleeping)

They cooked bacon in a frying pan. (a pan for frying)

Turn and Talk With a partner, find the adjectives that tell about the underlined nouns. Which adjectives tell *what kind*? Which tell *how many*? Which are *adjectives of purpose*?

❶ The brave <u>driver</u> looked at the muddy <u>road</u>.

❷ She tied one <u>horse</u> to a hitching <u>post</u>.

❸ She left three <u>horses</u> with her young <u>partner</u>.

❹ She stepped into a waiting <u>room</u>.

❺ She wanted the doctor to look at her bad <u>eye</u>.

Sentence Fluency To make your writing flow smoothly, you can move adjectives to combine sentences. If two choppy sentences tell about the same noun, try moving an adjective from one sentence to another. You can place an adjective before a noun to combine sentences.

Short, Choppy Sentences

The horses trotted along the dusty road.

There were five horses.

Longer, Smoother Sentence

The five horses trotted along the dusty road.

Connect Grammar to Writing

As you revise your writing, look for short, choppy sentences that may repeat a noun. Try combining these sentences by moving an adjective.

Write to Narrate

☑ **Ideas** In "Riding Freedom," the author creates a colorful simile—a comparison using *like* or *as*—when she says that the horses ran "like scared jackrabbits." When you revise a **description** for a personal narrative, add similes to paint vivid word pictures.

Claire drafted a descriptive paragraph about a bus ride during a rainstorm. Then she reread her draft and added some similes.

Writing Traits Checklist

☑ **Ideas**
 Did I use similes to paint vivid pictures?

☑ **Organization**
 Are all my details about one main idea?

☑ **Word Choice**
 Do my words say just what I mean?

☑ **Voice**
 Did I show how it feels to be in the place I describe?

☑ **Sentence Fluency**
 Did I combine short, choppy sentences so they read smoothly?

☑ **Conventions**
 Did I use correct spelling, grammar, and mechanics?

Revised Draft

Bang! The thunder ~~was really loud.~~ sounded like dynamite exploding

Everyone on the bus shrieked, and

then the older kids started laughing.

Some kindergartners burst out crying.

~~They were (scared.)~~ All of a sudden,

rain began hammering on the roof.

It grew louder and louder. like a drum roll

A Ride to Remember

by Claire Amaral

Bang! The thunder sounded like dynamite exploding. Everyone on the bus shrieked, and then the older kids started laughing. Some scared kindergartners burst out crying. All of a sudden, rain began hammering on the roof. It grew louder and louder like a drum roll. My window fogged up, and down in front, the windshield wipers were jerking back and forth like a conductor keeping time to some super-fast music. When the bus stopped and the door opened, the water in the street was up to the curb. The kids who got off had to leap to the sidewalk. For once, I was glad my stop was last!

> In my final paper, I added some similes. I also combined two short sentences by moving an adjective.

Reading as a Writer

What do Claire's similes help you see or hear? Where can you add similes in your own description?

✔ **TARGET VOCABULARY**

reward

graduate

symbol

foster

disobey

confidence

patiently

confesses

ceremony

performs

Vocabulary
Reader

Context
Cards

Vocabulary in Context

1
reward
Many dogs reward the hard work of their caretakers with affection.

2
graduate
Some dogs graduate to show they have completed obedience school.

3
symbol
For some dogs, a leash is a symbol, or sign, of outdoor fun.

4
foster
Some service dogs live with foster caretakers for a short time.

- **Study each Context Card.**
- **Use context clues to determine the meanings of these words.**

5 disobey

Well-trained dogs don't disobey, or ignore, their owners' commands.

6 confidence

Praising a dog helps it gain confidence that it is learning well.

7 patiently

Show dogs must remain calm and wait patiently for long periods.

8 confesses

This girl confesses, or admits, that daily care of a dog is hard work.

9 ceremony

Dogs who win awards may be honored in a special event known as a ceremony.

10 performs

This working dog performs its job by herding sheep.

Background

Service Animals Do you know dogs that show confidence, don't disobey, and behave patiently? Some dogs with these traits go into training to become service animals. Service animals help people with disabilities. They are a symbol of the cooperation between humans and animals. Not all service animals are canine, however. Cats, monkeys, and birds can be trained too!

A service animal trainer is part foster parent and part coach. The trainer must make sure the animal performs its tasks very well. If the animal doesn't succeed, the trainer confesses that it won't be a good service animal after all. But if all goes well, the trainer is glad to reward the animal with a ceremony so that it may graduate and get to work.

Using this chart, name some specific ways that a service dog might help someone.

Service Dog Tasks

	For a person with difficulty seeing:	▸ Find a clear path for the person. ▸ Help the person avoid obstacles such as low-hanging branches and large objects.
	For a person with difficulty hearing:	▸ Alert the person to doorbells and smoke alarms. ▸ Alert the person when someone is approaching from behind or from the side.
	For a person with difficulty moving:	▸ Pull the person in wheelchair. ▸ Help the person get up after a fall.

Comprehension

✔ **TARGET SKILL** **Sequence of Events**

As you read "The Right Dog for the Job," notice the sequence, or order, in which events take place. Some events may happen at the same time, but others follow one another. Look for dates and clue words, such as *next, then,* and *now,* to help you. Use a graphic organizer like this one to help you identify the sequence of events in the story.

Event:

↓

Event:

↓

Event:

✔ **TARGET STRATEGY** **Summarize**

As you read, use the sequence of events and your graphic organizer to help you summarize, or briefly restate, the most important events of the selection. You should use your own words in your summary to help make sure you understand the selection. Summarizing also helps to show how the author organizes events.

THE RIGHT DOG FOR THE JOB

reward	confidence
graduate	patiently
symbol	confesses
foster	ceremony
disobey	performs

✓ **TARGET SKILL**

Sequence of Events
Examine the time order in which events take place.

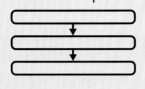

✓ **TARGET STRATEGY**

Summarize Briefly retell important parts of the text.

GENRE

Narrative nonfiction gives factual information by telling a true story.

Set a Purpose Set a purpose for reading based on the genre and your background knowledge.

MEET THE AUTHOR

Dorothy Hinshaw Patent

Dorothy Hinshaw Patent has always loved animals and the outdoors. As a child she kept snakes, frogs, and fish in her bedroom. She studied science in college and wanted to teach others to love nature. Like "The Right Dog for the Job," her book "The Buffalo and the Indians" describes a close relationship between people and animals.

MEET THE PHOTOGRAPHER

William Muñoz

William Muñoz has traveled around the United States, closely studying animals and the environment with his camera. Some of the animals he has photographed include grizzly bears, ospreys, and bald eagles. He and Dorothy Hinshaw Patent have worked together on more than sixty books.

THE RIGHT DOG FOR THE JOB
Ira's Path from Service Dog to Guide Dog

by Dorothy Hinshaw Patent
photographs by William Muñoz

Essential Question
What steps can you take toward success?

Ira was born on Shy Bear Farm in Montana, along with his sister, Ivy, and his brother, Ike. Like all newborn puppies, the three young golden retrievers have closed eyes, velvety ears, and very soft fur. But unlike most puppies, these three were born for a special purpose. By the time they are two years old, each is expected to have become a service dog, helping a person who has difficulty moving around on his or her own to lead a fuller life. Ira, Ivy, and Ike are part of PawsAbilities, Canine Partners for People with Disabilities.

Brea, the puppies' mother, and Kathleen Decker, PawsAbilities' foster puppy coordinator, take good care of the puppies. They grow bigger and stronger. Their eyes and ears open so they can take in the world around them. Soon they are romping and playing together, getting bolder each day. Kathleen begins to feed them puppy food when they are four weeks old. By the age of six weeks, they no longer need their mother's milk. Soon it will be time to leave home.

Before they can help people with disabilities, service dogs need to learn to deal confidently with the world and whatever it might present to them—loud noises, smelly buses, crowds of people.

Each puppy goes to live with a special person called a foster puppy raiser. The puppy becomes a member of the family, where it gets plenty of love, attention, and praise as the puppy raiser introduces it to the world.

When they are about eight weeks old, Ira, Ivy, and Ike meet their puppy raisers. Ira goes home with Sandy Welch, a sixth-grade teacher in Lolo, Montana. Sandy already has her own beautiful golden retriever, Laddy Griz. Laddy and Ira quickly become friends. Kathleen visits Ira and Sandy a month later. She wants to see how Ira is doing and check on his service-dog skills.

One of the most important tasks a service dog performs is retrieving things such as dropped keys. Sandy has already been working on this skill with Ira, so Kathleen throws her keys and tells Ira to fetch them. He runs over, picks them up in his mouth, and brings them back to Kathleen. Good news—Ira is already on his way to becoming a service dog!

> ☑️ **STOP AND THINK**
> **Sequence of Events** Explain, in chronological order, the events that happen to Ira on page 433.

Ira retrieves
Kathleen's keys.

All along, the puppy raisers meet as a group to learn how to teach the young dogs what they need to know. The puppies have to learn how to come or to sit on command and how to walk at heel on a leash.

Kathleen also shows them how to teach the puppies to press a wheelchair-access sign with their paw. The symbol appears on buttons that open doors automatically when pressed. Kathleen uses a plastic lid attached to a stick with a strip of cloth. On the lid is the wheelchair-access sign. She puts a dog treat on the deck and covers it with the lid. One by one, the puppies sniff and push the lid with their noses, trying to get at the treat. But only when they scratch at it with a foot does Kathleen lift the stick so the puppy is rewarded.

Ivy tries to figure out how to get at the treat under the plastic lid.

Ira gets off the bus.

Next, the group goes to the bus station. The bus company loans PawsAbilities a bus and driver. The puppies practice getting on and off over and over again. They ride around town and learn to stay calm on the bus as it stops and starts. By the end of the day, riding the bus has become as natural as a trip in the car.

The puppy raisers take the dogs wherever they can, such as to sporting events and the farmers' market. Every two weeks, the group meets at a different place somewhere in town. At the mall, the puppies learn not to be distracted at the pet store or by the crowds of people walking by. They also practice pushing the button with the wheelchair sign to open the door. At the university, they learn how to pull open a door using a tug made of rope tied to the knob. At the library, they learn to lie quietly under the table while the puppy raisers look through books. They also learn how to enter the elevator correctly, walking right beside the puppy raiser instead of going in front or behind. It would be dangerous if the elevator door closed on the leash.

Sandy brings Ira to her classroom two days a week. She explains to her students the importance of training Ira correctly.

"Ira needs to learn to lie down by himself and stay there, even if he gets bored," she says. "You have to leave him alone, even if he wants to be petted, so he doesn't get distracted from his job. You can also help teach the other children not to pet a service dog in training."

Ira has his own corner of the room, where he must lie quietly on his rug. If he gets up and wanders around, Sandy says in a firm voice, "Rug!" Then she tells Ira to sit, lie down, or stay. He must also learn to always stay close to the person he is helping.

When Sandy and the students work with Ira, they form a circle and bring Ira into the center. Then one of the children calls him. He knows he'll get a treat if he lays his head in the child's lap. The children take turns calling him, helping him learn to come reliably every time he is called. Then they help teach him to use his nose to push a light switch, another important job for a service dog to learn.

Ira learns to come when he is called.

It takes lots of practice for Ira to learn to flip a light switch with his nose instead of his mouth.

Ira goes all over the school, so he gets used to noisy places like the cafeteria and the gym during pep rallies. Sandy also takes him to other classrooms and tells the other students about service dogs.

As summer approaches, Sandy's students must say good-bye to Ira. Each child gets a chance to say what having Ira in the classroom meant to her or him.

"I feel special because I got to help train Ira," says one.

"I never liked dogs before Ira came, but now I like having him around," confesses another.

"Having Ira in the classroom has made me feel beyond wonderful," says a third.

To reward the children for their help, Sandy arranges a field trip to Shy Bear Farm. The students take turns making dog toys, working on scrapbooks for Ira's new companion, touring the farm, and playing with the six-week-old puppies. They also get to say one last good-bye to Ira.

✔ **STOP AND THINK**
Summarize Using your own words, summarize the skills Ira learns at Sandy's school.

As summer starts it's time for Ira to leave Sandy and go for more detailed service-dog training. But his assigned training facility isn't ready yet. Glenn Martyn, director of PawsAbilities, can't find another service-dog group that can use Ira. Everyone worries. What will happen? Can Ira learn a new career?

Though they rarely take dogs raised and trained elsewhere, Guide Dogs for the Blind in San Rafael, California, steps in. "Ira has lots of confidence, which is very important in a guide dog, so we'll give Ira a chance," says their coordinator. "But we'll have to change his name. Each dog we train has a different name, and we already have one called Ira. We'll just change the spelling to 'Irah' so he won't have to learn a new name."

Stacy works with Irah on the Guide Dogs for the Blind campus.

Now Irah needs to learn a whole new set of skills, which takes four to five months. He has to get used to wearing a guide-dog harness. Trainer Stacy Burrow helps him learn many things, such as stopping at street corners and crossing only when the way is clear.

The most important thing a guide dog must learn is intelligent disobedience. Knowing when to disobey can enable a guide dog to save its owner's life. For example, if the blind person tells the dog to go forward when a car is running a red light, the dog must refuse to obey. Irah is smart. He passes the program with flying colors.

STOP AND THINK

Author's Craft The author's **word choice** often includes signal words such as *next* and *all along* to explain the sequence of events. Find a signal word or phrase on page 439.

After training, Irah is paired with Don Simmonson, a piano tuner who had already retired two guide dogs after they got too old to work. Irah and Don work together for three weeks in San Rafael, learning to be a team. Then it's time to graduate.

Sandy comes from Montana for the graduation. She gets to see Irah and meet Don before the ceremony. Irah and Sandy are delighted to be together again, but Irah clearly knows his place is now with Don.

During the graduation ceremony, Don's name is announced when his turn comes. Sandy hands Irah over to Don. Irah is Don's dog now, and the two will be loving, giving partners. Sandy will miss Irah, but she is happy that he has found a home with someone like Don.

At home in Kennewick, Washington, Don and Irah continue to learn to work together. Grayson, Don's retired guide dog, also lives with them. Grayson and Irah become fast friends, playing together just like Irah and Laddy did.

Stacy, Sandy, and Irah stand by as Don speaks at the graduation.

When Don goes to work, Irah guides him. Once they enter the room with the piano, Don says, "Irah, find the piano," and Irah leads him to it. Then Don gets to work and Irah lies down nearby, waiting patiently, as he learned to do in Sandy's classroom. He is there for Don whenever he is needed.

"I'm so glad Irah and I found each other," Don says. "He's just the right dog for me."

Sandy and Don become friends, and, as a surprise, Sandy invites Don to the eighth-grade graduation of the children who helped train Irah.

Don's wife, Robbie, drives their motor home to Montana for the graduation. After Sandy talks to the audience about Irah and Don, she shows a movie of their graduation from Guide Dogs for the Blind. Then she announces that Don and Irah are in the auditorium, and Joey, Irah's favorite student, escorts them to the stage. The surprised students are delighted to see the results of their hard work and the hard work of so many others. Their own canine student, Irah, is now a working guide dog!

Joey escorts Don and Irah to the stage for their big moment.

Your Turn

Best Friends

Short Response Dogs and humans have been helping each other for thousands of years. Humans feed and shelter dogs. Dogs help herd animals and protect their owners. Write a paragraph about other ways dogs and humans help each other.

SOCIAL STUDIES

Train a Puppy

Make a Flyer With a partner, make a flyer inviting people to become foster puppy raisers. Briefly summarize what puppy raisers need to do. Be sure to include drawings of puppies.

PARTNERS

The Writer's Reasons

Turn and Talk With a partner, make a list of the steps it took to turn Ira into a guide dog. Discuss what you think is the most important thing a dog raiser can do to train a successful guide dog.

SEQUENCE OF EVENTS

Connect to
Traditional Tales

THE **STICKY COYOTE**

✓ TARGET VOCABULARY

reward	confidence
graduate	patiently
symbol	confesses
foster	ceremony
disobey	performs

GENRE

A **trickster tale,** such as this Readers' Theater, is a story with a character who plays tricks on other characters.

TEXT FOCUS

A **trickster** in a trickster tale moves the plot forward by playing a trick on another character and sometimes being tricked in return. What other stories have you read that contained tricksters? Compare and contrast their actions with Coyote's as you read this selection.

THE STICKY COYOTE

retold by Kate McGovern

CAST OF CHARACTERS

Narrator

Villager	Shoemaker
Coyote	Beekeeper

Narrator: Coyote is a trickster. He loves to disobey the rules and play tricks on people.

Villager: Coyote, you are always scaring our farm animals. It's time for you to stop!

Narrator: The villagers decide to capture Coyote and lock him up. But Coyote has confidence in himself. He knows that if he performs a good deed, the villagers will not want to capture him.

Coyote: Shoemaker, I can help you.

Shoemaker: How?

Coyote: I see you have made some special shoes for Beekeeper's daughter.

Shoemaker: That's right. She will wear them for a ceremony at school. She is going to graduate this year.

Coyote: I will deliver the shoes to Beekeeper for you.

Narrator: So Coyote takes the shoes and heads to Beekeeper's house. He hopes the villagers will want to reward him for his kindness. Suddenly, Coyote sees Beekeeper coming down the path carrying a big pot. On the front is a picture of a bee.

Coyote: That bee is a symbol. There must be honey in that pot. Yum!

Narrator: Coyote waits patiently for Beekeeper. Then Coyote drops the shoes to distract Beekeeper.

Beekeeper: Why are these shoes on the ground?

Narrator: When Beekeeper puts down her pot of honey, Coyote quickly grabs it and eats some honey.

Coyote: Mmm. Sticky and delicious. Wait, what's this? A fly is stuck on my snout!

Narrator: Coyote rolls on the ground to get the fly off, but his sticky fur gets covered with twigs and leaves. Some villagers see Coyote and think he is a monster. They run away.

Coyote: I am a mess! I will go into the river to clean myself off.

Narrator: Coyote washes the leaves off his fur.

Villager: There was a monster covered in leaves and sticks. Where did it go?

Coyote: That was no monster. It was I, Sticky Coyote. I was covered with honey and dirt and leaves.

Narrator: When Coyote confesses what he has done, the villagers laugh.

Villager: What would we do without you, Coyote? You make us laugh. Of course you can stay in our village.

Coyote: Thank you, friends. I am happy to stay. I will try not to cause so much trouble.

Narrator: Since then, Coyote often helps the villagers. He even protects them sometimes, like a foster parent. Every now and then, however, he still loves to play a good trick.

Making Connections

Text to Self

Working with Animals Have you ever cared for an animal or trained a pet? Write a paragraph about a lesson you have learned from working with an animal or watching other people work with animals.

Text to Text

Compare and Contrast Think about what you have read in "The Right Dog for the Job" and "The Sticky Coyote." Then research golden retrievers and coyotes to find out how they are similar and different. Make a poster that compares the two animals. Include a picture of each animal on your poster.

golden retriever

coyote

Text to World

Connect to Social Studies Ira was first trained as a service dog and then as a guide dog. What other jobs and services can dogs be trained to do? Work with a group to research other ways dogs are trained to help humans. Present your findings to the class.

Grammar

What Is an Adverb? An **adverb** is a word that describes a verb. Adverbs give us more information about an action verb or a form of the verb *be*. They tell *how, when,* or *where.* Most adverbs telling *how* end with *-ly.*

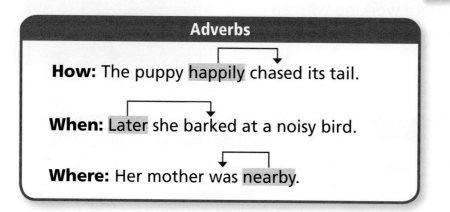

Adverbs
How: The puppy happily chased its tail.
When: Later she barked at a noisy bird.
Where: Her mother was nearby.

An **adverb of frequency** tells how often something happens. **Adverbs of intensity** tell to what degree or how much something happens.

Adverb of Frequency: Puppies usually love walks.

Adverb of Intensity: Our puppy almost caught a squirrel.

Try This! **Write the following sentences on a piece of paper and identify the adverbs. Note whether they tell about intensity or frequency.**

❶ A cat visits our yard often.

❷ Our dog barks loudly.

❸ She nearly jumps through the window.

Word Choice When you write, use precise adverbs to create clear pictures of how, when, and where things happen for your readers. Precise adverbs also help to make your writing more interesting and easier to understand.

Less Precise Adverb	More Precise Adverb
A well-trained dog often follows orders.	A well-trained dog reliably follows orders.

Less Precise Adverb	More Precise Adverb
A service dog does not get distracted.	A service dog rarely gets distracted.
My dog doesn't leave my side.	My dog never leaves my side!

Connect Grammar to Writing

As you revise your friendly letter, look for opportunities to use precise adverbs. Use descriptive language to help readers create clear pictures in their minds.

447

Write to Narrate

☑ **Voice** In "The Right Dog for the Job," Don lets his feelings come through when he says, "I'm so glad Irah and I found each other." When you revise your **friendly letter**, don't just tell what happened. Let your words show how you really feel. Use the Writing Traits Checklist as you revise your writing.

Anthony drafted a letter to his aunt about getting a dog. Then he revised some parts to let his feelings come through more clearly.

Writing Traits Checklist

☑ **Ideas**
Does my ending wrap up my main idea?

☑ **Organization**
Did I tell the events in chronological order?

☑ **Sentence Fluency**
Did I combine short, choppy sentences so they read smoothly?

☑ **Word Choice**
Did I choose vivid, interesting words?

☑ **Voice**
Did I sound like myself and show my feelings?

☑ **Conventions**
Did I use correct spelling, grammar, and mechanics?

Revised Draft

Dear Aunt Brenda,

Guess what! Last week I got the

~~Last week I got a dog. She is~~ smartest, most adorable dog. ~~a very good dog.~~ At the animal

shelter, I noticed a little brown and

white dog named Patsy. ~~I noticed~~

~~her~~ (immediately) She came right

to me, wagging her tail. When I

I can't
petted her, she licked my face. ~~So~~
wait until you meet Patsy.

~~I decided that I wanted her.~~

448

14 West Orchard Street
Nashville, Tennessee 37215
June 30, 2008

Dear Aunt Brenda,

Guess what! Last week I got the smartest, most adorable dog. At the animal shelter, I immediately noticed a little brown and white dog named Patsy. She came right to me, wagging her tail. When I petted her, she licked my face. After that, there was no way I was leaving the shelter without her. When we got home, I started teaching her, and she quickly learned to sit and stay. Now I'm teaching her to shake hands. I can't wait until you meet Patsy. Please visit us soon!

Love,
Anthony

In my final letter, I made changes to better show my feelings. I also combined two short sentences by moving an adverb.

Reading as a Writer

Which parts show how Anthony feels about his dog Patsy? Where can you show more feeling in your letter?

449

Moon Runner
CAROLYN MARSDEN

A Day for the Moon

✓ **TARGET VOCABULARY**

gigantic

miniature

especially

lapped

vanished

jealous

haze

lure

deliberately

crisp

Vocabulary Reader

Context Cards

The First Lady of Track

Vocabulary in Context

1 gigantic

Just one good play can make a gigantic, or very large, difference in a game.

2 miniature

Some people call miniature golf a sport, even though the course is small.

3 especially

This girl is especially proud that she won because she got a slow start.

4 lapped

After the swimming race, these kids rested as the water lapped gently at their legs.

- **Study each Context Card.**
- **Use a dictionary to help you understand the meanings of these words.**

5 vanished

The fly ball sailed over this outfielder's head and vanished, or disappeared.

6 jealous

Kids can be jealous. They might envy a friend's success in sports.

7 haze

The soccer game was cancelled because of this foggy haze that filled the air.

8 lure

The best pitchers can lure, or tempt, a hitter to swing at the next pitch.

9 deliberately

On most relay teams, the best runner goes last deliberately, or on purpose.

10 crisp

This sharp, crisp image is a good one for a team scrapbook.

Background

Being a Good Sport Does a game of baseball or soccer ever lure you and your friends outside? Many kids love outdoor sports, whether the sky is crisp and clear or filled with a rainy haze. Some people even have happy memories of playing in cold weather while the wind lapped against their faces.

Games give everyone a chance to compete and have fun, but what happens when you face a good friend in a contest? Do you deliberately keep from doing your best, or do you try especially hard to win? Many friendships have vanished because of jealous feelings. A contest can be miniature or gigantic in its importance. How would you try to be a good sport?

It's wise to be a good sport whether you're in a baseball game, a track meet, or a spelling bee.

Comprehension

✔ **TARGET SKILL** **Understanding Characters**

As you read "Moon Runner," try to figure out the characters' feelings and motives, or reasons for their behavior. Think about the ways they think and interact with each other. How would you or someone you know behave in similar situations? Make a graphic organizer like the one below. It will help you keep track of the characters' thoughts, actions, and words.

Thoughts	Actions	Words

✔ **TARGET STRATEGY** **Question**

Use your graphic organizer to help you ask important questions about a character's behavior and personality. For example, you might ask *why* a character acts a certain way or says certain things. It is useful to ask yourself questions before, during, and after reading a text.

✔ **TARGET VOCABULARY**

gigantic	jealous
miniature	haze
especially	lure
lapped	deliberately
vanished	crisp

✔ **TARGET SKILL**

Understanding Characters Use details to tell more about characters and their relationships.

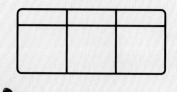

✔ **TARGET STRATEGY**

Question Ask questions before you read, as you read, and after you read.

GENRE

Realistic fiction is a present-day story that could take place in real life.

MEET THE AUTHOR

Carolyn Marsden

At the age of thirteen, Carolyn Marsden rewrote Jules Verne's *20,000 Leagues Under the Sea* with a spaceship instead of a submarine. Today, she keeps several projects going at once and makes a point of writing every day. "Through writing," she says, "I have the opportunity to live many lives."

MEET THE ILLUSTRATOR

Cornelius Van Wright

Art is not a matter of just picking up a brush and working, says this illustrator. A good painting takes time. "It is not a one-plus-one-equals-two process. You have to feel the painting taking shape." After a while, he says, your mind enters a "sweet spot" where ideas flow easily.

Moon Runner

by **Carolyn Marsden**

selection illustrated by
Cornelius Van Wright

Essential Question

How can people share their successes?

When Mina joins a new school, she quickly becomes "Fellow Friends" with Ruth, Alana, and Sammy. But things begin to change once track tryouts start. Mina suddenly discovers that she is a fast runner. Everyone is surprised, especially Ruth. Ruth has always been one of the best athletes at school, but during a tryout race, she and Mina tie for first place. Secretly, Mina knows that she is a faster runner than Ruth. Rather than hurt Ruth's feelings, Mina loses another tryout race deliberately. Now the girls know their friendship is in trouble. They sit outside of Ruth's house eating chips and drinking lemonade.

As Mina sat down in the lawn chair, she wished it was still the day the Fellow Friends had welcomed her into the group.

Little brown birds hopped along the branches of the walnut tree. Did they ever get jealous or scared ?

She wanted to hide from Ruth, covering her face with the glass of lemonade. Instead, she said, "Ruth, do you think . . ." She paused, not knowing how to put it. "Do you think the Fellow Friends group is falling apart?"

STOP AND THINK

Author's Craft Authors tell stories from different **points of view**. Sometimes they are actually in the story and sometimes they are outside the story, speaking as a narrator. From what point of view is this story told? How do you know?

Ruth looked up from her glass. "Why do you ask that?"

Mina shrugged and forced herself to go on. "Well, you and Sammy play alone a lot now. And Alana and I do, too."

"Yeah. I noticed." Ruth flicked a leaf off her forearm.

"This started when track started."

Ruth stared into her empty glass, as though studying the flecks of lemon pulp that clung to the sides.

Would she keep on staring into the glass, or set it down and leave? The conversation might end and never start up again. Mina had to keep talking. "I've never run before, at least not in races, or with anyone timing me," she said. "I didn't mean to tie you in the race. I didn't know I could."

"It wasn't your fault," Ruth said.

"But it still made you mad."

"Yeah. Sometimes."

Mina put down her glass and then picked it up again, needing something to hold on to. "But I didn't mean to tie you."

"Don't apologize."

A bird landed on the other side of the table. It cocked its head, first to one side and then the other, eyeing the bag of chips. *Just one, please? Just a nibble?*

Ruth reached into the bag and tossed a chip toward the bird. It began to tug at it, trying to break off a bite. Two more flew down to help.

✔️ **STOP AND THINK**

Question Why is it hard for Mina to talk to Ruth?

"You came out of nowhere and ran as fast as me," Ruth said. "I've worked all my life to be good at sports. I practice soccer three times a week. And here you come . . . But it's okay. Really, it's okay."

Mina felt like one of the tiny birds—out on the end of a branch, but with no wings. Yet she had to continue. "In the tryouts I tried to run slower."

"I know you did. And that was even worse. You know, Mina, when athletes compete, it isn't fair if someone doesn't try their hardest. You made me feel like I didn't really win. Or like at any time you could surprise me and beat me and I won't know what hit me."

"I didn't know what else to do."

"Yeah, I knew you lost on purpose because we're friends. A real athlete wouldn't have done that."

"But I'm not a real athlete," said Mina. "I'm a girlie girl."

Ruth laughed so loudly that the birds flew off. "You're one fast girlie girl."

Ruth's laughter made Mina laugh, too. Then she interlocked her fingers and looked down into the tight ball her hands made. She sighed and looked up. "I just want to be a Fellow Friend."

Ruth threw another chip to lure the birds back before turning to Mina. She squinted and screwed up her face against the bright sun. "It's too late. You're already more than a friend."

"What do you mean?"

"A friend is a friend. I've got lots. But there's not a lot of people I can race against." She paused. "I got an idea. I want to know something. Let's go over to the park right now and race."

Mina's legs suddenly felt as though they needed braces. She wondered if Wilma Rudolph had ever felt this weak. And yet there was no escaping this race.

"If you don't race, we'll never know if you can beat me. I'll never be able to think of myself as the fastest."

"Okay," Mina said slowly. "I'll race you."

Ruth held out her hands, the fingertips salty and greasy from the chips, ready for the Fellow Friends Handshake.

The park was just down the street from Ruth's house. As they walked, Mina thought of how the Chinese Moon Festival was a special time to celebrate friendship. If only it were fall instead of spring. If only she could just offer Ruth a simple moon cake. . . .

When they reached the spread of green grass, Ruth headed for an olive tree with a patch of bare dirt underneath. "Let's run from that pine tree over there to here." She marked a line with her toe. "That's about fifty meters."

Mina nodded. Would it really be okay to win? She followed Ruth to the pine, where she marked a second line.

Ruth leaned into the tree trunk and stretched one leg behind her, bouncing into the heel.

Not wanting to copy Ruth, Mina bent over to touch her toes.

"Hey, guys," Ruth called to two small boys crossing the grass. She cupped her hands around her mouth: "Can you help us with our race?"

The boys came closer, one in a striped T-shirt, the other wearing a purple baseball cap turned backward.

Ruth beckoned to the one with the cap. "You stand here." She pointed to the start line she'd drawn. "You'll count down for us." She pointed to the line by the olive tree. "You're over there," she told the other boy. "Watch who puts their foot across the line first. Watch closely because the race could be close."

Mina suddenly wished Ruth would offer another Fellow Friends Handshake, but Ruth was busy wiping her palms on her shorts.

The boy counted—"Three, two, one"—and then shouted: "Go!"

Mina plunged forward, shoving hard against the dirt with her toes. All her holding back vanished. She was off!

But the next moment, as though a whisper of wind had crossed her path, she found herself slowing—like in the tryouts when she had fallen behind on purpose. Way behind. That had felt awful.

She'd won once. It was time to win again.

At that moment, the world fell silent. The air filled with the smell of orange blossoms, a thick haze of sweetness. The sunshine cascaded, lovely and soft, around her head and shoulders. The tiniest breeze lapped at her as she ran. There was all the time in the world to complete the short distance between here and the tree.

She didn't turn her head to look, but Mina knew that Ruth was running beside her. They ran like the African antelopes she'd seen in a movie—loping over a yellow plain, beneath trees with flat, horizontal branches.

463

One gigantic leap took Mina sailing high and forward, over the line. The leap carried her past the boy in the striped shirt.

The silence broke. "You won!" shouted the boy, pointing at Mina.

She glanced down at herself. Then, even though her breath was coming in great heaving gulps, she looked at Ruth.

Ruth was leaning over, her hands on her knees, breathing hard. Finally, she lifted her face and managed to smile.

The boys wandered off, and Mina and Ruth lay down on the grass, cradled in a large nest of miniature white flowers. Their breathing calmed into the same rhythm.

The sun was still up, but Mina noticed a crisp crescent in the sky. For the next two weeks it would grow until it reached its night of complete fullness. Mina closed her eyes. She was glad she'd run against Ruth. Like the moon, she was beginning to feel round and whole herself.

"Thanks," said Mina after the shadow of the olive tree had edged across their faces.

"For what?"

"For helping me try my best."

STOP AND THINK

Understanding Characters Think about what Ruth said to Mina earlier in the story. What does Ruth's smile here tell you about her reaction to their race in the park?

Your Turn

In Their Shoes

Write About Friendship
Mina wished she could honor her friendship with Ruth by giving her a moon cake at the Moon Festival. Think about how you show your friends that you care about them. Write a paragraph that describes some of the caring things that you do for your friends.

PERSONAL RESPONSE

Everyone Wins

Make an Award Ruth doesn't win the race with Mina at the end of the story, but she shows she is a good sport. In a small group, design and make an award for Ruth. Include her name and three or four words that describe her good qualities. SMALL GROUP

Do Your Best

Turn and Talk With a partner, discuss why Ruth smiled at Mina after their race in the park. What do you think caused Mina to try to win the race instead of deliberately losing? Make a list of the character traits that drive both Ruth and Mina's actions in the story. Discuss with your partner how these traits influenced the story.

UNDERSTANDING CHARACTERS

File	Edit	View	Favorites

A Day for the Moon

For more than one thousand years, the people of China have celebrated a holiday for the moon. It takes place in September or early October (see the chart below). This is in the eighth month of the Chinese calendar. The holiday is known as the Mid-Autumn Festival or the Moon Festival. It honors the moon goddess, Chang E.

Date of the Moon Festival

Year	Day
2009	October 3
2010	September 22
2011	September 12
2012	September 30
2013	September 19
2014	September 8

The Legend of Chang E

The skill of Hou Yi (HOO YEE) with a bow and arrow made other archers jealous. Yet they cheered when his arrows erased nine gigantic suns that had been burning up the Earth. The emperor rewarded Hou Yi with a potion. If he drank half of it, he would live forever. But Hou Yi's wife, Chang E, found the potion first and drank it all. She floated up, up, up to the moon. You can still see Chang E whenever the haze clears around the full mid-autumn moon.

Lanterns and Moon Cakes

The Moon Festival is filled with customs. People still light candles in lanterns and deliberately float them in rivers. They look like miniature moons, gently lapped by the water. For many, the biggest treat of the holiday is the moon cake. It will lure you with its crisp coating and sweet filling. The moon cake is an especially favorite part of the holiday. Anyone wanting one by day's end usually finds that it has vanished.

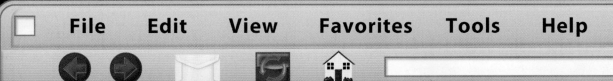
Many cities around the world celebrate Moon Festivals, including the United States. In 2007, the Chinatown Center in Austin, Texas held a Moon Festival on its birthday. To let the public know about it, the Center e-mailed press releases and posted information on its website.

Chinatown Center
中國城
1-Year Anniversary & Moon Festival Celebration
中秋佳節 TẾT TRUNG-THU 請來參加我們的週年慶 KỶ NIỆM 1 NĂM
SEPTEMBER 22-23, 2007
WWW.CHINATOWNAUSTIN.COM

FOR IMMEDIATE RELEASE:
Over 5,000 Attend
Chinatown Center's 1-Year Anniversary & Moon Festival Celebration

Austin, TX, September 27, 2007 — Central Texas's largest Moon Festival celebration was held at Austin's Chinatown Center on their 1-year Anniversary. The two-day event occurred Saturday, September 22nd and Sunday, September 23rd, 2007. This was the largest Asian celebration in Central Texas with over 5,000 people attending. The free event included singers from around the world, martial artists, Asian dancers, Japanese drumming, and Chinese guitar.

A Moon festival parade

Making Connections

Text to Self

Write About Friendship
Think of a time when you competed against a friend. Write a paragraph that describes what happened. What did you learn from the experience?

Text to Text

Ways to Succeed Does success always involve winning? Think about "Riding Freedom," "The Right Dog for the Job," and "Moon Runner." Tell what success means in each of these selections.

Text to World

Connect to Social Studies People celebrate the Moon Festival with moon cakes. Research another food that is used by a culture to celebrate a holiday. Find out how it is made and when it is eaten. Gather information from at least two different sources. Share what you learn with a partner. Then have your partner summarize the information for sense. Revise as necessary and present your findings to the class.

Grammar

What Is a Preposition? What Is a Prepositional Phrase? A **preposition** is a word that shows a connection between other words in a sentence. A **prepositional phrase** begins with a preposition and ends with a noun or pronoun. Prepositions are used to convey location, time, or to provide details.

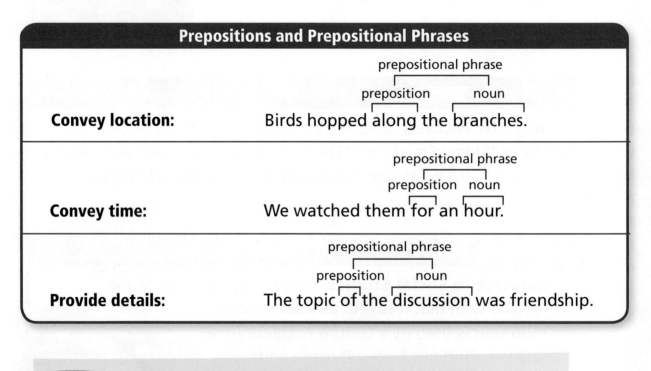

Prepositions and Prepositional Phrases	
Convey location:	*prepositional phrase* / *preposition* / *noun* Birds hopped along the branches.
Convey time:	*prepositional phrase* / *preposition* / *noun* We watched them for an hour.
Provide details:	*prepositional phrase* / *preposition* / *noun* The topic of the discussion was friendship.

Turn and Talk With a partner, find the prepositions in the underlined prepositional phrases. Tell whether each prepositional phrase conveys location, time, or provides other details.

➊ Both <u>of the girls</u> will race.

➋ The park is <u>down the street</u>.

➌ The race will begin <u>in ten minutes</u>.

➍ The boy <u>with a purple baseball cap</u> will help.

470

Ideas In your writing, you can use prepositional phrases to add helpful and interesting information to your sentences. Elaborating your sentences helps the reader visualize what you are describing in your narrative.

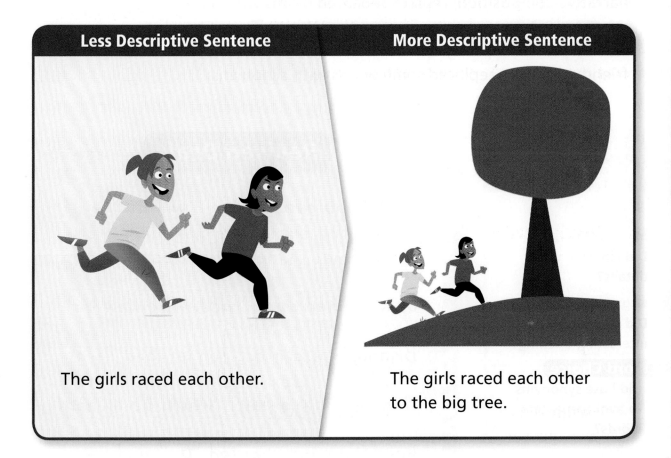

Less Descriptive Sentence	More Descriptive Sentence
The girls raced each other.	The girls raced each other to the big tree.

Connect Grammar to Writing

As you revise your narrative composition, look for sentences that you can make more descriptive by adding prepositional phrases.

Write to Narrate

☑ **Word Choice** In "Moon Runner," the author uses synonyms to avoid repeating words. For example, instead of repeating *looked*, she uses *stared* or *glanced*. When you revise your **narrative composition**, replace repeated words with more exact synonyms. As you revise, use the Writing Traits Checklist.

In "Moon Runner," the author uses synonyms to avoid repeating words. For example, instead of repeating *looked*, she uses *stared* or *glanced*. When you revise your **narrative composition**, replace repeated words with more exact synonyms. As you revise, use the Writing Traits Checklist.

Tina drafted a paragraph about how she made a new friend. Later, she replaced some words with synonyms.

Writing Traits Checklist

☑ **Ideas**
Did I include vivid details?

☑ **Organization**
Did I write an interesting opening?

☑ **Word Choice**
Did I use synonyms to avoid repeating words?

☑ **Voice**
Did I tell what I was thinking and feeling?

☑ **Sentence Fluency**
Did I vary the way my sentences begin?

☑ **Conventions**
Did I use correct spelling, grammar, and mechanics?

Revised Draft

Did you ever lose and win at the same time? One day at recess, six of us kids lined up to race. The new girl, Briana, was a great runner, and I was thinking how ~~great~~ terrific it would be to beat her. Someone shouted "Go," and we were off. Briana and I led the pack for a few seconds. Then, all at once, my foot hit a bump, and my two palms ~~hit~~ smacked the pavement hard.

When Losing Is Winning
by Tina Moore

Did you ever lose and win at the same time? One day at recess, six of us kids lined up to race. The new girl, Briana, was a great runner, and I was thinking how terrific it would be to beat her. Someone shouted "Go," and we were off. For a few seconds, Briana and I led the pack. Then, all at once, my foot hit a bump, and my two palms smacked the pavement hard. When I looked up, my classmates were speeding ahead. I turned my hands over and saw they were bleeding. That's when I noticed a pair of blue sneakers beside me. "Are you okay?" Briana asked. I gave her a grin as she helped me stand up. We had both lost the race, but at that same moment, we had each won a friend.

In my final paper, I replaced some repeated words with synonyms. I also varied a sentence by moving a phrase to the beginning.

Reading as a Writer

What synonyms did Tina use to avoid reusing the same words? What repeated words in your paper can you replace with synonyms?

473

overcome

association

capitol

drought

dedicate

publicity

violence

conflicts

horizon

brilliant

Vocabulary Reader

Context Cards

Vocabulary in Context

1 overcome
Cesar Chavez worked hard to **overcome**, or conquer, hardships.

2 association
These kids have formed a group, or **association**, that cleans up beaches.

3 capitol
A state **capitol** is a building where lawmakers can make and change laws.

4 drought
In the 1930s, a **drought**, or lack of rain, made life hard for many farmers.

● Study each Context Card.

● Use a dictionary to help you pronounce these words.

5 dedicate

Martin Luther King Jr. wanted to dedicate his life to equality. It was his life's work.

6 publicity

The media can spread publicity, or news, about events and causes.

7 violence

Many people believe change should come through peaceful ways, not violence.

8 conflicts

Most conflicts, or disagreements, can be solved by talking things over.

9 horizon

In the fields, Chavez often worked until the sun fell below the horizon.

10 brilliant

The bright, brilliant colors of the American flag symbolize freedom.

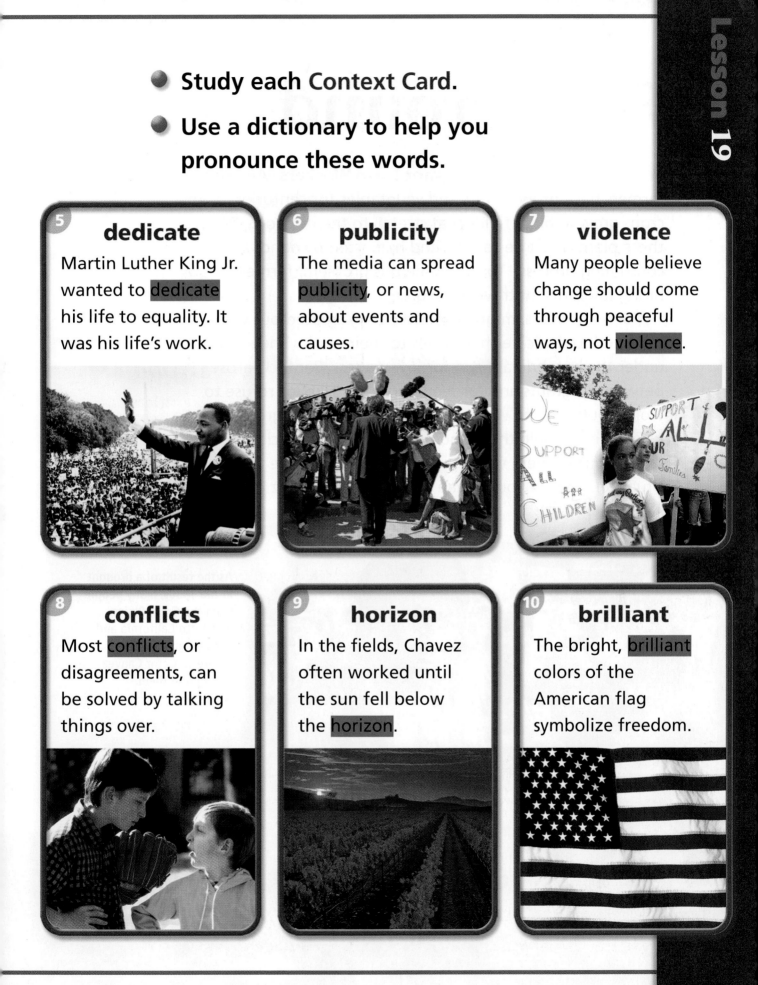

Background

Migrant Farm Workers American farmers have grown fruits and vegetables for centuries. Some crops grow in huge fields that stretch to the horizon. Often these plants must be tended and harvested by hand, a time-consuming process. To overcome this problem, farmers began hiring migrants, or traveling workers.

For many years, migrants were poorly treated but were expected to dedicate themselves to their work. They worked under the hot, brilliant sun for low wages. Conflicts arose between migrants and farm owners. To strike, or refuse to work, could lead to violence. For a long time, migrants had no association to help them and no contact with officials in the state capitol. There was no publicity to tell people about their situation. Then a young man named Cesar Chavez came along.

As the result of a drought in the 1930s, many people from the Great Plains moved to California and became migrant farm laborers. Cesar Chavez was one of them.

Comprehension

✓ TARGET SKILL Persuasion

As you read "Harvesting Hope," think about whether the author is trying to persuade, or convince, you to think or act in a certain way. Ask yourself, *What is the author trying to persuade me to do? How does the author use language to persuade me?* Use a graphic organizer like the one below to help you identify the author's goal and reasons.

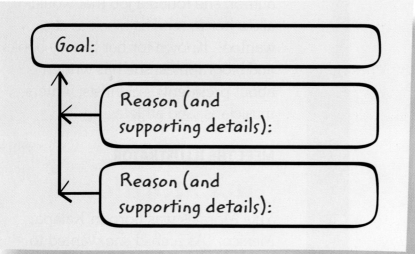

Goal:

Reason (and supporting details):

Reason (and supporting details):

✓ TARGET STRATEGY Infer/Predict

Sometimes the author's reasons are not stated directly in the text. Use your graphic organizer to infer those reasons by using details and evidence from the text. Inferring unstated details can help you decide if you agree with the author.

Main Selection

✔ TARGET VOCABULARY

overcome	publicity
association	violence
capitol	conflicts
drought	horizon
dedicate	brilliant

✔ TARGET SKILL

Persuasion Tell how an author tries to convince readers to support an idea.

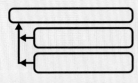

✔ TARGET STRATEGY

Infer/Predict Use text clues to figure out what isn't directly stated by the author.

GENRE

Biography tells about events in a person's life, written by another person.

Set a Purpose Before reading, set a purpose based on the genre and what you want to find out.

MEET THE AUTHOR
Kathleen Krull

As a teenager, Kathleen Krull was fired from her part-time job at the library for reading too much! When she went on to become an author, she found a job that would allow her to read as much as she wanted. Known for her history books and biographies, she has written about presidents, scientists, writers, musicians, and athletes.

MEET THE ILLUSTRATOR
Yuyi Morales

Yuyi Morales was born in Xalapa, Mexico. As a child she wanted to be an acrobat. Today she is a writer and an illustrator, and her books have been published in English and Spanish. Not all of her artwork is done on paper. She also makes puppets.

Harvesting Hope

The Story of Cesar Chavez

by Kathleen Krull   illustrated by Yuyi Morales

Essential Question

Why might a leader use persuasion?

As a boy, Cesar Chavez (SEH sahr CHAH vehz) lived on his family's big ranch in Arizona. His family had a big house and all the food they could want. Cesar loved to play with his cousins and his brother Richard. He liked to listen to his relatives' tales of life back in Mexico.

Then, in 1937, the summer Cesar was ten, the trees around the ranch began to wilt. The sun baked the farm soil rock hard. A drought (drowt) was choking the life out of Arizona. Without water for the crops, the Chavez family couldn't make money to pay its bills.

There came a day when Cesar's mother couldn't stop crying. In a daze, Cesar watched his father strap their possessions onto the roof of their old car. After a long struggle, the family no longer owned the ranch. They had no choice but to join the hundreds of thousands of people fleeing to the green valleys of California to look for work.

Cesar's old life had vanished. Now he and his family were migrants—working on other people's farms, crisscrossing California, picking whatever fruits and vegetables were in season.

When the Chavez family arrived at the first of their new homes in California, they found a battered old shed. Its doors were missing and garbage covered the dirt floor. Cold, damp air seeped into their bedding and clothes. They shared water and outdoor toilets with a dozen other families, and overcrowding made everything filthy. The neighbors were constantly fighting, and the noise upset Cesar. He had no place to play games with Richard. Meals were sometimes made of dandelion greens gathered along the road.

STOP AND THINK

Infer/Predict Why does the Chavez family tolerate the poor living conditions? What evidence from the text tells you this?

Cesar swallowed his bitter homesickness and worked alongside his family. He was small and not very strong, but still a fierce worker. Nearly every crop caused torment. Yanking out beets broke the skin between his thumb and index finger. Grapevines sprayed with bug-killing chemicals made his eyes sting and his lungs wheeze. Lettuce had to be the worst. Thinning lettuce all day with a short-handled hoe would make hot spasms shoot through his back. Farm chores on someone else's farm instead of on his own felt like a form of slavery.

The Chavez family talked constantly of saving enough money to buy back their ranch. But by each sundown, the whole family had earned as little as thirty cents for the day's work. As the years blurred together, they spoke of the ranch less and less.

The towns weren't much better than the fields. WHITE TRADE ONLY signs were displayed in many stores and restaurants. None of the thirty-five schools Cesar attended over the years seemed like a safe place, either. Once, after Cesar broke the rule about speaking English at all times, a teacher hung a sign on him that read, I AM A CLOWN. I SPEAK SPANISH. He came to hate school because of the conflicts, though he liked to learn. Even he considered his eighth-grade graduation a miracle. After eighth grade he dropped out to work in the fields full-time.

His lack of schooling embarrassed Cesar for the rest of his life, but as a teenager he just wanted to put food on his family's table. As he worked, it disturbed him that landowners treated their workers more like farm tools than human beings. They provided no clean drinking water, rest periods, or access to bathrooms. Anyone who complained was fired, beaten up, or sometimes even murdered.

So, like other migrant workers, Cesar was afraid and suspicious whenever outsiders showed up to try to help. How could they know about feeling so powerless? Who could battle such odds?

Yet Cesar had never forgotten his old life in Arizona and the jolt he'd felt when it was turned upside down. Farmwork did not have to be this miserable.

Reluctantly, he started paying attention to the outsiders. He began to think that maybe there was hope. And in his early twenties, he decided to dedicate the rest of his life to fighting for change.

Again he crisscrossed California, this time to talk people into joining his fight. At first, out of every hundred workers he talked to, perhaps one would agree with him. One by one—this was how he started.

At the first meeting Cesar organized, a dozen women gathered. He sat quietly in a corner. After twenty minutes, everyone started wondering when the organizer would show up. Cesar thought he might die of embarrassment.

"Well, I'm the organizer," he said—and forced himself to keep talking, hoping to inspire respect with his new suit and the mustache he was trying to grow. The women listened politely, and he was sure they did so out of pity.

But despite his shyness, Cesar showed a knack for solving problems. People trusted him. With workers he was endlessly patient and compassionate. With landowners he was stubborn, demanding, and single-minded. He was learning to be a fighter.

In a fight for justice, he told everyone, truth was a better weapon than violence. "Nonviolence," he said, "takes more guts." It meant using imagination to find ways to overcome powerlessness.

More and more people listened.

One night, 150 people poured into an old abandoned theater in Fresno. At this first meeting of the National Farm Workers Association, Cesar unveiled its flag—a bold black eagle, the sacred bird of the Aztec Indians.

La Causa (lah KOW sah)—The Cause—was born.

It was time to rebel, and the place was Delano. Here, in the heart of the lush San Joaquin (hwah KEEN) Valley, brilliant green vineyards reached toward every horizon. Poorly paid workers hunched over grapevines for most of each year. Then, in 1965, the vineyard owners cut their pay even further.

Cesar chose to fight just one of the forty landowners, hopeful that others would get the message. As plump grapes drooped, thousands of workers walked off that company's fields in a strike, or *huelga* (WEHL gah).

Grapes, when ripe, do not last long.

STOP AND THINK

Author's Craft Authors sometimes use **idioms**, or phrases that mean something different than the meaning of the individual words put together. An idiom used on this page is "Nonviolence takes more than guts." As you continue reading, look for other idioms. What do they mean?

The company fought back with everything from punches to bullets. Cesar refused to respond with violence. Violence would only hurt *La Causa*.

Instead, he organized a march—a march of more than three hundred miles. He and his supporters would walk from Delano to the state capitol in Sacramento to ask for the government's help.

Cesar and sixty-seven others started out one morning. Their first obstacle was the Delano police force, thirty of whose members locked arms to prevent the group from crossing the street. After three hours of arguing—in public—the chief of police backed down. Joyous marchers headed north under the sizzling sun. Their rallying cry was *Sí Se Puede* (see seh PWEH deh), or "Yes, It Can Be Done."

The first night, they reached Ducor. The marchers slept outside the tiny cabin of the only person who would welcome them.

Single file they continued, covering an average of fifteen miles a day. They inched their way through the San Joaquin Valley, while the unharvested grapes in Delano turned white with mold. Cesar developed painful blisters right away. He and many others had blood seeping out of their shoes.

The word spread. Along the way, farmworkers offered food and drink as the marchers passed by. When the sun set, marchers lit candles and kept going.

Shelter was no longer a problem. Supporters began welcoming them each night with feasts. Every night was a rally. "Our pilgrimage is the match," one speaker shouted, "that will light our cause for all farmworkers to see what is happening here."

Eager supporters would keep the marchers up half the night talking about change. Every morning, the line of marchers swelled, Cesar always in the lead.

On the ninth day, hundreds marched through Fresno.

The long, peaceful march was a shock to people unaware of how California farmworkers had to live. Now students, public officials, religious leaders, and citizens from everywhere offered help. For the grape company, the publicity was becoming unbearable.

And on the vines, the grapes continued to rot.

In Modesto, on the fifteenth day, an exhilarated (ihg ZIHL uh ray tehd) crowd celebrated Cesar's thirty-eighth birthday. Two days later, five thousand people met the marchers in Stockton with flowers, guitars, and accordions.

✔ STOP AND THINK

Persuasion What are some words and phrases that the author uses on this page to persuade the reader that the march is starting to affect people?

That evening, Cesar received a message that he was sure was a prank. But in case it was true, he left the march and had someone drive him all through the night to a mansion in wealthy Beverly Hills. Officials from the grape company were waiting for him. They were ready to recognize the authority of the National Farm Workers Association, promising a contract with a pay raise and better conditions.

Cesar rushed back to join the march.

On Easter Sunday, when the marchers arrived in Sacramento, the parade was ten-thousand-people strong.

From the steps of the state capitol building, the joyous announcement was made to the public: Cesar Chavez had just signed the first contract for farmworkers in American history.

Your Turn

Leading the Way

Write about History Cesar Chavez worked hard to gain rights for farm workers. Think about another leader who championed the rights of others. Write a paragraph describing what the person belived in and what he or she did to bring about change. SOCIAL STUDIES

Lift Every Voice

Write a Song People often sing during marches. With a partner, write words for a song the farm workers could sing during the march to Sacramento. Use the tune of a familiar song as your melody. In the song, say why they are marching and what they hope to gain. PARTNERS

Don't Fight—March!

Turn and Talk With a partner, discuss the result of the march to Sacramento. Why do you think Cesar Chavez used persuasion instead of violence to get what he and the farm workers wanted? What finally persuaded the grape growers to give in to his demands? PERSUASION

✓ TARGET VOCABULARY

overcome	publicity
association	violence
capitol	conflicts
drought	horizon
dedicate	brilliant

GENRE

Informational text, such as this magazine article, gives facts and examples about a topic.

TEXT FOCUS

Graph Informational text may include a graph, a diagram that shows how different facts and numbers relate to each other. What does the graph on page 492 tell you about nutrition?

The EDIBLE Schoolyard

by Ned L. Legol

The Edible Schoolyard program is part garden, part kitchen, and part classroom. It is all about the joy of learning. The large garden is right behind Martin Luther King, Jr. Middle School in Berkeley, California. Chef Alice Waters founded The Edible Schoolyard. She likes to dedicate a lot of her time to it.

FROM THE PAGES OF
WEEKLY READER

WR

Inside the Edible Schoolyard

Every year, the school's sixth-grade students plant, tend, and harvest the crops from the garden. They learn about the effects that changing climate and weather have on the plants. During a drought, for example, they must water the garden more often. This keeps everything alive and healthy.

The students grow many types of fruits, vegetables, and herbs. Brilliant colors surround the kids as they work in the garden that stretches toward the horizon.

Time to Get Cooking

The students also learn how to cook healthy meals with the food they grow. The school houses many different students and cultures. So, the meals vary from Indian curries to Mediterranean grape leaves. Some of the kids learn to overcome their fear of unknown foods.

If there are conflicts in the kitchen or the garden, students must work to solve them. The program fits with Martin Luther King, Jr.'s vision of inclusion, equality, and peaceful growth without violence.

The Edible Schoolyard has inspired similar programs around the country. These Florida students are part of the Plant a Thousand Gardens program.

Tastes Great and Is Healthy Too

The Edible Schoolyard program has received good publicity for teaching students about healthy food. Everything grown in the garden is organic. All meals the kids prepare are good for them.

Many other groups, such as The American Dietetic Association, also teach kids and adults about eating healthy. Because it is so important, a healthy school lunch is something that is often talked about in every state capitol.

Healthy Eating

According to the U.S. government, people should eat the following kinds and amounts of food each day.

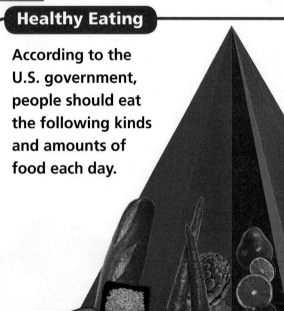

Grains	Vegetables	Fruits	Oils	Milk	Meat/ Beans
6 oz	2.5 cups	2 cups	5 tsp	3 cups	5.5 oz

Measurements
oz = ounces
tsp = teaspoons

Source: United States Department of Agriculture

Making Connections

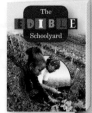

Text to Self

Write a Paragraph Think of a time when you had to be persistent to solve a problem. Describe that occasion. Explain the problem that you had to solve and how being persistent helped you solve the problem.

Text to Text

Compare and Contrast Think about some of the experiences had by Cesar Chavez in "Harvesting Hope" and Mina in "Moon Runner." How are they similar? How are they different? Record your thoughts in a Venn diagram.

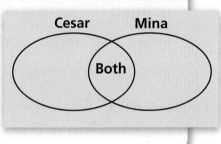

Cesar   Mina

Both

Text to World

Connect to Social Studies Farming is an important industry in many communities. Work with a partner to list the different agricultural products that are grown in or near your community. Share your findings with the class.

Grammar

What Are Transition Words? Transition **words** connect sentences and help readers make sense of what they read. Some transition words, such as *first, next, then, later,* and *finally,* can indicate time order. Others, such as *so, as a result,* and *to sum up,* can begin the conclusion of an article, speech, or essay.

Academic Language

transition words

Transition Words

Pilar, Arturo, and I stood beside the reporter in the fields. The camera operator pointed the camera at us. First the reporter asked Pilar about working conditions. Next, she asked Arturo about the shacks we live in. Finally, she asked me about our school. We answered her questions politely and honestly. As a result, the interviews were shown on the nightly news.

time-order transition words

transition words that indicate a conclusion

Turn and Talk **With a partner, identify the transition words in the sentences below. Tell which ones indicate time order and which one indicates a conclusion.**

❶ First the workers met in a hall.

❷ They next began their march to the north.

❸ During that time, they gained many supporters.

❹ After that, their leader met with the growers.

❺ The end result was recognition for the new union.

494

Sentence Fluency When you write, use transition words to make the order of events clear to the reader. If you include a conclusion at the end of a piece of writing, use a transition word to indicate this.

Unclear	Clear
I began eating the sandwich. I took it out of the bag.	I began eating the sandwich after I took it out of the bag.

Connect Grammar to Writing

As you revise your personal narrative next week, check to see that you have used transition words to indicate the order of the events. Also indicate to the reader when the narrative is coming to a conclusion.

Write to Narrate

✔ **Organization** Good writers organize their ideas before they draft. You can organize ideas for a **personal narrative** by using an events chart. In your chart, write the main events in order. Below each main event, write important or interesting details about it. Use the Writing Process Checklist below as you revise your writing.

Steve decided to write about a class adventure. First he jotted down some notes. Then he organized them in a chart.

Writing Process Checklist

▶ **Prewrite**

☑ Did I think about my purpose for writing?

☑ Did I choose a topic that I will enjoy writing about?

☑ Did I explore my topic to remember the events and details?

☑ Did I organize the events in the order in which they happened?

Draft

Revise

Edit

Publish and Share

Exploring a Topic

Topic: my class went on the Walk to End Hunger

discuss project with class

- my idea—Walk to End Hunger
- help people
- 20-mile walk
- vote—my idea won!!!

day of Walk

- bus ride
- big crowd
- balloons, food
- walked 5 hours
- TIRED!
- band
- felt really proud

collect pledges

- got people to donate money
- total—$425

Events Chart

Event:	My class discussed ideas for a community project.
Details:	Some kids gave ideas. Mine was to go on the Walk for Hunger to help people, walk 20 miles, and get free snacks. We voted and my idea won.

Event:	We collected pledges from people.
Details:	Friends and relatives pledge to donate money. We raised $425.

Event:	Class rode bus to the Walk on May 6.
Details:	At the starting place—big crowd, balloons, free water, granola bars, caps.

Event:	We walked for 5 hours.
Details:	Easy at first, hard later—tired, sore feet.

Event:	We finished the Walk.
Details:	A band was playing. I just wanted to go home. The next day I felt really proud.

In my chart, I put the events and details in an order that makes sense. I added some new details too.

Reading as a Writer

What kind of order did Steve use to arrange his events? Which parts of your events chart can you organize more clearly?

SACAGAWEA

Native American
NATURE POETRY

✓ TARGET VOCABULARY

territory

accompany

proposed

interpreter

duty

supplies

route

corps

clumsy

landmark

Vocabulary
Reader

Context
Cards

Lewis
and Clark's
PACKING LIST

Vocabulary in Context

1 territory

To many people, polar lands are unfamiliar territory.

2 accompany

Explorers going into a cave should find others to accompany them.

3 proposed

Some scientists have proposed, or suggested, further exploration of Mars.

4 interpreter

An interpreter, or translator, is helpful when people use different languages.

- **Study each Context Card.**

- **Use context clues to determine the meanings of these words.**

5 duty

Divers have a duty. They are required not to harm a marine area or its creatures.

6 supplies

Hikers need to carry supplies, such as food and water.

7 route

Backpackers should choose a safe route and stick to that path.

8 corps

On a research trip, every member of the corps, or team, must have valuable skills.

9 clumsy

A clumsy, or awkward, mistake can mean the loss of months of research.

10 landmark

Noting a landmark, or other recognizable object, makes the return trip easier.

Background

Exploring the West In 1803 President Thomas Jefferson did something amazing. He doubled the size of the United States! France sold him a huge section of land west of the Mississippi River in a deal known as the Louisiana Purchase.

Then Jefferson proposed that Captains Meriwether Lewis and William Clark lead an expedition called the Corps of Discovery. Their duty was to look for a route through this new territory by boat and to meet the Native Americans who lived there. Lewis and Clark knew the journey would be difficult. They found men to accompany them and gathered supplies. Soon they would need an interpreter to help them talk with the Native Americans and avoid clumsy communication errors.

The U.S. in 1803

As the Corps explored the unmapped region, they paid attention to every landmark.

Comprehension

✓ **TARGET SKILL** **Main Ideas and Details**

As you read "Sacagawea," figure out the most important ideas the author presents. Look for details that give facts or examples supporting those main ideas. Use a graphic organizer like this one to help you see the relationship between the main idea and supporting details and then summarize the most important ideas.

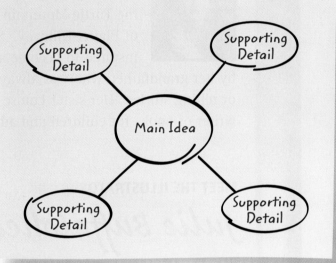

✓ **TARGET STRATEGY** **Visualize**

You can visualize various stages of Sacagawea's journey to help you identify the most important main ideas and supporting details of each stage. Descriptive details will help you create mental pictures that make the main ideas clearer.

✓ **TARGET VOCABULARY**

territory	supplies
accompany	route
proposed	corps
interpreter	clumsy
duty	landmark

✓ **TARGET SKILL**

Main Ideas and Details
Summarize a topic's key ideas and supporting details.

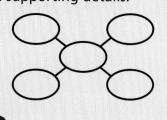

✓ **TARGET STRATEGY**

Visualize Use text details to form pictures in your mind of what you are reading.

GENRE

Biography tells about events in a person's life, written by another person.

Set a Purpose Before reading, set a purpose based on the genre and what you want to find out.

MEET THE AUTHOR

Lise Erdrich

Lise Erdrich is part Native American and a member of the Turtle Mountain band of Plains-Ojibway. She was inspired to become a writer by her grandfather, who was always writing or telling stories. Her sister Louise is also a writer of books for children and adults.

MEET THE ILLUSTRATOR

Julie Buffalohead

Part Ponca Indian, Julie Buffalohead researched traditional Native American art while in college. She often depicts Native American legends and traditions in her painting. She sometimes uses her painting as a way to explore important topics, such as prejudices some people may have about Native Americans.

SACAGAWEA

by Lise Erdrich illustrated by Julie Buffalohead

It is the early 1800s. Teenaged Sacagawea (sak uh juh WEE uh) is a Shoshone (shoh SHOH nee) Indian living in the Knife River villages, in what is now North Dakota. When she was a child, Hidatsa (hee DAHT sah) Indians kidnapped her from her home in the Rocky Mountains. Since then, she has lived with them on the Great Plains, far from her family. Sacagawea has learned many things from the Hidatsa, including how to grow food. She is now married to a French Canadian fur trapper named Toussaint Charbonneau (too SAN shahr bohn OH).

Meanwhile, Captains Meriwether Lewis and William Clark have been preparing for the Corps *(kohr) of Discovery. They and their team, which includes a large, black Newfoundland dog, are about to start a long journey of exploration, all the way to the Pacific Ocean.*

On May 14, 1804, a crew of more than forty men set off against the Missouri River current in a keelboat and two large canoes called pirogues (pih ROHGZ). The Corps of Discovery was under way.

The expedition arrived at the Knife River villages at the end of October. They were greeted with great excitement. Sacagawea heard tales of a gigantic black dog that traveled with the explorers. She heard that a fierce and awesome "white man" with black skin was among the crew. This was York, the slave of Captain Clark.

The explorers built a fort and called it Fort Mandan. Then they settled in to spend the winter at the Knife River villages. Lewis and Clark soon learned they would need horses to cross the Rocky Mountains. The people of the villages told them they could get the horses from the Shoshone when the expedition reached the mountain passes.

The wily Charbonneau proposed that they hire him as a guide and interpreter. He did not speak Shoshone, but Sacagawea did. He told her they would be joining the Corps of Discovery in the spring. This was exciting news, but Sacagawea's mind was on other matters. She was soon to become a mother.

In February, the time came for Sacagawea to have her baby. It was a long, difficult birth. Captain Lewis wanted to help her. He gave a crew member two rattlesnake rattles to crush and mix with water. Just a few minutes after drinking the mixture, Sacagawea gave birth to a baby boy. He was named Jean-Baptiste (zhawn bap TEEST) Charbonneau, but Captain Clark called him Pompy. Before long, the boy was known to everyone as Pomp.

On April 7, 1805, the Corps of Discovery started west, struggling upstream on the mighty, muddy Missouri in two pirogues and six smaller canoes. Pomp was not yet two months old. As Sacagawea walked along the riverbank, she carried Pomp on her back, in a cradleboard or wrapped up snug in her shawl.

Every member of the Corps of Discovery was hired for a special skill—hunter, blacksmith, woodsman, sailor. As an interpreter, Charbonneau was paid much more than the other crew members. But his skills as a sailor, guide, and outdoorsman were very poor. The only thing he did well was cook buffalo sausage.

Sacagawea did what she could to help the expedition, even though she was paid nothing. As she walked along the shore with Captain Clark, Sacagawea looked for plants to keep the crew healthy. She gathered berries or dug for wild artichoke roots with her digging stick. Her Shoshone childhood had prepared her well for this journey.

The Corps had been traveling less than two months when near disaster struck. Charbonneau was steering a boat through choppy waters when a sudden high wind tipped it sideways. He lost his wits and dropped the rudder while the boat filled with water. The expedition's valuables were spilling overboard! Charbonneau was ordered to right the boat or be shot.

Sacagawea stayed calm and rescued the captains' important things—journals, gunpowder, medicines, scientific instruments—every bundle she could reach. Without these supplies, the expedition could not have continued.

A few days later, they came to a beautiful river. The grateful captains named it after Sacagawea.

✔ **STOP AND THINK**

Main Ideas and Details Identify and summarize the main idea and supporting details in the last paragraph on page 506.

By June, the corps was entering mountain country. Soon they could hear the distant roaring sound of the Great Falls of the Missouri. Captain Lewis thought the waterfall was the grandest sight he had ever seen. But there was no way to get past it by boat. It would take the corps nearly a month to get around the Great Falls and the four waterfalls they found just beyond it.

The crew built creaky, clumsy wagons to carry their boats and supplies. Battered by hail, rain, and wind, the men dragged the wagons over sharp rocks and prickly pear cactus that punctured their moccasins.

One day, a freak cloudburst caused a flash flood. Rocks, mud, and water came crashing down the canyon. Sacagawea held on to her son as tight as she could while Clark pushed and pulled them both to safety. Pomp's cradleboard, clothes, and bedding were swept away by the rushing water, but all three were unharmed.

By the middle of July, the corps was once again paddling up the Missouri. They reached a valley where three rivers came together, a place Sacagawea knew well. If she was upset to see it again, she did not show it. The captains learned how Sacagawea had been captured and her people killed.

Sacagawea recognized a landmark that her people called the Beaver Head Mountain. She knew they must be nearing the summer camp of the Shoshone.

STOP AND THINK

Author's Craft In the first paragraph on this page is the word *roaring*. *Roar* is an example of **onomatopoeia**. That is, the sound and meaning of the word are similar. Find another example of onomatopoeia in the second paragraph on this page.

Nearly two weeks later, Sacagawea walked along the river, scanning the familiar territory. She spotted some men on horseback far ahead of them. Suddenly, Captain Clark saw Sacagawea dance up and down with happiness, sucking her fingers. He knew this sign meant that these were her people, the Shoshone.

An excited crowd greeted the explorers at the Shoshone camp. Although years had passed since Sacagawea had been captured, a Shoshone woman recognized her. She rushed up to Sacagawea and threw her arms around her.

Lewis and Clark had discovered that their need for Shoshone horses was even greater than they thought. There was far more mountain country between the Missouri River and a water route to the Pacific than they expected. A grand council was called to discuss the matter. Sacagawea was to be one of the translators.

Interpreting for the men at the chief's council was a serious responsibility. Sacagawea wanted to do her best. But when she looked at the face of the Shoshone chief, she burst into tears. He was her brother, Cameahwait (kah mah WAY uht)! Sacagawea jumped up, threw her blanket over her brother, and wept.

Cameahwait was moved, too. But the council had to continue. Though tears kept flooding back, Sacagawea kept to her duty until the council ended.

Sacagawea spent the last days of August with her people. The time passed too quickly. Before long, the expedition had to mount Shoshone horses and continue across the mountains, leaving their boats behind.

The next part of their journey almost killed them. The mountain paths were narrow and dangerous, especially once it started to snow. Their feet froze, they didn't have enough to eat, and the mountains seemed without end.

Finally, the expedition emerged on the Pacific side of the Rockies. There Nez Perce (nehz purs) Indians helped them make new boats and agreed to keep the horses in case they returned that way in the spring.

With great relief, the crew dropped their boats into the Clearwater River and let the current carry the expedition toward the ocean.

At the beginning of November, the explorers noticed a sound that could only be the crashing of waves. They had finally reached the Pacific Ocean!

The crew voted on where to make winter camp. Sacagawea was allowed to vote, too. She wanted to stay where she could find plenty of wapato roots for winter food. They set up camp not far from the ocean, in case a ship came to take them back home. But by now, people back east were sure the whole corps was long dead. No ship came for them.

A cold rain soaked the crew as they cut logs and built Fort Clatsop. The hunters went to find game, while Sacagawea dug for wapato roots in the soggy ground.

STOP AND THINK

Visualize As Sacagawea reunites with the Shoshone on pages 509–510, which phrases help you visualize what happens?

Christmas Day was rainy and dreary, but the corps was determined to celebrate. The men fired a salute with their guns and sang. Sacagawea gave Captain Clark a fine gift of two dozen white weasel tails.

In early January, Clark heard from some Indians that a whale had washed up onshore. He decided to go to the ocean to get blubber for the crew to eat. They were tired of their diet of lean spoiled meat and fish.

Sacagawea gathered up her courage and insisted that she be allowed to accompany Clark. She hadn't traveled so far to leave without ever seeing the ocean! And she wanted to see that monstrous creature. The captains agreed to let her go.

At last, Sacagawea saw the Pacific Ocean. She stood and stared at the great waters stretching endlessly in front of her. On the beach was the great skeleton of the whale. It was an amazing sight, nearly as long as twenty men lying end to end. The whale had been picked clean, but Clark was able to buy some blubber from the Indians to feed his men.

The crew stayed busy all winter, hunting, sewing moccasins, and making repairs on their equipment. Clark made maps, while Lewis worked on his report to President Jefferson.

Sacagawea watched over Pomp as he began to walk. Captain Clark called him "my little dancing boy." He had become very attached to Sacagawea and her son. When the time came, it would be hard for them to part.

Spring arrived, and it was time to go back the way they had come. In late March, the Corps of Discovery headed up the Columbia River to retrieve their horses from the Nez Perce.

At a place called Travelers' Rest, the expedition divided into two groups. Sacagawea would help guide Clark's group south to the Yellowstone River. Lewis's group would head northeast to explore the Marias River.

At the end of July, Clark's group came across an enormous rock tower on the banks of the Yellowstone. Clark named it Pompy's Tower in honor of his beloved little friend. In the side of the rock, he carved:

The two groups met up on August 12. Two days later, Sacagawea gazed once again upon the round earth lodges of the Knife River villages. She had been gone a year and four months.

Lewis and Clark prepared to return to St. Louis. Before they left, Captain Clark came to talk to Sacagawea and Charbonneau. He offered to take Pomp back to St. Louis with him. He would see that the boy had a good education and would raise him as his own son.

Sacagawea knew that Captain Clark would take good care of her child. But he was not even two years old. She couldn't let him go yet. Sacagawea and Charbonneau promised they would bring Pomp to visit Clark in a year or so.

On August 17, 1806, Sacagawea watched as the Corps of Discovery set off again down the Missouri River. Her journey of exploration was over, but the Corps of Discovery still had hundreds of miles to go.

Your Turn

Join the Corps

Write an Explanation
Imagine that you had been invited to go on Lewis and Clark's expedition. What qualities or skills would you have brought to the team? What would you have enjoyed most about the trip? What would you have found most difficult? Write a paragraph explaining your ideas.

PERSONAL RESPONSE

Action!

Act Out a Scene Work in a small group. Imagine that you are actors starring in a movie about the Corps of Discovery. Choose a scene from the selection and decide who will play the roles in that scene. Include a narrator, if necessary. Collect some props that will help bring your scene to life. Practice the scene and perform it for the class.

SMALL GROUP

Team Players

Turn and Talk With a partner, discuss what made the Corps of Discovery team successful. What challenges did they face? How did they work together to meet these challenges? How important was Sacagawea as a member of this team? Use details from the selection to support your thoughts.

MAIN IDEAS AND DETAILS

✓ **TARGET VOCABULARY**

territory	supplies
accompany	route
proposed	corps
interpreter	clumsy
duty	landmark

GENRE

Poetry uses the sound and rhythm of words to suggest images and express feelings.

TEXT FOCUS

Free verse is poetry without a regular rhyme or regular rhythm. As you read "The Wind," note how the poem does not have rhyme or rhythm like other poems you have read. How do the line breaks help create the poem's feeling of wind movement?

Native American NATURE POETRY

Nature and a person's relationship to nature are two important themes in Native American poetry. A poem might include details that describe a common territory, such as a forest with wind rustling through the trees. It might personify an object, giving human characteristics to it. Then again, a poem might tell what is important in life.

Here am I
Behold me
It said as it rose,
I am the moon
Behold me.
Teton Sioux

THE WIND

At night,
The wind keeps us awake,
Rustling through the trees.
We don't know how we'll get to sleep,
Until we do--
Dropping off as suddenly
As the wind dying down.
Crow

For centuries Native Americans passed their poems, songs, and stories orally from one generation to the next. People who did not speak Native American languages needed an interpreter to help them understand and write down these stories.

By the late 1800s, people could use cylinder recorders to record and play sounds. Compared to today's small electronic recorders, cylinder recorders were clumsy to use. Yet they preserved sounds exactly. In 1890 this recorder became important to scientist Jesse Fewkes, who was asked to accompany a corps of researchers to the southwestern United States. The cylinder recorder was among Fewkes's supplies. He used it to record and preserve Native American oral stories.

A cylinder recorder

You, whose day it is,
Make it beautiful.
Get out your rainbow colors,
So it will be beautiful.

Nootka

I THINK OVER AGAIN MY SMALL ADVENTURES

I think over again my small adventures,
My fears,
Those small ones that seemed so big,
For all the vital things
I had to get and to reach;
And yet there is only one great thing,
The only thing,
To live to see the great day that dawns
And the light that fills the world.

Anonymous
(North American Indian;
nineteenth century)

Write a Poem About Beauty

The poem "You, whose day it is" suggests that it is one's duty to make the day beautiful. How would you make your day beautiful? Would you help someone you care about? Would you take a special route to visit a favorite landmark? Would you make a picture or admire a sunset? Have friends proposed ideas to you in the past? Write a poem that tells what you would do.

Making Connections

Text to Self

Write a Journal Entry We know details of the Corps of Discovery expedition because Lewis and Clark kept journals. Recall an interesting trip you have taken. Write a journal entry about it. Explain why the trip was important to you.

Text to Text

Write a Poem Think about one of the natural sights that Sacagawea saw during her journey. Then write a poem about that sight. Include sensory details that help readers picture the scene. You may draw on the poems in "Native American Nature Poetry" for ideas.

Text to World

Research Native Americans Choose a Native American group that lived in your state in the past. Find at least three interesting facts about this group, and list them on a poster, along with drawings or photographs that help explain your facts.

The Cherokee Nation in Georgia

–The Cherokee migrated from the area around the Great Lakes to the Southeast. Cherokees lived in log houses in Georgia.

Grammar

What Is an Abbreviation? How Are Abbreviations Written? Some words have a shortened form called an **abbreviation**. An abbreviation stands for a whole word. Most abbreviations begin with a capital letter and end with a period. Use them only in special kinds of writing, such as addresses and lists.

Academic Language

abbreviation

Some Common Abbreviations			
Titles	Mr. → Mister Jr. → Junior	Capt. → Captain Dr. → Doctor	Mrs. → married woman Ms. → any woman
Addresses	Rd. → Road St. → Street	Ave. → Avenue Blvd. → Boulevard	Ct. → Court P.O. → Post Office
Months	Feb. → February	Aug. → August	Oct. → October
Days	Mon. → Monday	Wed. → Wednesday	Thurs. → Thursday
Measurements	in. → inch/inches	ft. → foot/feet	mi. → mile/miles

Try This! **Proofread the items below. On another sheet of paper, rewrite each group of words, using the correct abbreviations.**

❶ Andrew Perkins
438 Groat Avenue
Grapevine, TEX 76051

❷ 5280 feet = 1 mile

❸ Thursday, Feb'y 8, 2010

❹ Doctor Linda Cheung
4195 Buffalo Street
Chadron, Nebraska 69337

Conventions Good writers use abbreviations only in special kinds of writing, such as addresses and lists. When you use abbreviations, make sure you write them correctly.

Incorrect Abbreviations	Correct Abbreviations

Doct. James Sekiguchi
The Bradley Comp
127 Saratoga Boul.
Montgomery, Ala. 36104
Weds, Sep. 18
4 ft, 7 in

Dr. James Sekiguchi
The Bradley Co.
127 Saratoga Blvd.
Montgomery, AL 36104
Wed., Sept. 18
4 ft., 7 in.

Connect Grammar to Writing

As you edit your personal narrative, correct any errors in capitalization or punctuation that you discover. If you used any abbreviations, make sure you used proper capitalization and punctuation.

Write to Narrate

✔ **Ideas** In "Sacagawea," the author does not tell every detail about the explorers' journey. Instead, she includes only the most interesting and important parts. When you revise your **personal narrative**, look at each detail. Is it important to your story? Is it interesting? Use the Writing Process Checklist below as you revise your writing.

Steve drafted his story about a class adventure. When he revised it, he took out some uninteresting details and made other changes too.

Writing Process Checklist

Prewrite

Draft

▶ **Revise**

✔ Did I begin with an attention-grabber?

✔ Did I include only interesting parts and tell them in order?

✔ Did I use vivid details and dialogue?

✔ Do my feelings come through?

✔ Are my sentences smooth and varied?

✔ Does my ending show how the events worked out?

Edit

Publish and Share

Revised Draft

When Mrs. Kay asked our class to think of a community project, my hand shot up. ~~Mrs. Kay called on me fifth.~~ "Let's go on the Walk to End Hunger," I said. "We'll raise money to help people, plus it'll be <u>awesome</u> to walk twenty miles. ~~A~~nd you get free snacks along the way." We voted, and the Walk won! ~~A park clean-up came in second.~~

Our Walk to End Hunger
by Steve Jones

When Mrs. Kay asked our class to think of a community project, my hand shot up. "Let's go on the Walk to End Hunger," I said. "We'll raise money to help people, plus it'll be <u>awesome</u> to walk twenty miles, and you get free snacks along the way." We voted, and the Walk won!

Our first job was to ask relatives and friends to pledge money for needy families. They were generous and so was our principal, Mr. Desmond. When we added up our pledges, we burst into cheers. We had raised $425!

Then, on May 6, we went by bus to a street where the Walk would begin. Hundreds of people were there. We saw balloons, banners, and tables with juice and granola bars.

I took out some unimportant details. I also made sure to use correct punctuation.

Reading as a Writer

How did Steve keep his story interesting? What parts of your story could you make more interesting?

Read the next two selections. Think about how they are alike and different.

A Lesson Learned the Hard Way

Ryan and Ahmed sat on their bicycles at the start of the cyclocross course. Ahmed had been competing in cyclocross for three years, but this was Ryan's first race. He wished he could remember everything Ahmed had taught him.

Ryan reviewed the last six months in his mind. From the moment Ahmed had first asked whether he would like to try the sport, Ryan had been excited. Ahmed helped Ryan find safety gear. He also explained the importance of practicing and set up a schedule for the two friends to practice together.

Practicing was hard. Ryan soon grew bored with working on the same skills over and over. He was ready to race! Ryan ended up skipping many of the practices. When Ryan did go to practices, he spent more time doing tricks with his bike than he did listening to Ahmed's tips.

"Now the real fun begins," Ryan thought as he sat at the starting line.

"You need to get serious," Ahmed warned. "Cyclocross can be dangerous."

Bang! The starting gun went off. The boys exploded off the starting line. Ryan saw the first obstacle ahead. It was a series of small hurdles.

"Here I go!" Ryan yelled when he reached the hurdles. He jumped off his bike and landed hard on his foot. Next, he had to get his bike onto his shoulder. Ryan could not recall what Ahmed had said about shouldering the bike. He tried to pick it up by the wheels but dropped it. Finally, he got his bike off the ground. As he ran, he tried to balance the bike on his shoulder. The bike was heavy, and his ankle hurt. Before he knew it, he fell face-down into the mud.

"Are you okay?" Ryan heard his friend ask. Ahmed reached down to help Ryan. Ryan was grateful that Ahmed cared more about him than about the race. He grabbed Ahmed's hand and stood.

"Ouch!" Ryan shouted. It hurt to put weight on his ankle. "You were right, Ahmed. Cyclocross is about more than strength and speed. Can we spend a few more months training together? I want to finish my next cyclocross race!"

Is Cyclocross for You?

by Rick Spears, Staff Writer

Cyclocross is cross-country bicycle racing. Cyclocross racers spend only part of a race on their bikes because only part of the two-mile course is smooth. Other parts of the course present challenges such as sandpits, mud puddles, and piles of wood. When racers reach these obstacles, they have two choices. They can ride over them, or they can pick up their bikes and run.

You must be a strong athlete with good skills to compete in this sport. Here are some basics you should learn and practice before you enter a cyclocross race.

Dismounting

To be a top racer, you must dismount without slowing down at all. To do this, swing your right leg over the bike seat. At the same time, move the bike away from your body. This makes room for your right foot to hit the ground next to your left foot. As your right foot nears the ground, remove your left foot from the pedal. Put both feet on the ground and start running!

Carrying Your Bike

As soon as you are running, you have to decide what to do with your bike. You may shoulder it or lift it.

Sometimes you will need to run fast and jump over a series of obstacles. In these cases, you will probably want to shoulder your bike. As your feet hit the ground during a dismount, reach down and grab the bottom of your bike's downtube. Lift up gently and toss the bicycle frame onto your right shoulder. Hold on to the handlebar to keep the bike from bouncing while you run.

Sometimes you will want to lift your bike to get through obstacles. Lifting is like shouldering, except that you grab the bike's toptube instead of its downtube. Then you lift the bike high enough to get over the obstacles. After you have cleared the obstacles, gently set the bike on the ground.

Remounting

After you have successfully dismounted and carried your bike across an obstacle, you will need to remount. As soon as your bike is on the ground, push off with your left leg, swing your right leg over the bike seat, and slide into riding position. Remounting can be the hardest skill of cyclocross.

Imagine this: You are coming to a single, low obstacle. You want to clear it without taking time to dismount. You can do this with a bunny hop. To do a bunny hop, raise your whole body. This causes the bike to hop like a rabbit right over the obstacle.

Cyclocross is a great way to stay active and have fun. However, it can be dangerous. Make sure that you are well prepared and have the safety gear you need. Then, you will be ready and set. You'll just need to go!

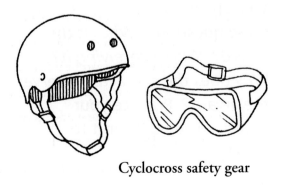

Cyclocross safety gear

Unit 4 Wrap-Up

The Big Idea

Recipe for Success Make a recipe card for achieving success. What is one accomplishment that would make you feel successful? List the qualities you need to achieve success. Then list the steps you would take to achieve it. Share your recipe with your class.

My Recipe for Success

Quantities Needed:
• •
Steps:
1.
2.
3.
4.

Listening and Speaking

Present an Award
The characters in Unit 4 are successful in different ways. Brainstorm an award to give to one of them. Prepare a short speech to present the award. Your speech should answer these questions: *What is the award? Who is receiving it? Why does the character deserve the award?* Practice your speech. Then deliver it to the class.

CHANGE
Is All Around

Unit 5

Big Idea

Change happens to us and because of us.

Paired Selections

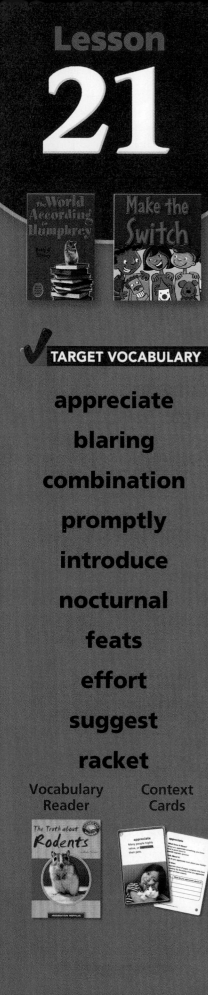

✓ TARGET VOCABULARY

appreciate

blaring

combination

promptly

introduce

nocturnal

feats

effort

suggest

racket

Vocabulary
Reader

Context
Cards

530

Vocabulary in Context

1 appreciate

Many people highly value, or **appreciate**, their pets.

2 blaring

If a dog barks at loud, **blaring** noises, it should be trained not to do that.

3 combination

People may feel a **combination** of love for and frustration with their pets.

4 promptly

If a dog needs to go out, it should be taken out **promptly**, or right away.

- ● **Study each Context Card.**

- ● **Use a dictionary to help you understand the meanings of these words.**

5 introduce

You should carefully introduce a new pet to the other pets in your house.

6 nocturnal

Some pets, such as cats and hamsters, are nocturnal. They're most active at night.

7 feats

Many people enjoy teaching their pets to perform tricks and other feats of skill.

8 effort

It takes effort, or hard work, to care for a pet, no matter what kind of animal it is.

9 suggest

Experts suggest, or recommend, that people remain calm when training a pet.

10 racket

Some pet birds can talk, but they can also create a loud racket by screaming.

Background

✓ TARGET VOCABULARY **Free Time** How do you spend your free time at home? Is the stereo playing at a blaring volume and making a racket? Maybe you are nocturnal, watching television heroes perform new feats each night. If you have a hamster or a guinea pig, perhaps you appreciate reading about rodents.

If you want to introduce a new hobby into your life, your parents can promptly suggest how to pursue it. With a combination of planning and effort, your free time can feel even richer.

Here are a few hobbies people pursue in their spare time. Some are common and some are not so common.

Common Hobbies

- Collecting things (such as stamps, coins, baseball or football cards, dolls)
- Taking photos
- Caring for pets
- Playing sports

Uncommon Hobbies

- Making art out of junk
- Bee keeping
- Making origami (paper folding)
- Doing calligraphy (artistic handwriting)

Comprehension

✓ **TARGET SKILL** **Theme**

As you read "The World According to Humphrey," ask yourself what important lesson the main characters learn over the course of the story. This lesson is the story's theme. Use a graphic organizer like this one to keep track of the characters' thoughts and actions as well as the ways in which they change and grow. This will help you figure out the story's theme.

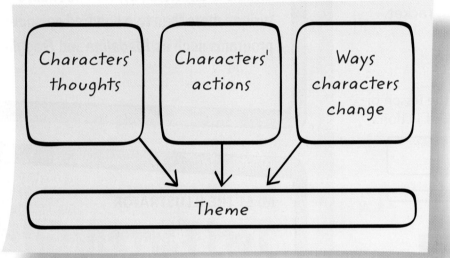

Characters' thoughts

Characters' actions

Ways characters change

Theme

✓ **TARGET STRATEGY** **Summarize**

You can use the information in your graphic organizer to help you summarize, or briefly describe, the main events in "The World According to Humphrey." At the end of each page, pause to briefly summarize what you have just read to make sure you understand it.

JOURNEYS DIGITAL — Powered by DESTINATIONReading®
Comprehension Activities: Lesson 21

✓ TARGET VOCABULARY

appreciate	nocturnal
blaring	feats
combination	effort
promptly	suggest
introduce	racket

✓ TARGET SKILL

Theme Explain the lesson or message in a work of fiction.

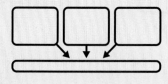

✓ TARGET STRATEGY

Summarize Briefly retell important parts of the story in your own words.

GENRE

A **fantasy** is a story with details that could not happen but seem real.

Set a Purpose Before reading, set a purpose based on the genre and what you want to find out.

MEET THE AUTHOR

Betty G. Birney

Betty G. Birney wrote her first "book," titled *The Teddy Bear in the Woods,* when she was seven years old. Now she is the author of more than twenty-five children's books, including several others in the *Humphrey* series. Although Birney criticizes television in this selection, she has written more than two hundred episodes of TV programs such as *Madeline* and *Fraggle Rock*.

MEET THE ILLUSTRATOR

Teri Farrell-Gittins

Teri Farrell-Gittins might not be an artist today if she had watched as much TV as the family in this selection does. She didn't have a TV in the house very often when she was growing up, so she drew a lot. Illustrating this selection has reminded her how important it is to unplug, use her imagination, and get outside to see the beauty of nature.

THE WORLD
ACCORDING TO
HUMPHREY

by Betty G. Birney
selection illustrated by Teri Farrell-Gittins

Essential Question

How would your day differ without TV?

The kids in Mrs. Brisbane's class love taking care of their hamster, Humphrey. The weekends are especially fun because one of them takes Humphrey home. This weekend, the lucky student is A. J.

The bus let us off close to A. J.'s house. It was a two-story old house with a big porch. As soon as I entered, I got a warm welcome from A. J.'s mom, his younger brother, Ty, his little sister, DeeLee, and his baby brother, Beau.

"Anthony James, introduce us to your little friend," his mom said, greeting us.

Anthony James? Everybody at school called A. J. by his initials or just "Aje."

"This is Humphrey," he answered.

"Hello, Humphrey," said Mrs. Thomas. "So how was your day, Anthony?"

"Lousy. Garth kept shooting rubber bands at me. He won't leave me alone."

"But you two used to be friends," his mother said.

"Used to be," said A. J. "Until he turned into a JERK."

Mom patted her son on the shoulder. "Well, you've got the whole weekend to get over it. Now take Humphrey into the den and get him settled."

Mrs. Brisbane called him Lower-Your-Voice-A. J. because A. J. always talked extra loud in class. I soon noticed that everybody at A. J.'s house talked extra loud. They had to, because in the background the TV was always blaring.

Now, every house I've been in so far has had a TV, and I've enjoyed some of the shows I've seen.

There's one channel that has nothing but the most frightening shows about wild animals attacking one another. I mean *wild*, like tigers and bears and hippopotamuses. (Gee, I hope that's not on our vocabulary test in the near future.) Those shows make me appreciate the protection of a nice cage. As long as the lock doesn't quite lock.

There's another channel that only has people in funny-looking clothes dancing and singing in very strange places. It makes me glad that I have a fur coat and don't have to figure out what to wear every day.

Mostly, I like the cartoon shows. Sometimes they have mice and rabbits and other interesting rodents, although I've never seen a hamster show. Yet.

Anyway, the difference at the Thomases' house is that the television is on *all the time*. There's a TV on a table across from a big comfy couch and a big comfy chair and someone's almost always sitting there watching. I know because they put my cage down on the floor next to the couch. I had a very good view of the TV.

I couldn't always hear the TV, though, because A. J.'s mother had a radio in the kitchen, which was blaring most of the time while she cooked or did crossword puzzles or talked on the phone. No matter what she did, the radio was always on.

When A. J.'s dad came home from work, he plopped down on the couch and watched TV while he played with the baby. Then A. J. and Ty plugged in some video games and played while Dad watched. DeeLee listened to the radio with her mom and danced around the kitchen.

When it was time for dinner, the whole family took plates and sat in the den so they could watch TV while they ate.

Then they watched TV some more. They made popcorn and kept watching.

Finally, the kids went to bed. The baby first, then DeeLee and later Ty and A. J.

After they were all in their rooms, Mr. and Mrs. Thomas kept watching TV and ate some ice cream.

Later, Mrs. Thomas yawned loudly. "I've had it, Charlie. I'm going to bed and I suggest you do, too," she said.

But Mr. Thomas just kept on watching. Or at least he kept on sitting there until he fell asleep on the couch. I ended up watching the rest of the wrestling match without him.

STOP AND THINK
Author's Craft An author often uses **idioms**, phrases that mean something different than the meanings of the words put together. Mrs. Thomas says "I've had it," which means she is tired. As you continue reading, identify other idioms the characters use and their meanings.

Unfortunately, the wrestler I was rooting for, Thor of Glore, lost. Finally, Mr. Thomas woke up, yawned, flicked off the TV and went upstairs to bed. Peace at last.

But the quiet only lasted about ten minutes. Soon Mom brought Beau downstairs and gave him a bottle while she watched TV. When Beau finally fell asleep, Mrs. Thomas yawned and flicked off the TV. Blessed relief.

Five minutes later, Mr. Thomas returned. "Sorry, hamster. Can't sleep," he mumbled to me as he flicked on the remote. He watched and watched and then dozed off again. But the TV stayed on, leaving me no choice but to watch a string of commercials for car waxes, weight-reducing programs, exercise machines and "Red-Hot Harmonica Classics."

The combination of being nocturnal and being bombarded with sight and sound kept me wide-awake.

At the crack of dawn, DeeLee tiptoed into the room, dragging her doll by its hair, and switched to a cartoon show about princesses.

She watched another show about cats and dogs. (Scary!) Then Mr. Thomas woke up and wanted to check some sports scores. Mrs. Thomas handed him the baby and his bottle and soon the older boys switched over to video games and their parents watched them play.

It was LOUD-LOUD-LOUD. But the Thomases didn't seem to notice.

"What do you want for breakfast?" Mom shouted.

"What?" Dad shouted louder.

"WHAT DO YOU WANT FOR BREAKFAST?" Mom yelled.

"TOASTER WAFFLES!" Dad yelled louder.

"I CAN'T HEAR THE TV!" Ty hollered, turning up the volume.

"DO YOU WANT JUICE?" Mom screamed.

"CAN'T HEAR YOU!" Dad responded.

And so it went. With each new question, the sound on the TV would be turned up higher and higher until it was positively deafening.

Then Mom switched on her radio.

The Thomases were a perfectly nice family, but I could tell it was going to be a very long and noisy weekend unless I came up with a Plan.

So, I spun on my wheel for a while to help me think. And I thought and thought and thought some more. And then it came: the Big Idea. I probably would have come up with it sooner if I could have heard myself think!

Around noon, the Thomases were all watching the football game on TV. Or rather, Mr. Thomas was watching the football game on TV while A. J. and Ty shouted questions at him. Mrs. Thomas was in the kitchen listening to the radio and talking on the phone. DeeLee played peekaboo with the baby in the cozy chair.

No one was watching me, so I carefully opened the lock-that-doesn't-lock on my cage and made a quick exit.

Naturally, no one could hear me skittering across the floor as I made my way around the outside of the room, over to the space behind the TV cabinet. Then, with Great Effort, I managed to pull out the plug: one of the most difficult feats of my life.

The TV went silent. Beautifully, blissfully, silently silent. So silent, I was afraid to move. I waited behind the cabinet, frozen.

The Thomases stared at the TV screen as the picture slowly went dark.

"Ty, did you hit that remote?" Mr. Thomas asked.

"Naw. It's under the table."

"Anthony, go turn that thing on again," Mr. Thomas said.

A. J. jumped up and hit the power button on the TV.

Nothing happened.

"It's broken!" he exclaimed.

Mrs. Thomas rushed in from the kitchen. "What happened?"

Mr. Thomas explained that the TV had gone off and they discussed how old it was (five years), whether it had a guarantee (no one knew) and if Mr. Thomas could fix it (he couldn't).

"Everything was fine and it went off—just like that. I guess we'd better take it in to get fixed," Mr. Thomas said.

"How long will it take?" DeeLee asked in a whiny voice.

"I don't know," her dad replied.

"How much will it cost?" Mrs. Thomas asked.

"Oh. Yeah," her husband said. "I forgot. We're a little low on funds right now."

The baby began to cry. I thought the rest of the family might start crying, too.

"Well, I get paid next Friday," Dad said.

A. J. jumped up and waved his hands. "That's a whole week away!"

"I'm going to Grandma's house. Her TV works," said Ty.

"Me, too," DeeLee chimed in.

"Grandma's got her bridge club over there tonight," Mom said.

"I know," said Dad. "Let's go to a movie."

"Do you know how much it costs to go to a movie?" Mom asked. "Besides, we can't take the baby."

"Oh."

They whined and bickered for quite a while. They got so loud, I managed to scamper back to my cage, unnoticed. Then I guess I dozed off. Remember, I had hardly had a wink of sleep since I'd arrived. The bickering was a nice, soothing background after all that racket.

I was only half-asleep when the squabbling changed.

"But there's nothing to do," DeeLee whined.

Her father chuckled. "Nothing to do! Girl, my brothers and I used to spend weekends at my grandma's house and she never had a TV. Wouldn't allow it!"

"What did you do?" A. J. asked.

"Oh, we were busy every minute," he recalled. "We played cards and board games and word games. And we dug in her garden and played tag." He chuckled again. "A lot of times we just sat on the porch and talked. My grandma . . . she could *talk*."

"What'd you talk about?" Ty wondered.

"Oh, she'd tell us stories about her growing up. About funny things, like the time her uncle was walking in his sleep and went to church in his pajamas."

Mrs. Thomas gasped. "Oh, go on now, Charlie."

"I'm just telling you what she told us. He woke up in the middle of the service, looked down and there he was, in his blue-and-white striped pajamas."

I let out a squeak of surprise and the kids all giggled.

STOP AND THINK

Then Mrs. Thomas told a story about a girl in her class who came to school in her slippers by accident one day. "Yes, the fuzzy kind," she explained with a big smile.

They talked and talked and Dad got out some cards and they played a game called Crazy Eights and another one called Pig where they put their fingers on their noses and laughed like hyenas. When Beau fussed, they took turns jiggling him on their knees.

After a while, Mrs. Thomas gasped. "Goodness' sakes! It's an hour past your bedtimes."

The children all groaned and asked if they could play cards tomorrow and in a few minutes all the Thomases had gone to bed and it was QUIET-QUIET-QUIET for the first time since I'd arrived.

Early in the morning, Ty, DeeLee and A. J. raced downstairs and played Crazy Eights. Later, they ran outside and threw a football around the yard.

The Thomases were having breakfast with Beau when the phone rang. Mr. Thomas talked for a few minutes, mostly saying "Uh-huh, that's fine." When he hung up, he told Mrs. Thomas, "We're going to have a visitor. But don't tell Anthony James."

Oooh, a mystery. I like mysteries because they're fun to solve. Then again I don't like mysteries because I don't like not knowing what's going on. So I waited and waited.

A few hours later, the doorbell rang.

The visitor turned out to be Garth Tugwell and his father!
"I really appreciate this," Mr. Tugwell told the Thomases.
"It was Mrs. Brisbane's idea. Since Garth can't have Humphrey
at our house right now, she suggested that he could help A. J.
take care of him over here."

Sounds like Mrs. Brisbane. As if I'm trouble to take care of.

But Garth had been crying because he couldn't have me.
So maybe—maybe—she was trying to be nice.

After Mr. Tugwell left, Mr. Thomas called A. J. in.

A. J. ran into the room and practically backed out again when
he saw Garth.

"We have a guest," said Mr. Thomas. "Shake hands, Anthony.
Garth is here to help you take care of Humphrey."

A. J. and Garth reluctantly shook hands.

"How come?" asked A. J.

Garth shrugged his shoulders. "Mrs. Brisbane said to."

"Well, come on. We'll clean his cage and get it over with,"
A. J. said.

The boys didn't talk much while they cleaned the cage. But
they started giggling when they cleaned up my potty corner.
(I don't know why that makes everybody giggle.)

After they stopped giggling, they started talking and kidding
around. They decided to let me out of the cage, so they took a set
of old blocks from DeeLee's room and built me a huge maze.
Oh, I love mazes!

✔️ **STOP AND THINK**

Theme A. J. learns a lesson when Garth
comes to his house. What message does
their new friendship teach?

544

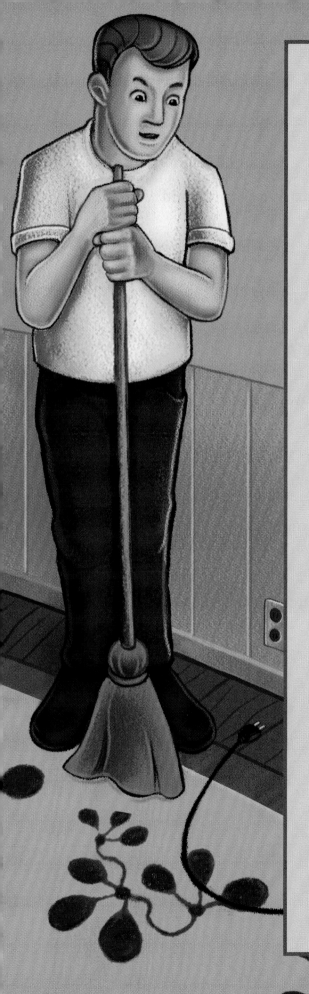

When we were all tired of that game, A. J. offered to teach Garth to play Crazy Eights and then Ty and DeeLee joined them in a game of Go Fish.

Nobody mentioned the TV. Nobody shot any rubber bands.

Later in the afternoon, the kids were all outside playing football. I was fast asleep until Mrs. Thomas came into the den with a broom and started sweeping. A minute later, Mr. Thomas entered.

"What are you doing, hon?"

"What does it look like? I'm sweeping. You know, all the snacking we do in here makes a real mess on the floor," she said.

"Beau's asleep?" her husband asked.

"Uh-huh."

Mr. Thomas walked over to his wife and took the broom away from her. "Then you sit down and rest a spell, hon. I'll sweep. Go on, don't argue."

Mrs. Thomas smiled and thanked him and sat down on the couch. Mr. Thomas swept all around the outside of the room.

Even behind the TV. Uh-oh.

When he got there, he stopped sweeping and leaned down.

"Well, I'll be," he muttered.

"What's wrong?" asked Mrs. Thomas.

"The TV is unplugged," he said. "It's unplugged!" He came out from behind the TV, plug in hand and a very puzzled look on his face.

"But it couldn't have just come unplugged while we were sitting there watching. I mean, a plug doesn't just fall out," he said.

"Plug it in. See if it works," his wife told him.

Well, you guessed it. The TV came on as bright and loud as ever.

"I don't get it," Mr. Thomas muttered. "But at least we don't have to pay to get it fixed."

Mrs. Thomas stared at the screen for a few seconds, then glanced out the window at the kids playing happily outside.

"Charlie, what do you say we keep it unplugged for a couple more days?" she asked. "We just won't tell the kids."

Mr. Thomas grinned. Then he bent down and unplugged the TV. "Couldn't hurt," he said.

He put down the broom and sat on the couch near his wife and the two of them just sat there in the den, giggling like— well, like Stop-Giggling-Gail!

Suddenly, Mr. Thomas looked over at me.

"You don't mind a little peace and quiet, do you, Humphrey?"

"NO-NO-NO!" I squeaked. And I promptly fell asleep.

Your Turn

Power Failure

Write a Response The Thomas family lose power for their TV for a short time. Choose another electrical device that you rely on, such as a personal computer, a washing machine, or a refrigerator. What would you do if this device stopped working? Write a paragraph describing how you would handle the situation.

PERSONAL RESPONSE

TV Time-Out

Make a Calculation With a partner, calculate how many hours you spend watching TV and playing video games in one week. Start by estimating how many hours you spend on these activities in one day. Once you have figured out the total, brainstorm some other ways you could spend that time. PARTNERS

What's the Message?

Turn and Talk What lesson does the Thomas family learn after Humphrey unplugs the TV? With a partner, discuss the lesson, or theme, expressed in "The World According to Humphrey." Be sure to use details from the story to support your thoughts. Then talk about how you might use this lesson in your own life. THEME

Social Studies

✓ **TARGET VOCABULARY**

appreciate	nocturnal
blaring	feats
combination	effort
promptly	suggest
introduce	racket

GENRE

Advertisements, such as these posters, are short announcements designed to grab the attention of the public in order to support an idea or action.

TEXT FOCUS

Persuasive techniques are the types of language and graphics an author uses to convince a reader to think or act in a certain way. How do the language and graphics work together to persuade the reader?

How many ads do you see on an average day? Chances are you see hundreds of them. They may be on billboards, T-shirts, and buses, in stores and magazines, and, of course, on television.

Ads may be selling a product, a service, or an idea, but they all have one thing in common. Their goal is to influence you. Ads use a combination of techniques to do this. Often they introduce ideas not just with words but with pictures and colors.

Be aware of the persuasive techniques used in ads. Sometimes ads try to convince you to do things you were not aware of or even things that you didn't want to do at all! On the following pages are two posters for you to study. How do they try to influence your thoughts and behavior?

Don't Just Sit There!
NEW
The jagged lines suggest the TV is making a blaring noise.
The dim light makes the scene look nocturnal, as if the boy stays up late watching TV. The dull colors suggest boredom.
Despite the racket, the boy looks bored. How do the different parts of this poster make you think a certain way?

The colors in this poster are very bright. The colors can help turn ordinary activities into great **feats** of adventure.

The goal of this poster is to make you **appreciate** the joys of activity.

How do these children feel? How do you know?

The drawings show movement and look lively. They show that the **effort** of finding something else to do will be rewarding.

TV OFF! LIFE ON!

Five Fabulous Things to Do

Read a Book!

Ride a Bike!

Talk with a Friend!

Create!

Play a Game!

These posters want to influence you. They want you to turn off the television and **promptly** find something else to do. What positive and negative effects might they have on the audience?

Making Connections

Text to Self

Express Your Opinion Would you rather watch TV in the evening or play games and tell stories like the Thomas family did when their TV was unplugged? Explain your thoughts in a paragraph.

Text to Text

Make a Poster Imagine that Humphrey created a "TV Off, Life On!" poster. What kinds of activities might Humphrey show? Draw such a poster and include captions for the images.

Text to World

Analyze Ads Find two print ads—one for a type of food and one for a game you enjoy. Then compare your ads with those of a partner. How do these ads try to convince you to buy or use their products? How do they make you feel? Discuss your responses with your partner.

Grammar

What Is a Comparative Adjective? What Is a Superlative Adjective? A **comparative** adjective compares two persons, places, or things. Add *-er* to most adjectives to make their comparative forms. A **superlative** adjective compares more than two persons, places, or things. Add *-est* to most adjectives to make their superlative form.

adjective:	The kids played a noisy video game.
comparative adjective:	Next they played an even noisier one.
superlative adjective:	Then the kids began playing the noisiest video game of all.

Many adverbs also have comparative and superlative forms. To make the comparative form of most adverbs, put the word *more* in front the adverb. To make the superlative form, use the word *most*.

adverb:	The family played Crazy Eights enthusiastically.
comparative adverb:	They told stories more enthusiastically.
superlative adverb:	The family played Pig the most enthusiastically of all.

Turn and Talk Work with a partner to identify whether each underlined word is an adjective or an adverb, and whether it is comparative or superlative.

❶ Our hamster is the <u>smartest</u> rodent in the world.

❷ He nibbles his food the <u>most happily</u> of all our pets.

❸ His fur is <u>thicker</u> than our mouse's fur was.

❹ He watches us <u>more frequently</u> than the mouse did.

552

Ideas When you write, you can sometimes make a sentence clearer and more descriptive by adding a comparative or a superlative adjective or adverb.

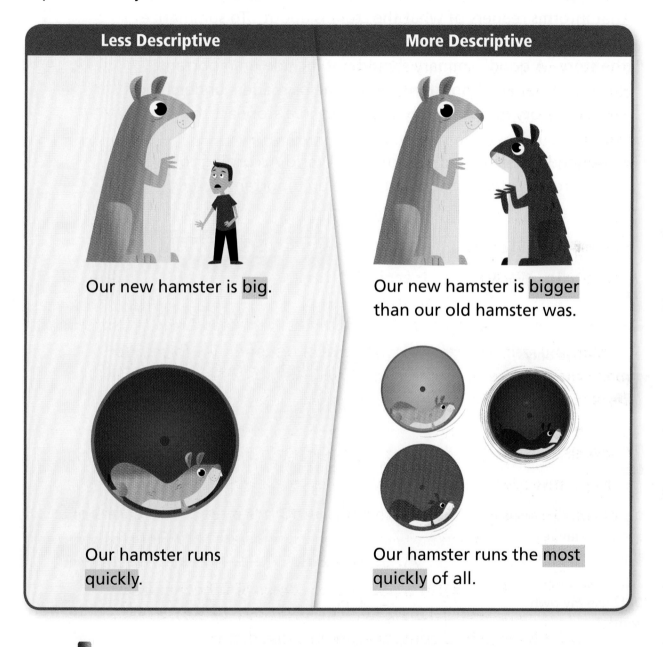

Less Descriptive	More Descriptive
Our new hamster is big.	Our new hamster is bigger than our old hamster was.
Our hamster runs quickly.	Our hamster runs the most quickly of all.

Connect Grammar to Writing

As you revise your summary this week, look for places to add more details and make your sentences clearer by using comparative and superlative adjectives and adverbs.

Write to Inform

☑ **Ideas** A **summary** of a fiction selection is a short retelling that informs readers of what the story is about. To summarize a work of fiction, tell about the main characters and events in the story. A good summary should not include unimportant details. A detail is important when it helps readers understand the main story events or why characters in a story act the way they do.

Amanda summarized part of "The World According to Humphrey." Later, she took out some unimportant details.

Writing Traits Checklist

☑ **Ideas**
Did I include only main events and important details?

☑ **Organization**
Did I tell the events in order?

☑ **Sentence Fluency**
Did I use comparative and superlative adjectives correctly?

☑ **Word Choice**
Did I use my own words?

☑ **Voice**
Did my summary sound interesting?

☑ **Conventions**
Did I use correct spelling, grammar, and punctuation?

Revised Draft

Humphrey is a hamster in Mrs. Brisbane's class. Each weekend, a different student in the class takes Humphrey home to care for him. One weekend, Humphrey goes home with A. J. Thomas. ~~A. J. has a little sister~~ ~~named DeeLee and a baby brother named~~ ~~Beau.~~ At A. J.'s house, Humphrey notices that everyone talks louder than normal.

554

Summary of <u>The World According to Humphrey</u>

by Amanda Farrell

Humphrey is a hamster in Mrs. Brisbane's class. Each weekend, a different student in the class takes Humphrey home to care for him. One weekend, Humphrey goes home with A. J. Thomas. At A. J.'s house, Humphrey notices that everyone talks louder than normal. He realizes that it's because the television is on constantly. The only time Humphrey can't hear the TV is when the radio in the kitchen is blasting even louder. Although Humphrey enjoys some TV, the noise begins to drive him crazy. He fears that it will be the longest, noisiest weekend ever! Then Humphrey has an idea. He sneaks out of his cage and secretly unplugs the TV!

In my final summary, I deleted unimportant details. I also made sure that I used comparative and superlative adjectives correctly.

Reading as a Writer

Why did Amanda take out certain details? As you write your summary paragraph, make sure you include only important or interesting details and remove unnecessary information.

✔ TARGET VOCABULARY

politics

intelligent

disorderly

approve

polls

legislature

amendment

candidates

informed

denied

Vocabulary
Reader

Context
Cards

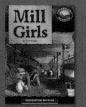

Vocabulary in Context

1 politics

Politics is the work of government. Running for office and voting are part of politics.

2 intelligent

Smart people make intelligent decisions when they vote.

3 disorderly

Without a set of rules or laws, society might be disorderly, or disorganized.

4 approve

People who run for office hope voters will like and approve of them.

- Study each Context Card.
- Use a dictionary to help you pronounce these words.

5 polls

Voters go to the polls, or election locations, to place their votes on Election Day.

6 legislature

A legislature is a group of elected officials who make laws.

7 amendment

Only in 1920 did an amendment to the Constitution allow all U.S. women to vote.

8 candidates

Candidates, or people trying to get elected to office, sometimes have public debates.

9 informed

Informed voters have learned about issues in order to decide how they will vote.

10 denied

People should not be denied, or refused, meetings with their elected officials.

Background

Women's Lives in the 1800s

Growing up as a girl was much different in the 1800s than it is now. Many people did not approve of education for girls. Even after girls grew up, they were denied control over much of their lives. Women were citizens, but they were not considered intelligent or informed enough to make good decisions. Polls were closed to them, so women could not vote. They could not become candidates themselves either. Some people feared society would become disorderly if women entered politics. Not until 1920 did the United States adopt an amendment to the Constitution, giving all women the right to vote.

> Use this timeline to summarize and explain important steps that led to voting rights for women.

1850   1860   1870   1880   1890   1900   1910   1920

1851: Susan B. Anthony and Elizabeth Cady Stanton meet and become leaders in the movement.

1869: The legislature of Wyoming passes a law allowing women to vote. Wyoming becomes the first U.S. territory (and later the first state) to grant this right.

1872: Susan B. Anthony votes in Rochester, New York. She is arrested and fined.

1920: Thirty-six states approve the Nineteenth Amendment, giving all U.S. women the right to vote.

Comprehension

Cause and Effect

As you read "I Could Do That!", note how some events cause, or lead to, other events, or effects. Sometimes several causes have one effect. At other times, one cause may have several effects or start a chain of events. A cause-and-effect relationship may be indicated by a signal word, such as *because*, *so*, or *when*. It could also be implied, or not stated directly in the text. Use a graphic organizer like the one below to show a chain of causes and effects.

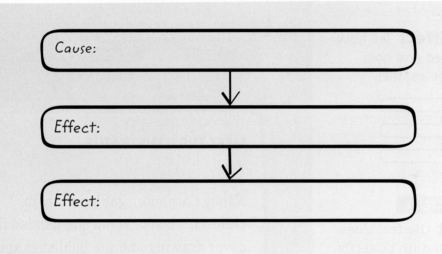

✓ TARGET STRATEGY **Infer/Predict**

When you make inferences, you use text clues to figure out what the author doesn't state directly. As you read, make inferences to help you figure out the cause-and-effect relationship between events in "I Could Do That!"

Main Selection

I Could Do That!

✓ TARGET VOCABULARY

politics	legislature
intelligent	amendment
disorderly	candidates
approve	informed
polls	denied

✓ TARGET SKILL

Cause and Effect Tell how events are related and how one event causes another.

✓ TARGET STRATEGY

Infer/Predict Use text clues to figure out what isn't directly stated by the author.

GENRE

Biography tells about events in a person's life, written by another person.

Set a Purpose Before reading, set a purpose based on the genre and what you want to find out.

MEET THE AUTHOR

Linda Arms White

Linda Arms White grew up in the wide open spaces of Wyoming, which is also known as the "Equality State." When she was a child, she heard inspiring stories about Esther Morris. As an adult, Linda began writing the day her youngest child was old enough to start school. Now her children are grown, and she has published many books for both children and adults, including *Too Many Pumpkins* and *Comes a Wind*.

MEET THE ILLUSTRATOR

Nancy Carpenter

Nancy Carpenter got her start in children's books when she handed in a cover drawing and the publisher spilled something on it. "So," she says, "I redid the job for free." The publisher soon gave her a whole book to illustrate. Ten more followed. She is the illustrator of *Apples to Oregon*, *Fannie in the Kitchen*, and *Abe Lincoln: The Boy Who Loved Books*.

560

I Could Do That!

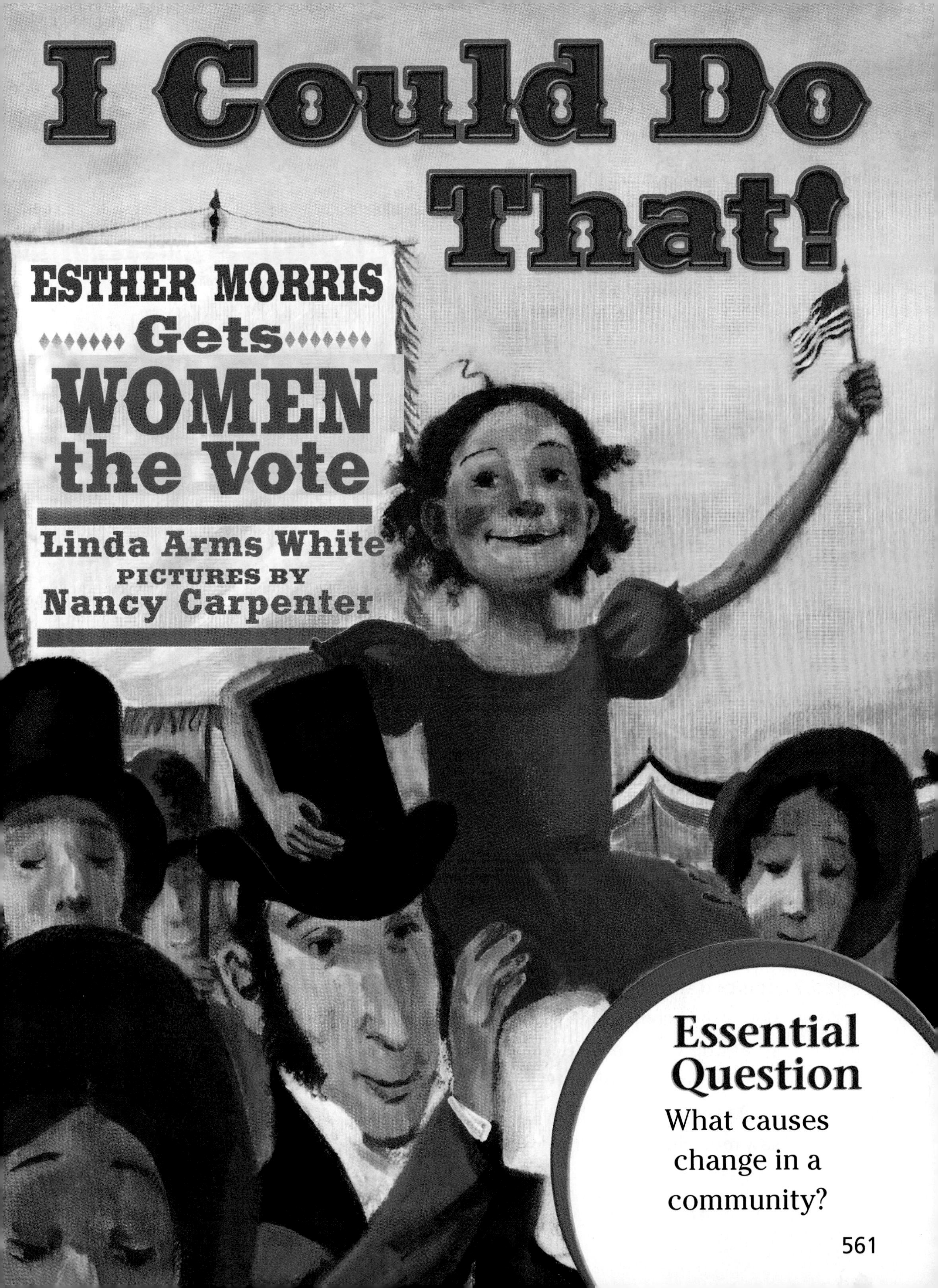

ESTHER MORRIS
◆◆◆◆◆◆ Gets ◆◆◆◆◆◆
WOMEN
the Vote

Linda Arms White
PICTURES BY
Nancy Carpenter

Essential Question

What causes change in a community?

In 1820, six-year-old Esther McQuigg studied her mother making tea. "I could do that," she said.

"Make tea?" asked Mama. "The older girls do that."

"But I want to learn," said Esther, and she did. She pumped water into the kettle and set it on the woodstove to boil. She scooped tea leaves into the teapot, then poured steaming water over them. Esther strained the tea into cups, one for her mother, one for herself.

As they sat near the window of their New York house, Esther saw men riding by in their best suits, some carrying flags.

"Where are those men going, Mama?" asked Esther.

"They are going to vote for the next president of the United States," Mama said.

"Will Papa vote?"

"Yes, Papa always votes."

"Will you vote, Mama?"

"No, dear, only men can vote."

When Esther was eight, she watched her mother sew a fine seam. The needle pulled thread in and out, in and out, tracking tiny, even stitches across the fabric. Esther felt her hands mimicking her mother's. "I could do that," she said. And she did.

She made clothes for her doll from scraps, and when her stitches became neat and straight, she sewed a shirt for Papa.

When Esther was eleven, her mother died, and for the first time she saw her father cry. He gathered his eleven children together. "I don't know what we'll do without your mama," he said. "I'm depending on each of you to be brave and to take care of one another." Esther, eighth of the eleven, cried, too. But then she said, "I can do that, Papa." And she did.

When Esther was nineteen, six feet tall, and on her own, she earned a living making dresses with leg-of-mutton sleeves for society ladies.

When the ladies wanted hats to match the dresses, Esther designed and made those, too. Soon, she thought of opening a millinery shop.

"You are much too young to run a business," she was told.

"I don't see why" was Esther's reply, and with that, she opened a hat shop in Owego, New York.

Esther started attending abolitionist meetings at her church. But a throng of people who believed in the right to own slaves threatened to stop the meetings even if they had to tear down the Baptist church where they were held.

"You can't do that," Esther said. "I'll stop anyone who tries."

When Esther was twenty-eight, she married Artemus Slack and, a few years later, had a son they called Archy.

But when Artemus died in an accident, Esther made a big decision. "I'm moving to Illinois," she told her friends. "I'll claim the land Artemus owned there and raise our son."

"You can't do that!" her friends cried. "Illinois is the very edge of civilization. It's full of dangerous people and wild animals."

"Yes," she said, "I can." And that was that.

In Illinois, she fought long and hard to claim Artemus's land, but was denied her inheritance because she was female. So Esther opened another hat shop.

Esther met and married John Morris, a merchant and immigrant from Poland, and in 1851 she gave birth to twin boys, Edward and Robert.

But John had a hard time making a living. So while Esther raised the children, cooked the meals, and washed the clothes, she helped earn the money, too.

When Esther was forty-six, she went with John to the presidential election polls and watched through the window while he voted.

"You know," she told him when he came out, "I could do that."

"Politics is the business of men, my dear," he said.

"Humph," said Esther. "It's our country, too."

When war broke out between the Northern and Southern states, Esther was proud that Archy joined the victorious fight of the North to end slavery. Soon after, an amendment to the Constitution granted African American men all rights of citizenship, including the right to vote.

When Esther heard Susan B. Anthony speaking out about women's rights, Esther began to hope that someday women might vote, too.

STOP AND THINK

Author's Craft "Making a living" is one example of an **idiom**. It means something different than the meaning of the words put together. Find other idioms throughout this selection.

565

In 1869, when Esther was fifty-five, she and her eighteen-year-old sons moved to the newly formed Wyoming Territory, where John and Archy, who'd gone there the year before, waited.

Esther and the boys traveled by train across miles of prairie, then by stage over rocky hills to South Pass City, a dusty, hurriedly built town where gold had been found. Most of the two thousand people who lived there were rowdy young men.

The Morrises moved their belongings into a small log cabin, and South Pass City became home. John tried his hand at another business.

Archy bought a printing press and started a newspaper. Esther opened another hat shop.

But with six men to every woman, there was always a need for someone to nurse the sick and wounded, sew clothes, help deliver babies, and give motherly advice to the few young women in town. "I could do that," Esther said.

And she did.

One day, Esther read a proclamation tacked to a wall: ALL MALE CITIZENS 21 AND OLDER ARE CALLED TO VOTE IN THE FIRST TERRITORIAL ELECTIONS. Esther looked around at the disorderly young men.

"It's time I did that," she said.

When Esther's sons watched her march toward home, they knew it was more likely that things were about to change than that things would stay the same.

Esther invited the two men running for the territorial legislature to her house to speak to the citizens. Then she sent out invitations to the most influential people in the territory: "Come for tea, and talk to the candidates."

She scrubbed her tiny home from top to bottom, washed the curtains, and ironed her best dress.

When the candidates and guests arrived, Esther served them tea. "One thing I like about Wyoming," she said, "is how everyone is important. It takes all of us to run the town, women as well as men."

"Yes," her guests agreed.

"And it's a place where people aren't afraid to try new things."

Her guests agreed again.

STOP AND THINK

Infer/Predict On page 567, why does Esther begin the meeting by serving tea and talking about the people of Wyoming? How do you know?

Esther smiled. She turned to the candidates. "Then, would you, if elected, introduce a bill in the legislature that would allow women to vote?"

Suddenly, in that tiny room full of people, not a sound was heard.

Finally, Colonel William Bright spoke. "Mrs. Morris, my wife would like to vote, too. She is intelligent and well educated. Truth be told, she would be a more informed voter than I. If I am elected, I will introduce that bill."

Not wanting to be outdone, the other candidate, Herman Nickerson, also agreed.

Applause broke out in that tiny cabin, and Esther dropped to her chair. "Thank you," she said.

People warned her that once the bill was introduced, the men of the legislature would have to approve it. And the governor would have to sign it. This had never happened anywhere. Why did she think it could happen here?

But Esther had seen that things that were not likely to happen, happened every day. She wrote letters and visited legislators to make sure this bill would happen, too.

And it did. On December 10, 1869, Governor John Campbell signed this bill into law! WYOMING WOMEN GOT THE VOTE!

Yee-haw!

Yippee!

Hurrah!

Hurrah!

Women across the country rejoiced for the women of Wyoming.

But some people didn't like it. Only eight days later, Judge James Stillman, the county's justice of the peace, turned in his resignation. He refused to administer justice in a place where women helped make the laws.

Word went out that a new justice of the peace was needed.

Esther's boys turned to her. "Mama, you could do that," they said.

And so she applied.

Archy, then clerk of the court, proudly swore his mother in, making Judge Esther Morris the first woman in the country to hold public office.

But Judge Stillman refused to turn over the official court docket to Esther.

"Never mind," she said. "Archy, will you please go to the Mercantile and buy me a ledger? I'll start my own docket."

And, of course, she did.

On September 6, 1870, one year after her tea party, Judge Esther Morris put on her best dress and walked with her husband, John, and her sons down the dusty street to the polling place. She would be one of a thousand Wyoming women voting that day, the first ever given that right permanently by any governing body in the United States.

As they walked, John, who still didn't think women should vote, tried to coach her on which candidates and issues to vote for.

Esther held up her hand.

"I can do this," she said.

And she did.

STOP AND THINK

Cause and Effect What events cause Esther Morris to become the first woman in the country to hold public office? What might have happened to her next?

Your Turn

I Could Do That!

Write a Response When facing a challenge, Esther Morris always said, "I could do that!" Think of a time when you did something nobody thought you could do. What was the challenge, and how did you overcome it? Write a short paragraph about your experience. PERSONAL RESPONSE

Esther Did It!

Make a Timeline Think about the many important things Esther Morris did in her life. With a partner, create a timeline that shows her accomplishments, as described in "I Could Do That!" PARTNERS

1820

1814

Cause for Applause

Turn and Talk Remember that a cause can have multiple effects. With a partner, discuss how Esther's actions changed the community of South Pass City, Wyoming. Then talk about the effects her actions had on communities across the country. CAUSE AND EFFECT

✓ **TARGET VOCABULARY**

politics	legislature
intelligent	amendment
disorderly	candidates
approve	informed
polls	denied

GENRE
A **play** tells a story through the words and actions of its characters.

TEXT FOCUS
Stage directions in a play identify a time or place, describe a setting, or tell about a character's feelings or actions. How do the stage directions help draw the reader into the play?

Set a Purpose Before reading, set a purpose based on the genre and what you want to find out.

WORKING FOR THE VOTE

BY ALICE CARY

CAST OF CHARACTERS

Narrator	Elizabeth Cady Stanton
Harriot Stanton	Susan B. Anthony

[*Setting: The living room in the home of Elizabeth Cady Stanton*]

Narrator: When Susan B. Anthony and Elizabeth Cady Stanton met in New York state in 1851, they became partners in politics. For years this intelligent pair worked to try to win women the right to vote. Susan often visited Elizabeth, who had many children. Little Harriot Stanton and her siblings, however, were a bit afraid of their mother's strict friend.

Harriot: Hide! Aunt Susan's here!

Elizabeth: [*hugging her friend*] I'm glad you're here, Susan! What's new from the New York legislature? What are those candidates up to?

Susan: First things first, my dear! Harriot, come here! How are those disorderly brothers of yours? No more climbing on the roof, I hope!

Harriot: *[shyly]* No.

Susan: Wonderful! Tell them I approve of good behavior. And tell everybody it's time for bed. Your mother and I have to figure out how to get women to the polls. One day you and your sister are going to be allowed to vote, just like your brothers.

Narrator: Harriot left but didn't go far. Her mother and Susan were too busy to notice.

[Harriot hides behind the door.]

Elizabeth: I've got an idea for an article. People need to be more informed about women's rights. We've been denied the vote long enough!

Narrator: The two women talked, argued, and wrote together, as they often did. On this night they kept busy until they heard someone sneeze.

Susan: *[moving toward the noise]* Harriot? What are you doing behind that door? I thought you were asleep!

Harriot: *[coming out, looking thoughtfully at her mother]* The boys must be right.

Elizabeth: What do you mean?

Harriot: They say Aunt Susan can see around corners. They say she sees everything.

Susan: *[laughing]* Well, they must be right, because I see voting in your future! Now go to bed and dream about that!

Narrator: Susan B. Anthony and Elizabeth Cady Stanton worked for women's rights for the rest of their lives. As an adult, Harriot helped her mother and Susan write a history of the women's movement. In 1920, an amendment to the Constitution was passed that finally gave women the right to vote. Sadly, Susan and Elizabeth had died by then, but Harriot finally got her chance to vote.

SUSAN B. ANTHONY

ELIZABETH CADY STANTON

HARRIOT STANTON

Making Connections

Text to Self

Write a Letter Imagine that you could talk to Esther Morris. What would you say to her? Write your thoughts in a short letter. Be sure to include a salutation, the date, and a closing.

Text to Text

Compare Texts Think of another selection you have read that features a strong female character, such as "Riding Freedom" or "Sacagawea." Compare the experiences of that female character to Esther Morris from "I Could Do That!" How are they similar? How are they different?

Text to World

Connect to Social Studies Esther Morris worked very hard to get women the right to vote because she thought it was very important. Work with a partner to research other elections that happen in your community and state. What is the role of the individual voter in these elections?

Grammar

What Is a Negative? A word that makes a sentence mean "no" is called a **negative**. The words *no, no one, nobody, none, nothing, nowhere,* and *never* are negatives. The word *not* and contractions made with *not* are also negatives. Never use two negatives together in a sentence.

Incorrect	Correct
There weren't no states in which women could vote.	There weren't any states in which women could vote. *OR* There were no states in which women could vote.
Esther Morris wouldn't never give up hope.	Esther Morris wouldn't ever give up hope. *OR* Esther Morris would never give up hope.

Turn and Talk **Work with a partner to read each sentence below and tell whether it has one or two negatives in it. If a sentence has two negatives, correct it by removing one negative and rephrasing the sentence if necessary. Say each corrected sentence aloud.**

❶ Long ago, women couldn't own no property.

❷ They generally weren't able to borrow money.

❸ Many men didn't want nothing to change.

❹ Many women were not happy with the situation.

Conventions Sometimes you can join a verb and the word *not* to make a contraction. As you edit your writing, make sure that you have not used two negatives in one sentence.

Sentence with Double Negative	Corrected Sentence
My aunt Leona hasn't let no one hold her back.	My aunt Leona hasn't let anyone hold her back.
No challenge isn't too big for her to accept.	No challenge is too big for her to accept.

Connect Grammar to Writing

As you edit your cause-and-effect paragraph this week, look for negatives. If you find two negatives in any sentence, rewrite the sentence to eliminate the double negative.

Write to Inform

✓ Sentence Fluency A good **cause-and-effect** paragraph uses transition words such as *therefore, thus, so, because, since,* and *as a result* to connect ideas and sentences clearly and smoothly. Use transitions like these when you explain cause and effect. Use the Writing Traits Checklist as you revise your writing.

Joel explained the chain of cause and effect that led Esther Morris to open a hat shop. Later, he added some transition words to his sentences.

Writing Traits Checklist

✓ **Ideas**
Did I use facts to explain?

✓ **Organization**
Are the events in a logical order?

✓ **Word Choice**
Did I use vivid words and expressions?

✓ **Voice**
Did I sound interested in the topic?

✓ **Sentence Fluency**
Did I use transition words?

✓ **Conventions**
Did I use correct spelling, grammar, and mechanics?

Revised Draft

The events that led Esther Morris to open a hat shop began when she was only eight. *Because* Esther's mother was skilled at sewing, Esther loved to watch her make clothes for the family. She wanted to try it herself. *Therefore,* She began to practice sewing by making doll clothes. *As a result,* She learned to sew very well, and soon she was even good enough to make her father's shirts.

A Hat Shop for Esther
by Joel Silver

The events that led Esther Morris to open a hat shop began when she was only eight. Because Esther's mother was skilled at sewing, Esther loved to watch her make clothes for the family. She wanted to try it herself. Therefore, she began to practice sewing by making doll clothes. As a result, she learned to sew very well, and soon she was even good enough to make her father's shirts. When she was nineteen, Esther earned money by making fancy dresses. Her wealthy customers wanted hats to go with their dresses, so Esther began making hats too. This gave her a wonderful idea. Why not open a hat shop? People told her that she was too young, but she didn't pay any attention.

In my final paper, I used transition words. I was also careful to not use double negatives.

Reading as a Writer

What cause-and-effect transition words did Joel use? Where can you add transitions in your own paper?

Towering Trees

The Ever-Living Tree
The Life and Times of a Coast Redwood

✔ **TARGET VOCABULARY**

resources

dense

evaporate

shallow

moisture

civilized

continent

opportunities

customs

independent

Vocabulary
Reader

Context
Cards

Forever
Green

Vocabulary in Context

1 resources

Trees and forests are among the earth's valuable resources, or supplies.

2 dense

Roots grow from a banyan tree's branches like a thick, dense forest.

3 evaporate

The broad leaves of some trees let water evaporate easily into the air.

4 shallow

Some trees have shallow roots. The roots don't go deep into the ground.

- Study each Context Card.
- Use context clues to determine the meanings of these words.

5 moisture

Over half the world's species live in rain forests, helped by the moisture, or wetness.

6 civilized

Most civilized, or advanced, cities set aside places for trees to grow.

7 continent

The continent of North America has the world's tallest trees, coast redwoods.

8 opportunities

A forest offers many opportunities, or chances, for a career or volunteer work.

9 customs

Some human customs, such as the practice of clearing trees, are ruining many forests.

10 independent

People cannot be independent from trees. We need the oxygen trees provide.

Background

✓ **TARGET VOCABULARY** **Does Time Rush or Creep?** What can you do in an hour? You might grab several opportunities to e-mail friends or finish a list of chores in that time. Now think about shallow drops of moisture in a sink. In one hour you probably won't see them change, yet they might evaporate by the next day.

The history of civilized humankind might seem to change more quickly than the history of the natural world. Sometimes they seem to be completely independent histories. Over hundreds of years, people's customs clearly change, while natural resources such as a dense forest or the landmass of a continent might seem not to change at all. Yet they do.

In one hour you might not see a flower bud move, yet in a day or two it's in full bloom.

Comprehension

✔ **TARGET SKILL** **Text and Graphic Features**

As you read "The Ever-Living Tree," notice the text and graphic features in the selection. These features include icons, timelines, maps, diagrams, and italic type. How do they help you understand the text? How do they help you locate information? Make a graphic organizer like this one to record the selection's text and graphic features and their purposes.

Text or Graphic Feature	Page Number	Purpose
•	•	•
•	•	•
•	•	•

✔ **TARGET STRATEGY** **Monitor/Clarify**

"The Ever-Living Tree" covers a number of centuries and switches between natural and human history. Use your graphic organizer to help you monitor your comprehension of the events and the passage of time in the selection.

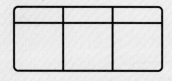

The Ever-Living Tree
The Life and Times of a Coast Redwood

✔ **TARGET VOCABULARY**

resources	civilized
dense	continent
evaporate	opportunities
shallow	customs
moisture	independent

✔ **TARGET SKILL**

Text and Graphic Features
Examine how text features
help you understand and
locate information.

✔ **TARGET STRATEGY**

Monitor/Clarify Notice
what is confusing as you read.
Find ways to understand it.

GENRE

Informational text gives
facts and examples about a
topic.

MEET THE AUTHOR

Linda Vieira

Linda Vieira uses writing
as a way to understand
something. She "prewrites" in her
head at dawn each morning while
walking the dog. What if she can't
begin writing immediately? "I trust
myself and let the thinking happen for
as long as it takes before starting,"
says Vieira.

MEET THE ILLUSTRATOR

Christopher Canyon

Can only talented people
become artists? This illustrator says no.
He believes working hard at your art is
much more important. "Some people
are naturally talented, but even if you
are not, you should *never give up* on
the things that you love or the dreams
that you have."

The Ever-Living Tree

The Life and Times of a Coast Redwood

by Linda Vieira

illustrated by Christopher Canyon

Essential Question

How do forests and trees show change?

It was a cool, foggy morning in a forest near the ocean when the little tree first poked itself up out of the ground. There were other trees in the evergreen forest just like it. Some were taller, some fatter, some older.

Eventually scientists would call this tree *Sequoia sempervirens*, an *ever-living sequoia*. It would also be known as a coast redwood.

More than 50 million years before this tree began to grow, different kinds of redwood trees grew all over the world. They lived at the same time as the dinosaurs until the glaciers came. Those slow-moving rivers of ice made many plants and animals extinct.

The long, narrow forest where the little tree grew stretched 600 miles along the western coast of the North American continent. It was bordered on the east by a huge mountain range and on the west by the Pacific Ocean.

The movement of cold air from the ocean toward the sheltering mountains saved the forest from the glaciers. The cold, heavy air created low-hanging fog, very important to the little redwood tree's survival.

MACEDONIA THRACE BLACK SEA RUSSIA

ASIA MINOR CASPIAN SEA PUNJAB

CYPRUS BACTRIA

MEDITERRANEAN SEA PHOENICIA PARTHIA

EGYPT

RED SEA PERSIAN GULF GEDROSIA INDIA

ALEXANDER'S EMPIRE

Halfway around the world Alexander the Great of Macedonia perfected the use of catapults in battle and became one of history's greatest generals. Using elephants as beasts of burden, he led his conquering army through Greece to India, and over much of the civilized world. Inspired by his teacher, Aristotle, he spread the ideals of Greek civilization throughout Europe and Asia.

On the other side of the world, the little tree kept growing bigger.

Time passed and the new tree grew quickly. It spread its shallow roots far out under the floor of the forest. Its bark grew thicker. Like an outer skin, it protected the living part of the tree, a thin circle of cells under the bark called the *cambium*.

Every year the cambium added a layer of bark toward the outside of the tree and a layer of new wood to the inside. The newest wood was called *sapwood*, where water and nutrients traveled up into the tree from the roots.

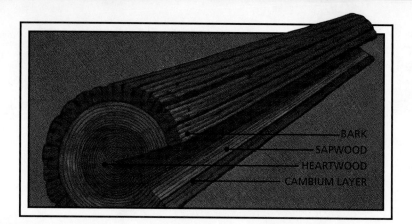

BARK
SAPWOOD
HEARTWOOD
CAMBIUM LAYER

The cambium added more and more rings of sapwood to the inside of the tree closest to its bark. The older sapwood became the heartwood of the tree. Its fibrous chambers, clogged with wastes, were no longer used to carry food and water, but the tree still needed the heartwood to help it stand straight and tall.

Time went on. Dozens of trapping spiders looked for spaces up and down the thick, uneven bark of the tree. They stretched their webs wherever they could. The outside of the tree looked like an apartment house for spiders. The webs didn't hurt the tree at all. It just kept growing.

Across the ocean in China, men began building a great stone wall along their borders for protection against their enemies. Built entirely by hand of earth, brick, and stone, it took millions of workers hundreds of years to complete. The Great Wall eventually stretched more than 1,500 miles across mountains and valleys.

Thousands of miles to the east, the little redwood tree grew and grew.

The cold morning air was heavy with moisture, but soon the sun found its way through the thick trees to the forest floor. The air became warmer and the moisture began to evaporate. The warmed air rose as it lost moisture and became lighter. The air currents gently pushed insects higher and higher. Some were trapped by the waiting webs along the bark.

A small group of native women came into the forest to collect acorns, pine nuts, ferns, and other plants beneath the tree. They belonged to a peaceful Native American tribe called *Ohlone* (oh LOH nee).

Although they gathered what they needed from the redwood forest, the natives did not live there. They considered the forest a sacred place, with its giant trees and ferocious grizzly bears. They did their gathering quickly and left, thanking the Great Spirit for such a bounty.

STOP AND THINK
Monitor/Clarify What role does cambium play in the development of the tree? Reread pages 587–588 if necessary.

589

A woodpecker landed on the tree, pecking a small hole into the thick bark. It ate the tiny insects living there.

A gray squirrel ran up the tree and hid an acorn in the hole left by the woodpecker. The squirrel hid lots of acorns that year. Later it forgot all about the one hidden in the woodpecker hole.

Years went by, and the cambium of the tree grew new bark over the hole. The little acorn was completely closed up inside the bark, and the tree kept on growing.

Time went on. Augustus Caesar became the first emperor of Rome, marking the start of the powerful Roman Empire. The Roman Empire ruled many lands until the late fifth century.

✔ **STOP AND THINK**

Text and Graphic Features How do the timelines at the top of the page and the icons work together to help you understand the text?

The tree was over 300 years old by then, still young for an ever-living sequoia. It stood almost 200 feet tall and measured about 20 feet around its base.

One day there was a big fire in the forest and many trees burned. Flames ate into the redwood tree near the ground. Fire-resistant elements in the heartwood finally stopped the fire, leaving a low, hollowed-out cave inside.

The cambium of the tree was not hurt badly by the fire. It continued to grow new bark around the opening of the cave. Over many years, the new bark almost closed up the opening, while the inside stayed hollow. The tree grew on and on.

Almost nine thousand miles southeast of the forest lay the continent of Africa. In a grassy savanna at the edge of the vast Sahara desert, the kingdom of Kanem flourished as a major commercial center. Caravans brought metalware, horses, and salt from North Africa and Europe to trade there for ivory and kola nuts from the south.

In the peaceful forest far away to the west, the redwood tree stood tall and strong.

Tiny striped chipmunks ran up and down the tree. They nestled on a branch that grew in a strange and different way. The branch had become a burl. Its wood was curled into a lump cozy enough for a chipmunk to rest upon. The burl didn't stop the tree from growing higher and wider. By now it was over 250 feet tall. It was more than 50 feet around the bottom. It grew and grew and grew.

A trader named Marco Polo traveled with his father and uncle from Europe to China. They were the first outsiders ever to be welcomed in China. They found gold, jewels, silks, and spices never before seen by Europeans.

When they returned home, Marco Polo described the advanced customs they had found in China—a postal system, paper money, and the use of coal as fuel.

The redwood tree grew taller and thicker. Its new rings of wood grew closer together like pages of a book. Its bark was almost a foot thick. Its twisted roots sent root crown sprouts up through the ground, encircling the tree in a fairy circle.

Another, smaller fire swept through the forest, clearing away loose brush from around the tree. Dense fibers in the tree snuffed out the flames again before there was any damage.

Redwood cones fell from the tree's high branches. Many burst open when they landed, and some of their tiny seeds sprouted into new trees.

STOP AND THINK
Author's Craft Authors use **similes** to compare two unlike things, using *like* or *as*. For example, in the sentence "The surface of the water looked as smooth as glass," *as smooth as glass* is a simile. Find another example of simile on this page.

An Italian explorer named Christopher Columbus wanted to find a new route to China. Inspired by the explorations of Marco Polo, he persuaded the queen of Spain to finance his voyage through uncharted seas to the west. Although Columbus did not reach China, he landed at the southeastern part of North America and called it the New World.

The redwood tree was almost 3,000 miles away from where Columbus landed, still growing in its sheltered forest far to the west.

Deer walked the trails of the forest and found hidden areas to protect them from their enemies while they grazed on the lush vegetation.

Gray foxes lived in the forest, too. Some of their babies were born inside the tree's sheltered cave.

Birds nested in the topmost branches of the tallest, oldest trees. Mammals, birds, insects, and reptiles lived together, replenishing their species every year according to a natural balance.

On the northeastern coast of North America, a small ship called the *Mayflower* brought a group of pilgrims to the New World. Many of them had been oppressed, and dreamed of a land where freedom of religion would prevail. The pilgrims struggled to live through their first terrible winter in the New World.

On the opposite coast, the tree provided a home for a mother raccoon and her babies. The cave kept them warm and dry, safe from the grizzly bears and mountain lions.

Time went on and on. The ever-living redwood tree kept growing bigger and bigger. It stood tall and silent in the middle of its fairy circle of younger trees.

The United States of America declared itself an independent nation in the New World with thirteen colonies along the eastern coast of North America. General George Washington led the colonists through the bitter Revolutionary War with Great Britain to establish that independence. After the war, General Washington became the first president of the United States.

The giant redwood tree was now more than 300 feet tall—one of the tallest living things on the face of the earth.

One day there was a terrible storm in the forest. Wind and rain lashed at the trees. Claps of thunder made the animals run and hide. A flashing bolt of lightning struck the base of the tree at its weakest part, near the cave. The tree fell over on its side with a tremendous crash. Its huge trunk broke into pieces when it hit the ground.

Gold was discovered in the western territories of North America. Thousands of people crossed the continent in horse-drawn wagons, dreaming of riches and new opportunities.

Boom towns and cities grew quickly. Hunters, loggers, tanners, and miners exploited the resources of the land. Soon a railroad reached across the continent from coast to coast. Trains carried settlers to places near the redwood forest, where the vigorous roots of the fallen tree kept growing.

Time went on. The life force of the ever-living sequoia would not die. Its roots gave life and strength to the smaller trees around it. Soon a new tree began to grow up from the broken trunk.

Millions of insects used the bark of the old tree for food. Over many years the wood began to change into a fine dust. Banana slugs changed the dust into organic elements, which went back into the soil as nutrients.

In outer space, a man walked on the moon for the first time. People watched him on television screens all over the world. Astronauts and cosmonauts from different countries traveled into space. Scientists planned to build a space station hundreds of miles from Earth.

Today people camp in the shelter of the tree, and children play games on its decomposing log. They are amazed at its length—longer than a football field.

In the narrow, ancient forest, the ever-living sequoias keep growing. They stand like giant statues as millions of visitors from all over the world come to marvel at their incredible height.

Tiny new trees poke themselves up out of the ground. Life in a coast redwood forest goes on and on.

Your Turn

Web of Life

Write About Nature Use facts from "The Ever-Living Tree" to write a paragraph describing how animals and insects depend on redwood trees over the course of their lives. Then tell about ways in which humans depend on trees. SCIENCE

Time Marches On

Add Historical Events With a partner, think of two recent historical events to add to the timeline in "The Ever-Living Tree." Write a short description and create a picture, or icon, for each event you have chosen. PARTNERS

Talk About Graphics

Turn and Talk The timelines, the icons, and the map of Alexander the Great's empire in "The Ever-Living Tree" help readers understand the text. With a group, discuss the purpose of each of these features. Then discuss which of the features was most helpful to you and why. TEXT AND GRAPHIC FEATURES

Connect to
Poetry

Towering Trees

✓ **TARGET VOCABULARY**

resources	civilized
dense	continent
evaporate	opportunities
shallow	customs
moisture	independent

GENRE
Poetry uses the sound and rhythm of words to suggest images and express feelings.

TEXT FOCUS
Narrative poetry focuses on telling a story, often about a particular event. Narrative poetry is broken into lines, and a section of lines is called a **stanza**. As you read each poem, note how each stanza relates to the meaning of the entire poem.

Towering Trees

The poems you will read next are about people and trees. "Ancestors of Tomorrow" compares children to growing trees, while "First Recorded 6,000-Year-Old Tree in America" and "Giant Sequoias" describe the majesty of towering trees.

Ancestors of Tomorrow

children are
the blooming
branches of trees

one day their seeds
will become
the roots

of other trees
bearing their own
blooming branches

by Francisco X. Alarcón

First Recorded 6,000-Year-Old Tree in America

The "Eon Tree"
- A coast redwood
- Humboldt County, California
- 250 feet tall
- About 6,200 years old

When Mother Nature held her ground,

When almost no one was around,

A redwood bud began to grow

And watch the seasons come and go.

For sixty centuries or more,

It stood upon the forest floor

And waved its arms about the sky

And sang a woodland lullaby.

December 1977;

The Eon Tree, so tall to heaven,

Bowed gracefully and bid farewell

To all its fellow trees,

and fell.

by J. Patrick Lewis

Humboldt Redwoods State Park

Visitors to Humboldt Redwoods State Park in California have numerous opportunities to see redwoods. Redwoods are important natural resources on the continent of North America. Plentiful rain and dense fog provide redwoods with moisture to grow. The trees' shallow roots take in water from the soil.

Cars can drive through some redwoods near the state park.

Giant Sequoias

these are the great-great-
great-great grandparents
of the Sierra Nevada

their many scars tell
of the storms and fires
they have survived

every year without fail
their huge trunks
add another ring

thick in a wet year
with plentiful rains—
thin in a dry one

it takes my whole
family holding hands
for us to give a hug

to the tallest
and oldest tree
in this grove

by Francisco X. Alarcón

Write a Tree Poem

Think of a tree you have seen in your corner of the civilized world. Write a poem about it. You might describe how it grows and changes through the year or how it makes you feel. Try to use the following words in your poem: customs, evaporate, and independent.

Making Connections

Text to Self

Write a Response Many animals depend on trees for survival and often stay with the same tree for many years. Do you have a favorite tree that you like to sit under or climb? Write a paragraph about how trees have had an impact on your life.

Text to Text

Compare Purposes Explain the difference between a stated and an implied purpose. Then use details from the texts to identify the purposes of "The Ever-Living Tree" and one of the poems in "Towering Trees," and note how they are similar. Tell whether the purposes are stated or implied.

Text to World

Construct a Timeline Research the dates of the historical events mentioned in "The Ever-Living Tree." Then use those dates to construct a timeline of events that occurred throughout the redwood tree's life.

Grammar

How Are Direct Quotations Written? When you are writing the exact words that a speaker says, you are writing a **direct quotation**. Use **quotation marks** (" ") before and after a speaker's exact words. Put a **comma** before the quotation marks to introduce the quotation. Put a comma right inside the quotation marks at the end of a quotation if the sentence doesn't end then. Write the words of each new speaker as a new paragraph. Indent the first line of a speaker's **dialogue**.

> "It's been foggy all summer," moaned Lesley. "I'm so tired of gray skies and drippy plants!"
>
> Simon joked, "Well, if you were a redwood tree, you wouldn't mind. You would cheer every gray day, and you would love the feeling of water dripping from your branches."

Try This! **Copy these sentences onto another sheet of paper. Add quotation marks and a comma to set off the direct quotation in each sentence.**

1. This tree is sixty feet around Laura announced.

2. Joe blurted I want to check that measurement.

3. Stretch this string around the base of the tree advised Laura.

4. Next, cut the string where it meets itself she continued.

5. Joe said Then I will measure the length of the string.

Word Choice Using exact words in your writing will give readers a clear picture of what you are writing about. When you write a quotation, try to use a word that is more exact than *said*. Make sure you use correct punctuation.

Less Exact	More Exact
Jackie said, "Don't scare the woodpecker in that redwood tree."	Jackie whispered, "Don't scare the woodpecker in that redwood tree."

Less Exact: "Hey, look at the spider webs on that tree trunk!" said Justin.

More Exact: "Hey, look at the spider webs on that tree trunk!" exclaimed Justin.

Connect Grammar to Writing

As you revise your writing, check the verbs in your sentences and direct quotations to make certain you have chosen exact words.

Write to Inform

☑ **Organization** In a **procedural composition** you explain a process, or series of events. Begin by introducing the topic and then explain each step in the process in order. Transition words such as *first, then,* and *finally* make the steps clear to readers. Supporting facts and details make the main idea of the composition clearer as well.

Erin wrote a procedural composition explaining how a redwood tree grows from a cone to a young, strong tree. Later, she reordered events and added transitions to better organize her ideas.

Writing Traits Checklist

☑ **Ideas**
Did I include enough details to make the process clear?

☑ **Organization**
Did I use transitions to make the order of events clear?

☑ **Word Choice**
Did I define unfamiliar words?

☑ **Voice**
Did I express my ideas clearly?

☑ **Sentence Fluency**
Did I vary the length of my sentences?

☑ **Conventions**
Did I use correct spelling, grammar, and mechanics?

Revised Draft

The magnificent coast redwoods are fast-growing conifers. Conifers are plants that bear seeds in a cone—and that's how some redwoods get their start. First, Cones on a redwood tree begin to open up. Next, the cones dry out. dry Then, They shed their seeds. Not many of the seeds sprout. But when they do, they are called seedlings.

How a Young Redwood Grows
by Erin Casey

The magnificent coast redwoods are fast-growing conifers. Conifers are plants that bear seeds in a cone—and that's how some redwoods get their start. First, cones on a redwood tree begin to dry out. Next, the dry cones open up. Then they shed their seeds. Not many of the seeds sprout. But when they do, they are called seedlings.

If the soil is rich, a young redwood seedling will continue to grow. As it grows, it spreads its roots outward through the forest. The roots will help the seedling continue to grow. Seedlings can grow more than a foot a year. Once a seedling becomes a strong young tree, it is known as a sapling.

In my final paper, I reordered steps in the process and added transitions.

Reading as a Writer

As you write your procedural composition, look for changes you can make in your paper to make the order of events clear.

TARGET VOCABULARY

bond

suffered

intruder

companion

enclosure

inseparable

charged

chief

exhausted

affection

Vocabulary
Reader

Context
Cards

DANGEROUS
WAVES

Vocabulary in Context

1 bond

Many people feel a very strong bond, or connection, with animals.

2 suffered

A veterinarian treats animals who have suffered injury or illness.

3 intruder

Animals are cautious when an intruder invades their territory.

4 companion

A pet is usually a companion of its owner. They spend a lot of time together.

● **Study each Context Card.**

● **Use a dictionary to help you understand the meanings of these words.**

5 enclosure

This ranch worker checks to be sure that an animal's enclosure is secure and safe.

6 inseparable

People and their service animals often become inseparable. They are never apart.

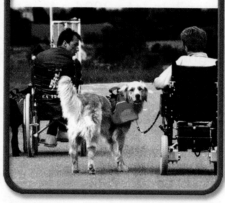

7 charged

This dog has charged, or rushed at, the ball that its owner has tossed.

8 chief

One of the chief jobs of an aquarium biologist is to educate visitors about sea life.

9 exhausted

This dog walker loves his job, but he will be exhausted, or worn out, by the day's end.

10 affection

This girl feels affection, or fondness, for the sheep on her family's farm.

Background

✓ **TARGET VOCABULARY** **What Helps an Animal Survive in the Wild?** Sometimes an inseparable bond between animals can make a difference. For instance, a helpless newborn needs the affection and care of a companion, such as a parent, to survive. An animal that is exhausted or one that has suffered an injury might need to rest in some kind of natural enclosure. While it rests, others in its group watch for signs of an intruder.

What happens if a young animal is separated from its parent or chief companion? In late 2004 a tsunami, a large ocean wave caused by an underwater earthquake, hit coastal areas on the Indian Ocean. Some animals charged off and escaped the tsunami. Others died. Still others were stranded, such as a young hippopotamus that was separated from his pod, or group.

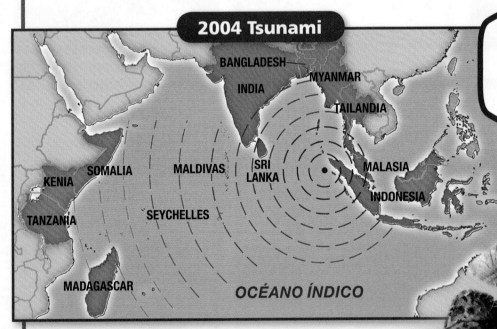

2004 Tsunami

BANGLADESH

INDIA

MYANMAR

TAILANDIA

SOMALIA

MALDIVAS

SRI LANKA

MALASIA

KENIA

INDONESIA

TANZANIA

SEYCHELLES

MADAGASCAR

OCÉANO ÍNDICO

During a 2006 flood in India, a mouse survived by catching a ride on the back of a frog.

Use the red lines on this map to understand how the 2004 tsunami affected many places on the Indian Ocean.

Comprehension

✔ **TARGET SKILL** **Compare and Contrast**

The authors of "Owen and Mzee" thought carefully about how to organize the facts they presented about two very different animals. As you read the selection, look for ways in which Owen and Mzee are alike and different. Use a graphic organizer to help you note their similarities and differences.

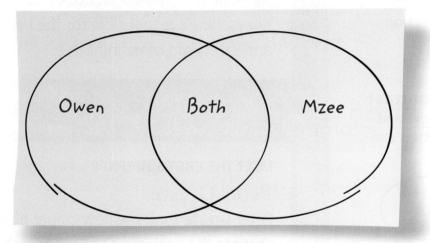

✔ **TARGET STRATEGY** **Analyze/Evaluate**

As you read, use your graphic organizer to help you analyze the relationship between Owen and Mzee. Why do you think these two animals have become friends, despite their differences? Ask questions while you read to help understand why Owen and Mzee's relationship is unique.

Main Selection

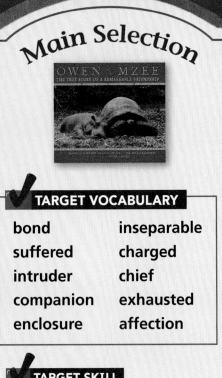

✔ **TARGET VOCABULARY**

bond	inseparable
suffered	charged
intruder	chief
companion	exhausted
enclosure	affection

✔ **TARGET SKILL**

Compare and Contrast
Examine the similarities and differences of characters and their actions.

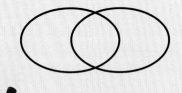

✔ **TARGET STRATEGY**

Analyze/Evaluate Think carefully about the text and form an opinion about it.

GENRE

Narrative nonfiction gives factual information by telling a true story.

Set a Purpose Before reading, set a purpose based on the genre and what you want to find out.

MEET THE AUTHORS

Isabella Hatkoff   **Craig Hatkoff**   **Dr. Paula Kahumbu**

Isabella Hatkoff was six years old when she saw a photo of Owen and Mzee in the newspaper. She decided to write about them with the help of her father, Craig. Dr. Paula Kahumbu is an ecologist in Kenya. She's responsible for the health and safety of Owen and Mzee.

MEET THE PHOTOGRAPHER

Peter Greste
Peter Greste took the newspaper photo that led the Hatkoffs and Dr. Kahumbu to write "Owen and Mzee." Greste works not only as a photographer but also as a radio news reporter. He travels the world covering important events.

612

OWEN & MZEE

THE TRUE STORY OF A REMARKABLE FRIENDSHIP

by Isabella Hatkoff, Craig Hatkoff, *and* Dr. Paula Kahumbu
photographs by Peter Greste

Essential Question
How can friendship help us find things in common?

This story began in Malindi, Kenya, on the east coast of Africa, in December 2004. A pod of hippopotamuses was grazing along the shore of the Indian Ocean. Suddenly, giant, surging waves from a tsunami (tsu NAH mee) rushed high onto the beach. The powerful waves caused destruction for miles around. After the water went down, only one hippo remained, and it was stranded on a reef. Hundreds of villagers worked for hours to rescue the six-hundred-pound baby. Finally, a man named Owen caught the animal, which was later named after him. The rescuers wrapped the hippo in a net and placed him in a pickup truck.

People weren't sure where Owen should be taken next. They called Haller Park, an animal sanctuary about fifty miles away, near the city of Mombasa. Dr. Paula Kahumbu, the manager, immediately offered Owen a place to live there. She explained that he could never be returned to the wild. Since he was still a baby, he wouldn't have learned yet how to fend for himself. And he would never be welcomed into another hippo pod—he would be seen as an intruder and attacked. But they would take good care of him in Haller Park. Dr. Paula offered to drive to Malindi herself to bring Owen to his new home.

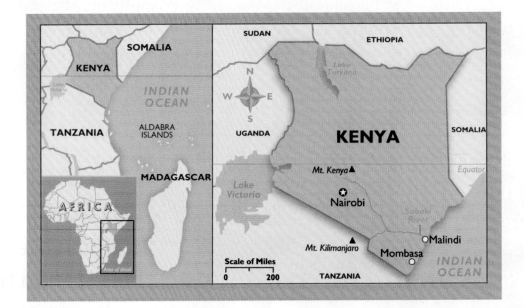

Dr. Paula, Stephen, and Sabine were eager to help the orphaned hippo.

Dr. Paula knew she would need help. She asked the chief animal caretaker, Stephen Tuei, to come along with her. She knew that Stephen had a special way with animals. Some people said he could even talk to them. Dr. Paula and Stephen quickly set off in her small truck to Malindi.

Meanwhile, ecologist Sabine Baer got to work with others at Haller Park to prepare for Owen's arrival.

When Dr. Paula and Stephen arrived in Malindi, they helped to remove the nets and lead Owen out of the pickup. But Owen became angrier than ever and charged at the people gathered around. They tried to help him calm down by wrapping a blanket around his head. That way, he wouldn't see the things that were upsetting him. But Owen was angry about that, too. After many hours, about a dozen rescuers managed to move Owen from the pickup into Dr. Paula's truck, tying him so that he would be safe during the long drive to Haller Park.

STOP AND THINK
Analyze/Evaluate Why do you think people are working so hard to move Owen to a new home?

Stephen tickles Mzee.

Meanwhile, Sabine and other workers prepared a large enclosure for Owen. They chose a part of the park that had a pond and a mud wallow, as well as tall trees and brush—everything a hippo could want. The area was already home to a number of bushbucks, vervet monkeys, and a giant Aldabra tortoise called Mzee (mzay).

Mzee, whose name means "wise old man" in the Swahili (swah HEE lee) language, was the oldest creature in the park. At about 130 years of age, he had been alive since before Stephen's great-grandmother was born. He wasn't very friendly, except to Stephen, who seemed to know just what he liked, such as getting tickled under the chin. Otherwise, Mzee kept to himself.

No one could have guessed how Mzee's life was about to change.

Finally, Dr. Paula and Stephen arrived with Owen, who was now weak and exhausted. As soon as the ropes that held him were untied, Owen scrambled from the truck directly to Mzee, resting in a corner of the enclosure. Owen crouched behind Mzee, the way baby hippos often hide behind their mothers for protection. At first, Mzee wasn't happy about this attention. He hissed at Owen and crawled away. But Owen, who could easily keep up with the old tortoise, did not give up. Slowly, as the night went on, Mzee began to accept his new companion. When the park workers checked on them in the morning, Owen was snuggled up against Mzee. And Mzee didn't seem to mind at all.

At first, Mzee crawled away, but Owen wouldn't give up.

Over the next few days, Mzee continued to crawl away, and Owen continued to follow him. But sometimes it was Owen who would walk away from Mzee, and Mzee who would follow. Bit by bit, Mzee grew friendlier.

At first, Owen wouldn't eat any of the leaves left out for him. Stephen and the other caretakers were worried that he would weaken even more. Then they noticed Owen feeding right beside Mzee, as if Mzee were showing him how to eat. Or perhaps it was Mzee's protective presence that helped Owen feel calm enough to eat. No one will ever know. But it was clear that the bond between Owen and Mzee was helping the baby hippo to recover from being separated from his mother and stranded in the sea.

With Mzee by his side, Owen began to eat.

Both hippos and tortoises love the water.

As the weeks went on, Owen and Mzee spent more and more time together. Soon, they were inseparable. Their bond remains very strong to this day. They swim together, eat together, drink together, and sleep next to each other. They rub noses. Owen leads the way to different parts of the enclosure, then Mzee leads the way. Owen playfully nuzzles Mzee's neck, and Mzee stretches his neck forward asking for more, just as he does when Stephen tickles him under the chin. Though both animals could easily injure each other, they are gentle with one another. A sense of trust has grown between them.

STOP AND THINK

Author's Craft The authors use careful **word choice** to shape your opinion about Owen and Mzee's friendship. They use specific adjectives and verbs. For example, they use the word *snuggled* on page 617. Find an example of word choice on pages 618–619 and explain how it shapes your opinion.

Owen nuzzles Mzee's ticklish neck.

Wildlife experts are still puzzled about how this unlikely friendship came to be. Most have never heard of a mammal, such as Owen, and a reptile, such as Mzee, forming such a strong bond.

Perhaps for Owen, it happened this way: Young hippos like Owen need their mothers in order to survive. An old, slow tortoise like Mzee can never protect Owen the way a fierce mother hippo could. But since Mzee's coloring and rounded shape are similar to a hippo's, it's possible that to Owen, Mzee looks like the hippo mother he needs.

Harder to explain is the affection that Mzee seems to show for Owen. Like most Aldabra tortoises, Mzee had always preferred to be alone. But sometimes these tortoises live in groups, and perhaps Mzee sees Owen as a fellow tortoise, the first tortoise he is willing to spend time with. Or perhaps Mzee knows that Owen isn't a tortoise, but likes him anyway.

The reasons are unclear. But science can't always explain what the heart already knows: Our most important friends are sometimes those we least expected.

News of Owen and Mzee's friendship quickly spread around the world. People all over have come to love Owen, who endured so much, yet never gave up, and Mzee, who became Owen's friend when he needed one most. Their photographs have appeared in countless newspaper and magazine articles. Television programs and even a film documentary have been made about them. Visitors come to Haller Park every day to meet the famous friends.

✔ STOP AND THINK

Compare and Contrast How are Owen and Mzee alike? In what ways are they different?

Owen and Mzee look out for each other.

Owen's future is bright.

Owen suffered a great loss. But with the help of many caring people, and through his own extraordinary (ihk STROHR dn ehr ee) resilience, Owen has begun a new, happy life. Most remarkable is the role that Mzee has played. We'll never know for sure whether Owen sees Mzee as a mother, a father, or a very good friend. But it really doesn't matter. What matters is that Owen isn't alone—and neither is Mzee.

And that is the true story of Owen and Mzee, two great friends.

Your Turn

An Unusual Pair

Write a Response Owen and Mzee's unusual friendship surprised many observers. Have you ever formed a friendship that seemed unlikely at first, perhaps because of a big difference in your ages, personalities, or interests? Write a short paragraph describing this friendship. PERSONAL RESPONSE

Animal Talk

Make a Comic Strip Imagine that Owen and Mzee can think and feel as humans do. What thoughts might have gone through Mzee's mind when Owen first showed up in the enclosure? What might Owen have thought when he first saw Mzee? With a partner, create a comic strip that shows their first day together. PARTNERS

What Leads to Friendship?

Turn and Talk Use a Venn diagram to compare and contrast the way hippos and tortoises normally interact with one another with the way Owen and Mzee interact. Then discuss your Venn diagram with a partner. Remember to use details from the story to support your thoughts.

COMPARE AND CONTRAST

GENRE

Informational text, such as this science article, gives factual information about a topic, organized around main ideas and supporting details.

TEXT FOCUS

Maps and diagrams help readers understand facts in informational text. What information does the diagram on page 626 add to the text of this selection?

SEA SANCTUARY

by Rob Hale

Monterey Bay National Marine Sanctuary

Monterey Bay

PACIFIC OCEAN

Monterey Bay National Marine Sanctuary covers more than 5,300 square miles.

A sea otter finds plenty of shellfish to eat in Monterey Bay. These animals suffered a drop in numbers because of being hunted for their fur in the early 1900s. Now, they are slowly starting to return to the area.

We often think of a wildlife sanctuary as a jewel of land that has been set aside to keep safe. But there are ocean sanctuaries, too.

The United States government has preserved thirteen important areas as marine, or sea, sanctuaries. The largest of them is California's Monterey Bay National Marine Sanctuary.

This sanctuary is an ecosystem. It is an environment whose nonliving parts, such as water and earth, work with its living parts. Each part is like a companion to another part. "Upwelling" is one example of this. Wind causes cold water to rise to the surface of the ocean. This cold water causes new plants to grow. Then, animals come to eat these plants. This food source is the chief reason why so many species are drawn to Monterey Bay. No enclosure, or closed space, keeps them there. The food does!

Seafood Chain

Each plant and animal in a sanctuary is part of a food chain. A necessary bond connects each hunter to its prey. The need for food is why a hungry orca might have charged at a sea lion. It is the same reason a sea lion might leave a rockfish exhausted after a chase. One animal depends on another for life.

Flower Garden Banks

You may think that coral reefs and ocean waters are inseparable. Yet coral reefs can be found 110 miles off the Texas and Louisiana coasts. They are protected by the Flower Garden Banks, a 36,000-acre marine sanctuary.

The coral reefs lie on top of two salt domes, old underwater mountains. Today Flower Garden Banks Sanctuary is home to 23 types of coral. Anyone with affection for marine creatures will find many animals there. One might see turtles, manta rays, or the odd intruder, such as the huge whale shark.

Texas
LA
Gulf of Mexico
Flower Garden Banks
National Marine
Sanctuary (FGBNMS)
Miles
0 100 200

Predators and Prey

A healthy environment keeps each member of the food chain well fed. Orcas eat sea lions. Sea lions eat rockfish. Rockfish eat krill. Krill eat tiny plankton.

Orcas eat
sea lions.

Sea lions
eat rockfish.

Rockfish
eat krill.

Krill eat tiny
plankton.

Making Connections

Text to Self

Write About an Animal Think about a time when you saw an animal in the wild, or in a zoo or aquarium. Describe the animal and its habitat. Tell how it interacted with any nearby animals.

Text to Text

Compare Nonfiction Both "Owen and Mzee" and "Sea Sanctuary" are nonfiction. With a partner, make a Venn diagram to compare and contrast the two selections. Include information about the organization of the texts, the types of graphics and photographs used, and the author's purpose.

Text to World

Connect to Science Think about another part of the world where a wildlife sanctuary might help to protect a threatened species or habitat. With a partner, use the Internet or other media to find out more information about that animal or habitat. Present your findings to the class.

Grammar

How Are Commas Used? A **comma** is needed after an introductory word in a sentence and to set off the name of a person being addressed. A comma separates the day and the year in a date as well as the city and the state in a place name. Commas are used to separate items in a series.

> to set off an
> introductory word   to set off a name
> No, Wardell, that is not a warthog.
>
>   in a place name
> It is the baby hippo that was rescued near Malindi, Kenya, on
> December 27, 2004.
>   in a date
>
>   to separate items in a series
> Villagers, fishermen, and visitors performed the rescue.

A comma is used with a conjunction to form a compound sentence. A comma is also used to introduce quotations.

>   to join parts of a
>   compound sentence
> The tortoise was not very friendly, but he loved being tickled under
> the chin.
>   in a direct quotation
> "I would love to see a baby hippo," remarked Ann.

Turn and Talk **Work with a partner. Read each sentence and tell how each comma is used.**

1. Leah said, "Our zoo has adult hippos, but none of them have babies."

2. "Hey, let's go on the Internet," yelled Ivan.

3. Leah, Ann, and Jed ran to the computer.

4. They found a baby hippo in a zoo in Seattle, Washington.

Sentence Fluency Sentences with missing commas can be difficult to understand. Check your work carefully to make sure you have used commas where they are needed.

Sentences with Missing Commas	Sentences with Correct Comma Usage
Sheila Billy and Lonnie flew into Mombasa Kenya on March 22 2007.	Sheila, Billy, and Lonnie flew into Mombasa, Kenya, on March 22, 2007.
"Look here Billy" said Sheila.	"Look here, Billy," said Sheila.
Billy exclaimed "The tortoise is eating, so the little hippo is eating, too!"	Billy exclaimed, "The tortoise is eating, so the little hippo is eating, too!"

Connect Grammar to Writing

As you edit your research report next week, make sure that you have used commas correctly. They should be used with introductory words, names, dates, places, direct quotations, compound sentences, and items in a series.

Write to Inform

☑ **Ideas** When you plan a **research report**, do research to answer your questions about the topic. Take notes on index cards. Then make an outline from your notes. Each main topic in your outline will become a paragraph in your report. Use the Writing Process Checklist below to help plan your writing.

Maya took notes to answer her questions about hippos. Then she organized all of her notes into an outline.

Writing Process Checklist

▶ **Prewrite**

☑ Did I choose a topic that will interest my audience and me?

☑ Did I ask interesting questions about my topic?

☑ Did I use dependable sources to find facts?

☑ Did I take notes on enough facts?

☑ Did I organize my outline with main topics and subtopics?

Draft

Revise

Edit

Publish and Share

Exploring a Topic

What is a hippo's habitat?
-in Africa by rivers and lakes
"spend much of the day in the water because the intense heat can rapidly dehydrate them" Langston, Kate. "Hippo Facts." Nature for Kids May 2003: paragraph 1.
www.onfourfeet.org/mammals/hippo
Nov. 7, 2010.

What do hippos eat?
- mainly plants
- eat at night on grasslands
- about 80 pounds of food a day
Deets, Wayne. The Hippopotamus.
New York: Kite Tail Books, 2009.
p. 14.

I.   Hippos' water habitat

    A. Live by rivers and lakes in Africa

    B. Spend day in water because "intense heat can rapidly dehydrate them"

    C. In water can watch for danger—eyes near top of head

    D. Walk on river or lake bottom—can hold breath about 5 minutes

II.   What hippos eat

    A. Eat on land at night

    B. Mostly plants

    C. Grab food with lips—sharp teeth only for fighting

    D. Eat about 80 pounds a day—small amount for size

III. How hippos care for their babies

    A. One born at a time

    B. Can nurse underwater

    C. Mother doesn't eat until baby strong enough to go on land

> In my outline, I grouped my facts by topic. I listed them in an order that makes sense.

Reading as a Writer

In what way do Maya's facts support her main topics? In your outline, where can you add interesting and specific facts?

progress

calculated

dispute

centuries

superior

insert

waste

inspector

mechanical

average

Vocabulary   Context
Reader   Cards

REMARKABLE
ROBOTS

Vocabulary in Context

1 progress

Today's many ways of learning may show society's progress, or improvement.

2 calculated

Using machines, many people have calculated answers to math problems.

3 dispute

People dispute the value of TV. Some argue that shows can be educational.

4 centuries

For centuries, or hundreds of years, we've learned a lot from books.

- Study each Context Card.
- Break the longer words into syllables.
  Use a dictionary to confirm.

5 superior

Some people find the Internet superior to, or better than, other ways of learning.

6 insert

If you insert a book on disc into a portable CD player, you can learn on the go.

7 waste

It's such a waste to throw away old computers. They could be recycled.

8 inspector

This inspector checks a disc to make sure there's nothing wrong with it.

9 mechanical

Typewriters are mechanical devices for writing that are hardly used anymore.

10 average

The average, or typical, reader might prefer printed books to electronic books.

Background

✓ TARGET VOCABULARY **Imagining the Future** Science fiction writers create worlds that are set many years, even centuries, in the future. Some writers might imagine a superior society that shows great progress in building mechanical objects. Such machines could take over tasks that are a waste of time for average humans to perform. Other writers might insert strange characters into a story. Imagine a government inspector who has calculated how much air each person is allowed to breathe! Some people dispute the possibilities that appear in science fiction, but who knows what might come to pass?

One illustrator has imagined a futuristic city that looks like this.

634

Comprehension

✔ **TARGET SKILL** **Author's Purpose**

As you read "The Fun They Had," think about the author's reasons for writing the story. Does he want to entertain, inform, or persuade you? For clues, look at the plot and character details. Use a graphic organizer like this one to help you figure out the author's purpose.

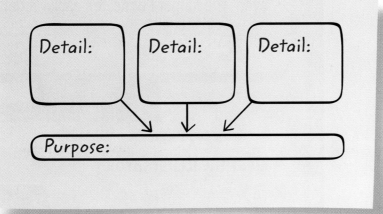

Detail: Detail: Detail:

Purpose:

✔ **TARGET STRATEGY** **Question**

As you make note of the story details from "The Fun They Had," ask yourself why the author included these details. Answering these questions by revisiting story details will help you figure out the theme of the story and discover the author's purpose for writing it.

Main Selection

✔ **TARGET VOCABULARY**

progress	insert
calculated	waste
dispute	inspector
centuries	mechanical
superior	average

✔ **TARGET SKILL**

Author's Purpose Use text details to figure out the author's reasons for writing.

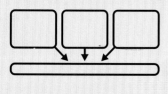

✔ **TARGET STRATEGY**

Question Ask questions before you read, as you read, and after you read.

GENRE

Science fiction is a type of fantasy story whose plot often depends on scientific ideas.

Set a Purpose Before reading, set a purpose based on the genre and what you want to find out.

MEET THE AUTHOR
Isaac Asimov

Isaac Asimov is one of the world's best-known science fiction writers. His work helped people take science fiction more seriously. Isaac saw his first science fiction magazine in his father's candy store. After writing his first three hundred books, he said, "Writing is more fun than ever. The longer I write, the easier it gets."

MEET THE ILLUSTRATOR
Alan Flinn

Alan Flinn has been an illustrator for more than twenty years. With author Jim Sukach, he created a book of detective stories called *Elliott's Talking Dog and Other Quicksolve Mysteries*. He has also illustrated *Constellations*, a glow-in-the-dark astronomy book.

The Fun They Had

from Isaac Asimov: The Complete Stories

by Isaac Asimov
selection illustrated by Alan Flinn

Essential Question

Why might an author write about change?

Margie even wrote about it that night in her diary. On the page headed May 17, 2157, she wrote, "Today Tommy found a real book!"

It was a very old book. Margie's grandfather once said that when he was a little boy *his* grandfather told him that there was a time when all stories were printed on paper.

They turned the pages, which were yellow and crinkly, and it was awfully funny to read words that stood still instead of moving the way they were supposed to—on a screen, you know. And then, when they turned back to the page before, it had the same words on it that it had had when they read it the first time.

"Gee," said Tommy, "what a waste. When you're through with the book, you just throw it away, I guess. Our television screen must have had a million books on it and it's good for plenty more. I wouldn't throw *it* away."

"Same with mine," said Margie. She was eleven and hadn't seen as many telebooks as Tommy had. He was thirteen.

She said, "Where did you find it?"

"In my house." He pointed without looking, because he was busy reading. "In the attic."

"What's it about?"

"School."

Margie was scornful. "School? What's there to write about school? I hate school."

Margie always hated school, but now she hated it more than ever. The mechanical teacher had been giving her test after test in geography and she had been doing worse and worse until her mother had shaken her head sorrowfully and sent for the County Inspector.

He was a round little man with a red face and a whole box of tools with dials and wires. He smiled at Margie and gave her an apple, then took the teacher apart. Margie had hoped he wouldn't know how to put it together again, but he knew how all right, and, after an hour or so, there it was again, large and square and ugly, with a big screen on which all the lessons were shown and the questions were asked. That wasn't so bad. The part Margie hated most was the slot where she had to put homework and test papers. She always had to write them out in a punch code they made her learn when she was six years old, and the mechanical teacher calculated the mark in no time.

The Inspector had smiled after he was finished and patted Margie's head. He said to her mother, "It's not the little girl's fault, Mrs. Jones. I think the geography sector was geared a little too quick. Those things happen sometimes. I've slowed it up to an average ten-year level. Actually, the over-all pattern of her progress is quite satisfactory." And he patted Margie's head again.

Margie was disappointed. She had been hoping they would take the teacher away altogether. They had once taken Tommy's teacher away for nearly a month because the history sector had blanked out completely.

STOP AND THINK
Question Which details in this section help you figure out what a *sector* is?

So she said to Tommy, "Why would anyone write about school?"

Tommy looked at her with very superior eyes. "Because it's not our kind of school, stupid. This is the old kind of school that they had hundreds and hundreds of years ago." He added loftily, pronouncing the word carefully, "*Centuries* ago."

Margie was hurt. "Well, I don't know what kind of school they had all that time ago." She read the book over his shoulder for a while, then said, "Anyway, they had a teacher."

"Sure they had a teacher, but it wasn't a *regular* teacher. It was a man."

"A man? How could a man be a teacher?"

"Well, he just told the boys and girls things and gave them homework and asked them questions."

"A man isn't smart enough."

"Sure he is. My father knows as much as my teacher."

"He can't. A man can't know as much as a teacher."

"He knows almost as much, I betcha."

Margie wasn't prepared to dispute that. She said, "I wouldn't want a strange man in my house to teach me."

Tommy screamed with laughter. "You don't know much, Margie. The teachers didn't live in the house. They had a special building and all the kids went there."

"And all the kids learned the same thing?"

"Sure, if they were the same age."

"But my mother says a teacher has to be adjusted to fit the mind of each boy and girl it teaches and that each kid has to be taught differently."

"Just the same they didn't do it that way then. If you don't like it, you don't have to read the book."

"I didn't say I didn't like it," Margie said quickly. She wanted to read about those funny schools.

They weren't even half-finished when Margie's mother called, "Margie! School!"

Margie looked up. "Not yet, Mamma."

"Now!" said Mrs. Jones. "And it's probably time for Tommy, too."

Margie said to Tommy, "Can I read the book some more with you after school?"

"Maybe," he said nonchalantly (nahn shuh LAHNT lee). He walked away whistling, the dusty old book tucked beneath his arm.

STOP AND THINK

Author's Craft The author uses funny details and dialogue to create a humorous **tone** in his story. For example, when Margie and Tommy first look at the book, their reaction is funny. Find other details on pages 642–643 that add to the humor.

Margie went into the schoolroom. It was right next to her bedroom, and the mechanical teacher was on and waiting for her. It was always on at the same time every day except Saturday and Sunday, because her mother said little girls learned better if they learned at regular hours.

The screen was lit up, and it said: "Today's arithmetic lesson is on the addition of proper fractions. Please insert yesterday's homework in the proper slot."

Margie did so with a sigh. She was thinking about the old schools they had when her grandfather's grandfather was a little boy. All the kids from the whole neighborhood came, laughing and shouting in the schoolyard, sitting together in the schoolroom, going home together at the end of the day. They learned the same things, so they could help one another on the homework and talk about it.

And the teachers were people. . . .

The mechanical teacher was flashing on the screen: "When we add the fractions ½ and ¼—"

Margie was thinking about how the kids must have loved it in the old days. She was thinking about the fun they had.

Please
Insert
Yesterday's
Homework
In The
Proper
Slot

✔ **STOP AND THINK**
Author's Purpose Why do you think the author wrote this story? Keep in mind that it was first published in 1951.

Your Turn

Now and Then

Write a Response How is the future school that the author imagined similar to schools today? How is it different? Write your ideas in a paragraph. Use your own experience as well as story details to support your points.
SOCIAL STUDIES

Future Fun

Draw a Scene School for Margie and Tommy is very different from school for kids today. With a group, brainstorm a list of other ways in which Margie and Tommy's lives might be different. Where do they meet their friends after school? How do they get around their neighborhood? Then draw pictures showing the activities you listed.
SMALL GROUP

Is Newer Always Better?

Turn and Talk The author imagined a future time when school would be very different from the way it is today. How do you think the author felt about the idea of learning only from a machine? With a partner, discuss what you think his purpose was for writing about this kind of change. Use evidence from the text to support your thoughts. AUTHOR'S PURPOSE

GENRE

Informational text, such as this magazine article, gives facts and examples about a topic.

TEXT FOCUS

Diagram Informational text may include a diagram, a kind of drawing that explains how something works or how the parts of a thing relate to each other. How does the diagram on page 647 relate to the text?

Technology for All Learners

by Mia Vosic

Each year, students miss many weeks of school from being sick. It has been calculated that this happens to more than six hundred thousand children in the United States. These children face challenges that the average child does not. Missing school is a waste of valuable time. Plus, these students miss being in class with their friends.

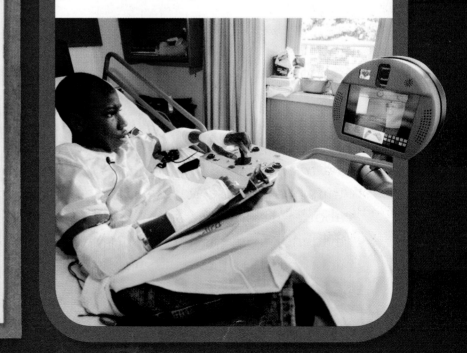

Meet PEBBLES

Luckily, the learning progress of these students does not have to stop. A robotic system called PEBBLES can insert them into their classrooms. *PEBBLES* stands for "Providing Education by Bringing Learning Environments to Students."

The PEBBLES system uses two small robots connected through the Internet. One robot sits beside the student. The other is in the classroom. The Internet sends "real-time" audio and video back and forth. This way, the absent student, the teacher, and the other students can see and hear each other. There is even a mechanical hand that can be raised to ask questions. The machine also has a scanner and a printer to send and print assignments.

The PEBBLES Robot

Video Screens

The student can see what's going on in the classroom. The teacher and the classmates can also see the student.

Camera

Robotic Hand

The student can raise the mechanical hand of the classroom robot to ask a question.

Microphone

Speakers

The student, the teacher, and the classmates can hear each other through the speakers.

Control Pad

The student can control the camera-fitted head of the classroom robot with the control pad to get a better view.

Technology That Hears and Speaks

For students who can't move their arms and legs, typing on a computer is impossible. Voice-activated software can help. It changes spoken words into text on a computer screen, so students can "type" with their voices. The speaker must watch the screen and act as an inspector to make sure there are no mistakes.

Another device helps students who have trouble speaking by changing text to speech. The student uses a keypad to type a text message. Then a voice delivers the text as a spoken message. It can also change pictures and symbols to speech for children who have not yet learned to read.

Other types of technology help students who cannot see. It lets them take notes in Braille, a language for people with visual impairment. There are also video phones for students with hearing problems.

Looking to the Future

In centuries past, students with disabilities did not attend school. Today, it's hard to dispute the fact that superior technology can help all students with their education.

Equipment such as this Braille keyboard helps people with visual impairment use computers.

Making Connections

Text to Self

Write a Response Think about a technology product you use often. What if this product had never been invented? Write a paragraph telling how life would be different for you if this product did not exist.

Text to Text

Compare Characters Both Opal in "Because of Winn-Dixie" and Margie in "The Fun They Had" learn about events in the past—Opal from Miss Franny and Margie from the old book. Using text details, compare and contrast how they react to what they learn.

Text to World

Learn About School Technology What technology can students at your school use to help them learn? Work with a group to make a list of all the machines and technologies used in your classroom and school. Discuss whether you think any other technologies could be used in your school.

Grammar

What Are the Mechanics of Writing? In writing, **mechanics** refers to the correct use of **capitalization** and **punctuation**. Capitalization should be used for proper nouns, such as titles and names of historical events. Documents, languages, races, names, states, and nationalities should also be capitalized. Correct punctuation must always be used at the end of a sentence. **Apostrophes** are needed in **contractions** and possessive nouns.

Academic Language

mechanics

capitalization

punctuation

apostrophes

contractions

---

          name   planet

The Amazon River Basin is home to the largest rain forest on Earth.

    contraction   book title   end punctuation

Why haven't you read the book *The Great Kapok Tree*?

     name   possessive noun

The Kapok tree is often a parrot's home.

Try This! **Write each sentence on another sheet of paper. Capitalize the proper nouns and important words in titles and names. Add end punctuation and apostrophes where they are needed.**

1. The book called *the amazon* is Mikes favorite

2. Isnt that a book about earths rainforests

3. Its also about the animals and the people who live in the amazon.

4. I would love for mrs. ortiz to read that book

5. You cant find it anywhere but the smithville library.

Conventions Readers will have an easier time reading and understanding what you write if you use correct capitalization and punctuation. Errors in capitalization and punctuation may confuse readers and they might not understand what you mean.

Sentences with Missing Commas

Incorrect Capitalization and Punctuation	Correct Capitalization and Punctuation
My sisters newest story is called "the strangest river" Its a story about an unusual mammal called the platypus How would you react to an animal that looks like a cross between a beaver and a duck	My sister's newest story is called "The Strangest River." It's a story about an unusual mammal called the platypus. How would you react to an animal that looks like a cross between a beaver and a duck?

Connect Grammar to Writing

As you revise your research report, correct any errors in capitalization or punctuation.

Write to Inform

☑ **Word Choice** In a **research report**, good writers do not copy from other authors. They write the facts in their own words. As you revise your report, be sure to reword any parts you copied from your notes. You can use synonyms—different words with the same meaning—to help you reword the facts. Use the Writing Process Checklist as you revise your report.

When Maya revised her report, she rewrote a sentence that she had accidentally copied. She made other changes too.

Writing Process Checklist

Prewrite

Draft

▶ **Revise**

☑ Did I introduce my main ideas in an interesting way?

☑ Did I give facts, not opinions, and use my own words?

☑ Did I write a paragraph for each main topic?

☑ Does my closing sum up my main ideas?

☑ Did I give an accurate list of sources?

Edit

Publish

Share

Revised Draft

Because their bodies quickly dry up in the strong sun, hippos stay in the water for many hours each day.

Hippopotamuses are huge animals. ~~They~~ are related to pigs. Their name
∧ that
means "river horse," and in many ways they are more like water creatures than land animals.

Hippos' habitats are by rivers and lakes in Africa. ~~They spend much of the day in the water because the intense sun can rapidly dehydrate them.~~ They can guard against danger above the water even while they are mostly underwater.

The Amazing Hippopotamus
by Maya Landon

Hippopotamuses are huge animals that are related to pigs. Their name means "river horse," and in many ways they are more like water creatures than land animals.

Hippos' habitats are by rivers and lakes in Africa. Because their bodies quickly dry up in the strong sun, hippos stay in the water for many hours each day. They can guard against danger above the water even while they are mostly underwater. That's because their eyes, ears, and nose are near the top of their head. Hippos can also sink to the bottom of the river or lake and walk underwater. They don't have to come up for air for about five minutes.

In my final paper, I wrote the facts in my own words. I also combined short sentences to make my writing smoother.

Reading as a Writer

How else could Maya have reworded the sentence that she copied? Find a way to reword any copied parts of your own paper.

Read the next two selections. Think about the author's message in each selection.

The Stonecutter
a Japanese folktale

Once there was a stonecutter who lived in a small house in the country. He was content with his life. Then one winter day, while he was in the city, he saw a house more splendid than his own. "I wish I had a house like this!" he cried.

When the stonecutter returned home, his little house was gone. In its place stood a palace. The stonecutter was delighted. Soon, however, summer came. The sun burned hotter each day. Even in his fine palace, the stonecutter could not bear the heat. "I am rich, but the sun is more powerful than I!" he cried. "I wish I were the sun!"

Instantly, the stonecutter became the sun. He felt mighty and powerful. His rays shone on Earth until the rice crops dried up in the field, and he burned the faces of rich and poor people alike.

Then one day, a cloud covered the face of the sun. The sun cried, "I am powerful, but this cloud is mightier! I wish I were a cloud!"

So the stonecutter became a cloud. He rained on Earth, and it grew green again. He poured down rain until floods ruined rice fields and villages. Only the great mountain stood firm and strong.

Seeing this, the cloud cried, "I am powerful, but the mountain is mightier! I wish I were the mountain!"

Suddenly the stonecutter was the mountain. He stood tall and proud, not bothered by sun or rain. Days turned into weeks. Weeks turned into months. Months turned into years. The mountain was lonely.

"I wish I were a man," the mountain said gloomily.

So the stonecutter became a man once more, living back in his little house. Never again did he wish to be someone or something else.

Changing His Tune

Once there was a bird named Twitter. Twitter loved to sing. He sang all day long. He had a very unusual voice, unlike any of the other birds. "T-t-t-witt! T-t-t-witt!" he warbled.

One day, Twitter stopped singing. He listened to the songs of the other birds. Twitter thought that their songs were better than his. He decided that he didn't like his own music. Right then, he decided that he would change his song. He decided to sing just like the other birds.

Twitter sat high in a tree. He listened to another bird's song and decided to repeat it. "Ta-weee! Ta-weee!" he sang out loudly.

Just then a blue jay landed beside him. It was Twitter's friend, Skye. "Hi!" Twitter chirped to Skye. "It's good to see you!"

"Twitter?" asked Skye. "Is that you? You don't sound like yourself. I thought it was someone else singing."

"That's because I'm singing like my friend Kiwi today," answered Twitter. "Tomorrow I plan to sing like Dove. The next day I'll sing like Marcella." Twitter paused. "Listen, Skye! I can sing like you!" He gave a harsh, jeering call. It hurt his throat and made him cough, but it *did* sound like Skye.

"Hah! That was good!" squawked Skye. "But why are you imitating other birds? Why don't you just sing like yourself?"

"I like the songs of the other birds," Twitter replied. He added sadly, "Their songs sound better than mine."

"That's too bad," Skye said. "I always thought your song was the best."

"Really?" Twitter asked in disbelief.

"Really!" answered Skye.

Twitter thought about what Skye had said. Could it be true? He thought about how imitating other birds had made his throat feel funny. He stretched out a wing to Skye. "Thanks!" he told him. "I'm going to change my tune – back to my old song!"

And from that moment on, Twitter sang in his own lovely warble. "T-t-t-witt! T-t-t-witt!"

Unit 5 Wrap-Up

The Big Idea

Friendship Friendships can change people's lives, just as it changes Owen's and Mzee's. Friends spend time together and learn from each other, too. Write about a friendship that has changed your life. Explain how it has changed your life. Draw a picture to illustrate the change.

Listening and Speaking

Interview In Unit 5, you read about many kinds of change. Interview an older person you know, about what life was like when that person was your age. Begin by writing five questions you would like answered. After your interview, compare your findings with those of your classmates.

Glossary

This glossary contains meanings and pronunciations for some of the words in this book. The Full Pronunciation Key shows how to pronounce each consonant and vowel in a special spelling. At the bottom of the glossary pages is a shortened form of the full key.

Full Pronunciation Key

Consonant Sounds

b	bib, cabbage	kw	choir, quick	t	tight, stopped
ch	church, stitch	l	lid, needle, tall	th	bath, thin
d	deed, mailed, puddle	m	am, man, dumb	th	bathe, this
		n	no, sudden	v	cave, valve, vine
f	fast, fife, off, phrase, rough	ng	thing, ink	w	with, wolf
		p	pop, happy	y	yes, yolk, onion
g	gag, get, finger	r	roar, rhyme	z	rose, size, xylophone, zebra
h	hat, who	s	miss, sauce, scene, see		
hw	which, where			zh	garage, pleasure, vision
j	judge, gem	sh	dish, ship, sugar, tissue		
k	cat, kick, school				

Vowel Sounds

ă	pat, laugh	ŏ	horrible, pot	ŭ	cut, flood, rough, some
ā	ape, aid, pay	ō	go, row, toe, though	û	circle, fur, heard, term, turn, urge, word
â	air, care, wear	ô	all, caught, for, paw		
ä	father, koala, yard	oi	boy, noise, oil		
ĕ	pet, pleasure, any	ou	cow, out	yo͝o	cure
ē	be, bee, easy, piano	o͝o	full, book, wolf	yo͞o	abuse, use
ĭ	if, pit, busy	o͞o	boot, rude, fruit, flew	ə	ago, silent, pencil, lemon, circus
ī	ride, by, pie, high				
î	dear, deer, fierce, mere				

Stress Marks

Primary Stress ´: bi·ol·o·gy [bī **ŏl´** ə jē]

Secondary Stress ´: bi·o·log·i·cal [bī´ ə **lŏj´** ĭ kəl]

Pronunciation key and definitions copyright © 2007 by Houghton Mifflin Harcourt Publishing Company. Reproduced by permission from *The American Heritage Children's Dictionary* and *The American Heritage Student Dictionary*.

A

ac·com·pa·ny (ə **kŭm′** pə nē) *v.* To go along with: *I was told to* **accompany** *them to the concert.*

ad·vanced (əd **vănst′**) *adj.* Highly developed or complex; beyond in progress: *The* **advanced** *high school student was able to take college courses.*

ad·ver·tise (**ăd′** vər tīz′) *v.* To announce to the public: *Posters sometimes* **advertise** *movies.*

af·fect (ə **fĕkt′**) *v.* To cause a change in something or someone: *Problems in the rain forest* **affect** *the animals living in it.*

af·fec·tion (ə **fĕk′** shən) *n.* A feeling of fondness or love for a person, animal, or thing: *My* **affection** *for my dog grew after he brought me the morning paper.*

a·lert (ə **lûrt′**) *adj.* Watching out for danger; attentive: *A good driver must always be* **alert.**

a·mend·ment (ə **mĕnd′** mənt) *n.* A change made to improve, correct, or add something: *An* **amendment** *to the United States Constitution limits the President to two full terms in office.*

an·gle (**ăng′** gəl) *n.* A way of looking at something: *There are many different* **angles** *from which we could film this movie.*

a·pol·o·gize (ə **pŏl′** ə jīz′) *v.* To make an apology; say one is sorry: *Did you* **apologize** *to your mother for burning the pancakes?*

ap·pre·ci·ate (ə **prē′** shē āt′) *v.* To be thankful for: *Will the child* **appreciate** *my help?*

ap·prove (ə **prōōv′**) *v.* To consent to officially: *The Senate is expected to* **approve** *the treaty.*

ar·range·ment (ə **rānj′** mənt) *n.* **1.** The act or an example of arranging; order in which things are arranged: *I studied the alphabetical* **arrangement** *of the books on the shelf.* **2.** Preparations for an undertaking; plan: *Pigeons find that living among people is a fine plan, or* **arrangement.**

as·sist (ə **sĭst′**) *v.* To give help; aid: *Did you* **assist** *him in moving the box?*

as·so·ci·a·tion (ə sō sē **ā′** shən) *n.* A group of people organized for a common purpose: *The students formed an* **association** *to help stop global warming.*

av·er·age (**ăv′** ər ĭj) *adj.* Typical or ordinary: *The* **average** *kid loves to play.*

B

ban (băn) *v.* To forbid by making illegal: *Fishing can be* **banned** *in certain areas to protect fish.*

amendment

The base word of *amendment* is the verb *amend*. It comes from the Latin word *emendare*, which means "to correct." The word *mend*, which means "to fix or repair," comes from the same Latin word root. When you *make amends*, you try to correct or mend a wrong you did to someone.

ă r**a**t / ā p**ay** / â c**a**re / ä f**a**ther / ĕ p**e**t / ē b**e** / ĭ p**i**t / ī p**ie** / î f**ie**rce / ŏ p**o**t / ō g**o** / ô p**aw**, f**or** / oi **oi**l / ŏŏ b**oo**k

bat·tle (**băt´** l) *n.* A fight between two armed forces, usually in war: *The two ants were in a **battle** over a breadcrumb.*

be·tray (bĭ **trā´**) *v.* To be unfaithful to: *When he heard the lie, Tom knew his friend had **betrayed** him.*

bi·o·log·i·cal (bī´ ə **lŏj´** ĭ kəl) *adj.* Of, relating to, or affecting living things: *She had a **biological** need to sleep.*

blar·ing (**blâr´** ĭng)) *adj.* Loud, harsh: *The concert began with a fanfare of **blaring** trumpets.*

bond (bŏnd) *n.* A force that unites; a tie: *I feel a close **bond** with my sister.*

bor·der (**bôr´** dər) *n.* The line where an area, such as a country, ends and another area begins: *The Americans had to cross the Mexican **border** on their way to South America.*

bor·row (**bŏr´** ō) *v.* To get from someone else with the understanding that what is gotten will be returned or replaced: *I want to **borrow** that toy.*

bril·liant (**brĭl´** yənt) *adj.* Very vivid in color: *The sky was a **brilliant** blue.*

bur·gla·ry (**bûr´** glə rē) *n.* The crime of breaking into a building with the intention of stealing: *The unlocked door led to many **burglaries**.*

C

cal·cu·late (**kăl´** kyə lāt´) *v.* To find by using addition, subtraction, multiplication, or division: *I **calculated** the amount of fabric I would need to make the bedspread.*

can·di·date (**kăn´** dĭ dāt´) *n.* A person who seeks or is put forward by others for an office or honor: *The **candidates** walked in the morning parade, shaking people's hands and asking for their votes.*

cap·i·tol (**kăp´** ĭ tl) *n.* The building in which a state legislature meets: *The governor went to the **capitol** to sign a bill that the legislature created.*

cap·ture (**kăp´** chər) *v.* **1.** To seize and hold, as by force or skill: *The play **captured** my imagination.* **2.** To get hold of, as by force or craft: *The enemy **captured** the general.*

cen·tu·ry (**sĕn´** chə rē) *n.* A period of 100 years: *The United States Constitution was written more than two **centuries** ago.*

cer·e·mo·ny (**sĕr´** ə mō´ nē) *n.* A formal act or series of acts performed in honor of an event or special occasion: *Our school had a graduation **ceremony** today.*

capitol

ōō b**oo**t / ou **ou**t / ŭ c**u**t / û f**u**r / hw **wh**ich / th **th**in / *th* **th**is / zh vi**s**ion / ə **a**go, sil**e**nt, penc**i**l, lem**o**n, circ**u**s

conclude
One meaning of *conclude* is "to bring to an end; close; finish." *Conclude* comes from the Latin: the prefix *com-* plus *claudere*, "to close." When you decide something or form an opinion, you *conclude* or reach a *conclusion*, bringing your thoughts to a close. The word *include* comes from the same Latin root. When you include people, you "enclose" them.

continent

cham·ber (**chām´** bər) *n.* An enclosed space in a machine or in an animal's living space; compartment: *The yellow jackets' nest was in a **chamber** in the soil next to the house.*

charge (chärj) *v.* To rush or rush at with force; attack: *The soldiers **charged** the fort.*

chief (chēf) *adj.* Most important: *The **chief** problem is to decide what to do first.*

churn·ing (**chûrn´** ĭng) *adj.* Moving forcefully: *The **churning** winds picked up dirt.*

civ·i·lized (**sĭv´** ə līzd´) *adj.* Having an advanced culture and society: *The **civilized** city had strict rules.*

clas·si·fy (**klăs´** ə fī´) *v.* To put together into groups or classes; sort: *The books were **classified** by reading level.*

clum·sy (**klŭm´** zē) *adj.* Done or made without skill: *The **clumsy** shelter fell apart.*

com·bi·na·tion (**kŏm´** bə **nā´** shən) *n.* The condition of being combined; union: *Salt and pepper make a good **combination**.*

com·fort (**kŭm´** fərt) *v.* To soothe when sad or frightened: *She tried to **comfort** the lost child.*

com·pan·ion (kəm **păn´** yən) *n.* A friend or associate: *My dog Sam was my favorite **companion**.*

con·cerned (kən **sûrnd´**) *adj.* Worried or anxious: *The **concerned** citizens went to the town meeting.*

con·clude (kən **klōōd´**) *v.* To think about something and then reach a decision or form an opinion: *I have **concluded** that the best way to make a friend is to be one.*

con·di·tion (kən **dĭsh´** ən) *n.* General health and fitness: *Athletes train before a competition so they are in good **condition**.*

con·fess (kən **fĕs´**) *v.* **1.** To admit that one has done something bad, wrong, or illegal: *This woman **confesses** to eating the apple.* **2.** To own or admit as true: *This girl **confesses**, or admits, that daily care of a dog is hard work.*

con·fi·dence (**kŏn´** fĭ dəns) *n.* Trust or faith in someone else or in something: *The coach had a brief moment of **confidence** in his team before they started losing again.*

con·flict (**kŏn´** flĭkt´) *n.* A clash or struggle, as of ideas, feelings, or interests: *The differences between the rich and the poor cause many **conflicts** about taxes.*

con·sist (kən **sĭst´**) *v.* To be made up: *The biology class today **consisted** of a pop quiz and a lecture on always doing your homework.*

ă ra**t** / ā **pay** / â **c**are / ä **f**ather / ĕ **p**et / ē be / ĭ **p**it / ī **p**ie / î **fie**rce / ŏ **p**ot / ō **go** / ô **p**aw, fo**r** / oi **oi**l / ŏŏ **b**ook

debris

con·struct (kən strŭkt´) v. To make by fitting parts together; build: *We constructed a book-case.*

con·ti·nent (kŏn´ tə nənt) n. One of the main land masses of the earth: *North America and South America are two continents.*

corps (kôr) n. A group of people acting or working together: *We belong to a drum and bugle corps.*

crisp (krĭsp) adj. Brief and clear: *It was a crisp picture in which I could see every hair on my dog's head.*

crit·ic (krĭt´ ĭk) n. A person whose work is judging the value of books, plays, or other artistic efforts: *There were many critics at the premier of the movie.*

crush (krŭsh) v. To press, squeeze, or bear down on with enough force to break or injure: *The tree fell, crushing the car.*

cus·tom (kŭs´ təm) n. Something that the members of a group usually do: *Shaking hands when meeting someone is one of many customs our society has.*

D

de·bris (də brē´) n. The scattered remains of something broken or destroyed: *The man used a bulldozer to clear away the debris after the storm.*

de·but (dā´ byōō´) n. A first public appearance, as of a performer: *The juggler had his debut on television that night.*

ded·i·cate (dĕd´ ĭ kāt´) v. To set apart for a special purpose; devote: *The scientists will dedicate themselves to research after graduating from college.*

de·fend (dĭ fĕnd´) v. **1.** To protect from attack, harm, danger, or challenge: *They defended themselves from the wolves with spears.* **2.** To support or maintain, as by argument; justify: *The child defended taking the cookie, saying he was hungry.*

de·lib·er·ate·ly (dĭ lĭb´ ər ĭt lē) adv. Done or said on purpose; intentional: *She told a lie deliberately to fool him.*

dense (dĕns) adj. Having the parts packed together closely: *I could not move in the dense crowd.*

de·ny (dĭ nī´) v. To refuse to give; withhold: *He denied the rabbit the carrot.*

de·serve (dĭ zûrv´) v. To be worthy of or have a right to; merit: *You deserve the reward.*

di·rect·ly (dĭ rĕkt´ lē) adv. In a direct line or way; straight: *My teacher is directly responsible for my interest in science.*

ōō b**oo**t / ou **ou**t / ŭ c**u**t / û f**u**r / hw **wh**ich / th **th**in / th **th**is / zh vi**s**ion / ə **a**go, sil**e**nt, penc**i**l, lem**o**n, circ**u**s

dis-

The prefix *dis-* has several senses, but its basic meaning is "not, not any." Thus *disbelieve* means "to refuse to believe" and *discomfort* means "a lack of comfort." *Dis-* comes ultimately from the Latin adverb *dis,* meaning "apart, asunder." *Dis-* is an important prefix that occurs very often in English in words such as *discredit, disrepair, disrespect,* and *disobey.*

dis·be·lief (dĭs´ bĭ **lēf´**) *n.* The refusal or unwillingness to believe: *The audience was in* **disbelief** *after the magician pulled the rabbit from the hat.*

dis·cour·aged (dĭ **skûr´** ĭjd) *adj.* Less hopeful or enthusiastic: *After getting a nail in the foot, the* **discouraged** *child stopped running barefoot.*

dis·o·bey (dĭs´ ə **bā´**) *v.* To refuse or fail to obey: *Why did you* **disobey** *a direct order to eat your spinach?*

dis·or·der·ly (dĭs **ôr´** dər lē) *adj.* Not behaving according to rules or customs; unruly: *The classroom became* **disorderly** *after the substitute teacher did not tell the students the rules.*

dis·play (dĭ **splā´**) *n.* A public showing; exhibition: *A* **display** *of moon rocks is in the museum.*

dis·pute (dĭs **pyōōt´**) *v.* To argue about; debate: *In the debate, did the students* **dispute** *the question of a dress code?*

dream (drēm) *n.* Something hoped for; aspiration: *I have a* **dream** *of world peace.*

drought (drout) *n.* A period of little or no rain: *The farmers' crops could not grow because of the* **drought.**

du·ty (dōō´ tē) *n.* The obligation to do what is right: *The president had a* **duty** *to serve his country.*

E

ef·fort (ĕf´ ərt) *n.* The use of physical or mental energy to do something: *Doing it this way will save time and* **effort.**

en·clo·sure (ĕn **klō´** zhər) *n.* An enclosed area: *I kept my pets in an* **enclosure** *made of wood.*

en·coun·ter (ĕn **koun´** tər) *n.* **1.** An often unexpected meeting with a person or thing: *I had many* **encounters** *with animals as a kid.* **2.** A hostile confrontation: *The two armies had several* **encounters** *on the battlefield.*

en·cour·age·ment (ĕn **kûr´** ĭj mənt) *n.* The act of encouraging: *He gave his son* **encouragement** *to do the right thing.*

en·deared (ĕn **dîr´**) *v.* To make beloved or very sympathetic: *The child* **endeared** *himself to everyone who met him because of his charming personality.*

en·ter·tain·ing (ĕn´ tər **tān´** ĭng) *adj.* Holding the attention in an agreeable way: *The movie was* **entertaining.**

es·cort (ĕs´ **kôrt´**) *v.* To go with as an escort: *Police* **escorted** *the senator during the parade.*

es·pe·cial·ly (ĕ **spĕsh´** ə lē) *adv.* In a special way; specifically: *These coats are designed* **especially** *for tall people.*

ă r**a**t / ā p**ay** / â c**a**re / ä f**a**ther / ĕ p**e**t / ē b**e** / ĭ p**i**t / ī p**ie** / î f**ie**rce / ŏ p**o**t / ō g**o** /
ô p**aw**, f**o**r / oi **oi**l / ōō b**oo**k

e·vap·o·rate (ĭ **văp´** ə rāt´) *v.* To change into a vapor or gas: *The water will* **evaporate** *quickly under the hot sun.*

ex·am·ple (ĭg **zăm´** pəl) *n.* Someone or something that should be copied; model: *Their courage was an* **example** *to all of us.*

ex·cess (**ĕk´** sĕs´) *adj.* More than is needed or usual: *I brushed the* **excess** *salt off my pretzel.*

ex·change (ĭks **chānj´**) *n.* A giving of one thing for another: *I did not feel that the several* **exchanges** *I had with that man were fair.*

ex·haust·ed (ĭg **zôst´** əd) *adj.* Worn out completely; tired: *I was* **exhausted** *from the long swim.*

ex·plode (ĭk **splōd´**) *v.* To burst or cause to burst with a loud noise; blow up: *The fireworks were* **exploding** *over the hotel.*

ex·traor·di·nar·y (ĭk **strôr´** dn ĕr´ ē) *adj.* Very unusual; remarkable: *Landing on the moon was an* **extraordinary** *event.*

F

faint (fānt) *v.* To lose consciousness for a short time: *She* **fainted** *after he took off his mask.*

fault (fôlt) *n.* Responsibility for a mistake or an offense: *Failing the test was my own* **fault** *because I did not study.*

fav·or (**fā´** vər) *n.* A kind or helpful act: *She granted him a* **favor.**

feast (fēst) *n.* A fancy meal; banquet: *We prepared a* **feast** *for the wedding.*

feat (fēt) *n.* An act or accomplishment that shows skill, strength, or bravery: *The gymnasts performed remarkable* **feats.**

foam·ing (**fō´** mĭng) *adj.* Full of bubbles that form in a liquid such as soap; frothing: **Foaming** *bubbles from the puppy shampoo spilled outside the tub.*

fo·cus (**fō´** kəs) *v.* To concentrate or center; fix: *I could not* **focus** *on the test.*

fos·ter (**fô´** stər) *adj.* Receiving, sharing, or giving care like that of a parent, although not related by blood or adoption: *There are three* **foster** *children in our home.*

frac·tured (**frăk´** chərd) *adj.* Broken: *The* **fractured** *television had to be thrown away.*

G

gen·er·ate (**jĕn´** ə rāt´) *v.* To bring about or produce: *Water and steam* **generated** *electricity.*

gen·u·ine (**jĕn´** yo͞o ĭn) *adj.* Sincere; honest: *They showed* **genuine** *interest in my work.*

gi·gan·tic (jī **găn´** tĭk) *adj.* Being like a giant in size, strength, or power: *Some of the dinosaurs were* **gigantic** *creatures.*

explode

Explode comes from a Latin word meaning "drive out or off by clapping." It was originally used in theatres to mean "to drive an actor off the stage by making noise."

feast

---

o͞o b**oo**t / ou **ou**t / ŭ c**u**t / û f**u**r / hw **wh**ich / th **th**in / *th* **th**is / zh vi**s**ion / ə **a**go, sil**e**nt, penc**i**l, lem**o**n, circ**u**s

glance (glăns) *v.* To take a quick look: *She glances outside to make sure it isn't snowing yet.*

glo·ri·ous (glôr´ ē əs) *adj.* Having great beauty; magnificent: *We saw a glorious sunset.*

grace·ful (grās´ fəl) *adj.* Showing grace, as in movement: *The deer is a graceful animal.*

grad·u·ate (grăj´ ōō āt´) *v.* To finish a course of study and receive a diploma: *My cousin will graduate from high school next Saturday.*

H

hab·i·tat (hăb´ ĭ tăt´) *n.* The place where a plant or animal naturally lives: *When ecosystems change, animals often have to leave their habitats.*

has·ten (hā´ sən) *v.* To move or act swiftly; hurry: *I hastened home to tell my family the news.*

haul (hôl) *v.* To move from one place to another, as with a truck: *I was hauling the bed from my house to hers when I heard the news.*

haze (hāz) *n.* Fine dust, smoke, or water vapor floating in the air: *The haze along the beach did not allow the lifeguard to see who was swimming.*

hid·e·ous (hĭd´ ē əs) *adj.* Very ugly or disgusting: *The man looked hideous after he put on the Halloween mask.*

hire (hīr) *v.* To use the work or services of; employ: *He was hired to mow the grass, but instead he fell asleep.*

hon·or (ŏn´ ər) *n.* Special respect or high regard: *We display the flag to show honor to the United States.*

ho·ri·zon (hə rī´ zən) *n.* The line along which the earth and the sky appear to meet: *The sun dropped beneath the horizon and the day grew into the night.*

hor·ri·fy (hôr´ rə fī´) *v.* To surprise unpleasantly: *The farmer was horrified to find his cows in the neighbor's field.*

hud·dle (hŭd´ l) *v.* To crowd close or put close together: *We huddled around the campfire to keep warm.*

I

im·mense (ĭ mĕns´) *adj.* Of great size, extent, or degree: *Antarctica is covered by an immense sheet of ice.*

in·ci·dent (ĭn´ sĭ dənt) *n.* An event that causes trouble: *The newspaper reported the fire incident.*

in·clude (ĭn klōōd´) *v.* To put into a group, set, or total: *She was included in the kids' package even though she was too old.*

graduate

graduate
Graduate comes from the Latin word root *gradus,* meaning "step." The word *grade,* meaning a slope that changes a little at a time, also comes from the same word root. *Gradual,* which means "occurring in small steps over time," is another related word.

ă rat / ā **pay** / â **care** / ä **father** / ĕ **pet** / ē **be** / ĭ **pit** / ī **pie** / î **fie**rce / ŏ **pot** / ō g**o** / ô p**aw, fo**r / oi **oil** / ōō b**oo**k

in·de·pend·ent (ĭn´ dĭ **pĕn´** dənt) *adj.* Not dependent: *My brother is not **independent** of mom and dad. He receives a monthly check to help pay his rent.*

in·formed (ĭn **fôrmd´**) *adj.* Having or prepared with information or knowledge: *The **informed** driver knew the correct directions to the city.*

in·jus·tice (ĭn **jŭs´** tĭs) *n.* Unfair treatment of a person or thing: *They protested the **injustice** of not having a snow day.*

in·no·cent (ĭn´ ə sənt) *adj.* Not guilty of a crime or fault: *The jury found them **innocent**.*

in·sep·a·ra·ble (ĭn **sĕp´** ər ə bəl) *adj.* Impossible to separate or part: *The two best friends were **inseparable**.*

in·sert (ĭn´ **sûrt´**) *v.* To put, set, or fit into: ***Insert** the key in the lock.*

in·sist (ĭn **sĭst´**) *v.* To demand: *I **insisted** on going to the beach.*

in·spec·tor (ĭn **spĕk´** tôr) *n.* A person who makes inspections: *The **inspector** found mold in the walls.*

in·tel·li·gent (ĭn **tĕl´** ə jənt) *adj.* Having or showing the ability to learn, think, understand, and know: *The **intelligent** man read the whole book in five minutes.*

in·tend (ĭn **tĕnd´**) *v.* To have in mind as an aim or goal; plan: *He **intends** to bake his friend a cake for her birthday.*

in·ter·pret·er (ĭn **tûr´** prĭ tər) *n.* A person who translates orally from one language to another: *An **interpreter** was needed to find out what the foreign president was saying.*

in·tro·duce (ĭn´ trə **doōs´**) *v.* To bring or put in something new or different: *Will you **introduce** the cat to the dog?*

in·trud·er (ĭn´ **troōd´** ər) *n.* A person who intrudes, especially into a building, with criminal intent: *I called the police after the **intruder** refused to leave my house.*

in·vis·i·ble (ĭn **vĭz´** ə bəl) *adj.* Not capable of being seen; not visible: *Air is **invisible**.*

J

jeal·ous (jĕl´ əs) *adj.* Having a bad feeling toward another person who is a competitor; envious: *Were you **jealous** of the winner?*

jolt (jōlt) *n.* A feeling or something that causes a feeling of sudden shock or surprise: *The audience felt a **jolt** every time the car turned a corner in the movie.*

invisible
The word *invisible* comes from the Latin prefix *in-* ("not") and the Latin word root *vis*, meaning "sight." *Visual*, "relating to the sense of sight"; *visible*, "able to be seen"; *envision*, "to picture in the mind"; and *television*, "a device that receives and reproduces visual images" all contain the word root *vis*.

oō b**oo**t / ou **ou**t / ŭ c**u**t / û f**u**r / hw **wh**ich / th **th**in / *th* **th**is / zh vi**s**ion / ə **a**go, sil**e**nt, penc**i**l, lem**o**n, circ**u**s

L

land·mark (lănd´ märk´) *n.* A familiar or easily seen object or building that marks or identifies a place: *The Golden Gate Bridge is a landmark of San Francisco.*

lap (lăp) *v.* To wash or splash with a light, slapping sound: *The waves lapped at his feet as he stared across the ocean.*

leg·is·la·ture (lĕj´ ĭs lā´ chər) *n.* A body of people with the power to make and change laws: *The legislature made a law that forced people to throw away their trash.*

lo·cal (lō´ kəl) *adj.* Of a certain limited area or place: *The town has its own local government.*

lure (loŏr) *v.* To attract by offering something tempting: *He can lure the mouse out of the hole with cheese.*

miniature

M

me·chan·i·cal (mə kăn´ ĭ kəl) *adj.* Of or relating to machines or tools: *It takes mechanical skill to repair a clock.*

mem·o·ra·ble (mĕm´ ər ə bəl) *adj.* Worthy of being remembered: *Our class trip to the circus was a memorable event.*

men·tion (mĕn´ shən) *v.* To speak of or write about briefly: *I mentioned my idea during class.*

min·i·a·ture (mĭn´ ē ə chər) *adj.* Much smaller than the usual size: *We have a miniature train.*

mis·judge (mĭs jŭj´) *v.* To judge wrongly: *I misjudged the distance to the boat and fell into the ocean.*

mod·el (mŏd´ l) *adj.* Serving as a model: *Since we have to move, we looked at a number of model homes.*

mois·ture (mois´ chər) *n.* Liquid, as water, that is present in the air or in the ground or that forms tiny drops on a surface: *I wiped away the moisture on the window so I could see outside.*

mood (moōd) *n.* A person's state of mind: *Playing with my friends puts me in a happy mood.*

mourn·ful (môrn´ fəl) *adj.* Feeling, showing, or causing grief; sad: *The mournful owner buried his dog in the back of the yard.*

N

na·ture (nā´ chər) *n.* The basic character or quality of a person or thing: *She has a friendly nature.*

neg·a·tive (nĕg´ ə tĭv) *adj.* Lacking in positive qualities such as enthusiasm and hope: *Your negative attitude is not helping you to make friends.*

noc·tur·nal (nŏk tûr´ nəl) *adj.* Active at night: *Owls are nocturnal birds.*

ă rat / ā pay / â care / ä father / ĕ pet / ē be / ĭ pit / ī pie / î fierce / ŏ pot / ō go / ô paw, for / oi oil / oŏ book

nour·ish·ing (**nûr´** ĭsh ĭng) *adj.* Helping to promote life, growth, or strength: *The vitamins were parts of a **nourishing** diet.*

nu·mer·ous (**no͞o´** mər əs) *adj.* Including or made up of a large number: *They have **numerous** problems.*

O

ob·serve (əb **zûrv´**) *v.* To say; remark: *"This hot dog is tasty," the man **observes**.*

ob·sta·cle (**ŏb´** stə kəl) *n.* Something that blocks or stands in the way: *Fallen rocks and other obstacles made it impossible to use the road.*

op·por·tu·ni·ty (ŏp´ ər **to͞o´** nĭ tē) *or* (ŏp´ ər **tyo͞o´** nĭ tē) *n.* A good chance, as to advance oneself: *That summer job offers many **opportunities**.*

or·gan·ism (**ôr´** gə nĭz´ əm) *n.* An individual form of life, such as a plant or animal: *On the field trip, we looked at sea **organisms** under the microscope.*

out·cast (**out´** kăst´) *n.* A person blocked from participation in a group or society: *Stormy felt like an **outcast** because he had outgrown Cape Cod.*

o·ver·come (ō´ vər **kŭm´**) *v.* To get the better of; conquer: *I had to **overcome** my fear of heights to climb the mountain.*

P

pa·tient·ly (**pā´** shənt lē) *adv.* Putting up with trouble, hardship, annoyance, or delay without complaining: *He waited **patiently** for his food to arrive.*

pe·cu·liar (pĭ **kyo͞ol´** yər) *adj.* Not usual; strange or odd: *I smell a **peculiar** odor.*

per·form (pər **fôrm´**) *v.* To carry out; do: *She **performs** very well onstage after a lot of practice.*

per·mis·sion (pər **mĭsh´** ən) *n.* Consent granted by someone in authority: *Our parents gave us **permission** to go to the movies.*

pol·i·tics (**pŏl´** ĭ tĭks´) *n.* The science, art, or work of government: *My father felt **politics** got in the way of people doing their regular jobs.*

poll (pōl) *n.* Often **polls**. The place where votes are cast: *I went to the **polls** to vote for the President of the United States.*

pos·i·tive (**pŏz´** ĭ tĭv) *adj.* Having no doubts; sure: *I'm **positive** that we've met before.*

pos·ses·sion (pə **zĕsh´** ən) *n.* Something that is owned; belonging: *They fled the burning building, leaving their **possessions** behind.*

pounce (pouns) *v.* To seize swiftly or as if by swooping: *The kitten **pounced** on the ball.*

---

o͞o b**oo**t / ou **ou**t / ŭ c**u**t / û f**u**r / hw **wh**ich / th **th**in / *th* **th**is / zh vi**si**on / ə **a**go, sil**e**nt, penc**i**l, lem**o**n, circ**u**s

pre·fer (prĭ fûr´) *v.* To like better: *I preferred dancing to jogging.*

pre·pare (prĭ pâr´) *v.* To put together the ingredients of: *I prepare my lunch each morning.*

pres·ence (prĕz´ əns) *n.* The fact or condition of being present: *Your presence is not required.*

pri·or (prī´ ər) *adj.* Coming before in time or order; earlier: *Tell me about your prior grades.*

prog·ress (prŏg´ rĕs´) *n.* Steady improvement: *After I passed the test, I realized I was making very good progress.*

pro·mote (prə mōt´) *v.* To try to sell or make popular, as by advertising; publicize: *Television ads promote many products.*

prompt·ly (prŏmpt´ lē) *adv.* Done or given without delay: *I promptly sent my message.*

proof (proof) *n.* Evidence of truth or accuracy: *We have no proof that the money was stolen.*

prop·er·ly (prŏp´ ər lē) *adv.* In a proper manner: *Jim did not hold his fork properly.*

pro·pose (prə pōz´) *v.* To put forward for consideration; suggest: *I proposed a trip to Florida. We went to Ohio instead.*

pub·lic·i·ty (pŭ blĭs´ ĭ tē) *n.* Information that is given out to let the public know about something or to get its approval: *There was no publicity for the new movie, so few people watched it.*

R

rack·et (răk´ ĭt) *n.* A loud, unpleasant noise: *The several parrots outside my window made a racket this morning.*

ra·di·a·tion (rā´ dē ā´ shən) *n.* Energy that travels through space as rays or waves: *Sunscreen helps protect people from the sun's radiation.*

re·call (rĭ kôl´) *v.* To bring back to mind; remember: *I can't recall their phone number.*

ref·er·ence (rĕf´ ər əns) *adj.* A book, such as an encyclopedia or dictionary, that gives special information arranged according to a plan or system: *This book has a reference glossary.*

re·fuse (rĭ fyōoz´) *v.* To decline to do or give: *The cat refused to go out in the snow.*

re·gret·ful·ly (rĭ grĕt´ fə lē) *adv.* Full of regret: *Looking down regretfully, she cancelled the party.*

re·in·force (rē´ ĭn fôrs´) *v.* To make stronger with more material, help, or support: *The construction crew will reinforce this building with a single beam.*

re·ly (rĭ lī´) *v.* To be dependent for support, help, or supply: *I relied on my brother to give me money for dinner.*

ă rat / ā pay / â care / ä father / ĕ pet / ē be / ĭ pit / ī pie / î fierce / ŏ pot / ō go / ô paw, for / oi oil / ōo book

rep·u·ta·tion (rĕp´ yə tā´ shən) *n.* The general worth or quality of someone or something as judged by others or by the general public: *The senator has a very good* **reputation.**

res·cue (rĕs´ kyōō) *v.* To save from danger or harm: *Lifeguards learn how to* **rescue** *swimmers.*

re·source (rē´ sôrs´) *or* (rĭ sôrs´) *n.* Something that is a source of wealth to a country: *Our forests and trees are great natural* **resources.**

re·ward (rĭ wôrd´) *v.* To give a reward for or to: *The son* **rewarded** *his mother with breakfast in bed.*

route (rōōt) *n.* A road or lane of travel between two places: *The hikers climbed the mountain, using a well-known* **route.**

rub·ble (rŭb´ əl) *n.* Broken or crumbled material, as brick, that is left when a building falls down: *The building exploded and left* **rubble** *everywhere.*

ru·in (rōō´ ĭn) *v.* To damage beyond repair; wreck: *She* **ruined** *the clay castle by stepping on it.*

S

sat·is·fy (săt´ ĭs fī´) *v.* To fulfill or gratify: *The steak* **satisfied** *my hunger.*

scarce (skârs) *adj.* Not enough to meet a demand: *Food is* **scarce** *in many countries.*

sched·ule (skĕj´ ōol) *n.* A program of events, appointments, or classes: *We have a full* **schedule** *of activities after school.*

scheme (skēm) *n.* A plan or plot for doing something: *He created a* **scheme** *to break out of prison.*

sea·far·ing (sē´ fâr´ ĭng) *adj.* Earning one's living at sea: *The* **seafaring** *life of a fisherman is dangerous.*

seg·re·ga·tion (sĕg´ rĭ gā´ shən) *n.* The act of segregating or the condition of being segregated: *Laws on* **segregation** *once kept African Americans and white Americans separate.*

sen·si·tive (sĕn´ sĭ tĭv) *adj.* Easily affected, influenced, or hurt: *Don't be so* **sensitive** *to criticism.*

shal·low (shăl´ ō) *adj.* Measuring little from bottom to top or from back to front; not deep: *The fish swam in the* **shallow** *end of the river.*

short·age (shôr´ tĭj) *n.* An amount of something that is not enough: *We donate items to a food pantry when there is a food* **shortage.**

reference

ōō **b**oot / ou **out** / ŭ **cut** / û **fur** / hw **which** / th **thin** / *th* **this** / zh **vision** / ə **ago,** sil**e**nt, penc**i**l, lem**o**n, circ**u**s

sit·u·a·tion (sĭch´ o͞o ā´ shən) *n.*
A set of circumstances: *The child
knew he was in a bad* **situation**
*when his mother caught him with
his hand in the cookie jar.*

slab (slăb) *n.* A broad, flat, thick
piece, as of bread, stone, or meat:
My mother threw a **slab** *of steak
on the grill to cook.*

sli·my (slī´ mē) *adj.* Like slime
in appearance or texture: *The*
slimy *mud made him slip.*

smear (smîr) *v.* To become
spread or blurred: *The ink*
smeared *easily.*

so·cial (sō´ shəl) *adj.* Living
together in communities or
groups: *Bees and ants are* **social**
insects.

spe·cies (spē´ shēz´) *n.* A group
of animals or plants that are
similar and are able to mate and
have offspring: *Scientists discover new* **species** *of sea life in
the deepest ocean.*

spec·u·late (spĕk´ yə lāt´) *v.* To
think deeply; ponder; reflect: *I*
speculated *on whether to have
fries or mashed potatoes.*

stan·dard (stăn´ dərd) *n.*
Something that is accepted as a
basis for measuring or as a rule or
model: *Americans have
different* **standards** *of living than
the Japanese.*

stor·age (stôr´ ĭj) *n.* A space or
place for storing things: *I kept
my belongings in* **storage** *when I
went away.*

strand (strănd) *v.* To leave in
a difficult or helpless position:
They were **stranded** *on the mountain when their car broke down.*

streak (strēk) *v.* To mark or
become marked with streaks:
The light seemed to **streak** *across
the sky.*

stub·born (stŭb´ ərn) *adj.*
1. Continuing to exist; lasting:
I have the **stubborn** *idea that
I want to be a teacher when I
grow up.* **2.** Unyielding; difficult
to deal with: *A* **stubborn** *stain
ruined the tablecloth.*

stu·di·o (sto͞o´ dē ō´) *n.* The
place where an artist works: *The
artist was working on his
painting in his* **studio.**

suf·fer (sŭf´ ər) *v.* To feel pain
or distress: *The drought victims*
suffered *from malnutrition.*

sug·gest (səg jĕst´) *v.* To offer
for consideration or action: *I*
suggest *going to a movie tonight.*

su·pe·ri·or (so͞o pîr´ ē ər) *adj.*
Considering oneself better than
others; conceited: *Don't take
a* **superior** *attitude toward the
younger students.*

sup·plies (sə plīz´) *n.* Necessary
materials used or given out when
needed: *After a month of bad
weather, the explorers'* **supplies**
ran out.

storage

ă rat / ā pay / â care / ä father / ĕ pet / ē be / ĭ pit / ī pie / î fierce / ŏ pot / ō go /
ô paw, for / oi oil / o͞o book

sus·pect (səs′ pĕkt′) *n.* A person suspected, as of a crime: *When I was a child, I was always the* **suspect** *when anything broke.*

swell (swĕl) *v.* **1.** To increase in size or volume as a result of internal pressure; expand: *The injured ankle* **swelled. 2.** To increase in force, size, number, or degree: *The army* **swelled** *from 100 soldiers to 150 soldiers.*

sym·bol (sĭm′ bəl) *n.* **1.** Something that stands for or represents something else: *The dove is a* **symbol** *of peace.* **2.** A printed or written sign used to represent an operation, action, quantity, and the like: *A red traffic light is a* **symbol** *to stop.*

T

tal·ent (tăl′ ənt) *n.* A natural ability to do something well: *If you stop taking music lessons, you'll waste your* **talent.**

tar·get (tär′ gĭt) *adj.* Established goal: *The* **target** *date for finishing our report was May 6th.*

tempt (tĕmpt) *v.* To appeal strongly to; attract: *Your offer* **tempted** *me to leave the office.*

ten·e·ment (tĕn′ ə mənt) *n.* An old apartment house that is badly maintained: *My grandfather grew up in a* **tenement** *that had holes in the roof.*

ter·ri·to·ry (tĕr′ ĭ tôr′ ē) *n.* An area of land; region: *I have never* been to any **territory** *south of the equator.*

thrill·ing (thrĭl′ ĭng) *adj.* Exciting: *The movie was* **thrilling.**

tid·al (tīd′l) *adj.* Relating to or affected by tides: *An earthquake can cause a* **tidal** *wave.*

tim·ber (tĭm′ bər) *n.* A long, heavy piece of wood for building; beam: *The carpenter laid down several* **timbers** *that he was going to use to build the house.*

tour (to͝or) *v.* To go on a tour: *We* **toured** *through Spain.*

tow·er (tou′ ər) *v.* To rise very high: *The basketball hoop* **towered** *over the child.*

trace (trās) *n.* A very small amount: *After Julian ate the candy bar, there were* **traces** *of chocolate on his fingers.*

trans·fer (trăns fûr′) *v.* To cause to move from one place to another: *Who* **transfers** *the money from the house to the bank?*

trans·port (trăns pôrt′) *v.* To carry from one place to another: *Can you* **transport** *this box to China?*

trem·ble (trĕm′ bəl) *v.* To shake: *He* **trembles** *in the winter when he doesn't wear a hat.*

tri·umph (trī′ əmf) *n.* The fact of being victorious: *Becoming a star is a* **triumph** *most performance artists long for.*

trans-
The prefix *trans-* comes from the Latin preposition *trans,* meaning "across, beyond, through." Many common English words begin with *trans-* and have base words from Latin: *transfer, transfuse, translate, transmit, transpire,* and *transport.* Another large group of words has *trans-* in combination with English adjectives, as in *transatlantic, transcontinental,* and *transoceanic,* meaning "across" or "through" a particular geographic element.

ō͞o b**oo**t / ou **ou**t / ŭ c**u**t / û f**u**r / hw **wh**ich / th **th**in / th **th**is / zh vi**s**ion / ə **a**go, sil**e**nt, penc**i**l, lem**o**n, circ**u**s

U

un·spoiled (un spoyld) *adj.* To be not lessened or diminished by flaws or imperfections: *The snow was **unspoiled** until Jimmy made a snow angel.*

ut·ter (ŭt′ ər) *v.* To express out loud: *Did she **utter** a sigh of relief after the test?*

V

van·ish (văn′ ĭsh) *v.* To disappear or become invisible: *My smile **vanished** when I heard the bad news.*

va·ri·e·ty (və rī′ ĭ tē) *n.* A number of different things within the same group or category: *The market sells a **variety** of bread.*

vast (văst) *adj.* Very great in area; huge: *The Amazon River flows through a **vast** rain forest.*

vi·o·lence (vī′ ə ləns) *n.* The use of physical force to cause damage or injury: *The **violence** of war caused many to die.*

vi·sion (vĭzh′ ən) *n.* A mental picture produced by the imagination: *I had a **vision** of a pink elephant bouncing on a trampoline.*

W

war·ri·or (wôr′ ē ər) *n.* A person who is involved or experienced in war or fighting: *The **warrior** went to battle without armor.*

waste (wāst) *n.* The act of wasting or the condition of being wasted: *If you aren't going to read the newspaper, you should recycle it. It would be such a **waste** if you do not.*

wealth·y (wĕl′ thē) *adj.* Having wealth; rich: *She came from a **wealthy** family.*

wea·ri·ness (wîr′ ē nĕs) *n.* Temporary loss of strength and energy resulting from hard physical or mental work: *Chasing the dog for hours caused great **weariness**.*

wel·comed (wĕl′ kəmd) *adj.* Greeted, received, or accepted with pleasure: *She was a **welcomed** visitor.*

wor·thy (wûr′ thē) *adj.* Having merit or value: *We contribute to **worthy** causes.*

wreck·age (rĕk′ ĭj) *n.* The remains of something that has been wrecked: *The **wreckage** of the car was hauled away.*

Y

yank (yăngk) *v.* To pull with a sudden, sharp movement: *We **yanked** the heavy door open.*

yearn·ing (yûr′ nĭng) *n.* A deep longing or strong desire: *Grandfather felt a **yearning** to visit his childhood home in the mountains.*

ă rat / ā pay / â care / ä father / ĕ pet / ē be / ĭ pit / ī pie / î fierce / ŏ pot / ō go / ô paw, for / oi oil / o͞o book

Acknowledgments

Main Literature Selections

"Ancestors of Tomorrow/Futuros ancestros" from *Iguanas in the Snow and Other Winter Poems/Iguanas en la nieve y otras poemas de invierno* by Francisco X. Alarcón. Copyright © 2001 by Francisco X. Alarcón. Reprinted by permission of the publisher, Children's Book Press, San Francisco, CA, www.childrensbookpress.org.

Antarctic Journal: Four Months at the Bottom of the World written and illustrated by Jennifer Owings Dewey. Copyright © 2001 by Jennifer Owings Dewey. Reprinted by permission of Houghton Mifflin Harcourt Publishing Company and Kirchoff/Wohlberg, Inc.

Because of Winn-Dixie by Kate DiCamillo. Copyright © 2000 by Kate DiCamillo. Reprinted by permission of the publisher Candlewick Press Inc., and Listening Library, a division of Random House, Inc.

"Over 5,000 attend Chinatown Center's 1-Year Anniversary & Moon Festival Celebration." Copyright © 2007 by Tan International Group, Ltd. Reprinted by permission of Red Velvet Events, Inc. on behalf of Tan International Group, Ltd.

Coming Distractions: Questioning Movies by Frank E. Baker. Copyright © 2007 by Capstone Press. All rights reserved. Reprinted by permission of Capstone Press.

Dear Mr. Winston by Ken Roberts. Copyright © 2001 by Ken Roberts. Reprinted by permission of Groundwood Books Limited, Toronto.

"Dreams" from *The Collected Poems of Langston Hughes* by Langston Hughes, edited by Arnold Rampersad with David Roessel, Associate Editor, copyright © 1994 by The Estate of Langston Hughes. Reprinted by permission of Alfred A. Knopf, a division of Random House, Inc., and Harold Ober Associates, Inc.

"The Dream Keeper" from *The Collected Poems of Langston Hughes* by Langston Hughes, edited by Arnold Rampersad with David Roessel, Associate Editor, copyright © 1994 by The Estate of Langston Hughes. Reprinted by permission of Alfred A. Knopf, a division of Random House, Inc., and Harold Ober Associates, Inc.

The Earth Dragon Awakes: The San Francisco Earthquake of 1906 by Laurence Yep. Copyright © 2006 by Laurence Yep. All rights reserved. Reprinted by permission of HarperCollins Publishers and Curtis Brown, Ltd.

Ecology for Kids by Federico Arana. Originally published as *Ecologia para los ninos*. Text copyright © 1994 by Federico Arana. Text © 1994 by Editorial Joaquin Mortiz, S.A. DE C.V. Reprinted by permission of Editorial Planeta Mexicana, S.A. DE C.V.

The Ever-Living Tree: The Life and Times of a Coast Redwood by Linda Vieira, illustrations by Christopher Canyon. Copyright © 1994 by Linda Vieira. Illustrations copyright © 1994 by Christopher Canyon. All rights reserved. Reprinted by permission of Walker & Company.

"First Recorded 6,000-Year-Old Tree in America" from *A Burst of Firsts* by J. Patrick Lewis. Published by Dial Books for Young Readers. Copyright © 2001 by J. Patrick Lewis. Reprinted by permission of Curtis Brown, Ltd.

The Fun They Had by Isaac Asimov. Copyright © 1957 by Isaac Asimov from Isaac Asimov: The Complete Stories of Vol. 1 by Isaac Asimov. Reprinted by permission of Doubleday, a division of Random House, Inc.

"Giant Sequoias/Secoyas gigantes" from *Iguanas in the Snow and Other Winter Poems/Iguanas en la nieve y otras poemas de invierno* by Francisco X. Alarcón. Copyright © 2001 by Francisco X. Alarcón. Reprinted by permission of Children's Book Press, San Francisco, CA, www.childrensbookpress.org.

Harvesting Hope: The Story of Cesar Chavez by Kathleen Krull, illustrated by Yuyi Morales. Text copyright © 2003 by Kathleen Krull. Illustrations copyright © 2003 by Yuyi Morales. Reprinted by permission of Houghton Mifflin Harcourt Publishing Company and Writer's House, LLC, acting as agent for the author.

How Tía Lola Came to (Visit) Stay by Julia Alvarez. Copyright © 2001 by Julia Alvarez. Published by Dell Yearling and in hardcover by Alfred A. Knopf Children's Books, a division of Random House, New York. Reprinted by permission of the Susan Bergholz Literary Services, New York, NY and Lamy, NM. All rights reserved.

I Could Do That! Esther Morris Gets Women to Vote by Linda Arms White, illustrated by Nancy Carpenter. Text copyright © 2005 by Linda Arms White. Illustrations copyright © 2005 by Nancy Carpenter. Reprinted by permission of Farrar, Straus & Giroux LLC.

José! Born to Dance By Susanna Reich, illustrated by Raúl Colón. Text copyright © 2005 by Susanna Reich. Illustrations copyright © 2005 by Raúl Colón. All rights reserved. Reprinted by permission of Simon & Schuster Books for Young Readers, an Imprint of Simon & Schuster Inc., and Adams Literary.

The Life and Times of the Ant written and illustrated by Charles Micucci. Copyright © 2003 by Charles Micucci. All rights reserved. Reprinted by permission of Houghton Mifflin Harcourt Publishing Company.

"Lightning Bolt" *from Flicker Flash* by Joan Bransfield Graham. Copyright © 1999 by Joan Bransfield Graham. Reprinted by permission of Houghton Mifflin Harcourt Publishing Company.

Excerpt from "Lines Written for Gene Kelly to Dance To" from *Wind Song* by Carl Sandburg. Copyright © 1960 Carl Sandburg and renewed 1998 by Margaret Sandburg, Janet Sandburg, and Helga Sandburg Crile. Reprinted by permission of Houghton Mifflin Harcourt Publishing Company.

Me and Uncle Romie: A Story Inspired by the Life and Art of Romare Bearden by Claire Hartfield, illustrated by Jerome Lagarrigue. Text copyright © 2002 by Claire Hartfield. Illustrations copyright © 2002 by Jerome Lagarrigue. Reprinted by permission of Dial Books for Young Readers, a Division of Penguin Young Readers Group, A Member of Penguin Group (USA) Inc., 345 Hudson Street, New York, NY 10014. All rights reserved.

Moon Runner by Carolyn Marsden. Copyright © 2005 by Carolyn Marsden. Reprinted by permission of the publisher Candlewick Press Inc.

My Brother Martin: A Sister Remembers Growing Up with the Rev. Dr. Martin Luther King Jr. by Christine King Farris, illustrated by Chris Soentpiet. Text copyright © 2003 by Christine King Farris. Illustrations copyright © 2003 by Chris Soentpiet. Reprinted by the permission of The Permissions Company and Simon & Schuster Books for Young Readers, an imprint of Simon & Schuster Children's Publishing Division.

Once Upon a Cool Motorcycle Dude by Kevin O'Malley, illustrated by Kevin O'Malley, Carol Heyer, and Scott Goto. Text copyright © 2005 by Kevin O'Malley. Illustrations copyright © Kevin O'Malley, Carol Heyer, and Scott Goto. All rights reserved. Reprinted by permission of Walker & Company.

Owen and Mzee by Isabella Hatkoff, Craig Hatkoff, and Dr. Paula Kahumbu, photographs by Peter Greste. Copyright © 2006 by Turtle Pond Publications, LLC and Lafarge Eco Systems, Ltd. Photographs copyright © 2006, 2005 by Peter Greste. All rights reserved. Reprinted by permission of Scholastic Press, an imprint of Scholastic Inc., and Turtle Pond Publications, LLC.

"Race Day" excerpted from *Ice Marathon 2006*, by Evgeniy Gorkov. Text and photographs © 2006 by Evgeniy Gorkov. http://run.gorkov.org/antarctica2006.html. Reprinted by permission of the author.

Riding Freedom by Pam Muñoz Ryan. Text copyright © 1998 by Pam Muñoz Ryan. Reprinted by permission of Scholastic Press, a division of Scholastic Inc.

The Right Dog for the Job: Ira's Path from Service Dog to Guide Dog by Dorothy Hinshaw Patent, photographs by William Muñoz. Copyright © 2004 by Dorothy Hinshaw Patent. Photographs copyright © 2004 by William Muñoz. All rights reserved. Reprinted by permission of Walker & Company.

Sacagawea by Lise Erdrich, illustrated by Julie Buffalohead. Text copyright © 2003 by Lise Erdrich. Illustrations copyright © 2003 by Julie Buffalohead All rights reserved. Reprinted by permission of Carolrhoda Books, a division of Lerner Publishing Group, Inc.

"The Screech Owl Who Liked Television" from *The Tarantula in My Purse and 172 Other Wild Pets* by Jean Craighead George. Copyright © 1996 by Jean Craighead George. Reprinted by permission of HarperCollins Publishers and Curtis Brown, Ltd.

"The Song of the Night" by Leslie D. Perkins from *Song and Dance*, published by Simon & Schuster.

"Stormalong" from *American Tall Tales*, by Mary Pope Osbourne. Text copyright © 1991 by Mary Pope Osbourne. Reprinted by permission of Alfred A. Knopf, a division of Random House, Inc.

"Three/Quarters Time" from *Those Who Rode the Night Winds* by Nikki Giovanni. Copyright © 1983 by Nikki Giovanni. Reprinted by permission of HarperCollins Publishers.

"To You" from *The Collected Poems of Langston Hughes* by Langston Hughes, edited by Arnold Rampersad with David Roessel, Associated Editor, copyright © 1994 by The Estate of Langston Hughes. Reprinted by permission of Alfred A. Knopf, a division of Random House, Inc., and Harold Ober Associates, Inc.

"Weather" from *Always Wondering* by Aileen Fisher. Copyright © 1991 by Aileen Fisher. Reprinted by permission of the Boulder Public Library Foundation, Inc., c/o Marian Reiner, Literary Agent.

"Weatherbee's Diner" from *Flamingos on the Roof* by Calef Brown. Copyright © 2006 by Calef Brown. Reprinted by permission of Houghton Mifflin Harcourt Publishing Company and Dunham Literary as agent of the author.

The World According to Humphrey by Betty G. Birney. Copyright © 2004 by Betty G. Birney. Reprinted by permission of G. P. Putnam's Sons, A Division of Penguin Young Readers Group, A Member of Penguin Group (USA) Inc., and Faber & Faber, Ltd.

Credits

Photo Credits

TOC Norbert Wu/Getty Images; **TOC** Three Lions/Getty Images; **TOC** Alan and Sandy Carey/Photo Researchers Inc.; **TOC** Travis Rowan/Alamy; **TOC** Creatas Images/Jupiter Images; **TOC** Courtesy of the Pebbles Project, www.pebblesproject.org; **TOC** Yellow Dog Productions/Getty Images; **TOC** © CORBIS; **TOC** © Bettmann/CORBIS; **TOC** ©SHOUT/Alamy; **TOC** Diane Ferlatte; **TOC** © Robbie Jack/Corbis; **TOC** © Royalty-Free/CORBIS; **TOC** GoodShoot/SuperStock; **TOC** © Mapi/age fotostock; **TOC** Richard Donovan/www.IceMarathon.com; **TOC** © Buddy Mays/Corbis; **TOC** © Bettmann/CORBIS; **2** (bl) Yellow Dog Productions/Getty Images; **8** b © Buddy Mays/Corbis; **9** c ©Jeff Greenberg/ The Image Works; **9** c © Oote Boe Photography / Alamy; **17** c © Charles Bowma/age fotostock; **18** tl Yellow Dog Productions/Getty Images; **18** cl Juan Silva/Getty Images; **18** cr Butch Martin/Alamy; **18** bl Image Source Black/Getty Images; **18** br Creatas Images/Jupiter Images; **19** tl Blend Images/Alamy; **19** tc © Myrleen Ferguson Cate/PhotoEdit; **19** tr © Brian Pieters/Masterfile; **19** bl © Hill Street Studios/AgeFotostock; **19** bc Terry Vine/Getty Images; **19** br © Terry Vine/age fotostock; **20-21** © Andersen Ross/Blend Images/Corbis; **22** © Kate DiCamillo; **23** "BECAUSE OF WINN-DIXIE"©2005 Twentieth Century Fox. All rights reserved.; **24** "BECAUSE OF WINN- DIXIE"©2005 Twentieth Century Fox. All rights reserved.; **25** "BECAUSE OF WINN- DIXIE"©2005 Twentieth Century Fox. All rights reserved.; **27** "BECAUSE OF WINN- DIXIE"©2005 Twentieth Century Fox. All rights reserved.; **29** "BECAUSE OF WINN- DIXIE"©2005 Twentieth Century Fox. All rights reserved.; **31** "BECAUSE OF WINN- DIXIE"©2005 Twentieth Century Fox. All rights reserved.; **32** "BECAUSE OF WINN- DIXIE"©2005 Twentieth Century Fox. All rights reserved.; **33** (br) PhotoDisc / Getty Images; **34** br Purestock/Getty Images; **34** tl Yellow Dog Productions/Getty Images; **35** Yellow Dog Productions/Getty Images; **36** © Houghton Mifflin Company/School Division; **37** c © Frank Siteman / PhotoEdit; **37** b Getty Images/Stockdisc Premium; **37** tr

Illustration

Cover Brandon Dorman. **5** (bl) © Scott Goto; **7** (tml) Ann Boyajian; **8** (ml, b) Peter Grosshauser, (b) Tim Bower; **9** (ml) Gerardo Suzan, (bl) Linda Bronson; **10** (bl) Lisa Perrett; **12** (ml) Jackie Stafford-Snider, (bl) Renee Graef, (bc) Alan Flinn. **17** Sally Vitsky; **38–39** Rob McClurken; **63** (mr) Kristine Walsh; **63** (tr) Lesley Withrow; **64** Rob McClurken; **72–81** David Diaz **83** Lesley Withrow; **85** Lesley Withrow; **86** Rob McClurken; **115** LesleyWithrow; **116** Rob McClurken. **116** Rob McClurken; **122** Ortelius Design Inc; **134–137** © Scott Goto; **138** Rob McClurken **143** Sally Vitsky; **144** Tim Johnson **148** Argosy **168–169** Rob McClurken **191** Ken Bowser; **192** Rob McClurken **214–217** Ann Boyajian **218–219** Rob McClurken **226–237** Andy Hammond **241** Tim Johnson **242–243** Rob McClurken **265** Lesley Withrow **266** Rob McClurken **270** Sally Vitsky. **272** Sally Vitsky; **278–291** Tim Bowers **292–295** Peter Grosshauser **296–297** Rob McClurken; **304–315** Yuan Lee. **316–317** Patrick Gnan; **318–319** Patrick Gann; **320–321** Rob McClurken; **326** Susan Carlson. **341** Ortelius Design Inc; **343** Daniel Delvalle; **344–345** Rob McClurken; **366–368** Gerardo Suzan; **370** Rob McClurken; **390–391** Linda Bronson. **392** Sally Vitsky; **394–395** Rob McClurken; **398** Sally Vitsky; **400** Sally Vitsky; **404** Peter Bull; **406–417** Marc Scott; **422** Steve Mack; **442–444** Lisa Perrett; **445**. Kristine Walsh; **446-447** Rob McClurken. **454–465** Cornelius Van Wright; **470–471** Rob McClurken; **494–495** Rob McClurken; **500** Susan Carlson; **521** Kristine Walsh; **522** Rob McClurken. **526** Sally Vitsky; **528** Tim Johnson; **534–546** Teri Farrell-Gittins; **548–550** Jackie Stafford-Snider; **551** Tim Johnson; **552** Rob McClurken. **553** Rob McClurken; **572–575** Renee Graef. **576–577** Rob McClurken; **604** Rob McClurken; **610** Ortelius Design Inc; **624** Rob McClurken. **624** Robert Schuster; **628** Rob McClurken; **636–645** Alan Flinn. **650-651** Rob McClurken. **654-655** Sally Vitsky.